Drugs in South Asia

Also by M. Emdad-ul Haq

COMPARATIVE POLITICAL ANALYSIS

DRUG ADDICTION: National and World Perspectives

Drugs in South Asia

From the Opium Trade to the Present Day

M. Emdad-ul Haq
Professor
Department of Political Science
University of Chittagong
Bangladesh

First published in Great Britain 2000 by
MACMILLAN PRESS LTD
Houndmills, Basingstoke, Hampshire RG21 6XS and London
Companies and representatives throughout the world

A catalogue record for this book is available from the British Library.

ISBN 0–333–75465–4

First published in the United States of America 2000 by
ST. MARTIN'S PRESS, INC.,
Scholarly and Reference Division,
175 Fifth Avenue, New York, N.Y. 10010

ISBN 0–312–22379–X

Library of Congress Cataloging-in-Publication Data
Emdad-ul Haq, M.
Drugs in South Asia : from the opium trade to the present day / M. Emdad-ul Haq.
p. cm.
Includes bibliographical references and index.
ISBN 0–312–22379–X
1. Drug traffic—South Asia. 2. Drug Traffic—South Asia—History—20th century.
I. Title.

HV5840.S64 E45   2000
363.45'095—dc21
                                                          99–059428

This book is printed on paper suitable for recycling and made from fully managed and sustained
forest sources.

10   9   8   7   6   5   4   3   2   1
09 08 07 06 05 04 03 02 01 00

Printed and bound in Great Britain by
Antony Rowe Ltd, Chippenham, Wiltshire

To Dolly, my wife,
who endured many hardships for this work

Contents

List of Tables, Figures and Maps

Tables

Figures

Maps

Preface

In mid-January 1997, the ABC evening news unveiled the biggest seizure of hashish in history by the local enforcement authorities along the Australian seaboard. Weighing about ten metric tons, with a market value of A$100 million, the hashish had been smuggled from Pakistan by a yacht. Understanding the significance of this information, my 8-year-old daughter Nazifa asked me curiously: 'Why can't the people in Pakistan stop the supply?' To find an answer for such a subtle yet simple inquisition was hard for me. I replied 'that's a long story'! In South Asia this problem is not confined to Pakistan alone. The present work is an attempt to provide an explanation for the above question and examine whether ordinary people have any control over the drug problems in the region. It illustrates a range of issues that are pertinent to the origins and development of drug abuse and illicit trafficking in Pakistan, India and Bangladesh.

This study, originally the politics of narcotics in South Asia, I undertook as my Ph.D. dissertation in the Department of Politics at La Trobe University, Melbourne, Australia. My initial aim in writing a Ph.D. thesis was far from the present topic. This project came about after discussions with my supervisor, Professor Robin Jeffrey, who had stressed my previous work in the area. My first step in this current research developed from consulting the voluminous report of the *British Royal Commission on Opium of 1893–95*. This document was used as a powerful instrument in defense of the British opium trade in South Asia until an international control was adopted in 1925. Using the raw materials derived from this report, I was able to establish clear links between colonial revenue and drug policies, and their influences in South Asia during the post-independence era. My investigation is extensive, both in length and depth. South Asian drug issues are closely connected with the external policies of a dozen western and Asian countries, ranging from Afghanistan and Australia, to the US. Due to international control and underworld connections, present day drug-related issues in South Asia have attained a complexity that makes it difficult to trace the role of the secret agencies which are sometimes the hidden players in geo-strategic games.

To Professor Robin Jeffrey, I am grateful for his tireless help that enabled me to produce this work. I have great respect and admiration for his scholarship and academic integrity, and these qualities have been of extensive benefit in the completion of this project. I am thankful to Professor Frank F. Conlon, Department of History and International Studies, Director of the South Asia Center, University of Washington, valuable for his comments on my work. Professor Peter B. Mayer, Head, Department of Politics, the University of Adelaide, Australia, also helped contributed on some specific issues. Thanks are due to John Robinson for his continued support in collecting many current materials on India. Thanks are also due to the inter-library loan section of the La Trobe University Library for collecting rare documents from diverse sources in Australia, and from overseas. My relatives and family members helped me in many ways in collecting documents from Bangladesh. The present discourse has been fortunate to have many well-wishers in Australia, in South Asia and around the world. Finally, I extend gratitude to my mother Begum S. Nahar, my wife Dolly, and our daughters Raisa and Nazifa, for their lasting support and understanding towards the completion of this work.

M. EMDAD-UL HAQ

List of Abbreviations

AA:	Acetic anhydride
ANTF:	Anti-Narcotics Task Force
ASF:	Airport Security Force
BCCE:	Bank of Credit and Commerce Emirates
BCCI:	Bank of Credit and Commerce International
BDR:	Bangladesh Rifles
BIDS:	Bangladesh Institute of Development Studies
BJP:	Bharatiya Janata Party
BNP:	Bangladesh Nationalist Party
BOP:	Border Observation Post
BSF:	Border Security Force
BPC:	Basic Principles Committee
BPLF:	Baluchistan People's Liberation Front
CAA:	Civil Aviation Authority
COFEPOSA:	Conservation of Foreign Exchange and Prevention of Smuggling Activities
CND:	Commission on Narcotic Drugs
CPS:	Concentrate Poppy Straw
DEA:	Drug Enforcement Agency
DNC:	Department of Narcotics Control
ECOSOC:	Economic and Social Council
FATA:	Federally Administered Tribal Areas
FIA:	Federal Investigation Agency
JUI:	Jamiatul Ulema-i-Islam
IDA:	Islamic Democratic Alliance
INCB:	International Narcotics Control Board
INCSR:	International Narcotics Control Strategy Report
IRS:	Internal Revenue Service
ISI:	Inter Service Intelligence
MLR:	Martial Law Regulations
MNA:	Member of National Assembly
MP:	Madhya Pradesh
MPA:	Member of Provincial Assembly
MQY:	Minimum Qualifying Yield

NCB: Narcotics Control Bureau
NCD: Narcotics Control Division
NDP: National Democratic Party
NDPSA: Narcotic Drugs and Psychotropic Substances Act
NOPE: National Organisation of Postal Employees
NLC: National Logistic Cell
NSL: National Security Council
NWFP: North West Frontier Province
PAF: Pakistan Air Force
PBUH: Peace be upon Him
PIA: Pakistan International Airlines
PNA: Pakistan National Alliance
PNCB: Pakistan Narcotics Control Board
PITNDPS: Prevention of Illicit Traffic in Narcotic Drugs and
            Psychotropic Substances
PPP: Pakistan People's Party
PTV: Pakistan Television
SAARC: South Asian Association for Regional Cooperation
SSOT: Society for the Suppression of Opium Trade
TREVI: Terrorism, Radicalism, Extremism and International
            Violence
UAE: United Arab Emirates
UNDCP: United Nations Drug Control Program
UNFDAC: United Nations Fund for Drug Abuse Control
UP: Uttar Pradesh

Prelude

To tell the compound nature of the present-day drug[1] menace in South Asia, it is important to scrutinize the historical context of the opium trade in the eighteenth and nineteenth centuries. Trade in non-medicinal opium evolved through a long process of competition amongst western trading companies and the extensive administrative experiments of the British colonial authorities. To manage the cross-regional opium trade, the East India Company established its monopoly in Bengal in 1773. Through this measure the colonial authorities excluded other European companies, including local private traders in Patna (capital of modern Bihar), from the government-run monopoly in opium. To support its opium enterprise the government enacted numerous laws on drugs from 1797 to 1878.

In an effort to protect and expand the opium industry, the colonial government annexed some strategically important areas, both coastal and poppy growing, between the 1820s and 1850s. To safeguard the interests of the opium trade in foreign markets, the government imposed a transit duty on Malwa opium in 1830. As a result of the above policies the British government derived a huge amount of revenue that contributed to the maintenance of the colonial administration in India. During the late nineteenth century opium exports provided over 16 per cent of the total revenue in India.[2] Moreover, the marketing of excise opium in India also contributed a revenue of £175,000 per annum to the colonial authorities.[3] The present work argues that the British policy for the maximization of revenue from drugs largely helped in the promotion of opium addiction and drug trade in South Asia.

Ignoring the catastrophe of opiate abuse in the region, the *Final Report of the Royal Commission on Opium* of 1895 endorsed the British opium trade and credited the government monopoly as the finest system for regulating the production of opium.[4] The present work takes this moment as an attempt by the British Imperial government to suppress anti-opium opinion in Britain, India, Burma and Sri Lanka. In an attempt to alleviate the anti-opium pressures both at home and abroad, the British House of Commons on 30 June 1893 set up a Royal Commission for investigating major issues that were pertinent to the working of the government opium monopoly in India. The Commission, which was composed of eight British and two Indian Members, examined about 725 witnesses in England, India and Burma, and presented its Report to Parliament on 25 April 1895. In its closely printed seven-volume report, about 29,000 questions, a huge number of appendices, valuable reports, and memoranda were incorporated. Although ingenious in manipulating facts, this document provides priceless materials for a critical study of the colonial drug trade in South Asia.

Nevertheless, recognition of the abuse of drugs in South Asia and efforts to deal with the issue began with the US, where a large drug addiction problem stemmed from the Civil War era. The classification of opiates as dangerous drugs occurred as a result of the spread of medical awareness in the US during the late nineteenth century, and the existence of a massive opium addiction problem in the Philippines, a colony occupied by the US in 1898. Under the US's leadership, diplomatic pressure was mounted in opposition to British opium policy in South Asia. To overturn the British approach, global opium summits, during the first quarter of the twentieth century, linked Indian opium revenue more than ever with international politics. In an attempt to limit the consumption and trafficking in South Asian drugs, 13 nations met at an international summit in Shanghai in 1909. This was the first endeavour to ban non-medicinal opium trade internationally. For centuries, western countries were not publicly aware of, or had ignored, the drug addiction problem in South Asia, China and the Asia-Pacific region. As public opinion in the US, Britain, India, and China expanded to oppose the colonial opium trade, it became imperative for the major opium producing countries, including the British government, to limit the supply of opium from India and elsewhere.

The British government joined in international summits, but delayed the execution of regulations. In the International Opium Commission in Shanghai the British government guarded the legality of the colonial opium trade in South Asia. Nevertheless, this Commission for the first time examined accounts of the British opium trade and questioned its legitimacy. After this initial diplomatic victory, the US government organized a second round of international summits at The Hague during 1912–14. Facing defeat, the government of British India boycotted the Hague international summits and remained reluctant to ratify the articles of the International Convention until 1919. The outbreak of the First World War in 1914 temporarily eased international pressure on the colonial opium trade. Overall, the government of British India pursued complex tactics in order to counteract immediate international pressure and to slowly shift its revenue sources away from opium exports to other forms of excisable drugs. However, Gandhi's political agitation in opposition to the official distribution of drugs pressurised the colonial authorities to sign the Geneva Convention of 1925. The findings of the Assam Opium Inquiry Committee in 1924 also expedited this ratification. Under international agreements then in place and domestic pressures, the government finally adopted the Dangerous Drugs Act of 1930, and allowed some provincial governments to adopt opium smoking legislation by 1935. This legislation marginally met current demands.

In South Asia, every major religion – Islam, Hinduism and Buddhism – has restrictions on the use of intoxicating liquor. In India, liquor has been a target of prohibition policies since 1937. However, the absence of any international regulations on liquor and other so called 'soft drugs' allowed the colonial authorities to draw an increasing amount of revenue from these items and undermined a uniform prohibition programme throughout the region. Following independence, for revenue purposes the prohibition of liquor was either partially implemented or sidelined as an issue. The lack of unified prohibition programme largely resulted in confusion, and the effort was doomed to failure. Recent anti-drug laws in Bangladesh and Pakistan have incorporated liquor as a banned item. Considering the above factors, liquor is included amongst the list of drugs. As in the case of liquor, the post-independence governments in India, Pakistan and Bangladesh barely changed the existing colonial drug laws until the mid-1980s. This continuance of colonial legislation was an outcome of a lack of political determination by the ruling authorities, whose revenues depended to a considerable extent on excise from various intoxicating drugs. The post-independence government in India protracted colonial drug policies, and by the early 1980s India had re-emerged as a major international consumer and supplier of drugs. By the late 1950s, India had revived the traditional opium industry for medicinal and quasi-medicinal purposes. However, Indian authorities continue to claim that the country is used in the northeast by drug traffickers from Burma, in the west by those from Pakistan, and from the north (the Himalayan region) by those from Nepal. They further maintain that the transit traffic from Pakistan and Burma has had links with the insurgent wars in the Punjab, Kashmir and the northeastern states in India. The present work demonstrates that India, geographically located at the heart of three opium-producing regions,[5] is in the grip of colonial habits of thought. India had been a traditional supplier of contraband opium to China and the Asia-Pacific region, and it re-emerged as the major supplier of illicit drugs in the 1980s. Under its century-old drug laws and confused prohibition policies, it was unable to handle either the flow of illicit supply from the cross-border sources, or to control the management of the licit opium industry. In the late 1980s, in belated recognition of the need to combat illicit production and trafficking, the Indian government adopted strict anti-drug laws. The results of the recent enactment, however, are not promising.

Unlike India, the fruitless attempts of the Pakistani authorities to revive the licit opium industry, coupled with the geo-strategic changes in southwest Asia at the beginning of the 1980s, helped to increase the illicit production and transit trafficking of heroin. Instead of adopting tougher anti-drug laws, as in India, successive governments in Pakistan (erstwhile West Pakistan) retained the colonial drug policies until the late 1970s. Except for the government of Field Marshal Ayub Khan during 1958–69, most of the post-independence governments were reluctant to instil any meaningful anti-drug legislation either in accordance with current international conventions or the religious spirit of the country. Aiming to create political credibility for his regime amongst the *ulema* (religious leaders), Prime Minister Zulfikar Ali Bhutto attempted to introduce

Islamic prohibition in early 1977. Later in 1979, with the increase of the illicit production of opium poppy in NWFP and along the border between Pakistan and Afghanistan, General Zia-ul Haq adopted the *Shariah* approach (Islamic prohibition) and banned poppy cultivation to help prevent the domestic consumption of drugs.

The rise of the Afghan crisis slyly encouraged intelligence agencies in Pakistan and the US to deflect money from heroin trafficking to support the war in Afghanistan. As a result of the US's Cold War strategies in Afghanistan, combined with the Pakistani perception of a threat to its territorial integrity in NWFP and Baluchistan, the *Pathan* cultivators produced record-breaking illicit opium in 1979. The funnelling of drug money into the politics of insurgency has helped to institutionalize the drug trade in Pakistan. With the intro-duction of heroin technology to help finance the Afghan war, Pakistan eventually emerged as the world's largest consumer and supplier of illicit heroin by the late 1980s. The boom in poppy cultivation, and in the manufacture of heroin in the tribal areas and across the border in Afghanistan, ensured Pakistan's prominence in underground trafficking. Due to international pressure, General Zia in 1985 amended Pakistan's drug laws, including the Dangerous Drugs Act of 1930. Pakistan also adopted property seizure laws for drug traffickers, and imposed life imprisonment for drug related offences. To satisfy the interests of the US and other western countries, the Pakistan government introduced a death penalty for drug trafficking in 1993. While the laws have been made more stringent, they have remained largely unendorsed, thereby rendering them ineffectual. The problems of drugs in southwest Asia have now become international.

The legacies of the colonial opium trade and then US Cold War strategy have created a relentless situation from which no country in the region, including Bangladesh, is immune. Bangladesh (erstwhile East Pakistan) emerged as a major consumer of, and geo-graphical crossroads for, illicit drugs in the 1980s, largely because of the influence of the colonial and post-colonial drug policies of Pakistan, India and Burma. To derive revenue from the sale of intoxicating drugs, the Pakistani authorities continued the colonial excise policies during the 1950s and 1960s, when Bangladesh was still the eastern wing of Pakistan. No significant change in the government's drug policy occurred immediately after Bangladesh's independence in 1971. In the 1980s, when an abundance of illicit supplies started to arrive from the neighbouring countries of Burma, India and Pakistan, the drug menace in Bangladesh began to go out of control. In accordance with the UN Convention of 1988, the Ershad regime in 1990 adopted strict anti-drug policies. Similarly, the government of Khaleda Zia during the early 1990s undertook an anti-narcotics drive. Due to political instability, lack of sufficient logistic support and administrative corruption, Bangladesh has been unable to deter trans-border traffickers and the spread of drug addiction in the country.

This work is extensive and delicate in nature. Because of the political sensitivity of the topic, it was not easy for me to handle what became a gigantic task. There are many examples where contemporary writers have carefully evaded discussions about the involvement of some Pakistani top brass in the drug trade. General Fazle Haq, otherwise known as the 'Poppy General' in Pakistan, was interviewed in the late 1980s by Emma Duncan, a journalist with the *Independent Television News*, and by Christina Lamb, a correspondent of *The Financial Times*. These young ladies, who stayed in Pakistan for about two years, pin-pointed many vital issues of Pakistani politics in their books *Breaking the Curfew: Journey Through Pakistan* and *Waiting for Allah: Pakistan's Struggle for Democracy*, respectively. However, they did not comment on General Fazle Haq's association with the Pakistani heroin trade. It is highly unlikely that they did not find any alliance between General Haq and the Pakistani drug trade during the Cold War era. Most likely, both Duncan and Lamb chose to ignore the 'dark side' of the powerful Pakistani General. During the early 1990s, a Pakistani journalist was assassinated while he was searching for material on the drug trade. In 1990, BBC reporters were attacked by the 'bodyguards' of the leading Pakistani trafficker Iqbal Baig, whilst on an official mission in Lahore. The above examples reveal that any sensitive work on drugs is susceptible to risks. As a result of this, it was not possible to contact questionable political figures or to clarify some issues pertinent to my drug-related research. It was equally impracticable to contact those beneficiaries who know about the trade, because they would not speak for the sake of their own interest.

Above all, drug policies are often related to the financial and political interests of the national governments. For example, during colonial rule the British government was heavily dependent on revenue from intoxicating drugs. For similar reasons, after 50 years of independence, the Narcotics Control Bureau in India still comes under the umbrella of the Ministry of Finance. In Pakistan, the leading military intelligence agency, ISI, has allegedly been involved in the strategic use of drug money in insurgency wars in Afghanistan and India. Similar allegations were evident about the CIA's underhand connection with the promoters of the heroin trade in Pakistan and Afghanistan during the Cold War era. At times, these shady links are exposed, but normally they remain concealed. It was impossible to get any evidence from primary sources about the alleged activities of the leading secret agencies in Pakistan, India or the US. Given the political sensitivity of the issue, it was also difficult to collect some official and rare documents from overseas sources.

I depended for my work mostly on published materials and documents prepared by specialized agencies, both local and international. I verified the 'soft data' provided by newspapers and official reports, and tried to avoid misinformation, fabricated stories and twisted facts made for political propaganda. For the nineteenth-century materials I mostly consulted the *British Parliamentary Command Papers*, *Hansard*, concurrent newspaper reports and publications both by anti-opium writers and pro-opium bureaucrats in the Indian Civil Service. For current information, I examined narcotics reports published in three-dozen daily newspapers from Bangladesh, India, Pakistan, Australia, the US and UK. In dealing with my sources, I tried to carefully avoid the cloud of misinformation and emotion. I paid careful attention to reports, which were aimed at manipulating information, and politically motivated to promote national interests or prejudice. I depended mostly on published and unclassified documents, letter correspondence and personal discussions. This work has greatly benefited from personal letters by David Guinane, Executive Officer of the Australian Poppy Advisory and Control Board, who was an Australian delegate to the Commission on Narcotic Drugs meeting in Vienna in 1988. His letters provided important indications about the Indo-Australia trade competition in the international opium market and helped me to understand the repercussions among the poppy growers in India.

The current task scrutinizes the findings of the world's major inquiry commissions or committees both in regard to legalization and criminalization of drugs during the nineteenth and twentieth centuries. To compare the findings of the nearly 2,600-page *Royal Commission Report on Opium* of 1893–5, I consulted the *Philippines Opium Commission Report* of 1906, and the tiny *Report of the Ceylon Committee on Opium* of 1908 and the *Report of the Assam Opium Enquiry Committee* of 1925. Besides these, I consulted approximately 30 other reports on narcotics conducted by diverse national and international bodies. As regards the role of the colonial government and the post-independence national authorities in the international anti-drug drive, I examined almost all the major treaties and agreements conducted by the world bodies or reached between countries on a bilateral basis. To characterize the shifts in government policies, I checked over 60 central and provincial/state drug laws enacted by governments in South Asia throughout the nineteenth and twentieth centuries. For verification of the US position in the South Asian drug trade, I used extensively the relevant US State Department reports and the congressional reports of the twentieth century. Besides these, I read a huge number of contemporary journal articles and books written by experts on drugs.

This project contributes to an area where no factual work has previously been done. A generation of historians, who emerged during the late nineteenth and early twentieth centuries, dealt with the Indo-China opium trade and produced some studies on the Anglo-Chinese Opium Wars. Most of these works were either arrogantly in favour of the colonial opium trade or maintained an anti-opium position with moral emotions. Taking a pro-opium stand, Maurice Collis in his book *Foreign Mud* provided the rationale of British offensive during the Opium Wars.[6] Following the British withdrawal from Hong Kong, a strategic colony established in 1842 to promote opium trade in the region, Chinese film-makers have released a factual movie on the Opium Wars. However, after 50 years of independence the current generation of analysts has not conducted serious studies of the opium trade in South Asia. They have shown little concern with drug issues in South Asia from a historico-political perspective.

Only a handful of publications are obtainable on the medical or social aspects of drugs in Bangladesh, India and Pakistan. Writings on the political implications of the opium trade in South Asia are rare. Alfred W. McCoy is perhaps the foremost authority on the region, but his works have covered mainly the areas to the east and west of South Asia. In his analysis McCoy ignored the importance of the Durand Line in the Pakistani security perception and its influence in the spread of the drug trade in the region in recent years. As a ground-breaking attempt, the present investigation explains and identifies the political heritage, nature and connections of the so-called Golden Crescent's drug trade from the late nineteenth century to the present.

Except for a handful of sub-regional or country studies, there is no general work available concerning the drug threat in South Asia. Existing studies mostly deal with the physical hazards and social consequences of drug abuse in Bangladesh, India or Pakistan, but ignore discussions of the political implications of the drug trade in the region. In 1991, Ikramul Haq, a Pakistani journalist, provided brief explanations of the drug threat in Pakistan in his book *Pakistan: from Hash to Heroin*. In 1993, I published a book entitled *Drug Addiction: National and World Perspectives* [*Madokashakti: Jatio O Bishwa Poriprekhhit*]. It examined the trends of the cross-border drug trade in Bangladesh and their connection in the country's recent emergence as a major user of illicit drugs and important corridor in international drug trafficking. From this survey it is clear that there is no work available that comprehensively treats the danger of drugs in the countries of South Asia. Given this lacuna, the current study focuses on the colonial and post-colonial history of the drug trade in South Asia and highlights many of the delicate issues which are pertinent to the current geo-political experience in the region.

In recent years, some authorities argue that a legal approach has failed to combat the drug menace in many countries, including Australia. The legalization of opium that had been recommended by the Royal Commission on Opium of 1895 has drawn renewed attention from many enforcement authorities, political leaders and academics. This enterprise contributes, if not totally, to an understanding of the motive of current debates about the decriminalization of harmful drugs in some parts of the western world. It is often argued that in the past prohibition policy did not work anywhere in the world. This study helps understand some of the constitutional weaknesses of the prohibition measures that have been implemented to deal with drug offenders in Bangladesh, India and Pakistan. The present work argues that the lack of political will of successive governments in South Asia, both colonial and post-colonial, has helped the drugs problem flourish throughout the region.

Eagerness for revenue from drugs encouraged many governments to compromise with the evils of intoxicating drugs. This project examines the potential of the stringent anti-drug laws adopted by the governments of South Asian countries during the 1980s and early 1990s, and demonstrates how the contradictory policies pursued by the ruling authorities have prevented the proper implementation of anti-drug laws. It maintains that the strategic use of drug money allowed some leading intelligence agencies in the region to become promoters of cross-border drug trafficking. It also examines the contradictory role pursued by the CIA during the Cold War era in actually curing the problem of drugs in southwest Asia. I demonstrate the flaws in the drug laws of South Asia and argue that the lack of political commitment of the ruling authorities has been one of the major impediments to the successful implementation of anti-drug legislation.

1
The Colonial Drug Trade

Through the dealings of the British East India Company, opium, traditionally used medicinally, became a non-medicinal business commodity during the late eighteenth and throughout the nineteenth centuries. At the time of growth and development of the opium monopoly in Bengal from 1773 to 1856, the economic condition of the poppy farmers (*ryots*) had deteriorated and tension had erupted between the local *zamindars* (landlords) and the colonial authorities. This conflict aided in the eventual uprising of 1857, also known as the Indian 'Sepoy Mutiny'. In an attempt to further control the private cultivation of opium poppies and the free trade in opium, the government adopted the Opium Act of 1857 and the Opium Act of 1878.

The colonial drug laws applied a double standard, as they allowed the imperial authorities to appropriate revenue from the state-run opium monopoly, while pushing the private traders to become involved in the contraband trade. The Indian opium trade flourished until the late nineteenth century, when China emerged as a major market for the supply of opium from India. By the end of the century, the colonial rulers progressively increased local consumption of intoxicating drugs in South Asia through the establishment of an official distribution system. Thus, the history of the drug trade in South Asia has a complex political background with numerous cross-regional connections.

Bengal opium traffic 1773–1856

The growth and development of an opium trade in South Asia between the late eighteenth and early nineteenth centuries has a sensational political history. The Arab physicians, who had learnt the medicinal application of opium (*Papaver Somniferum*) from the Greeks,[1] came in contact with India from the eighth century AD. The knowledge of medicine that they brought with them had a profound impact in later history. Eventually, in collaboration with Dutch, Portuguese and then the English trading companies, a group of private traders evolved in sporadic poppy cultivation in some parts of India in the sixteenth and seventeenth centuries. With the establishment of political rule, the British East India Company eventually expelled all other parties from the opium trade and came in conflict with the local zamindars that attempted to resist the large-scale conversion of fertile land into poppy cultivation. This rift eventually contributed to the great uprising of 1857 in the poppy growing areas.

The war on opium trade

In 1986, in an interview with Lt. Col. James B. Gritz (Ret.), an official envoy of the White House, the Burmese drug lord Khun Sa' maintained:

> We must remember the opium trade is originally a creation of the west. The British fought major wars with Asian nations to ensure their monopoly on, and freedom to trade in opium.[2]

This bitter claim by an infamous drug dealer was made probably in regard to the Anglo-Chinese Opium Wars in the late 1830s and 1850s. However, an academic inquiry into the origin of major wars in Bengal and other parts of South Asia in the eighteenth and nineteenth centuries and their relevance to the opium trade has never been conducted. The following discussion illustrates the commercial policies of the western maritime powers, especially those of the British East India Company, that eventually inspired them to seize political power in Bengal, largely for the benefit of opium trafficking.

The Arabs first traded opium in India as a medicinal commodity. They studied and practised Greek medicine, and opium became well known to them as *afyun*, a word that is quite close to the Greek *opion* (οπιον) meaning opium. Abu-l-ali-ibn-Sina or Avicenna, a renowned Arab physician, recommended it especially for pain relief and as a cure for eye diseases.[3] The Arab traders, who came to know of the drug during the Roman Empire, introduced it to Persia. They brought medicinal opium into India, China and elsewhere around the eighth century AD.[4] E.H. Walsh wrote:

> The use of opium spread eastwards from Arabia, through Persia, and into India with the Arab invaders who conquered Sindh from the sea in the eighth century, and was extended through the country by successive waves of Mahomedan [Mohammedan] conquest, each of which extended further than the last.[5]

In 1927, Richard M. Dane argued that the Arabs controlled the trade from the Red Sea and Persian Gulf to Malaya and carried opium from Turkey, India and Iran.[6] It was through Arab traders and travelling physicians[7] that the medicinal use of opium was introduced into India, and then became known under various Sanskrit and vernacular names: *afim, afyun, afyuni, afimi, afimchi, afiun, aphin,* and *apeem,* in various parts of South Asia. In the Punjab, opium was known as *khash-khash, khis-khash,* which had derived presumably from the Persian *cash-cash.* In Nepal, opium was introduced as *aphim,* while the Chinese adopted *af-yun* or *a-fu-yong,* which are very close to the Arabic form. Opium was initially incorporated in the *Bharaprakasha,* a Sanskrit text, and other *Ayur-Vedic* works during the eleventh century.[8] The use of opium continued in traditional India in secret (*tantric*) rituals and herbal (*hakimi*) treatments, as a remedy for diarrhoea, dysentery, incontinence, and fever. With the promotion of quasi-medicinal opium, western trading companies eventually became involved with the commercial opium trade in South Asia.

During the sixteenth century a growing trade in opium in India exhilarated many western travellers and business-minded people. The Portuguese traveller Duarte Barbosa, who accompanied Vasco da Gama as his secretary in 1500, made early reference to the Indian opium trade at Calicut and Cannanore until 1515. In the memorandum submitted before the Opium Commission, Dane provided evidence that opium was listed in the articles sent from India to Lisbon with Cabral's fleet in 1501.[9] Writing of the flourishing demand for medicinal opium in India, D'Albuquerque in a letter to King Manuel of Portugal in December 1515 requested that opium poppies 'be sown in all the fields of Portugal' to make money from India.[10] Europeans like Garcia D'Orta and John Huyghen van Linschoten, who visited India in the sixteenth century, noticed a sprouting trade in opium in many parts. Caesar Fredrick, a Venetian, wrote in 1518 that he made profits in opium supplies from Cambay and the port of Chawl on the West Coast of India to Burma. Thus, a trade in medicinal opium flourished in different parts of pre-Mughal India without much regulation.

Alongside the flourishing opium trade, the recreational and semi-medicinal use of opium was evident amongst the Mughal nobility and Rajputs in medieval India. It is known from the *Babur-Nama* that Qasim-i-Ali, one of the associates of Emperor Babar, was an opium eater.[11] Abu'l Fazl, a learned adviser of the Emperor Akbar, mentioned the use of *kuknar* (a mixture of opium and hemp) by some Mughal dignitaries including Akbar.[12] The *kuknar* in *A'in-I-Akbari* appears to be closely associated with another Persian name *kouknar*. Bernier, who traveled in the Mughal Empire in the midseventeenth century, noted that the warrior Rajputs were greatly 'accustomed to the use of opium'.[13] With the rise in demand for non-medicinal opium within and outside India, the cultivation of opium poppy gradually increased. (See below for a discussion about the controversy on Mughal opium monopoly.) During the eclipse of the Mughals some Patna traders, in collaboration with western trading companies, became involved in the organized opium trade. In partnership with Dutch, Portuguese and then English trading companies, a group of Patna free traders became involved in the production of opium poppies in the sixteenth and seventeenth centuries.

Portuguese merchants embraced the trade in the early sixteenth century. As a result of their dealings, opium became an exportable product of India, poppies being grown in parts of modern Uttar Pradesh (UP), Rajasthan, Gujarat and Madhya Pradesh.[14] Their greater involvement also made Cambay an important centre in the South Asian opium trade.[15] At Goa, the Portuguese seized the major share of that trade from the Arabs,[16] and exported Indian opium to

China.[17] Following the Portuguese, the Dutch, Spanish and British traders became involved in 'a tug of war', as they competed for the Indian opium trade and other commodities. With the formation of the Dutch East India Company in 1602, Dutch factories were established at Hooghly, in Bengal. Dane noted that the Dutch East India Company sent about 100 kilos of Malwa opium annually from 1613 to Malaya (Malacca) and then sold it in Thailand (Siam), Burma (Pegu) and China for a profit.[18] After occupying Malaya in 1649, and wresting control over the Indian Ocean from the Portuguese, the Dutch carried Indian opium to Batavia. The Dutch began to trade Bengal opium from 1659.[19] Tavernier, who was in India during this period, mentioned that Dutch traders traded in opium in 'exchange for their pepper'.[20] The islands of the East Indies were the chief markets for the Dutch opium trade.

To expand their trade interests in opium, the British East India Company competed with the existing local and foreign opium traders in Patna throughout the seventeenth century. Between 1583 and 1591 Ralph Fiche, an Englishman, visited Bengal and described the culture of opium present in Patna.[21] In 1600, the British merchants founded the British East India Company to facilitate taking part in the flourishing opium trade. In his recent work, Om Prakash maintains that by the middle of the seventeenth century the British East India Company carried opium from Bengal to Sumatra in Indonesia for sale.[22] Dane maintained that the British traders competed with the Dutch East India Company, which received permission from the Mughal Emperor in 1676 for licitly trading in opium by 'paying a tax'.[23] In 1683, the management of the British East India Company, 'to make opium a part of the Company's investment', issued orders.[24] Nevertheless, the Patna opium dealers and petty traders (*paykars*), who due to their connections with the Dutch traders had attained a dominant position in the trade, confronted the British merchants.

With the eclipse of the Mughal Empire by the mid-eighteenth century, the British East India Company forcefully established a substantial influence in the Indian opium trade. In March 1757, in a letter to the President and Council of Fort William in Bengal, P. Godfrey and his associates indicated that the East India Company had achieved exclusive control over the opium trade on the West Coast by October 1754, and had 'prohibited' all other parties 'from trading therein'.[25] The strategic importance of the east coast due to its geographical proximity to the Asia-Pacific region, a major market for opium trade, also influenced British merchants to expand their military influence in the region. In an attempt to expand their commercial facilities, the British East India Company increased military power along the coastline in Bengal in the mid-eighteenth century. The adoption of defence strategies, in violation of the Mughal trade rules (*dastak*), generated an armed conflict between Nawab Seraj-ud Daula of Bengal[26] and the East India Company authorities. In an 1891 document George Watt maintained that the attack of Nawab Seraj-ud Daula over the Kashimbazar military base (*Kuti*) in 1756, and the disruption in the supply of opium from the Patna Opium dealers'[27] to the British East India Company, led to the Battle of Plassey in the following year. In 1894, providing similar evidence, James F. Finaly noted:

> The destruction of the English settlements by Sura-jud-Daula in 1756 drove the English merchants out of the market; and in defaunt [defiant] of competitors, the native dealers were compelled to dispose of their opium to the Dutch at Rs70 a maund. This low rate led to the cultivation being greatly restricted.[28]

To break this circumscription, the leaders of the East India Company went into a secret deal with some of the rival ministers of Nawab Seraj-ud Daula. The *Fort William–India House Correspondence* indicated that under a 'trade agreement' Omichund, an influential merchant within the Nawab's government, helped in ousting the youthful Nawab from power.[29] The victory of Plassey in 1757 provided the British East India Company with a stronger political hold over the opium trade in Patna and the surrounding poppy-growing areas.

After establishing its political control in Bengal, the British East India Company founded the government opium monopoly that eventually ousted the Patna opium dealers and the Dutch, Spanish and Portuguese companies from the trade. In a letter addressed from the Court of Directors to the Council in Bengal, it was admitted that the initial experiments over the establishment of the opium monopoly were responsible for 'all the bloodshed, massacres, and confusions' in Patna in 1763.[30] The situation deteriorated further

after conflicts between the agents of the newly installed ruler
Mir Kashim and the merchants of the British East India Company.
In order to establish its total control, the East India Company
authorities finally seized political power in the Boxer War in 1765.
Following this, the colonial rulers swiftly established their exclusive
power in the opium trade.[31] The beginnings of political control in
the late 1750s allowed the colonial authorities to set up a despotic
type of state-run opium monopoly that expelled all competitors
from the existing free trade.

Mughal opium

In an attempt to justify the establishment of an opium monopoly in
Bengal, colonial historians maintained that the monopoly had
existed in India for centuries and they inherited it from the Mughal
rulers. In 1890–1, Watt argued that the poppy cultivators paid Rs4
per *bigha*[32] in Agra and Rs1 and 4 *anna* in Malwa[33] as highest and
lowest rent rates to the Mughal authorities during the sixteenth
century. Watt did not mention whether a similar tax was applicable
for other agricultural products in India.

Dane, formerly of the Indian Civil Service, asserted that the Mughal
Emperor in 1676 granted 'a monopoly' of the trade to the Dutch, who
in turn paid a tax to the government.[34] He further debated that the
opium monopoly was conducted for many years by Fakhr al Tujar, a
local merchant, who enjoyed absolute freedom for supplying it to the
European companies, in exchange for an annual payment to the
government. Dane's assertions were contradictory and do not testify to
the running of an opium monopoly by the Mughal rulers. It is more
plausible that the British East India Company was inspired by the
Dutch opium monopoly that had been established in Ceylon in
1675.[35] Through this measure the Dutch colonial rulers prohibited
local people and all other private traders from taking part in the
commercial activities in opium.

The claim about the existence of a Mughal opium monopoly was
written during the late nineteenth century when the official policy
was attacked by the anti-opium crusaders as morally indefensible.
Being engaged in the propaganda battle, some of the imperialist
writers attempted to justify the colonial drug trade in South Asia
from an historical point of view. In a parliamentary monograph,
Watt maintained that the poppy-growing areas of Fatehpur,

Allahabad, Ghazipur and Ahmedabad came under Mughal administration during the time of Emperor Akbar.[36] In defence of the government policy George H. Batten, formerly of the Bengal Civil Service, argued that the Mughal rulers started manufacturing and selling the drug as the 'most convenient and successful' example of opium monopoly.[37] To stimulate the pro-opium sentiment, Batten's paper was read before the Society of Arts in London in March 1891 and then presented to the British Royal Commission in 1893.

The colonialist writers held that in some towns the right to sell opium was taxable, in the same way that certain other luxury articles were taxed. Referring to Abu'L Fazl, the celebrated historian of Akbar's time and the writer of the *Akbarnamah*, Robert Needham Cust in 1893 claimed that poppy was 'one of the most valuable crops' and 'an important source of revenue' during the time of Emperor Akbar.[38] Consulting *A'in-I Akbari*, *Alamgirnama* and Bernier's *Travels in Mughul India*, I have found no evidence of the existence of an opium monopoly in medieval India. However, from the *A'in-I Akbari* it is apparent that Akbar's governor in Kandahar, Shahbaj Khan, was known as *char bughra khur* for his dependence on four drugs: opium, cannabis, wine and *khuknar*.[39] In his book on *Storia Do Mogor*, Niccolao Manucci, an Italian traveller who visited India between 1653 and 1708, mentioned opium as one of the exportable commodities of the Mughal Kingdom.[40] Scattered information from contemporary sources does not certify the claims made by colonial writers about the Mughal control on opium revenue.

The sporadic cultivation of opium poppies in different parts of medieval India was outside the general revenue system of the state authorities. The *Final Report of the Opium Commission* maintained that under the Mughal and other dynasties which had successively held power in various parts of India, there does not seem to have been any system of excise on opium.[41] In 1853, Nathan Allen argued that to mislead the public opinion both in England, India and elsewhere, the Imperial authorities had fabricated stories about the peerless growth of the opium trade under the Mughal rulers.[42] Given the varied information, it is a bit difficult to arrive at a conclusion that the Mughals had any monopoly in the trade. As a rule, therefore, there was no control on the cultivation of opium poppies and opium revenue in medieval India. The policy adopted by the Dutch in Ceylon appears to have been duplicated by the British in Bengal from 1773.

British opium monopoly

The establishment of the government opium monopoly in Bengal evolved through a process of autocratic administrative experiments between the early 1770s and 1800s. In a 1957 study, G.N. Chandra provided a chronological account of the growth and development of the opium monopoly in Bengal.[43] In 1983, *The Cambridge Economic History of India* maintained that poppy cultivation was profitable to farmers and they enthusiastically took part in production.[44] These works failed to demonstrate the nature of the political struggle between the colonial authorities and the dominant social groups, or the hostility amongst the European trading companies that resulted from the enforcement of the monopoly. The following discussion illustrates the social dimensions of the political battle that occurred during the consolidation of the opium monopoly in Bengal, and its eventual outcome as a mass uprising in the poppy-growing areas.

To organize the opium enterprise, the government of the East India Company in 1763 established the so-called 'Gentlemen's monopoly' run by the Patna Council. It consisted of Company officials, who entered the business directly and distributed money through Indian agents (*gumastas*) amongst farmers to grow opium poppies. The employees received their salaries from the profits they made individually in the opium monopoly.[45] However, the tendency to maximize personal benefits from the trade often led to conflict and misunderstanding between the rival Indian agents. The Gentlemen's monopoly also experienced competition from the French and Dutch merchants, who received opium supplies from the Patna traders.

In an attempt to establish a business consortium in opium, the East India authorities in 1765 allowed other European companies to participate in a joint venture under one general agent. Malpractice and corruption of officials affected this system,[46] when the respective companies started to 'trade clandestinely on their own account in the drug'.[47] Under the joint venture, the land under poppy cultivation was increased from 283,000 hectares in 1765–6, to 303,500 hectares in the following year.[48] This large-scale conversion of paddy fields into poppy cultivation contributed to a famine in Bengal in 1770. This famine caused the death of 10 million people[49] in an area that had been traditionally known as the 'Golden Bengal' due to its natural resources.[50] As a result of official malpractice and famine caused by the joint venture, the legal and moral control in the maintenance of the opium monopoly fell into a deep crisis.

To manage the outcomes of the fragile monopoly, governor-general Warren Hastings in 1772 withdrew the opium monopoly from the Patna Council, and leased the whole business for a fixed amount, to two local businessmen who had previous experience in the management of an opium factory at Patna. This attempt was followed by the creation of a separate Board that helped create the government monopoly of opium in Bengal in 1773.[51] Explaining the attempt, Hastings wrote:

> We have prohibited all other persons under our protection from interfering with it and we have determined to sell it by public auction for the benefit of the Company.[52]

As a result of this policy, the Dutch and French Companies lost their authority in the Patna opium trade, and the production management came under the control of the British East India Company.[53] To stop the diversion of monopoly opium into private channels, Cornwallis expelled the agents of French and Dutch companies from their possessions in India and Sri Lanka by 1795. In July 1799, the management of the opium industry was left in the hands of two senior bureaucrats, one with headquarters in Patna (Bihar Agency), and the other in Ghazipur (Benares Agency). This system eventually helped the colonial authorities to consolidate the opium administration, and achieve greater benefits from the opium industry.

During the early years of the opium monopoly, contractors were involved in the forceful engagement of poppy farmers to produce the maximum amount of opium. In 1777, the *Bengal Revenue Consultations* reported 'forcible destruction' of crops in Bihar to make land available for poppy cultivation.[54] In 1789, the *Bengal Board of Revenue Proceedings* maintained that after paying a high price to the Company authorities, contractors forced the farmers 'to increase their poppy cultivation beyond their means and convenience'.[55] The *Bengal Board of Revenue Proceedings* of 1790 maintained that the 'rapacity' of the contractors also led to conflict with zamindars or headmen (*chaudhuries*), who with interests in alternative crops, opposed poppy cultivation in their areas.[56] To prevent local zamindars from interference in the poppy cultivation, the contractors used the influence of the state power, the Patna Council.

The tension between the contractors and the zamindars was a major impediment to the growth of poppy cultivation and the revenue income derived from opium. The royalty paid by the contractors under the monopoly system was unconvincing to Lord Cornwallis, who arrived in Bengal as governor-general in 1786.[57] On his arrival, Cornwallis established a government opium monopoly in Benares, and urged zamindars to refrain from encouraging farmers in alternative crops, or to offer them better incentives. Thus, frequent mention occurs in the records of the period that under the opium monopoly, injury and oppression were inflicted upon poppy-growing farmers, and tension erupted between zamindars and contractors. To secure the confidence of the poppy cultivators, Cornwallis introduced an official purchasing system in 1789, and fixed a rate of remuneration in Bihar. Despite the measure, the government failed to increase opium production or to secure a good price from foreign markets.[58] To upgrade the opium monopoly as an important branch of the public revenue, the government in 1799 abandoned the contract system and adopted the agency system instead.

Under the new system the government imposed repressive regulations on poppy cultivation and urged poppy farmers to 'refund threefold' the advances for any land, which they did not cultivate according to their undertaking.[59] The leading contemporary economist Adam Smith criticized the intimidation of the farmers by the official authorities:

> A rich field of rice or other grain has been ploughed up; in order to make room for a plantation of poppies; when the chief foresaw that extraordinary profit was likely to be made by opium.[60]

Smith also indicated that Company officials, in certain cases, forced unwilling farmers to accept advance money to grow poppies instead of other crops in their paddy fields. Assessment by Indian officials while converting agricultural land into poppy cultivation often provoked disagreement by farmers. Once a farmer started poppy cultivation, invariably he had to continue production year after year. Considering the crop unprofitable, the farmers were less than enthusiastic about growing poppies and neglected to water them.

Despite the unwillingness of the farmers, poppy cultivation continued with greater control by the colonial bureaucracy. The hierarchy of the opium administration was constituted in five categories: (1) the Collector, a senior British administrator; (2) the *gumastas*, a group of local commercial agents directly attached to the administration; (3) the *sudder mattus*, members of the landed aristocracy; (4) the village *mattus* or *khatadars*, agents of the villagers; and (5) the poppy farmers. Negotiations between the manage-ment and the poppy growers were conducted through village intermediaries, who received a commission for their services in the implementation of opium policies in rural areas. The arbitrary role of the middlemen and coercion of the field officers often caused frustration and suffering among the poppy farmers. Every cultivator was bound to sell the whole of his produce to the Opium Departments, at a rate fixed by the government.

As a result of state patronization, the opium monopoly emerged as one of the largest economic activities in colonial India. To maintain and promote the trade in opium, the government increased the cultivation of poppy to those areas where the quality was superior. Under the Regulation of 1816, the police and the excise officers were authorized to take action against the zamindars and other landed aristocrats if there was any indication found that they had encouraged clandestine cultivation of poppy and illicit sale of opium.[61] To encourage maximum production by the poppy farmers, the governor-general increased the incentives for the poppy growers once in 1822, and again in 1830.[62] This measure helped expand poppy cultivation in 49 sub-divisions of the Benares agency and 11 districts in the Bihar agency[63] (see Map 1). By the mid-1850s, the total area engaged under the Bengal opium monopoly was about 31 million hectares (120,000 square miles), where under the licensed system 1.25 million cultivators were engaged in poppy cultivation.[64] In 1857, a British parliamentary paper documented that the production of opium under the Bengal monopoly rose from 1,600 metric tons in 1845–6 to 3,200 metric tons in 1854–5.[65] Out of this total production, the Bihar agency contributed the two-thirds of the amount.

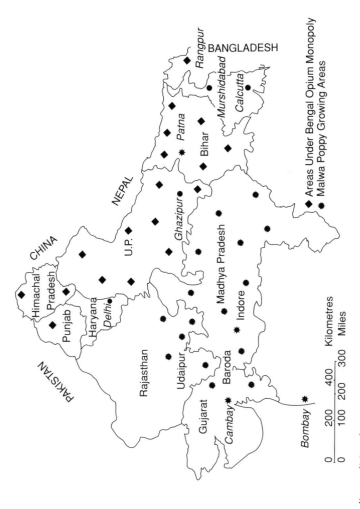

Map 1 India: traditional poppy growing areas (1997 boundary)

During the 1820s and 1830s the British government either conquered or physically blocked the strategically important poppy-growing areas to help expand the opium enterprise in Bengal. It annexed areas along the eastern side of Punjab in 1801 and some parts of UP in 1803, and subsequently expanded the Bengal opium monopoly system in northern India. Opium poppies had been grown sporadically without official control in Punjab under Sikh rule, and in Oudh under the Nawab's rule. Following the annexation of Punjab in 1849, the British government extended the opium monopoly to certain districts there and poppy was then grown under the licence system. A similar system was also adopted in Jammu and Kashmir after these areas were annexed from the Sikh rulers. In Kashmir, the average area under this crop was roughly 760 hectares in the mid-1850s.[66] The total area under the government opium monopoly system in northern India including the UP was about 26 million hectares (100,000 square miles).[67] Poppy cultivation was extended to these areas under the Benares Opium Agency. With the creation of this agency, Ghazipur emerged as the second largest opium producing centre after Patna. The total area engaged in poppy cultivation in northern India gradually increased to match the Bihar agency.

Following the British invasion, the government adopted mechanisms to forcibly involve farmers in poppy cultivation, and to prevent local zamindars from intervening in the opium monopoly. There was a growing body of public opinion in India that to bring about a change in the policy the government should abolish the system of opium monopoly. Aggregating the opinions of the poppy cultivators, the British Indian Association, in a petition to the House of Commons in 1853, urged:

> Justice requires that the interference of the government with the cultivation should cease, and that revenue derived from the drug should be in the shape of fixed duties on manufacture and exportation. ... By the adoption of this principle, the cultivators will posses that freedom of action which all men possess under governments.[68]

This appeal for the emancipation of poppy farmers from forced cultivation of opium was unsuccessful.[69] Ignoring the appeal, the colonial authorities increased indirect control over the cultivation of the opium poppy in central India. In 1856–7, the government regulated about 117,000 hectares engaged in poppy cultivation in that region.[70] Despite the resentment and suffering of the poppy growers, the opium monopoly in Bengal and private poppy cultivation in central India flourished. Under the opium monopoly, the economic conditions of the poppy farmers deteriorated and the strength of the zamindars was undermined.

The culmination of a long-term conflict between the local zamindars and the promoters of poppy cultivation helped to provoke rural people to join hands against the colonial authorities. In his work *Reminiscences of the Great Mutiny 1857–59* William Forbes-Mitchell, a sergeant who took part in the suppression of the uprising in UP, argued that the introduction of forced poppy cultivation sparked mass rebellion in the region.[71] Mitchell contended that the mass uprising was more serious in the poppy-growing areas of northern India. People in the south, on the other hand, generally aided the colonial government. The most vulnerable areas were Oudh, Rohilkhand, Doab, Meerut, Bengal, Bihar, Benares, Gujarat, Bombay and Allahabad, where the rural population extensively took part with urban people in the uprising. The war was deadly in Oudh, where over 100,000 civilian-armed men joined in the rebellion.[72] The annexation of Oudh in August 1856 was described by Ralph Moore as 'the blackest crime' that England ever committed, and was the 'immediate cause' of the so-called Sepoy Mutiny of 1857.[73] The revolt of 1857 can largely be ascribed to the discontents of local zamindars and poppy cultivators who persistently opposed the colonial opium monopoly system.

The events of the uprising in India in many ways were comparable to the Chinese Opium Wars of the mid-nineteenth century. (I shall discuss the Anglo-Chinese opium wars later). While in India, the unwilling farmers were compelled to cultivate the opium poppy, in China the ruling authorities were forced to open their ports to accept opium from India. In both cases, the pro-revenue claims of the colonial power were triumphant.

Pro-revenue actions

Throughout the nineteenth century the colonial authorities pursued double-standard narcotics laws to eliminate the private traders from the opium trade and help the Bengal opium monopoly system flourish. Under Regulation 3 of 1816, clauses agreeable to the monopoly system were incorporated.[74] In his contemporary work, Donald Matheson argued that, practising the 'worst form of Machiavellian policy',[75] the colonial authorities appropriated revenue from opium exports and the domestic consumption of intoxicating drugs. After the uprising of 1857, the government adopted further legislation banning poppy cultivators from growing opium poppies for private profit. Under the Opium Act of 1878, the government imposed penalties for smuggling contraband opium. The following discussion considers the extent of the political control that assisted colonial authorities to draw multiple revenues from harmful drugs.

'Blood money'

For capital formation, as well as to run the administration, the colonial government in India continued the supply of opium to China throughout the nineteenth century. As early as 1800, the Chinese Emperor issued an edict prohibiting the import and abuse of the Indian drug altogether.[76] Although the Chinese rulers treated opium as a vice, it was officially treated by the Indian customs as a 'medicinal drug'.[77] Its use in England was regulated by the Poisonous Drugs Act of 1819. Despite the fact, the continued supply of opium from India was creating socio-economic and political concerns for the Chinese authorities.

Pursuing an unrelenting policy, British opium trade to China and the Asia-Pacific region expanded at the turn of the eighteenth century. The Annual Reports for the *Proceedings of the Board of Trade (Opium)* during 1794–1805 maintained that the net amount of revenue from opium exports increased from Rs414,869 in 1794–5 to Rs983,514 in 1797–8 and it shot up to Rs2,370,706 in 1798–9.[78] Compared to the Portuguese and the Dutch, who never had exported over '200 chests [13 metric tons] in any year' to China, the sending of opium by the East India Company broke all previous records.[79] Manufactured under the supervision of qualified staff, Indian opium was dearest to Chinese addicts, who were prepared to pay a premium for the drug.[80] In violation of the Chinese ban but in line with the government's pro-revenue policies, the export of opium from India consecutively increased until the late nineteenth century.

In an attempt to technically continue the export of so-called 'provision opium' by individual companies, the British government prevented its marines from participating in the Indo-China opium trade, but set up a public auction system in Calcutta. The British owners ran most of the private companies, who took part in the prospering opium trade, while Americans and local Parsees operated some.[81] Dane argued that British merchants and free traders, 'many of whom were lawless men', smuggled opium to China in open violation of Chinese regulations.[82] To give this contraband trade a legal status, the British Parliament in 1833 unilaterally extended the Charter of the Indo-China opium trade for twenty years. The Chinese authorities attempted to stop the contraband supply of opium from India, but through the Opium Wars of the early 1840s and late 1850s China was forced by the maritime powers to legalize the opium trade. In these Wars, China lost about 20,000 soldiers and paid a huge penalty for the forceful resistance to Indian opium.

As a result of the First Opium War of 1839–42, opium exports from India to China increased tremendously by the mid-nineteenth century. In 1857, Donald Matheson indicated that opium exports rose from 127 metric tons in 1800, to 2,485 metric tons in 1837, but following the First Opium War it rose to 6,372 metric tons in 1857.[83] Table 1.1 shows that the export of opium under the Bengal government opium monopoly during 1845–55 increased by 51 per cent, while the total receipts from the Bengal opium monopoly increased by 30 per cent during 1845–53. However, as a result of the price reduction in the Chinese market during the mid-1850s, the receipts from that market dropped by 5 per cent. The British Parliamentary Paper *East India (Opium)* in 1857 maintained that the government of India earned a total land revenue of £15.07 million in 1854–5 followed by opium revenue of £4.42 million.[84] These statistics did not include the export of Malwa opium supplied from the non-British territories in central India. While throughout India land revenue was the number one revenue item, the opium revenue in Bengal exceeded it. Official statistics indicate that in 1854–5 the land revenue in Bengal was £3.33 million, whereas opium revenue was £3.37 million.[85] In 1854–5, the Bengal monopoly alone contributed 76.24 per cent of the total opium revenue earned in the country. Including the revenue from the hemp (*ganja*) monopoly in north Bengal, the total drug revenue in Bengal was far greater than any other revenues in colonial India.

Table 1.1   *Bengal government opium monopoly, 1844–55*

Year	Total exports (in metric tons)	Total receipts (in million Rs)
1845–6	1572	26.68
1846–7	1577	27.80
1847–8	2230	27.26
1848–9	2612	35.47
1849–50	2500	35.72
1850–1	2334	32.62
1851–2	2213	37.74
1852–3	2557	38.73
1853–4	3144	37.22
1854–5	3241	37.11

Source: 'Returns Relating to the Growth, &c; of Opium', British Parliamentary Papers, *East India (Opium)*, *1857*, Session 1 (60), volume 11, p. 124.

During the late nineteenth century, the British government adopted two important pieces of legislation that helped consolidate its control on opium trade. Under the Opium Act of 1857, the cultivation of poppy and manufacture of opium went under the direct control of the Bengal administration and the Board of Revenue at Calcutta. The Act repealed existing regulations on narcotics of 1793, 1795, 1816 and 1824,[86] and prohibited private traders, including local zamindars, from engaging in the opium trade.[87] The law forbade unauthorized poppy cultivation, and made it a punishable offence. Opposing the government policies on 'moral' grounds, some official members demanded the cessation of poppy cultivation under a monopoly.[88] However, for economic reasons their proposal was opposed by the Bengal government, and by the Bengal Board of Revenue. The colonial rulers denied a similar submission, for the withdrawal of authoritative control on poppy cultivation, in 1864, in 1868–9, and in 1881. In response, the government only adjusted the real value of rupees by increasing incentives to the poppy growers from Rs3 per *seer*[89] in 1850–1, to Rs5 in 1881–2 and Rs6 in 1894–5, for the promotion of the trade. This policy helped assist the colonial government to boost opium exports that had fallen almost 50 per cent in 1958, by about 90 per cent by the early 1870s.

The government enacted further legislation to deal with smugglers who undermined the opium laws and encouraged cultivators to divert extra quantities of opium at a handsome price. In May 1870, a river trader, Ram Dass, was caught in possession of about 508 kilos of illicit opium on the Hooghly River.[90] To control smuggling, the private possession and trade in opium became punishable under the Opium Act of 1878.[91] Under this Act, a maximum imprisonment of one year or a fine for Rs1,000 or both was imposed for illegal cultivation and trade of opium poppy.[92] The objectives of the above policies were to keep control over poppy cultivation both in British and non-British territories, and to ensure that the cultivators delivered to the state the whole of the produce without diverting it into illicit channels.

As a result of British Imperial policies, the annual revenue from opium exports rose dramatically. Referring to the Revenue Minister, the *Medical Times and Gazette* in 1873 indicated that the government of India at the beginning of the 1870s earned about £7.75 million from the Indian opium trade annually.[93] After a verification of the facts and surplus receipts from the estimated budget, the journal further contended that the actual receipts from the opium trade were £8.66 million. While the official reports celebrated this revenue increase, opponents condemned the policy, both at home and abroad, as 'a revenue of blood'! Nevertheless, the opium export continued, mostly to Hong Kong, China (Treaty Ports), the Straits Settlements, the Philippines, Singapore, Java (Indonesia), Cochin China, Ceylon (Sri Lanka), Mauritius, Mozambique and Zanzibar.[94] Amongst these areas, Hong Kong was the biggest centre for the colonial opium trade from where opium was smuggled into Mainland China, and also sent elsewhere in the Asia-Pacific region. The trade in opium, that also included opium from central India (Malwa), was continued by the British government until 1935.

Malwa toll

Through a series of wars, the British government forced the central Indian rulers and traders to hand over a substantial transit fee for their opium exports. In order to earn an extra revenue and protect the export market of the Bengal opium monopoly, the import of

Malwa opium[95] into or transport through British territory was prohibited except on payment of the bypass duty. A similar transit duty
had been in force in the 1780s on opium produced in the
Gorakhpur district of Oudh under the Nawab's dominion.[96] In line
with Oudh, the British government in 1830 adopted a transit duty
on Malwa opium (opium produced in the non-British territories in
central India) passing through British territories on the way to
foreign markets.[97] The following discussion outlines the geostrategic
objectives that inspired the British government to control opium
exports from central India.

The opium grown in Malwa had emerged as a rival to the Bengal
opium monopoly by the late eighteenth century. Malwa opium was
traditionally exported to China via Baroda and Cambay from the ports
of Diu and Daman, which were Portuguese possessions. By the end of
the century the colonial authorities came to realize that the increase of
opium supplies from central Indian states was compelling the Bengal
government to sell monopoly opium to China at very low prices. In
1796, the *Fort William–India House Correspondence* maintained that to
sell the Company's opium at a competitive price, merchants of the
East India Company gave Rs1.2 million 'remittance to China'.[98] Four
years later, the *Fort William–India House Correspondence* again indicated
that due to greater demand for opium from Bombay and Madras,
Bengal opium was facing a 'large deficit'.[99] To respond to this trade
competition, the British government pursued both military and
diplomatic solutions.

In an attempt to block the central Indian states, the British
government invaded some of the strategically important areas.
At the beginning of the nineteenth century the colonial
authorities annexed South Gujarat and obtained greater control
over the West Coast. Following this invasion, the colonial
authorities between 1824 and 1826 achieved the purchasing rights
of opium from Baroda, Holkar, and a number of small States.
However, the poppy cultivators refused to sell their produce to
the British Opium Agent at an arbitrarily fixed price. This measure
also failed to stop the indigenous rulers from engaging in
opium exports to China. In defiance of British policies, cultivators
in central India passed a large amount of opium to the Portuguese
ports of Diu, Daman and Goa, or used transit facilities in Karachi.
In a memorandum to the Royal Commission James F. Finlay,

Secretary of the Department of Finance and Commerce in India, maintained that 'Scindia, Jeypore, and other important Chiefs refused from the beginning to join in the arrangement', and used Karachi port for exporting opium into the China market.[100] In order to compel the central Indian farmers and authorities to submit to British policies, and to expand trade facilities in the Indus valley, the British government annexed Sind in 1843.[101] The annexation of Sind provided them with the ability to control exportable opium grown in the small central Indian states of Rajputana, Baroda, and other areas.

The conquest of Sind, amongst other strategic gains, gave the British government an opportunity to collect an increasing amount of revenue from central Indian opium exports. The headquarters for the Malwa transit duty was Indore, with sub-agencies in Bhopal, Udaipur, Jaora, Ratlam, Chittore and Mandsaur. In 1883–4, the amount of opium passing through the Indore agency was 2,566 metric tons.[102] The opium from these places was sent directly to Bombay for export. Transit duty on Malwa opium was levied at points on the border between the central Indian States and the Bombay Presidency, which were invaded during the previous century. In 1876, D.W.K.B. indicated that the average revenue from Malwa opium in 1875–6 was about £2.25 million, while the sales of Bengal opium were £4 million during this period.[103] In a contemporary paper, Batten maintained that the value of average exports of Malwa opium for the five years ending 1890–1 was Rs4 million.[104] Thus, without having any direct control over the cultivation or manufacture of Malwa opium, the British government derived a huge amount of revenue through the Malwa transit system. Alongside its revenue from the opium export, the colonial authorities increased the amount of revenue obtained from the domestic consumption of intoxicating drugs.

Excise revenue

In line with the promotion of export trade in opium, the pursuit of 'maximum revenue' was the core principle of the Excise (*Abkari*) policy of the government of British India. Rajeshwari Prasad, in his book entitled *Some Aspects of British Revenue Policy in India: 1773–1833*, provides a detailed account of the British government's major drives in three vital areas: for example, salt, opium and customs. In 1858, *Meliora* maintained that amongst all these sources, the trade in opium was 'particularly lucrative'. In 1922, G.S. Bajpai argued that as part of their 'civilized' culture,[105] the colonial authorities in Bengal established a branch of excise revenue for the retail sale of opium, cannabis and liquor in the early 1790s.

During the early years of their rule, the Imperial rulers in Bengal adopted policies that expanded excise revenue from deleterious drugs. As early as 1793, the government adopted excise duty on licensed vendors and on the transit of cannabis from north Bengal to Dhaka (formerly Dacca), and other urban areas.[106] In an attempt to earn revenue from liquor trade, the colonial authorities in 1789 introduced an auction system for selling the 'right to distil liquor' in Dhaka, and as a result of this policy the liquor revenue in Dhaka district by 1837 had reached Rs41,000.[107] A similar trend in the sale of country liquor was evident in all other big cities and district headquarters in Bengal. Following these initial measures, licensed shops were introduced in different city centres for the distribution of excise opium and cannabis to local customers. Under Regulation 6 of 1800, an excise duty was introduced on the consumption of cannabis, while excise duty had been imposed on opium and liquor by 1797.[108] The excise opium was manufactured in, and supplied from, Bihar and Benares government factories to licensed vendors for local consumption. Depending on local demands, the availability of illicit supplies, and the effectiveness of the administrative machinery, the retail price was set by the revenue department. The number and the location of licensed opium shops was determined by the local authorities under the control of the Board of Revenue, and the license fee for each shop was fixed annually by public auction.

The colonial authorities, in the early stages of their rule, also attempted to appropriate excise revenue from the production and consumption of cannabis in some parts of East Bengal (now Bangladesh). In line with the contemporary opium monopoly in Patna, the British government by the early 1790s tried to regulate the cultivation and distribution of cannabis (*ganja*) by private traders. Farmers in Jessore district produced excisable cannabis, and for its taste consumers throughout the region praised the '*Jessori ganja*'. An official wrote in 1809:

Ganja was largely cultivated within the district, principally about [in] Keshubpore, in pergunnahs Ramchunderpore and Taragonia, but also to a small extent in the north-western corner. The duty was collected upon it at the time of its purchase or export from the producing districts, of which Jessore was then a principal one.[109]

The same report indicated that the annual production of cannabis in Jessore ranged between 1,900 and 2,200 metric tons. Due to under-hand connections between the cannabis producers and the private traders (*byaparies*), the taxation on cannabis did not provide sufficient revenue for the colonial authorities. To break this nexus, the colonial authorities in the mid-1850s introduced the *Ganja Mahal* system (monopoly under licensed traders) in Naogaon in Rajshahi district, and in some parts of Bogra and Dinajpur districts, and banned hemp cultivation in Jessore in 1875. A London publication in 1891, however, claimed that cannabis production was continued in Jessore and Pabna districts during the 1880s.[110] By the early 1890s, the total area under official cannabis cultivation reached over 24,000 hectares, Naogaon being the headquarters of the administration.[111] Given the administrative arrangements, the government maintained a monopoly system in cannabis production in north Bengal, and most of the yield was exported to other parts of the region.

Nevertheless, in support of the export revenue from opium the colonial authorities pursued contradictory measures during the early nineteenth century. In an attempt to receive foreign currency, especially from China, the colonial authorities discouraged local consumption of opium and encouraged opium exports. In 1813, Collectors were warned about the sale and consumption of opium, 'except for medicinal purposes'.[112] Under Regulation 13 of 1816, the government declared a 'maximum revenue with minimum con-sumption' policy that contradicted the facilitation of opium distribution through licensed vendors.[113] The availability of excise opium (for example, poppy heads, *madak* and *chandu*) through licensed vendors made the government's regulatory measures doubtful. In India, where public opinion was generally reluctant to endorse the medicinal and recreational use of opium, licensed vendors were encouraged to distribute increasing amounts of opium through licensed shops.

As a result of the government's pro-revenue drug policy, the distribution and consumption of excise opium increased significantly. The sale of excise opium through the licensed vendors in Bengal in 1873–4 raised an amount of Rs1.75 million[114] that rose to Rs2.75 million in 1892–3.[115] It is likely that these figures also include excise revenue from other forms of intoxicating drugs. In 1892–3, Bengal licensed vendors distributed about 210 metric tons of excise opium among the local population. In Assam, the excise revenue rose from Rs1.17 million in 1873–4 to Rs1.87 in 1892–3.[116] In 1873–4, the licensed vendors in Assam sold about 70 metric tons of excise opium to local consumers. In Chattishgarh Division of the Central Provinces, the net revenue after deducting the cost price from excise opium in 1874–5 was over Rs100,000.[117] The number of opium shops for retail sale in the Central Provinces was 1,133 in 1892–3, and the quantity of opium issued to these shops was about 30 metric tons. A similar trend in the distribution of intoxicating drugs continued in other parts of South Asia. (I shall discuss the distribution of excise opium in Sri Lanka and Burma in Chapter 2.) Figure 1.1 shows that during 1880–94, the revenue from excise opium cautiously increased while the revenue from export opium and Malwa transit duty gradually fell from Rs7.68 million to Rs5.46 and from Rs2.53 million to Rs1.65 million respectively. This decline occurred largely as a result of the growing of opium in China to counteract supplies from India. The above statistics also show that due to political pressure created by the anti-opium lobbies in England and in South Asia, the sale of excise opium declined during 1892–4. As a result of the government's revenue 'maximization' policies, the consumption of opium, cannabis and liquor increased implicitly. While the British government had essentially controlled its own drug problem through the Pharmacy Act of 1868, a large amount of opium abuse continued among the South Asian population with little regulation.

None the less, the drug policies pursued by the government were increasingly attacked by the anti-opiumists and temperance workers in England, in China, and in South Asia as both reckless and immoral. In an attempt to overcome anti-narcotics public opinion, the British government in 1893 set up a Royal Commission on Opium that lauded the opium monopoly and recognized moderate use of opium as good for health. But the medical evidence provided

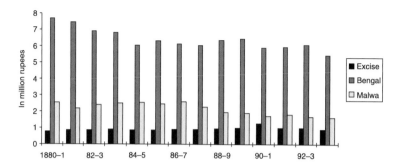

Figure 1.1 Gradual increase in excise revenue and decrease in opium exports in India, 1880–94
Source: Based on data provided by the *British Royal Commission on Opium*, 1894, vol. 61, p. 348

in defence of the Indo-China opium trade was attacked by pressure groups in the US, and refuted by subsequent Opium Committees in accordance with their observations in the Asia-Pacific region, in Sri Lanka and in India. Despite the resistance, the official distribution of excise opium and other intoxicating drugs proceeded when the principle of 'maximum revenue with minimum consumption' was still in force during the post-Royal Commission period.

2
Anti-opium Pressures

As public opinion in the US, UK, India, Ceylon (Sri Lanka), Burma and China started to rally against the colonial opium trade, the adoption of international control on the supply of drugs from India, Hong Kong and elsewhere became imperative. Many domestic and cross-regional pressures contributed to the initial direction of international control of South Asian opium in the first decade of the twentieth century. Driven by its socio-economic objectives, the US government initiated an international move to regulate the opium trade in South Asia. The US attempt connected the Indian opium trade more than ever with global politics. Besides the US push, a political demand for amending the colonial drug policies had persisted in South Asia from the late nineteenth century. Finally, the anti-opium battle launched by Christian missionaries, especially in England, compelled the British government to set up a Royal Commission on Opium in 1893. The British government, the most powerful Imperial government on earth at that time, eventually joined in the US-sponsored initiative at the expense of its Indian opium revenue, and risked the efficacy of the Royal Commission.

US concerns on opium traffic

At the dawning of the twentieth century, the US drug policy towards South Asia was the culmination of domestic and external elements. Besides the political influence of US missionaries in China, who vehemently opposed the British opium trade, the material interest of the US in China was an important factor. The findings of the Philippines Commission, that outlined the hazards of opium use in Burma and the Asia-Pacific region, provided a rationale to the US to become involved in the South Asian drug debate. Above all, an increasing trend in the abuse of opiates in the US became a concern for the government.

Opiate addiction in the US

To review the twentieth-century international regulations on drugs in South Asia, an understanding about the nineteenth-century opiate abuse in the US is essential. Two major aspects dominated the US political mind: (1) the increase of addiction to opium smoking (mostly adulterated) in the big cities, and (2) the misuse of semi-synthetic and synthetic opiates like morphine and heroin. Opium poppies, adapted for smoking purposes, were not commercially grown to any great extent in the US. Opium came from India, mostly by licit ways, through the 'Golden Gates' of Hong Kong and Macao. In 1890, the annual importation of prepared opium in San Francisco was 28,662 metric tons, providing over $758,000 revenue to the Federal government.[1] This capricious importation created a 'vicious indulgence' both for the Chinese immigrants and the Afro-American community, which smoked prepared opium. White Americans were progressively acquiring the habit.

Chandu smoking, a habit that first spread in China as a result of Anglo-American trade policies, now backfired to the US by Chinese in the form of addicted Chinese immigrants. The US was involved in the events leading to the Opium War between China and England from 1839 to 1842, and received an equal share in the 'spoils of victory'.[2] In 1858, the US government accepted the Tientsin Treaty and tariff arrangement with China, and allowed Americans to freely participate in the opium traffic. Nonetheless, the Chinese immigrant labourers, who crossed the Pacific in the 1850s and 1860s and brought their opium pipes and *chandu* smoking habit with them to the US West Coast, transmitted this habit.[3] About 70,000 railroad workers, those settled in Chinatown in San Francisco, established their opium dens and spread the habit amongst the 'gamblers and adventurers' of the society.[4] The first opium smoking in the Chinese dens in San Francisco began in 1868, and by 1880 about 6,000 US citizens, both male and female, became victims of the vice.[5] An 1898 study estimated that about 30 per cent of the Chinese residents in the area were addicted to opium smoking and that 10 per cent of the entire population of Chinatown were habitual opium drunkards.[6]

Opium dens were later established in many large and small cities, where the Chinese managers unobtrusively served opium pipes to both Afro-Americans and white residents in their locality. In 1877–8, in his report about the opium fiends in Deadwood, a gold mining town of the Black Hills in South Dakota, the Deputy Sheriff noted that 'after smoking only a few times', the devotees of opium have found it almost impossible to break to the dependence.[7] By the 1890s the proclivity was increasing amongst the white population. Describing the situation in California, Frederich J. Masters, in a contemporary study, wrote:

> It is no uncommon thing to see young men and even women of our race stealing into Chinatown at night for 'dope'. It is appalling to see the number of depraved women upon whose discolored faces opium has stamped its indelible brand. Frequent arrests are made by the police of youths found in opium resorts.[8]

Similar arrests took place in San Francisco, New Orleans, and occasionally in Chicago under the state and police regulations of 1895. Following the ban on white people visiting Chinatown, this targeted group established their own 'joints' to sell and smoke the drug. From these centres, the habit was soon transmitted amongst the anti-social and criminal groups 'that existed on the periphery of society and frequented the gambling saloons and brothels'.[9] In a similar way, it spread eastwards across the country, causing 'the threat of social upheaval' and moral degradation.[10] In August 1882 the *Evening Post* maintained that in 20 opium dens in New York city, opium smokers gathered in groups from all backgrounds.[11] In 1900, some 3.3 million doses of opium were sold every month in dens in the State of Vermont, the quantity being 'enough to provide' a minimum daily supply to the total population.[12]

The abuse of opiates in the US took place in two forms: opium eating and the maltreatment of morphine injection. Without realizing the tranquillizing properties of opium, physicians used it as a therapeutic agent.[13] The blended opium was sold by pharmaceutical industries under numerous trade names: for example, Dover's Powder, Laudanum, Ayer's Cherry Pectoral, Mrs Winslow's Soothing Syrup, McMunn's Elixir, Magendie's Solution, Godfrey's Cordial, and Hamlin's Wizard Oil. These medicines could be purchased in any pharmacy without prescription, or even in a grocery store.[14] The 'magic' central substance of these medicines was morphine, an alkaloid named after Morpheus, the Greek god of sleep. However, knowledge of the working of this agent in the nervous system remained unclear and often contradictory until the 1870s.[15] Ignorance of the opiate disease resulted in many, including physicians, becoming victims of opium eating.[16] In 1872, explaining his own experience of the opium habit, a US physician, James H. Brown, noted that he had 'the most terrible suffering of both mind and body' under the influence of this drug.[17] However, by prescribing opium as a tranquillizer and pain-killer in the symptomatic treatment of various diseases, unwary and unscrupulous physicians were contributing in the abuse of this drug.

Blended opium, and the invention of morphine and the hypodermic needle to administer the drug, helped drive hundreds of thousands of Americans to drug addiction. In 1853, Alexander Wood in Edinburgh invented the hypodermic syringe, and it was subsequently brought to North America. The chronic use of morphine became widespread during the American Civil War of 1860–5, when soldiers and prisoners of war injected the drug in large quantities on the battlefield and in prison camps. In 1868, Horace B. Day, in his book *The Opium Habit With Suggestions as to the Remedy*, wrote:

> Maimed and shattered survivors from a hundred battlefields, diseased and disabled soldiers from hostile prisons, anguished and helpless wives and mothers, made so by the slaughter of those who were dearest to them, have found, many of them, temporary relief from their sufferings in opium.[18]

The practice was particularly noticeable among ex-soldiers for the relief of pain and suffering from injuries received on the battlefield, and this gave rise to the term for the habit, 'the army disease'.[19] Following the war, thousands of ex-soldiers returned to civilian life addicted to morphine, and applauded it to friends and relatives. 'Habit-forming drug use in America was first recognized in 1864,' and the Civil War eventually produced about 400,000 opiate addicts in the country.[20] In 1867, describing the extent of opiate abuse during the post-Civil War era, Fitzhugh Ludlow wrote:

> The habit is gaining fearful ground among our professional men, the operatives in our mills, our weary sewing women, our fagged clerks, our disappointed wives, former liquor-drunkards, our very day-laborers, who a generation ago took gin; all our classes, from the highest to the lowest, are yearly increasing their consumption of the drug.[21]

After about eight and a half decades, H.J. Anslinger and William F. Tompkins claimed that drug dependence in the US in 1877 was 'almost eight times' higher than in 1953.[22] As the destructive qualities of morphine became evident amongst armies, physicians, and commoners, warnings about the dangers of opiate addiction was given in medical science in the 1870s and 1880s.[23] Medical reports and studies by a number of eminent medical experts clearly indicated the increasing trend of opiate abuse.

Nevertheless, the availability of opiates and the ignorance of consumers about the hazards of the drugs had pushed thousands of Americans to physical dependence and addiction by the end of the century. Lewis H. Lapman, in his contemporary study on 'Drug Prohibition and the Conscience of Nations', maintained that the number of morphine addicts in the US, in 1895, represented 2 to 4 per cent of the total population.[24] Consulting parallel sources, Jessica de Grazia in her book *DEA: The War Against Drugs* estimated that, in 1900, there were about 250,000 drug addicts in the US countryside from middle-class, middle-age, female backgrounds.[25] The above information reveals that despite the growing concern of the medical scientists, drug abuse was on the rise among different sections of people in the urban and rural areas.

The emergence of heroin, as a remedy for morphine addiction, contributed to the worsening of opiate abuse in the US. In 1890, Diacetylmorphine, or heroin, the 'great shadow' substance of morphine, was invented in Germany. It was imported to the US in 1898 for use in the treatment of tuberculosis and morphine addiction. The properties of the drug, which is ten times more powerful than morphine, were initially completely misunderstood. Consequently, the tides of heroin addiction swept onto consumers who took the drug for medicinal purposes. After dependency on the drug became recognized, many physicians recommended that heroin be prohibited entirely in the US. The ever-increasing use of non-medicinal opium derivatives – morphine, heroin, codeine, laudanum, barbiturates, etc. – in US society created great concern in many professional and scientific groups, including government bodies.

The growing magnitude of the drug menace gradually awakened the US mind to the fact that dependence somehow developed from the abuse of opiates. Physicians and workers in the public health movement described the obsession as the 'dubious legacy of the East', and demanded that opiates be outlawed in the US.[26] This resulted in the passage of opiate laws to control the sale and use of opium in Massachusetts, New York, Nevada, and Georgia around the turn of the twentieth century. Every large city in the US adopted police regulations governing the sale and use of smoking opium. To institute a nation-wide regulation on opiates, the US government passed the National Food and Drugs Act in June 1906. Nonetheless, in the absence of international regulations, domestic efforts in the US failed to limit the sale or consumption of these drugs.

A cognizance in the US government about the importance of stopping the supply of crude opium from the source countries, especially India, influenced its leaders to take international initiatives at the beginning of the twentieth century. The US government perceived that the promotion of a collective security to deter the drug threat was vital for its own interests. To make the domestic anti-opiate moves successful, the government felt that other countries, especially the UK, should take the same stand.[27] Thus, medical awareness in the US of the use of opiates resolved the century-long debate amongst colonial medical experts in South Asia. This development was aided by another organized group, the ex-China missionaries, many of whom themselves were medical practitioners.

Missionary politics

In harmony with their British counterparts, the US Protestant missionaries went to China during the mid-nineteenth century to preach Christianity amongst the Chinese. They suffered heavy losses, both in men and materials, during the Boxer rebellion in 1899. While critics blamed ex-China missionaries for the Boxer turmoil and rejected their claim to reimbursement, missionary leaders sought to use this incident to influence US government policy against narcotics.

In a decisive attempt to arrest the British opium trade, the local Chinese indiscriminately attacked the missionary barracks and burnt down most of their properties. Following the out-burst, some of the leading US newspapers became highly critical about the role of the missionaries in China. In 1900, the *New York Times* editorial criticized the expectation of missionary leaders that they would have US armed protection in China.[28] The role of the missionaries, during these years, was randomly attacked by political analysts, diplomats and secular forces in the US and elsewhere.

In an attempt to pass the blame, the missionaries raised many serious questions about the legality of Indian opium traffic in China. They constituted an anti-opium lobby in the US, and tried to influence the government to interfere in the South Asian opium trade. Through this organized platform, they argued that British Imperial drug trafficking was chiefly responsible for the Boxer massacre and accused the imperialist powers of 'encroaching on Chinese territory and sovereignty'.[29] The missionaries asked for the withdrawal of all foreign troops from China and termination of the Anglo-Chinese treaties which had 'forced' the opium traffic upon China following the Opium War of 1840.[30] They also reiterated that 'the legal status enjoyed by the missionaries in China was an outcome of imperialist wars and of treaties dictated at the cannon's mouth'.[31] Their leaders made contact with British religious leaders, and convinced the Archbishop of Canterbury to approach the British government on the subject.[32] In October 1891, about 500 Methodist churches of Australia, Europe and North America gathered in Washington under their auspices.[33] With this campaign, the missionary movement in the US received widespread public support, and attempted to portray the situation as a struggle for mankind.

Missionaries established a political connection with the State Department and influenced the government not to use its marines for the dismemberment of the Chinese Empire in retaliation for the

Boxer insurrection, even though the US marines could be sent from the Philippines. In 1900, ex-China missionaries, having support from other temperance and pressure groups, started a campaign against the British opium trade in China. Agreeing to the missionaries' demands, the International Reform Bureau in October 1904 suggested that British Prime Minister Balfour deliver China from her unequal treaty obligations.[34] In November 1904, the Rev. Wilbur F. Crafts, superintendent and treasurer of the Bureau, organized a hearing on the issue at the US State Department. Representatives attended this hearing from missionary and temperance societies. They put forward the demand that 'diplomatic efforts' be used to force the UK to free China from treaty bondage. In a letter to the US President the missionaries argued that before seeking an 'extension of commercial privileges' in China, the government should help release the country 'from the multiplied evils of the opium traffic'.[35] The ex-China missionaries urged the government to symbolize American rational ideals, and they sought to influence US foreign policy against the South Asian opium trade.

By raising the issue as a moral question, the ex-China missionaries created a convenient political ambience for the US government to pursue broader diplomatic pressure regarding an international ban on the immoral trade. The ex-missionaries, who involved their government in global diplomacy on intoxicating drugs, augmented the anti-opium agitation originally initiated by the SSOT in the UK in the late nineteenth century. In line with the missionaries, the relatively small share of US entrepreneurs in the Chinese export market also played a pivotal role in encouraging the US government to help free China from British trade captivity.

US trade interests

The US drive against the South Asian opium trade was significantly shaped by its growing need for an external market for its manufactured goods in China and the Asia-Pacific region. At the turn of the nineteenth century, the US economy was expanding, and required external markets to nurture industrial products. To help expedite this development, the leaders of the Chamber of Commerce joined in the anti-opium struggles with diverse temperance societies.

With the promotion of the US export trade in China during the late nineteenth century, US diplomats increasingly discouraged the Indian opium traffic. Following the signing of the Sino-American Commercial Treaty in November 1880, US trading companies sent manufactured goods from the ports of Boston and New York to Canton, and derived a handsome profit margin.[36] In 1967, Foster Rhea Dulles argued that with the industrialization of the US's economy, US entrepreneurs considered China 'as a major outlet' for US products.[37] In 1920, the *Commercial Handbook of China* indicated that the shift in the US policy largely occurred because of the 'mounting surplus' of manufactured goods that resulted from US industrial growth.[38] As a result of the increasing necessity to expand foreign market, US foreign policy experts perceived that a change in the Indo-China opium trade was cardinal for them to have any permanent influence in the region.[39] Thus the US government attempted to liberate these areas from their colonial bonds with British India. As Indiana Senator Beveridge, in January 1900, observed:

> Our largest trade must henceforth be with Asia. The Pacific is our ocean ... And the Pacific is the ocean of commerce of the future. Most future wars will be conflicts of commerce. The power that rules the Pacific, therefore, is the power that rules the world.[40]

As a result of US strategies the South Asian opium trade emerged as a crucial point of understanding in the Anglo-US power relationship. In 1894, the US government invited the UK to join in drawing up a universal agreement on the issue. To oppose British supremacy in the region the US government, during the aftermath of the Boxer uprising, provided diplomatic support for the territorial integrity of China, and a guarantee of commercial privileges. In October 1903, the US government signed a Commercial Relations Treaty with China. It became a diplomatic unanimity in the Sino-US efforts to control the drug trade in South Asia. Under the Commercial Treaty the US declared its approval of the 'prohibition' policy[41] that had been adopted by China as early as 1800.

US conformity gave China hope for its liberation from British opium traffic, and the US a more substantial footing in the Chinese economy than ever before. The growth of US trade links with China witnessed a decline in the supply of British opium from India. It fell from 3,200 metric tons in the mid-1850s, to 1,780 metric tons in

1903, with a further reduction to 210 metric tons in 1906. To help free China from opium threats, William W. Rockhill, the US Minister in Beijing, played an extraordinary diplomatic role at the beginning of the twentieth century. Thus, influenced by many factors, the State Department undertook some major diplomatic initiatives for a concerted international approach to help free China from the British opium trade. To be successful in such a gigantic task, it became imperative for the US government to invalidate the findings of the British Royal Commission on Opium, the finest document in defence of the colonial opium trade in China, India and elsewhere.

The Philippines move

Intent on winning a diplomatic battle against British Imperial power, the US government set up a Philippines Opium Commission that provided a rationale for a world-wide ban on the non-medicinal trade in opium. At the end of Spanish rule in the early 1890s, the supply of opium to the Philippines from India had increased significantly. In 1897, *British Parliamentary Papers* indicated that opium imports from India rose from 1.27 metric tons in 1889–90 to 30 metric tons in the next two years.[42] There were over 200 opium dens in the Visayan and Southern Islands, where opium smoking was mostly prevalent amongst the Chinese and local Filipinos. In the aftermath of the Spanish–American war in 1898, the US government annexed the Philippines from Spain and perceived a drug threat in its new colony. Before launching an international move on South Asian opium traffic, the US appointed an Opium Commission to the Philippines.

The US Opium Commission was a response to the Royal Commission on Opium in India. The Philippines commission consisted of two doctors and the islands' principal bishop, H. Brent. Between August 1903 and January 1904, Committee members visited most of the southeast Asian countries including China, Burma and Japan. They paid a great deal of attention to Taiwan (Formosa), where the Japanese government had gradually extinguished the opium habit.[43] The Committee submitted its 'unanimous' report on 15 June 1904. Published during the same decade as the British Royal Commission, the report outlined the 'gravest' results of opium abuse in the investigated areas. The Philippines Opium Commission recommended strict prohibition on the import, sale and use of opium. In early March 1905, the Filipino Progess Association appealed to the Congress for the enactment of legislation in accordance with the Commission's recommenda-tions.[44] In line with this proposal, the US Congress banned the opium trade in the Philippines in mid-1905, and vowed to suppress the problem on the island by March 1908.

The recommendations of the Philippines Opium Committee were almost exactly the opposite of those of the British Royal Commission on Opium and corresponded very closely to those uttered by Henry J. Wilson, a Member and MP, who filed a minority report to that Commission. The British Royal Commission strongly defended the government opium monopoly in India and technic-ally supported the contraband traffic in China. On the contrary, the Philippines Commission for the first time studied the opium legisla-tion of a number of countries where this drug had been a major concern. It recognized that the imposition of strict control over the colonial opium trade was vital for the very survival of Asians. Referring to medical opinion, the Royal Commission concluded that the effect of opium upon the human body was zero, and its moder-ate use by the Sikhs and Rajputs was good for health.[45] Compared to the British Royal Commission report, the Philippines Opium Commission made a thorough and extensive investigation of nine Asian countries including China. It raised many remarkable issues, including those that were either missed or ignored by the 'baffling' report of the Royal Commission.[46] Given the merits of the Philippines Commission report, the Australian government in late 1904 urged the British Imperial authorities to respond agreeably to the US anti-drugs initiatives in the region. In May 1906, in his state-ment, Lord Morley admitted that:

Its the Royal Commission on Opium's findings had failed to satisfy public opinion in Great Britain and to ease the conscience of those who had taken up the matter. What was the value of medical views as to whether opium was a good thing or not when we had the evidence of nations, who knew opium at close quarters. The Philippine Opium Commission, in the passage of their report ... recognized the use of opium as an evil ... that she [the US government] would not allow her citizens to encourage it even passively.[47]

While the evidence in the Royal Commission was 'either garbled or so twisted as to be useful in supporting some pro-opium conclusion',[48] the Philippines Committee investigated how the opium traffic could be suppressed in the Philippine islands. Unlike the Royal Commission, which had 'white-washed' and 'rubber-stamped' Indian opium revenue,[49] the Philippines Committee investigated the social aspect of the opium habit. It gave systematic suggestions to control the abuse of opium by the Filipinos. While the Royal Commission glorified Indian opium revenue, the Philippines Committee recommended a government monopoly system and discontinuance of the 'use of opium and the traffic therein'.[50] The Royal Commission Report repressed discussion of the opium problem, but the Philippines report gave to it a renewed impulse. Finally, the Royal Commission bent the medical evidence in favour of opium consumption in India and elsewhere, but the Philippines Committee understood the medical hazards of opium consumption and suggested the banning of the opium habit permanently.

The Philippines Commission looked at the opium problem largely the way the greater part of the world observes it today. Unlike the Royal Commission, which concluded that total prohibition was entirely beyond the power of the government, the Philippines Commission recommended prohibition of opium, except for medical purposes.[51] In defence of the colonial opium trade, the Royal Commission was the conclusive official act of the British Imperial government. However, the latter Commission urged the government 'to punish and, if necessary to remove from the Islands, incorrigible offenders'.[52] To deter young boys from contracting the habit, the Philippines Commission recommended licences only to males over 21 years of age, until the prohibition came into effect. The Philippines Committee Report laid the groundwork for future anti-drug policies throughout the world. The findings of the Philippines Commission granted the government an opportunity to proclaim the evils connected with the flow of opium and provided justification for US resistance to a trade from which the government of British India was deriving great material benefits. Backed by the US State Department, the missionaries in China distributed the translated version of the Philippines Committee Report throughout the country.[53] This Report enlivened the hopes and aspirations of the Chinese people, and they were able to take part in an organized international struggle against the colonial opium trade in South Asia.

Bishop H. Brent's role and the initiative taken by the US government provided renewed impetus to international measures concerning the drug trade. To create a concerted movement in accordance with the Philippines Commission Report, Brent, the only missionary member of the Committee, sought the US President's help. Brent perceived the issue both as a moral and 'global concern',[54] and on 24 July 1906, in a personal letter to President Theodore Roosevelt, he wrote:

> My experience on the Philippine opium investigating committee leads me to believe that the problem is of sufficient merit to warrant an endeavour to secure international action. ... We have the responsibility of actually handling the matter in our own possessions, to promote some movement that would gather in its embrace representatives from all countries where the traffic in and use of opium is a matter of moment.[55]

Brent argued that the Philippines Commission had provided sufficient rationale for conducting an international summit, and that such an action would be the single hope of the Chinese. He also suggested that the revival of anti-opium agitation in England, and the electoral victory of the Liberal Party, which had long proposed to expel Indian opium exports to China, has ushered in a unique opportunity for the US to approach the Britain on the topic. President Roosevelt acknowledged Brent's anti-opium attitude, and instructed the State Department in September 1906[56] to raise the issue with the British.

The perspective of the British government on international control of the South Asian opium trade was totally different to that of US. In October 1906, US Ambassador Reid asked the British Foreign Secretary, Sir Edward Grey, about the prospect of a joint Commission to investigate the consequences of the opium trade and the opium habit in the Asia-Pacific region. The British government, which had a completely different position on the issue, termed the US move 'interference' that would involve a 'great sacrifice' of Indian revenue.[57] Nevertheless, Grey pointed out that with the concurrence of the India Office the British government might consider the issue, if 'the result would be to diminish the opium habit'.[58] Grey's reference to the India Office contradicted Lord Salisbury's earlier statement, where he had argued that 'responsibility did not lie with the government of India, but with the Cabinet'.[59] Nevertheless, John Morley, the Secretary of State for India, cautioned Grey to be 'very *non-committal* as to the views and intentions of His Majesty's government on the question of Indian opium'.[60] Considering the merits of the US proposal Grey in November 1906 replied to Reid accepting his government's proposal for a joint Commission to investigate the South Asian opium trade. The anti-opium pressure and agitation in India, Burma, Sri Lanka and China had significantly contributed to this breaking of the ice in British opium diplomacy.

Struggle in South Asia

As in the US, resentment against British opium policies grew amongst organized groups and political forces in South Asia. By the end of the nineteenth century, anti-opium feeling, either latent or exposed, had transmitted amongst diverse professional groups. Poppy growers, missionary groups, and promoters of the temperance movement, some medical professionals, civil servants and local political leaders, expedited anti-narcotics demands and continued to oppose colonial drug policies. Their chief concern was the spread of the opium habit and its hazards throughout the region. This worry became evident in India, Burma and Sri Lanka, where people from all walks of life demanded a modification in the government's pro-revenue policy.

Resentments in India

In harmony with the missionary protests in the US and elsewhere, various professional groups in India expressed discontent in opposition to the government's drug policies during the late nineteenth century. In 1892, a declaration signed by 5,000 medical professionals demanded that the government of India 'prohibit the growth of the poppy and the manufacture and sale of opium, except for medical purposes'.[61] In 1908, after a visit to India, Meysey Thomson, British MP for Staffordshire, informed the House of Commons that there were people of all ages who wanted to bring the opium traffic to an end and close the opium dens as soon as possible.[62]

Christian missionaries in India generally opposed the colonial opium policy on ethical and moral grounds. Criticizing the 'Indo-China' opium trade and the disastrous results of opium in India, Dr Somerville, a missionary from Jodhpur in the 1880s, demanded 'an entire withdrawal of government from all share in this trade, and in the production of the drug'.[63] In 1882, in a revolutionary attempt, the Anglican Bishop of Bombay urged members of the clergy to refrain from their duties under the existing laws, until India got freedom from the opium trade.[64] In April 1891, the Bishop, at a large public meeting in Bombay, condemned colonial opium traffic as 'morally indefensible'. In a representation to the British Royal Commission, the missionaries in India noted that they were strongly opposed to participation by government in the demoralizing traffic in opium.

The missionaries were also concerned about the increase of drinking and liquor trafficking in India. In a letter to Lord Ripon, the Rev. Evans, a Baptist missionary at Monghyr in Bengal, expressed his anxiety about the 'enormous increase of drunkenness among hitherto sober populations'.[65] Anti-drugs public opinion was also dispersed amongst the followers of the Brahmo Samaj and other theistic organizations, as well as the pioneers of the Temperance Movement in India.[66] The 301 temperance associations at the First All-India Temperance Conference held in Bombay in 1904 raised a demand for a complete prohibition. As the result of a global missionary network, the temperance sentiment in India received attention in Canada, where resolutions were passed in public meetings, and leaflets and letters circulated in support of the issue in India.[67] The fraternity of Christian missionaries across the globe created moral pressure on colonial authorities to surrender their freedom in the opium trade.

Medical professionals from missionary backgrounds in India also resented colonial drug policies. In pursuance of medical opinion provided by US experts, and the legislation that had been passed in the UK, the missionary practitioners claimed that addiction developed from the non-medicinal use of opium. They asserted that opiates and other intoxicating drugs had been declared 'poison' in the UK in 1868. Dr George Smith, in his evidence to the Select Committee in 1871, explained the harmful physical and mental effects of the opium habit.[68] Dr John Wilson also stressed the injurious effects of *bhang* and of excessive indulgence in intoxicating liquors.[69] Every medical witness from a missionary background gave an opinion against the opium habit before the Royal Commission.

Indian medical opinion was greatly concerned about the abuse of opium amongst infants and children, and held that the habits of opium smoking and opium eating created a grave danger to the region. In his evidence to the Royal Commission, Sir William Roberts claimed that 60–90 per cent of newborns in the provinces in northwest India and in the central Indian states dosed with opium.[70] In recognition of their claims and evidence, Dr Rutherford argued in parliamentary debate in 1906:

> It was absolutely impossible for any man to say how much opium taken day by day and month by month a man could take without bringing about disastrous effects. Every vital function was reduced and destroyed, various diseases engendered, and life was curtailed.[71]

Condemnation of the use of opium also came from Sir Benjamin Brodie, who warned that opiates 'inflict a most serious injury on the human race'.[72] The missionary medical practitioners were critical about the recreational use of opium, and the way that it had contributed to the rise of drug addiction in different parts of India.

Many British officials, who had long working experience in India, expressed concern in their official reports and letters about the abuse of opium. Denying the financial excuses of the government, Sir Bartle Frere, Governor of Bombay, asserted that the trade could be abolished without any major 'financial embarrassment'.[73] K.G. Gupta, the Excise Commissioner in Bengal, in his evidence to the Royal Commission maintained that smoking *madak* and *chandu* was regarded in India 'as a degrading habit'.[74] F.W. Brownrigg, an officer in Oudh (UP), said that the practice of opium smoking was generally viewed in India as 'a low vicious habit'.[75] Referring to the banning of opium smoking by the central Indian rulers, R.J. Crosthwaite, the agent to the Governor-General in Central India, stated:

They did not condemn it on moral grounds; they merely said it destroys the man, and on that ground they felt bound to prohibit the smoking of opium.[76]

Impressed by the central Indian experience, a good number of bureaucrats, in their depositions to the Royal Commission, asserted that Indian 'public opinion generally condemns the habit as disreputable'.[77] Nevertheless, opium smoking continued unabated in India. These officials were also concerned about the increasing non-medicinal use of cocaine during the same period in India.[78] All these reports indicated that many government officials in India hoped to reduce the necessity for drug management.

Eminent political leaders in India demanded an end to poppy cultivation and its trafficking, which was degrading India in the eyes of the outside world. It had been asserted by the Royal Opium Commission Report of 1895 that the Indian National Congress was 'silent with reference to opium'.[79] Indeed, in the dearth of any organized socio-political group, party or intelligentsia capable of reflecting public opinion, there was no large anti-opium political agitation or popular movement in India. Nevertheless, aggregating anti-drug sentiments, the Indian National Congress, as a dominant political party, expressed its strong reservation about drug abuse once the party changed its loyalist policy towards the colonial administration. Alongside the aspirations for national independence, there were indications that anti-opium sentience was taking solid shape in India. In 1907, explaining the impairment done by intoxicating drugs in India, a member of the Legislative Council demanded action to reduce cultivation of the poppy.[80] Gopal Krishna Gokhale, an eminent leader of the Indian National Congress, in a speech in the Indian Legislative Council in March 1907 argued:

I confess I have always felt a sense of deep humiliation at the thought of this [opium] revenue, derived as it is practically from the degradation and moral ruin of the people of China. And I rejoice that there are indications of a time coming when this stain will no longer rest on us.[81]

Gokhale regarded opium revenue as 'a great stain' on Indian finances, because it was drawn from the 'moral degradation' of the people of a neighbouring country. Indeed, he was delighted to envisage the situation which the loss of opium revenue would create. Gokhale urged the government to withdraw from the 'melancholy business' and to cover the financial losses within a 10 year period. In 1908, British parliamentary Debate documented that South Asian students at Oxford, many of whom later became active in Indian politics, strongly opposed the opium trade.[82] Thus, political leaders and organizations in India at the beginning of the twentieth century expressed their growing concern on the promotion of the drug habit in the country.

Many critics of the government's opium policies, in their contemporary writings and reports, expressed resentment against the forced poppy cultivation that caused famine in Bengal and other poppy growing areas. Evidence provided before a Parliamentary Committee in 1871 by Dr John Wilson, Vice-Chancellor of the University of Bombay, and Sir Cecil Beadon and Dr George Smith, both having long working experience in India, asserted the connection between poppy cultivation and famine.[83] Their assertion came true in 1873–4, when a great famine hit Bengal and Bihar, affecting 17 million people.[84] Bengal, a great alluvial plain with the richest soils, the finest climates and rivers, suffered repeated famine mainly after its paddy fields were converted into poppy cultivation. In 1883, John F. Hurst admitted that the colonial authorities engaged about 354,681 hectares (876,454 acres) of fertile land to poppy cultivation in Bengal, and prevented the farmers from growing other precious food crops.[85] Commenting on this state of affairs in 1891, *Our Day* argued:

> The 700,000 acres of choice land, now given to the poppy, could be far more profitably devoted to food culture; and the destructive famines of India, which are now a standing demonstration of the economical unwisdom and inefficiency of the British government, would cease to exist.[86]

In 1904, Romesh Dutt, in his book, *India in the Victorian Age: An Economic History of the People*, argued that the poppy cultivators had continually, year after year, protested to the authorities against this cultivation, but their proposals were frequently ignored.[87] These writings about the forceful cultivation of opium poppies drew the attention of political leaders in UK at the beginning of the twentieth century.[88] With the growing awareness among public health campaigners, addiction specialists and political leaders, both in India and England, alertness developed amongst British legislators and civil servants of the need to impose restrictions on the abuse of opiates in South Asia. This political attention on opium in the UK was accelerated by anti-opium agitation that had taken place in Burma.

Anti-opium lobby in Burma

In contrast to the British government's drug policies, anti-opium public opinion prevailed in Burma after opium addiction spread amongst the local population in the late nineteenth century. The invasion of Burma by the British East India Company had started through the First Anglo-Burmese War of 1824–6. Before Burma fell under the British rule, opium smoking was treated as an offence, with the death penalty as the maximum punishment.[89] Under King Thibaw, the last Burmese ruler defeated by the Third Anglo-Burmese War of 1886, Sir Charles Aitchison reported that 'no one' smoked or chewed opium.[90] As in Japan, the drug was wiped out in Burma through the principles of Buddhism[91] and the adoption of stringent laws during 1853–71.

Following the Second Anglo-Burmese War of 1852, opium shops were opened in Lower Burma by junior officials, for the distribution of opium amongst young people. Until the 'taste' for opium was fixed, it was sold at a low price; and once users became addicted, the price was raised.[92] Thus creating dreadful results for the people, the colonial authorities generated large profits from harmful drugs. In 1891 *The Times* reported that by the end of the century demoralization, impoverishment and ruin created a fearful situation in Lower Burma, and that the Arakanese had been made into 'a race of haggard wretches'.[93] The local population became concerned to rescue themselves from further degradation.

Public opinion in Burma strongly preferred the stopping of the supply of Indian opium to that area altogether. In 1996, Ronald D. Renard, in his book *The Burmese Connection: Illegal Drugs and the Making of the Golden Triangle*, explained in detail the traditional attitude of the Burmese population about the abuse of intoxicating drugs.[94] There was a social hatred in traditional Burma against opium smokers, who were considered thieves, liars, and outcastes. In 1881, C.U. Aitchison, Chief Commissioner of Burma, referred to the Burmese protests. In his official report he noted:

> On a visit to Akyab, I was waited upon by a large deputation of the most influential natives of the town, who presented a petition describing, in very forcible language, the misery entailed on the population by opium, and praying that the traffic in opium might be altogether abolished in Arakan.[95]

This report also contained the personal opinion of the eight District Commissioners and three Divisional Commissioners of British Burma. In his concluding remarks, the Chief Commissioner appealed to the government of British India 'to adopt vigorous measures to discourage and restrict the consumption of opium', which was degrading 'the very life of this young and otherwise prosperous province'.[96] The report of the Chief Commissioner certified anti-opium agitation in Burma, and criticized the opium policy pursued by the British.

In an attempt to ease public discontent, the colonial authorities introduced revised opium laws in 1885. Under the new regulations, the selling of opium was to be allowed amongst the non-Burmese population, but restrictions were placed on Burmese consumption. This partial prohibition did not halt Burmese opium consumers from claiming to be Chinese and then buying opium. To stop this practice, the Society for the Suppression of the Opium Trade in England in 1886 urged the British Imperial authorities to ban all opium exports from India to Burma.[97] Despite this appeal, the distribution of opium continued unabated from licensed shops. In Lower Burma in 1892–3, the licensed vendors volunteered Rs53,082 in licence fees and Rs154,597 in excise duty. Under the Regulations of March 1893, subject to registration, the colonial authorities allowed both Burmese and non-Burmese addicts to buy and possess opium.[98] In 1902, the policy was revised further and a higher duty was levied on opium and licence fees, and consumption was increaced from 60 metric tons in 1894–5 to 68 metric tons by 1904–5.[99] Without regard for public opinion, a similar pro-revenue excise regulation was enacted in Upper Burma in 1904–5. As in

Burma, strong anti-drug opinion prevailed in Sri Lanka, where the British government partly continued the opium policies inherited from the Dutch colonial authorities (1656–1796).

Agitation in Sri Lanka

As in India and Burma, in Ceylon (Sri Lanka) protest against the distribution of opium through the licensed shops grew. In line with the growing anti-opium and temperance movement in South Asia and elsewhere, representatives of a cross-section of the population gathered at a large public meeting in Colombo in December 1893. Their aim was to oppose licences for the distribution of intoxicating drugs. The meeting, presided over by John Ferguson, an authority on narcotics, was addressed by some non-official members of the Legislative Council and Buddhist priests, and demanded restriction on the import and sale of opium in the island. The increase in opium imports to Sri Lanka, which had risen about fifteen-fold since 1840, was their prime concern.

A majority of the Singhalese community is Buddhist, and as Buddhist principles oppose the use of opium, the agitation drew popular support. In condemnation of abuse of the drug from the religious point of view, the Buddhist High Priest urged the colonial authorities to close the opium shops in Sri Lanka.[100] A resolution was adopted at the meeting and signed by over 27,000 inhabitants of the island.[101] People from all walks of life – the Singhalese, Tamils, Euro-Asians, Europeans and other nationalities – attended the gathering. They claimed that there was nothing in the case of Ceylon or its people to stop the abuse or sale of harmful drugs, whereas in the UK legislation had already been passed in 1868 declaring opium a poison. Public opinion in Sri Lanka was also influenced by the new Opium Regulations of Lower Burma in 1885. Citing the British and Burmese examples, the anti-drug crusaders appealed to the President of the Legislative Council for the same sort of legislation in Sri Lanka.

The reason for this agitation was partly the growth of distribution in opium and other hard drugs. In 1885–6 the supply of opium from India was five metric tons, and in 1892–3 it was increased to over eight metric tons.[102] As a result of public agitation the allotment of drugs fell slightly during 1893–5, but increased again during subsequent years. Except for the doubling the import duty on opium, no substantial changes were made in the Sri Lankan legislation to satisfy the local population. In November 1897 the colonial authorities, in a cosmetic attempt, banned the importation of *bhang* and cannabis onto the island, but continued increasing the supply of opium from India.

To propitiate the distribution of intoxicating drugs, the colonial government progressively increased the number of licensed shops from 39 in 1894, 56 in 1898 and 65 in 1906. Under this policy, the government received Rs191,306 from licences in 1906, as against Rs41,400 in 1893.[103] The authorities claimed that the purpose of this revenue collection was part of an attempt to combat the contraband supplies.[104] In 1894, Mary and Marg Leitch maintained that the licensed vendors contributed to the government Rs43,000 in opium revenue, while the total turnout of the trade was Rs200,000.[105] This paper indicated how secretly the opium vendors distributed enormous amount of opium to their addict customers. In 1905, licensed shops issued about 8.6 metric tons of crude opium to the colony's 20,000 addicts.[106] Given the abundance of official and contraband supplies, public opinion in Sri Lanka was dissatisfied with the colonial drug policies. The return of the British Liberal Party to power in 1906 facilitated the presentation of Singhalese feeling about opium through the setting up of the Ceylon Commission in the following year.

The Ceylon recommendations

In an attempt to mitigate the political pressure in its colonies, the British government set up its Opium Commission in Sri Lanka and sought gradual solutions to the issue. On 15 April 1907, Dr Rutherford, MP, placed a resolution in the House of Commons as to 'whether His Majesty's government will take steps to suppress the opium traffic' in Sri Lanka. The Secretary of State, Elgin, finding no point in defending the traffic after the publication of the Philippines Commission, asked for the establishment of a parallel commission to investigate the issue, and to submit a report on opium consumption in the Crown colony. In mid-1907 the colonial authorities set up the Ceylon Commission, with a similar purpose to the Philippines Commission. D.C. Jayasuriya, in his 1986 book

Narcotics and Drugs in Sri Lanka: Socio-Legal Dimensions, explains the evolution of colonial drug policies and their subsequent influence on recent legislation. The following discussion treats the Ceylon Opium Commission as a milestone in British drug policies that Jayasuriya totally ignored or omitted.

The Report of the Ceylon Opium Committee, which almost duplicated that of the Philippines Opium Committee, allowed the British Government to take a face-saving measure in alleviating political pressure both at home and abroad. The Ceylon Commission, which was set up four years after the Philippines commission, refuted many important conclusions of the Royal Commission Report. The terms of reference of the Ceylon Commission were quite different from those of the Royal Commission. The latter commission was aimed at examining the effects of banning opium on the Indian economy,[107] but the former was appointed chiefly to study the prohibitive measures on opium. Explaining the objective of the Ceylon Commission, Elgin wrote:

> I do not see how the introduction of apparently ever-increasing quantities of opium into Ceylon is to be defended, and I regret that I must ask for further inquiry and report. I would suggest that another Committee should be appointed to take evidence and make recommendations; or I am prepared to consider any other course, which you may be able to recommend as likely to minimise and eventually prevent, except for medicinal purposes, the consumption of opium in Ceylon.[108]

By contrast, the Royal Commission investigation was to determine 'whether the growth of the poppy and the manufacture and sale of opium in British India should be prohibited except for medicinal purposes.'[109] Unlike the British Royal Commission, the Ceylon Commission proposed the closure of opium shops on the expiration of existing licences, because these were creating an artificial 'taste for the drug'.[110] In line with the Bengal Regulation of 1813, the Ceylon Commission admitted the tranquillizing effects of opium, but the Royal Commission had twisted the observation in its closely printed seven volumes. As it was conducted by the Colonial Office, the findings of the Ceylon Opium Commission were the opposite of those of the Royal Opium Commission of 1895 staged by the India Office.

Compared to the grand Royal Commission Report, the Ceylon Commission Report was brief but drastic. The Royal Commission concluded that drawing a distinction between medical and non-medical uses of opium was impracticable. However, public witnesses who appeared before the Ceylon Opium Commission, unanimously declared that opium was an evil. The Royal Commission contended that the use of opium for smoking or addiction purposes in India was rare, and that it was used extensively for oral consumption and as a sedative for children.[111] (This assertion is countered by Virginia Berridge and Griffith Edwards, who argued that the primary objective of the Royal Commission was aimed at 'whitewashing' the opium habit.[112]) The Ceylon Commission reported that it could find no evidence of any Singhalese or Tamil desire to have opium shops in village localities. On the basis of public reports, the Ceylon Commission argued that opium had demoralized villagers, who never knew its evil results until they had become slaves to the habit.[113] In line with the popular demand, the Ceylon Commission recommended that the use of the drug, except for medical purposes, should be entirely prohibited after a definite period.

The recommendations of the Ceylon Commission were almost a duplication of the findings of the US-led Philippines Commission. Unlike the Royal Commission Report, which according to Joshua Rowntree, was as, 'trackless as an Indian jungle',[114] the Ceylon Commission echoed the recommendations of the Philippines Commission. In accordance with the advice made by the Philippines Commission, the Ceylon Commission recommended that the existing licence system of opium distribution for smokers be abandoned.[115] Government monopoly, like that established by Japan to control the opium habit on the island of Formosa (Taiwan), was initially incorporated by the Philippines Commission and then duplicated in the Ceylon Commission.

The Ceylon Commission Report appeared to be a combination of diverse radical measures: Japan's opium policy in Formosa, the proposals of the Philippines Opium Commission and the regulations adopted in Lower Burma. Chiefly influenced by the Philippines Commission, the Ceylon Commission proposed the banning of the non-medicinal use of opium after a definite period. Following the example in Lower Burma, the distribution of the drug was confined only to registered adult users. The Secretary of State accepted all these recommendations, and closed all opium dens and shops in Ceylon. In a letter of 15 May 1908 to the Governor of Ceylon, he wrote:

> It affords me much gratification to note that the Colonial Government have spontaneously recognised the necessity of taking adequate measures to restrict the use of opium within the narrowest possible limits.[116]

Thus, the Report of the Ceylon Commission and the Report of the Governor himself led to the end of an era of opium traffic in one of the Crown's colonies. The findings of the Ceylon Opium Commission provided the Imperial Government with the impetus to take part in a US proposed Opium commission. Thereafter, it became obligatory for the Imperial Government to rescue its subjects in India and Burma from the same evils, which has had such dreadful results in Sri Lanka. Besides the development of awareness in South Asia and Burma, anti-opium pressures also began in other countries, especially China. In line with anti-drugs opinion overseas, pressure from missionary groups erupted in the UK.

The battle in British democracy

The political agitation in India, Sri Lanka and Burma, in opposition to the colonial opium policy, became a cause for concern for the British Government during the early twentieth century. Widespread opiate abuse in India, China and the Philippines offered anti-opium crusaders a rational basis to mobilize public opinion in the UK. They protested against the contradictory medical opinions presented to the British Royal Commission on opiates. This movement, which opposed the government share in the opium trade, actively started with the formation of the Society for the Suppression of Opium Trade (SSOT) in November 1874. Through this organized activity, the minority missionary groups in England declared their fraternity with their fellow colleagues who, due to British involvement in the opium trade, faced tremendous difficulties in converting to Christianity local people in China and elsewhere.

Movement to end opium trade

The emergence of SSOT marked a greater solidarity amongst the minority Christian communities in England, and created new organized opposition to the South Asian opium trade. The SSOT leaders launched a powerful propaganda campaign to help free China from Imperial opium bondage, and to emancipate Indian farmers from their engagement in the government's opium monopoly. In October 1875, *The Friend of China* indicated that the campaigners were able to exert 'a distinct and significant influence on the whole Kingdom'.[117] As a result of their collective strength, the forum gained greater political weight in British parliamentary politics.

Patronized by Joseph Pease, a Birmingham Quaker and industrialist, the SSOT demanded the British Government amend its South Asian opium policy. In an attempt to mould British public opinion, the SSOT workers explained in their writings and speeches the evils of opium indulgence in China, India, Burma and elsewhere. To arouse British public sentiment in favour of the Chinese cause, F. Stross Turner, an eminent SSOT leader, wrote:

> We can not recount the hideous series of massacres, which at last compelled China to submit to our terms in 1842. The treaty of peace included a heavy indemnity for war expenses and the payment of six million dollars for the destroyed opium. Hong Kong, now [until July 1997] a British free port, became the headquarters of opium smuggling, and for fifteen years the trade returned to its old character prior to 1820.[118]

Aided by many high officials and diplomats, such as Sir John Jordan, British Minister in Beijing, Sir Robert Hert, and Dr Burdon, the SSOT movement blamed the British Government for deriving huge revenue from opium. In October 1881 the SSOT leaders claimed that the Imperial opium trade was against Christianity and international morality.[119] In May 1882, at a Church Missionary Society annual meeting in London, Dr Burdon, Bishop of Victoria (Hong Kong), said:

The story of the opium traffic is a long and bitter story; and I am rejoiced to think that there has been an agitation against it. (Cheers). I would say go on agitating until you stop all connexion of our Government with it – (Cheers) – but until India has taken the land from the growth of opium for the growth of cereals for her own famine–stricken people there is no hope of stopping the traffic. Let us go on agitating to remove this blot from England.[120]

In response to this call, people from diverse Christian denominations passed resolutions on the subject and forwarded them to parliament. During 9–11 March 1891, anti-opium workers met for a two-day conference in London. In 1892, A.P. Harper maintained that, finding human efforts feeble, the crusaders had prayed to 'the God of Israel' to help release China from this 'terribly destructive plague'.[121] Their worship strategy and persistent attacks helped influence the British Government to pass an anti-opium resolution in the House of Commons in the following month. However, without the banning of poppy cultivation in India, the mere passing of a resolution was ineffectual. Sir Joseph Pease, the President of the Anti-Opium Association, commented emphatically in the House of Commons:

As a moral and as a Christian nation, we have no right to trade in that which does others harm, and which is one of the greatest causes of misery to the human race.[122]

The commotion compelled the Gladstone Government to set up a Royal Commission on Opium in 1893 to investigate the subject. The Royal Commission published its report in 1895 in favour of the government monopoly. Prominent members of parliament discussed and denounced the Commission's report at a public meeting in London, commenting that it was 'full of falsehoods and machinations'.[123] Protestant missionaries, including diverse anti-opium organizations, Quakers, politicians and public officials, discredited the data of the Royal Commission on many grounds. They held that 'Lord Brassey and the majority of the Commission were thoroughly pro-opium'.[124] Henry J. Wilson, one of the anti-opium Commissioners and an MP from Yorkshire, declined to put his signature to the Report, as he regarded the Commission's findings as an 'elaborate defence of the opium trade of the East India Company'.[125]

Along with the political battle against the South Asian opium trade, criticism also persisted against the hemp policy of the Government of British India. Under the existing policy, moderate use of *bhang, ganja* and *charas* was considered 'harmless', and their excessive use was regarded as less harmful as the excessive use of alcohol.[126] These views, held by the Indian Hemp Commission of 1893, also came under attack by the SSOT workers. They criticized the report for its failure to prohibit opium consumption in India and recommending a permanent system of taxation on cannabis, by raising the duty from 4 to 8 *anas* per *seer* at the existing rates.[127] The SSOT leaders regarded the cultivation and sale of cannabis under government licences in India as the double-standard policy of the British government. In 1894, criticizing the government's banning of cannabis in England and its legality in India, W.S. Caine, a British MP, in his address at Exeter Hall in London argued:

> Yet the Government of India allows it [cannabis] to be retailed to anybody who wants to buy it, although it is one of the most deadly intoxicants the world has ever been able to produce.[128]

Thus, criticism of the Indian hemp policy went hand in hand with the contemporary anti-opium movement in England. However, to hasten the movement, Joseph G. Alexander, a Quaker and the Secretary of the SSOT, in a paper in 1896 wrote:

> We [the British people] are responsible, not only for supplying the Chinese with an enormous quantity of poison from India, but also for setting agoing its widespread cultivation in China. ... The opium war gave an impulse to the cultivation, and, since the legalization of the traffic, the poppy, like a noxious weed, has been running over the whole land.[129]

Joshua Rowntree, in his *The Imperial Drug Trade*, a well-documented book that was published in 1905, analysed the entire British drug policy from an anti-opium point of view. Rowntree and other anti-opium writers helped influence British public opinion to accept the judgement that the Royal Commission as a 'non-judicial commission' which had rubber-stamped the opium monopoly and the contraband trade. The Commissioners were also attacked for failing to examine the social effects of opium use, for placing great importance upon its medical use, and for recommending continuance of the opium policy.

In response to the financial questions raised by the pro-opiumists, the SSOT workers repeatedly put forward the legal and moral arguments against the opium trade. While some colonial officials employed in India and traders involved in opium upheld the financial 'benefits' of the issue, the anti-opiumists were committed to putting an end to the trade. They argued that the Government of British India had never approached the question on moral grounds, but only as a matter of finance and revenue. The SSOT leaders urged MPS through letters and telegrams that it was their duty to stop the traffic as speedily as possible. They argued that if the British Government gave up this trade, other forms of its trade would have easier access in the region. Through this 'backstage politicking',[130] the anti-opiumists were essentially broadcasting the evils of the government's South Asian opium policy to the public.

The SSOT workers, with the blessing of church leaders who placed virtue before money, attempted to convince British public opinion in favour of their cause. The persistent efforts and incessant political battle of the anti-opiumists and Christian missionaries after over half a century had created a climate in the British Parliament in 1906 for the abolition of the monopoly in India, and for the withdrawal of pressure on the Chinese Government to admit Indian opium.

Opium in the British Parliament

The origins of the parliamentary politics on South Asian opium trade go back to the mid-nineteenth century, when the British Government launched an offensive against China for its refusal to accept contraband opium from India. Some of the early Liberal leaders, especially W.E. Gladstone, strongly attacked government policy. In 1843, Lord Ashley moved a resolution in the House of Commons to abolish the immoral opium trade from British India.[131] Later, after becoming the Earl of Shaftesbury, Ashley renewed his attack in the House of Lords in 1857 and sought judicial opinion on the issue.[132] Similar anti-opium motions were raised in 1875, 1876, 1880, 1881, 1883 and 1886, but every time, on economic grounds, they were either withdrawn or met with parliamentary defeat.

At the peak of the anti-opium agitation in April 1891, Sir Joseph Pease tabled a revolutionary resolution that declared the mechanism by which Indian opium revenue was raised, 'morally indefensible'.[133] The British Government was 'disturbed by this resolution',[134] however, the motion was carried by 190 to 160 votes.[135] In 1893, the same resolution was defeated by a counter-resolution from Liberal Prime Minister Gladstone, who in 1840 had declared the Opium War with China 'unjust' and a 'permanent disgrace for Britain'.[136] The failure of the SSOT resolution provided for the establishment of a Royal Commission on opium. Its report was published in 1895, and there was no discussion of the issue under Conservative rule for nearly 11 years.

The return to power of the Liberal Party in 1906, and the inclusion of some leaders sympathetic to the SSOT in the British Cabinet, produced a goodwill environment for the anti-opium lobby. The anti-drug feeling was stoked up during the election, and helped the Liberals to achieve a landslide victory. However, the issue has largely been ignored by leading academics on the subject.[137] The entry of over 250 anti-opium members to the House of Commons, and their new interest in South Asian drug policies, created a profound impact on British opium policy. MPs who had voted for earlier anti-opium resolutions now held many Cabinet posts. John Morley, the Secretary of State for India (1906-11), had 'consistently supported' anti-opium efforts since his entry into Parliament in 1883; his Under-Secretary, John Ellis, was for years a leader of the Anti-Opium Society; and the Indian Viceroy, Lord Minto, was also in favour of substantial change in India.[138] Moreover, the combination of a Viceroy and a Secretary of State who desired to do 'full justice'[139] to the Indian population, created a positive ambience for reform in South Asian opium policy.

A motion by Liberal MP T. Taylor on 30 May 1906 condemned the traffic as 'morally indefensible' and exhorted the government to 'take such steps as might be necessary for bringing it to a speedy close'.[140] Dealing exhaustively with the economic aspects of the issue, Taylor argued that the Indian Government's revenue from the opium traffic came mainly at the cost of the 'misery, vice and poverty of many millions of the Chinese people'.[141] He further asserted that although the government would lose opium revenue, it was their duty to 'stop this traffic as speedily as possible'. The resolution was seconded by Dr Rutherford, who acknowledged that Britain was to a large extent the 'architect of this evil', and that Britons were 'responsible for their deed'.

John Viscount Morley, authorized by the Cabinet to effect a *rapprochement* of divergent opinions, engrossed a unique position in the Parliament over the trade question. During the debate, Morley blended the feelings of the civil servants in the India Office and his 'good friends, the philanthropists'. Unlike Kimberley, the Secretary of State for India, who had declared in 1893 that he would resign from office rather than consent to a resolution to surrender Indian opium revenue, Morley pragmatically admitted the harmful effects of opium. Giving much attention to the Philippines Commission Report, which had called the use of opium 'an evil', he praised the US Government's decision to outlaw its use in the Philippines after 1908. To win the conservatives' support, he criticized the motion on the grounds that the opium trade was a declining source of Indian revenue. He pointed out that over the 14 years ending in 1894, the average annual revenue had fallen from £5 million to £3 million in 1894–1905, and £2.30 million in 1906.[142] He further maintained that in 1880 the opium revenue had represented 14 per cent of the aggregate revenue of India, while in 1906 it represented only 7 per cent. Morley suggested to the House that opium revenue was an uncertain source over which the government could exercise no control.

To convince the Conservative Party members, including other members within his own camp, Morley argued that the Bengal monopoly was generally an adequate way of regulating opium production. In this tacit statement Morley approved the findings of the Royal Commission report. Like many others who had defended the trade during the previous 70 years, he said that the central Indian authorities conducted the cultivation and manufacture of Malwa opium. Morley suggested that the sudden cutting of opium revenue, in line with the 'righteous sentiments' of the anti-opiumists, would inflict harm on the people of India.[143] From his sensible experience, Morley approached the issue cautiously and supported the process of 'gradualism' for a total withdrawal from the trade.[144] His attitude was reflected in his advice to the anti-opium delegation in 1907:

> When you are at the top of the house and want to get to the bottom there are two ways of doing so. You can throw yourself out of a window, or you can go downstairs. I prefer to go downstairs.[145]

Following a pragmatic policy, Morley thus concluded that any plan for restricting the abuse of opium, 'if brought forward in good faith, would be agreed to by the Government of India and His Majesty's Government even though it might cost us some sacrifice'.[146] With his cautious and rational approach, Morley's motion was carried without a division, and gave the anti-opium opinion another moral victory over the government's long-standing South Asian opium policy.[147] Recalling the motion, Morley in 1917 stated that 'if the anti-opium motion had gone to a division, it would have been carried by a majority of 200'.[148] This parliamentary resolution was not followed up by any immediate measures to close the South Asian opium trade.

Nonetheless, the opponents of the trade were eager to speed up the process of opium reform in South Asia. To expedite Government action another resolution was moved in the British Parliament by W. Johnson, MP for Warwickshire, on 6 May 1908, who urged:

> That this House, having regard to the Resolution unanimously adopted on 30th May, 1906, that the Indo-Chinese opium trade is morally indefensible, welcomes this action of His Majesty's Government in diminishing the sale of opium for export.[149]

The second half of this resolution was about the immediate closure of opium dens in the Crown's colonies. It was inserted in accordance with the policies of Japan and China, with US legislation in the Philippines, and with the recommendations of the Ceylon Commission. Johnson questioned the delay in regard to the International Opium Commission, which the US had proposed in October 1906; he urged the Indian Colonial and Foreign Offices not merely to reduce the traffic, but to put a quick end to it.

Taylor, who seconded the motion, and had recently visited China to study this question, had observed that anti-opium reform in China was 'distinctly a great national movement'.[150] He demanded complete suppression of the consumption of opium in the British Kingdom. By this resolution, both the mover and seconder of the motion were intending to wipe the stain from the 'national character' and to rescue the British soul from future 'hell fire'.[151] They asked the British Government to honour the 'sacrifice' that had been committed by John Morley in 1906, as the British people would be behind them. The House then agreed unanimously with the resolution in support of Government action on the withdrawal of the trade. Thereupon, John Morley, at the invitation of President Theodore Roosevelt, expressed willingness to participate in the international meeting in Shanghai in 1909.

The US initiative for joint action, combined with the pressure of British public opinion and the anti-opium pressure from South Asia and China, led the British Government to participate in an international move to put an eventual end to the Imperial opium trade. The US proposal to convene an anti-opium international summit created a delicate situation for the Liberal Government, which faced the financial loss of opium revenue in India.[152] Throughout the negotiations with the US, the importance of opium revenue to India's finances was a major concern of the British Government. Nevertheless, embarrassed by public opinion at home and abroad, and urged on by the US Government, the British Government agreed to take part in international moves against drug trafficking. The US proposal for the dropping of opium trade also created a threat to the viability of British colonial rule in India.

3
British Narco-diplomacy, 1909–46

In retort to US-led international actions, the government of British India pursued a 'one step forward and two steps backward policy' on drug control during the early twentieth century. As a result of the Shanghai requirements, the government gradually reduced opium exports by the 1920s; however, its heavy reliance on excise revenue accelerated the dispersal of stupefying drugs for local consumption. After its initial disappointment in Shanghai, the government of British India boycotted the Hague Conferences during 1912–14, and launched repressive measures during the early 1920s against Non-Cooperation workers who agitated against the distribution of drugs from government stores. Under political pressure at home, and due to diplomatic strain abroad, the colonial authorities ratified the Geneva Convention of 1924–5, yet refrained from introducing any uniform anti-drug legislation. As a result of the varied laws at the provincial level, the distribution of drugs continued both from licit and illicit channels during the 1930s and 1940s. To elude further pressure against drug trafficking, the government of India convened an anti-opium summit in 1927, while contraband trade in harmful drugs persisted after the withering of the formal opium trade in 1935.

The government of British India emerged as an important player during the early twentieth century, when South Asian opium trade became a focal point in international narco-diplomacy. During all the major international summits in Shanghai, The Hague and Geneva, the British delegates from Britain and India played diplomatic chess against the Sino-US alliance to protect their revenue interests in India. Through a delicate process of bargaining and negotiations, especially amongst three key players, the US, Britain and China, international agreements were reached about the role of the British government in the South Asian opium trade. These agreements laid the foundation for nearly all the international measures that compelled the government of India to reduce the size of its century-old opium industry and the amount of opium traffic to China. Nevertheless, it was a difficult task on the part of the government of India to accommodate the diplomatic tremor that resulted from the global summits on opium. Given the financial dependence on revenue from drugs, and constitutional arrangements for collecting 'maximum revenue' from opium export, the pursuit of a whole-hearted anti-drug policy was almost impossible for the government of India.

The Shanghai opium conference

In response to the US initiative the British government attended the International Opium Summit in Shanghai from 1 to 26 February 1909, and defended colonial drug policies in South Asia. To cover up the financial loss that occurred as a result of the Shanghai agreements, the government sought solutions by excise revenue from local sources. S.K. Chatterjee, in his 1981 book *Legal Aspects of International Drug Control*, completely set aside the impact of the Shanghai Conference in the ensuing drug policies of the government of British India. The following discussion examines the role of British diplomats in the Shanghai Opium Conference, and its bearing on subsequent drug policies in South Asia

To express their solidarity with international opinion on drugs, the delegates from India took part in the Shanghai Opium Commission, and provided clarification in regard to the Bengal opium monopoly. Chaired by Bishop Charles H. Brent, an American who piloted the idea in 1906, the conference examined reports on the production of opium, revenue statistics, and excise policies submitted by the participating countries. The delegates from British India presented the longest report, covering almost 25 per cent of the conference's total documents. In line with findings of the Royal Commission on Opium, the delegation from India enlisted a detailed account of the history and formulation of the opium industry, and tried to justify their government's position in the South Asian opium trade. They asserted that poppy cultivation in Bengal and opium export from India were conducted within government regulations, and that the government enjoyed a 'treaty control' over the opium exports from central India.[1] The Indian report indicated little government will to execute anti-opium measures in the region.

To counter US fault finding, Brunyate, the delegate from India, argued that the opium statistics available were capricious. Referring to Lord Morley, the Secretary of State for India, he asserted that opium revenue had been ebbing. Replying to a US proposal for the urgent banning of opium smoking, the envoys from British India asserted that the problem was trifling in the region.[2] They reiterated that, under the regulations in 1897–8, opium smokers were prohibited from using opium dens and were compelled to make personal arrangements for the indulgence of their habit. They argued that under the principle of 'maximum revenue with minimum consumption' the government of India was trying to control opium abuse. Emphasizing defensive arguments, the British delegates succeeded in the adoption of a compromise resolution calling 'for the gradual suppression of the practice of opium smoking'[3] in their colonies and elsewhere.

Nevertheless, the admission of progressive termination in the resolution particularly touched the revenue interests of the British government in India. To avoid further pressure on opium trade, the delegation from India claimed that China had 'entire satisfaction' with the 10 per cent reduction of opium supply under the Indo-China Ten Years' Agreement of 1907.[4] The Chinese delegates, who demanded 'a modification' of the Agreement, contested this assertion.[5] However, the envoys from India refused to let the conference discuss the issue and sought a bilateral solution with China. Given this stalemate, the Sino-US delegation failed to exert enough pressure to curb British dominance, the then superpower of the world. Instead, they accepted a British proposal in support of China's 'unswerving sincerity' in its efforts to eradicate the production and consumption of opium throughout the country. The summit failed to apply adequate pressure on the government of British India for an immediate withdrawal of the opium trade from China.

As a result of the rigidity of the British delegates, the Shanghai conference provided a limited diplomatic opportunity for the US and China to discuss the socio-economic and moral aspects of the opium trade. The scholar Vladimir Kusevic maintains that due to the unwillingness especially of Britain, the Shanghai conference had 'accomplished little'.[6] Despite that unwillingness, the conference insisted that the British government make 'large financial sacrifices' in South Asian opium trade.[7] The British agreed in principle to ensure a 'careful regulation' of the medicinal use of opium, and to take 'reasonable measures' to prevent opium exports to countries where its import was forbidden.[8] Since the delegates in the Shanghai conference were not authorized to sign an international treaty, implementation of these resolutions in South Asia was entirely dependent on the political will of the British government. Thus, the British delegates were generally satisfied with the outcomes of the summit, because there was no specific resolution that addressed British opium policies.[9] Just the same, the summit mandated the British government to produce some immediate changes in its colonial drug policies in South Asian.

Morley–Minto Reforms

Coinciding the Shanghai prescription for an immediate cessation of the South Asian opium trade, the British government under the Morley–Minto reforms of 1909 allowed the Indian members to cooperate in the law-making process. Lord Morley, who was under strong pressure from the Conservatives not to cause any major change in Indian opium policy, together with Lord Minto, introduced a range of political reforms. These amendments included incorporating Indians in non-official seats in the provincial and central legislatures so that they could partake in the decision of public interests. This measure provided an opportunity for non-official members to move resolutions and to ask supplementary questions on opium and excise policy.

Under the Morley–Minto reforms, the local members participated enthusiastically in the central legislative debates to increase indigenous financial claims from the declining opium trade. In March 1911, G.K. Gokhale demanded the creation of an 'Opium Fund' amounting to £2 million, for expenditure on education, sanitation and medical relief. Gokhale's resolution was withdrawn as it was opposed by the Finance Member in the government as 'tricky cargo in the financial ship'.[10] From time to time local members raised questions that were against the government's revenue policy, thereby creating unpleasant situations for the ministers concerned. In 1911, when asked by the Raja of Dighapatia about the prospect of the abandonment of Indian opium revenue, Sir Guy Fleetwood Wilson expressed his inability to make any satisfactory statement on the issue.[11] In 1913, Sir Gangadhar Chitnavis proposed a tax on opium exports from India to Britain.[12] After a lengthy debate, the Chitnavis's resolution was withdrawn. In 1914, Sir Gangadhar Chitnavis queried whether there was a possibility of the government granting 'compensation for the loss of Indian opium revenue', and Sir William Meyer replied 'no'.[13] While the constitutional reforms of 1909 provided an opportunity for the non-official members to raise key issues in connection with opium policy, it denied them authority to pursue any nationalist policy.

The Indian legislative assembly, under the Morley–Minto reforms, was kept under the official majority, to ensure the dominance of the colonial authorities over the 'non-official' members. When the Indian members placed any resolution on opium or excise revenue, the calm British members effectively carried the government measure and turned down the indigenous move. Explaining this situation, the report on *East India (Constitutional Reforms)* in 1918 noted:

> The Indian members' views are therefore rarely placed on record as the opinion of the Council, because the Council's decision is in a majority of cases the decision of the government.[14]

The same document indicated that during 1910–17 the Indian legislative council passed 131 laws, of which 59 per cent were passed without any considerable discussion. While members from India tried to maximize their share of a declining trade, the government's policy was to overcome the 'dislocation of financial arrangements'[15] in the post-Shanghai era. Thus, the Morley–Minto reforms provided authority to the Indian members to safeguard their national interests, and to allocate funds from the decaying opium revenue for welfare activities in their localities.

A parallel 'tug of war' continued in the provincial legislative councils, where the colonial authorities introduced numerous Excise Bills and regulations that denied the claims of indigenous members. During 1909–17 the provincial legislatures passed many laws to promote excise revenue from the distribution of intoxicating drugs.[16] Most excise laws that proved detrimental to the interests of the people were validated even when the 'non-official' members protested. To magnify revenue from intoxicants, Meston on 25 February 1910 approved a Bill in the legislative council with an official majority. Through this Bill the government amended the Excise Regulation of 1813 and the Indian Tariff Act of 1894, and brought them under the control of a general excise policy. The policy increased taxation upon all kinds of intoxicants including opium, liquors, and hemp drugs. Under the Burma Opium Law Amendment Act of 1909 the colonial authorities inverted the existing laws on opium, which had been introduced during the 1890s to control the vice.[17] The government further adopted the Burma Excise Act of 1917 to draw revenue from opium and other intoxicants.[18] Under the UP Excise Act of 1910, the UP government authorized police officers to collect revenue.[19] It was clearly outside their normal functions, because their prime function was controlling criminal activities.

The Morley–Minto reforms witnessed the consolidation of excise revenue resulting from the highest distribution of intoxicating drugs through the licensed vendors. To alleviate the financial loss from declining opium exports, the government of India reversed its policy of export maximization and 'minimum consumption', which had prevailed since 1813. This new step also aimed at arresting the declining trend in the distribution of excise opium. In 1909–10, the distribution of excise opium in Bengal fell by 16 per cent, in UP by 12 per cent, while in Assam it increased by 10 per cent.[20] Except for Assam, the consumption of excise opium declined in most of the provinces. Figure 3.1 shows that as a result of the new excise policies, the average distribution of official opium increased throughout India during 1909–14. In pursuance of this policy, the colonial authorities abandoned the Shanghai prescription for the reduction of opium consumption and continued their reliance on the appropriation of excise revenue from other intoxicating drugs. In 1911, the *Bengal District Gazetteer* observed that the excise

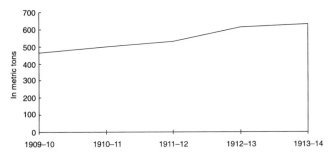

Figure 3.1 Distribution of excise opium in India, 1909–14
Source: *The Calcutta Review*, Dec. 1946, pp. 204–5

revenue was 'increasing more in proportion than the population'.[21] Consequently, at the end of 1911 there was public agitation against the government's policy and the increased domestic consumption of drugs.[22] The agitators drew attention to the fact that the British administration had made arrangements to stop all opium exports to China by 1917, and protested that if the drug was harmful for China, then it was equally ruinous for India. Disregarding the protesters, Hardinge wrote:

> The opium habit as a vice scarcely exists in India, opium is extensively used for non-medical and quasi-medical purposes, in some cases with benefits and for the most part without injurious consequences, the non-medical uses are so interwoven with the medical uses that it would not be practicable to draw a distinction between them.[23]

The Harding government was reluctant to implement any active measures to curtail domestic production and sale of opium as suggested by the Shanghai summit. In accordance with the findings of the Royal Commission on Opium, on the contrary, the government defended its traditional policy and tried to justify domestic consumption of narcotics on medical grounds. However, as a sign of ending the supply of opium to China, the government brought about some changes within the opium administration in India.

The closing of Patna factory

To adjust the Shanghai resolutions the British government in 1911 closed the Patna opium factory, but continued until 1917 to supply opium to China under the intended agreements. As I discussed in Chapter 1, Patna opium had played a historic role in the colonial opium trade since 1773. As a result of China's zeal for opium reform and British commitments for service to this cause, the government of India reduced its poppy cultivation in Bihar and the surrounding areas, and shifted the greater portion of poppy culture into the UP.

As a sign of Shanghai compatibility the government transferred its traditional opium headquarters from Patna to Ghazipur in UP, where it had maintained an opium factory for about three-quarters of a century. The official papers claimed that 'having the bulk of the cultivation in that province and the great majority of the establishment permanently employed there,'[24] it was considered a matter of administrative convenience for the government to transfer direct control of the department to UP. While the Bengal Board of Revenue continued to manage the sale of export opium in Calcutta, its other functions related to processing of opium were taken over by the Board in the UP[25] Under this new arrangement, poppy cultivation was continued in a number of remote districts in UP, while the government factory was run at Ghazipur.

In line with the closing of Patna opium factory, the amount of poppy cultivation as well as the size of the opium industry was drastically reduced. As a result of the reduction of poppy cultivation in Bihar, the total area under government poppy cultivation dropped from 304,000 hectares in 1906–7, to about 110,000 hectares in 1911–12, with a further reduction to only 68,000 hectares in 1913–14. In connection with the reduction in opium industry, the government dismissed the less efficient opium employees and transferred skilled officers and staff. To encourage the retirement of senior officers, the government offered full pensions to all those who were within five years of completing their qualifying period of service. The government dealt along these lines 'with every rank, from the highest paid departmental officer down to the humble peon', to bring about a drastic reduction of the opium industry.[26] During the constriction of the opium industry, the British government reached an agreement with China for a continuance of opium supplies until 1917.

In response to the Chinese proposal made in the Shanghai summit, the British government consolidated its bilateral trade arrangements with China for another six years. In May 1911, the government signed an agreement with China, and stated that India's supply of opium to China would gradually be terminated on condition that China demonstrated its sincerity in stamping out its local production.[27] The agreement reflected an official decision by the government of India to bring to an end to the century-old opium trade, and at the same time confirmed the continuance of the trade until the agreement expired. Given this situation, another international summit was called by the US to finalize outstanding issues connected with an imposition of a total ban on the South Asian opium trade.

The Hague opium conference

After its initial disappointments in Shanghai, the government of India boycotted the second round of international opium summits at The Hague during 1911–14, and was reluctant to ratify the Articles of the Hague Convention until the early 1920s. To formalize the recommendations of the Shanghai summit, US President Taft in September 1909 extended a proposal to India and some other major powers to meet at The Hague and to make arrangements to sacrifice their 'serious financial interests' in production and trafficking in opium.[28] By the middle of May 1910, all other countries had responded positively, except the government of British India, which insisted that morphine and cocaine be incorporated in the agenda before it would participate. Due to strong opposition from morphine producing countries, especially Germany and Japan, the conference was convened without India.

In the absence of India, one of the biggest producers of opium, the Hague summit held a series of meetings and undertook diplomatic discussions amongst the attending countries on drugs. It took over two and half years (December 1911 to July 1914) for the concurring countries to come to an agreement and to adopt the Final Protocol at the third Hague summit. The following discussion examines the reasons for the non-appearance of India at the Hague summits and examines the proxy role of the British delegates in favour of the government of India. It also examines the political response of the government of India to the implementation of the Hague principles on drugs until further international regulations were imposed in 1924–25.

The Indian boycott

The absence of India in The Hague Opium Conference was linked to its bargaining for the inclusion of morphine and cocaine on the agenda. During the first Hague summit, between December 1911 and January 1912, the British delegates successfully represented the interests of the government of India. In line with the pre-summit dialogue, they asserted that morphine smuggled from Germany, Japan and elsewhere was causing addiction problems in the large coastal cities of Madras, Bombay and Calcutta in India, and in Akyab in Burma. The British delegates also held that cocaine was smuggled into India and was causing 'a major problem'. They expressed the inability of the government of India to enforce banning of opium consumption in India. Referring to Lord Harding's recent dispatch, the British delegate Sir William Stevenson Meyer maintained that:

> The prohibition of opium eating in India we regard as impossible, and any attempt at it as fraught with the most serious consequences to the people and the government. We take our stand unhesitatingly on the conclusions of the Royal Commission for India which reported in 1895, viz.: that the opium habit as a vice scarcely exists in India.[29]

Refuting the anti-opium resolution of the Shanghai summit, he maintained that 'we cannot admit the total suppression of the opium habit in India', but consider a 'subject of careful regulation'. Meyer also referred to some of the token measures taken by the Indian government against the smoking habit in Burma and the rest of India. In accordance with the instructions of the British government, the British delegates resisted any resolution that particularly addressed the production and use of opium in India or any of the Crown colonies. Through a proxy role, the British delegates in the Hague Conference made successful representation in favour of the government of British India.

In keeping with the Hague narco-diplomacy, the government of India at once adopted some legal measures on cocaine. But for example, Roy K. Anderson, a high official from the Burma Excise Department, in a 1922 book called *Drug Smuggling and Taking in India and Burma*, provided only a little evidence of morphine and cocaine addiction in the region.[30] Justifying their measures, however, the government claimed that morphine and cocaine were inflicting more damage in India and China than opium. Sir Guy Fleetwood Wilson, immediately after the First Hague summit, reiterated in the legislative council that 'the evil done by these drugs is already great; their spread is rapid and insidious'.[31] To validate British claims in The Hague, the government of India banned the 'possession' of non-medicinal cocaine in all the provinces, but permitted opium. In support of India's diplomatic stand, the government maintained that the summit was 'comparatively unimportant' because it had already reached a mutual understanding on opium supply with China in 1911. The colonial authorities in India also claimed that opium consumption in South Asia was a matter of domestic concern, which did not require international attention.

Nevertheless, the summit urged India to review and improve its opium policy under The Hague principles. The first Hague summit adopted an international resolution to stamp out South Asian narcotic drugs.[32] In order to regulate the abuse of Indian hemp, the summit expressed its desire to study the question from a statistical and scientific point of view. The signatory countries of the first Hague Convention failed to ratify the major recommendations of the summit, until the third Hague summit met in June 1914. In the absence of India and Turkey, the two principal opium producing countries, many of the participating delegates, who had virtually nothing to do with the opium traffic, were apathetic during the second Hague summit. France declared that its ratification of the Hague Convention would be subject to the further ratification of India.[33] The UK also expressed unwillingness to put the Convention into force unless all signatory countries concurred. Given these unresolved controversies, the second Hague summit ended fruitlessly.

However, with the signing of the Final Protocol at the Third Hague Opium Summit in June 1914, an environment was created to make the anti-opium Convention of 1912 effective, with ratification of the Convention by the end of December 1914. Enactment of national legislation for the control of the production and distribution of opium became obligatory for the participating countries.[34] Limitations on the use of morphine, heroin and cocaine for medical purposes, licensing of manufacturers and distributors of narcotic drugs, and control over international drug trafficking also became mandatory. The inclusion of morphine and cocaine in the Final Convention of the Hague summit was a diplomatic victory for India. The UK ratified the Convention in July 1914; however, as an absentee from the summit, the government of India was not under any immediate obligation to give effect to the Convention's final resolutions.[35] The outbreak of the First World War created further reason for Indian reliance on revenue from drugs and delayed the implementation of the international regulations in South Asia.

Pursuit of drug revenue

The British morphine and cocaine positions at the Hague summits allowed the government of India to continue its opium supply to China until 1917, and to resurrect opium production after First World War. With the gradual reduction of poppy cultivation in India and of opium exports to China, the price of the drug increased both in China and in India.[36] Given this price rise the government of India during 1911–13 received about £10 million, an extra amount, which originally had been projected for the whole withdrawal period of 9 years.[37] As the importance of the trade increased tremendously and as the second Hague summit was coming closer, the supply of India's opium to China became a matter of Westminster politics.

In early May 1913, Towyn Jones, a Liberal MP, tabled a resolution in the House of Commons that 'the Chinese be at once formally and finally released from all further obligation to admit Indian opium'. Describing the iniquity of the trade, he argued that 'what is morally indefensible must be politically wrong'.[38] He further claimed that while China had by 1910 reduced its domestic production by between 70 and 80 per cent, India had decreased its opium supply to the latter by only 30 per cent. In condemnation of the treaty provisions, Taylor maintained that the Chinese government was restricted from any direct resistance to the wholesale traffic in Indian opium, and at the same time India's export privilege was guaranteed. Montagu, the Under-Secretary of State for India, replied:

> We have in India abandoned altogether the revenue derived from the sale of opium to China from this year, and we are to day selling no opium for China at all.[39]

The motion was withdrawn as a result of Montagu's untrue statement about the cessation of Indian opium trade. Despite the pronouncement, the government of India, under the guarantee provision, sent to China 1,147 metric tons of opium in 1913, 446 metric tons in 1914, and 255 metric tons in 1915.[40] In April 1916, *The Chinese Social and Political Science Review* indicated that six provinces of China were technically 'open' for the importation of Indian opium.[41] W.T. Dunn, a contemporary authority on the subject, argued that the government of India sent 127 metric tons in 1917 to collect ultimately $25 million from the opium traffic in China.[42] On receipt of the last consignment of opium, the Chinese government publicly burnt the whole shipment to symbolically mark the formal ending of the British drug trafficking.

The absence of India from the Hague summit, and the lack of unified stand amongst the participating countries, allowed India to accumulate increasing revenue from consumption of opium in South Asia. Ignoring the injurious effects of opium, the government allowed an increase in internal consumption between 1912 and 1920. The sale of excise opium during this period was higher than in any other period, with record sales in 1913–14 (as shown in Figure 3.1). Criticizing the government's domestic opium distribution policy, W.W. Willoughby in 1925 wrote:

> Neither Great Britain nor the British Indian Government has ever entered into any international agreement with reference to the manner in which the consumption of opium in India shall be controlled.[43]

In accordance with the Shanghai formula, the British government did not devise any sufficient way to control the abuse of opium in South Asia. The situation was aggravated with the outbreak of the First World

War in 1914. Indian manpower and resources were called upon for the war effort, and this slowed down 'further progress' in the international controls on drugs. The war contributed to a shortage in the supply of excise opium, which produced a price rise and spread opium trafficking in the region.

Moreover, the poppy cultivators in India in district after district abandoned their traditional occupation, due to the gradual extinction of the British opium trade after 1911, and caused a shortage in the production of licit opium. In 1934, L.E.S. Eisenlohr indicated that the manufacture of opium during 1910–14 fell from 2,810 metric tons to 1,150 metric tons, and the number of cultivators decreased from some 700,000 to less than 500,000.[44] Eisenlohr's figures included opium produced in central Indian states. In 1938, H.B. Dunnicliff maintained that due to the reduction policy, the opium export decreased from 1,711 metric tons in 1912 to 580 metric tons in 1914, with a corresponding decline from Rs74.8 million to Rs19.2 million.[45] Alongside the shortfall in the production, an additional demand was created for medicinal opium, as a result of the war. To encourage the cultivators to return to their previous occupation, the Opium Agency raised the purchase price between 1914 and 1917 from Rs5 *annas* 3 to Rs9 per *seer*. The prospect of increased financial returns finally succeeded in inducing the cultivators to grow the requisite amount of opium needed to meet the new demand. L.E.S. Eisenlohr wrote:

> Old districts of cultivation, closed when the China trade ended, were reopened, and a new department of research was instituted for improving the quality of the opium produced, the medicinal opium and morphine manufactured for war purposes required expensive new machinery, and all of these developments meant a large increase in staff.[46]

To resume its poppy cultivation, the government in 1915 utilized special lands in the Malwa territory and grew additional poppies for the purposes of the Opium Agency. Given these measures, the exports of opium increased by 28 per cent in three years.[47] The net receipt from this revised revenue activity in 1918–19 was over £2 million,[48] which was higher than the previous record in 1914–15.

Reviving the opium production, the colonial authorities increased the distribution of excise opium for local consumption. Anti-drug commentators placed the blame on government policy for 'forcing opium down the throats of a reluctant people, corrupting souls and ruining bodies for its own selfish purposes'. Applying new provincial excise policies the government of India received in 1918–19 a total of £3 million or Rs4.6 million, which rose further in the following year to £3.4 or Rs5.2 million.[49] To control this trend, Rai Bahadur B.N. Sharma urged in the Indian legislative assembly in February 1917 that non-official MLAs 'should be consulted with regard to all questions relating to the local administration of excise, and that no additional shops should be opened without their express sanction.'[50] Sharma's resolution was defeated by 38 to 20, with every vote in favour being cast by an indigenous member and every vote against by the British members. The supremacy of the official members further prevailed in the central legislature and provincial legislative assemblies under the constitutional reforms of 1919.

The constitution of 1919

Under the Montagu–Chelmsford (Montford) Reforms of 1919, the provincial governments were authorized to control excise revenue on drugs, but with no other alternative financial help from the central government. The Montford Reforms retained finance, customs, poppy cultivation and opium exports under the control of the central government, while allocating to the provincial governments the collection of excise duties from intoxicating drugs.[51] Given this arrangement the government of India claimed that the restrictions on opium consumption were no longer within the power of the central government, but were vested in the provincial authorities. It further maintained that the 'possibility of further' control on drug addiction lay with members of the provincial legislatures.[52] This shared authority on the distribution of drugs often led to conflict between the provincial and the central governments, or between the executive and legislative branches of the provincial authorities.

Under the Montford Reforms provincial governments were provided authority to control the sale of intoxicating drugs, while these governments for their welfare activities depended heavily on excise revenue. The sources of revenue assigned to the provinces were extremely limited, and excise was by far the most important source of income. If provincial governments wanted to develop education, public health services and public works, drug revenue was one of the biggest sources of funds. As a result of this financial dependency, the receipts from intoxicating drugs in Assam in 1921–2 were Rs10 million, while financial support from the central government for an annual budget was Rs5.8 million. Therefore, whatever may have been their wishes on the issue, neither the people nor their elected representatives in the provincial legislatures had any choice, but to continue to promote the sale and consumption of drugs. Figure 3.2 shows that the governments of Bombay and Assam, out of their total revenue income, received the highest amount of excise revenue in seven provinces, while the government of Punjab was the lowest excise revenue earner. Amongst the excisable items *tari*, *pachwai*, hemp (*ganja, charas, bhang and majum*), cocaine, liquor (both foreign and local) were intoxicating drugs. Except for licence fees from opium vendors, for technical reason, the earning of revenue from the domestic consumption of opium was excluded from the above list. Nevertheless, the Indian Statutory Commission in 1930 indicated that in every province excise revenue was next to the size of land revenue.[53] It was a

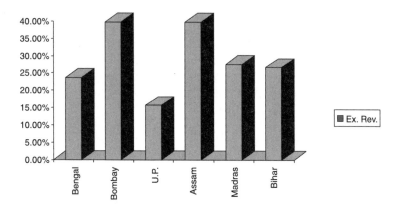

Figure 3.2   Excise revenue in seven provinces in India, 1921–2
Source: *The Indian Annual Register*, vol. 2, 1925, p. 112(i)

contradictory policy of the government of India, that provincial ministers were authorized to take measures to reduce the consumption of drugs, while they were not provided with an adequate budget to accomplish their development and welfare activities. Thus, under the Montford Reforms there was a conflict between provincial excise policy and the general financial policy of the central government, in which the latter was dominant.

Contradictions also persisted in India over the ratification of the Hague Convention. In accordance with the Versailles Peace Treaty and other post-First World War peace treaties,[54] the central government became accountable to the League of Nations for the implementation of the Hague principles. However, the central government remained reluctant to urge the provincial authorities to change policies that generated 'maximum revenue' from opium consumption. As a result of this, the distribution of excise opium declined over 50 per cent during 1913–26, while liquor revenue increased in most of the provinces.[55] This occurred largely in the absence of international control on liquor consumption, as well as through excise policies at the provincial level.

Under the Montford Reforms, central government dominated the provincial assemblies through the powers of provincial executives and governors, who appointed and dismissed Indian ministers and also selected some members of these legislatures. The provincial governors used their enormous influence on these ministers and members to ensure support for the government's drug policy. Using veto power, the governors dominated the provincial legislatures when the local members voted for a reduction of opium or liquor licences. Thus, the Montford Reforms did not bring about a major shift in the government's drug policy, although officially India claimed that its policy was in total accord with that of the League of Nations. W.W. Willoughby wrote:

> It would seem to be the fact that the Indian peoples themselves are allowed to exercise no control whatever over the cultivation and manufacture of opium, nor over its sale for exportation.[56]

Under the constitutional reforms of 1919 the ultimate authority of drug control was retained by central government, which was not yet prepared to allow any radical change in its traditional drug policy. In

1924, Dr S.K. Datta and several other members in the central legislature attacked the 'conservative' drug policy, which they claimed promoted drug addiction. Given the duplicity in the legal provisions on domestic consumption of drugs, the colonial authorities also attempted to suppress the anti-drug agitation created by the Non-Cooperation workers in different parts of India.

Crusaders' in chains

In line with the international summits, the Hindu and Muslim legislators, despite differences in their socio-political and economic interests, opposed the drug policies of the colonial authorities. The censure and attacks of local members both within and outside the legislative assemblies seriously undermined the British official position on opium. Facing tremendous pressure from the Non-Cooperation Movement led by Mahatma Gandhi in the early 1920s, the colonial rulers continued with repressive measures against anti-drugs campaigners in India.

G.K. Gokhale, one of the most influential leaders of the Indian National Congress Party, initiated the anti-opium campaign in India in 1911. As I discussed before, Gokhale and other non-official members in the central and provincial legislatures several times opposed the pro-revenue excise bills. After fruitless attempts to end the dominance of the official majority members in the legislative assemblies, the local members brought this issue to the public. Gokhale described opium revenue as 'a great stain on Indian finances',[57] and advocated total prohibition of all other intoxicating drugs, as they were rejected by the vast majority of people of India. The proclamation by Gokhale coincided with the contemporary temperance movement in India, and was then picked up by Mahatma Gandhi following his assumption of the Congress leadership after 1918.

Gandhi, an Indian Bar-at-Law, who suffered repression and disgrace at the hands of colonial authorities in South Africa, now linked the current anti-drug issues with the Non-Cooperation Movement to overthrow the Imperial powers in India. The harmful effects of government liquor and opium policies were strongly denounced by him. He provided his support to a campaign to picket liquor and *toddy* shops. Launching a publicity war against intoxicants, he told the public in Assam in early August 1921 that they could not achieve *Swaraj* without giving up their drug habits. Gandhi appealed to addicts to break their chains of addiction, and urged his audience to extend their love and affection towards these 'down-trodden' people.[58] In 1930, H.G. Alexander wrote:

> From August to November hundreds of young men, fired with enthusiasm, took up the temperance work and preached against opium, *ganja*, and other drugs; they stood outside the shops and implored the people not to buy; no violence was committed.[59]

However, the official authorities claimed that violence occurred during the Non-Cooperation campaign. In 1925, the Deputy Director of the Indian Intelligence Bureau, P.C. Bampford, maintained that the anti-drug campaigners attacked licensed vendors and this sometimes led to the 'looting and burning of the drugs shops'.[60] The Non-Cooperation workers organized a boycott and picketing of liquor and other drugs shops as a part of the programme of political unrest. They condemned the drinking habit on moral and religious grounds, and persuaded addicts that it was wasteful and harmful for family life. Information was provided in 1921 in a Parliament Report, which stated:

> Throughout India, ... pickets were placed around [liquor] shops and drinkers subjected to various forms of insult and degradation. They were excommunicated from their caste, deprived of the services of barbers and washermen, beaten, garlanded with shoes, tied to poles, or driven through the streets on the backs of donkeys with their faces to the tails.[61]

Gandhi-men, believing in Gandhi's *Sattagraha* political ideals and wearing handspun, hand-loom cloth (*khaddar*), protested against government provision of drug on people's doorsteps. During the Non-Cooperation Movement, Gandhi's followers aligned their anti-drug campaign with the anti-drink movement of the Koli peasants of the coastal region.[62] They tried to dissuade their countrymen from dangerous drug habits, especially the use of opium.

As a result of the anti-drug crusade, excise revenue declined substantially and many people in Assam and other parts of India gave up their drug addiction. During 1921–2, as Gandhi and his followers decided to refuse to cooperate with licensed vendors and officials dealing with the drug laws, there was a great decrease in both drug consumption and excise revenue all over India. Bamford, in his book *Histories of the Non-Cooperation and Khilafat Movements*, indicates that during the agitation excise revenue fell dramatically, especially in Bihar, Orissa and Bombay.[63] In 1924–5 the Finance Minister acknowledged that as a result of political agitation opium consumption fell during 1910–11 to 1922–3 by about 50 per cent. The Excise Department of Assam indicated that due to picketing of opium shops by the non-cooperators, opium consumption reduced from 60 metric to 39 metric tons between 1921 and 1922.[64] The Report of the Assam Inquiry Committee maintained that in 1920–1, 60 metric tons of opium, 24 metric tons of cannabis and 304,572 gallons of country liquor were consumed; but that in 1923–4 the figures dropped to 33 metric tons, 13 metric tons and 191,421 gallons respectively.[65] In 1934, Eisenlohr asserted that Gandhi's campaign was responsible for the 20 per cent reduction of drug consumption in Assam, one of the worst drug-affected areas in British India.[66] In Bombay Presidency, liquor consumption fell by 19 per cent as a result of picketing during the Non-Cooperation Movement.[67]

Alarmed by the strength of the anti-drug campaign, and by its spread to various parts of India, the government adopted repressive measures. The colonial authorities tried to suppress picketers by applying laws that had been introduced in 1898 to deal with criminals and drug traffickers. Perceiving a greater political threat, the colonial authorities promulgated new criminal laws in 1921, and arrested many anti-drug activists on the ground that they were 'inciting civil disobedience'.[68] Through this Act, the government practically made picketing illegal as an activity. In an attempt to restrict the campaign, the police intelligence kept watch on the anti-drug workers, and 'threw thousands of temperance workers into jail' in 1921.[69] Anti-drug activists suffered heavy repression after pro-drug persecution began in Assam, with the confinement of 1,100 Assamese lawyers, tea-planters, graduates, college students and patriotic young men.[70] Through these repressive measures, anti-drug agitation gradually was controlled and excise revenue returned to its normal scale by 1923. The use of force to suppress the anti-drug campaigners was an indication of the avowed revenue principle of the government's drug policy.

The repressive measures made the Non-Cooperation leaders more committed in their anti-drug struggle. In order to stop the government's supplies, the anti-drug activists formed subdivisional and district committees that were parallel to the Local Congress Committees. government officials also tried their best to counteract the campaigners' efforts by organizing anti-Non-Cooperation leagues, like the *Aman Sabhas*.[71] However, Gandhi workers preached temperance in the villages, held meetings all over Asssam, and delivered lectures at social and religious gatherings where 'they carried the message of prohibition which *Mahatmaji* had preached' to them. The people in the villages heard with profound interest and devotion the temperance words of Gandhi's followers; and the movement spread steadily and peacefully and with great zeal to other parts of British India. In line with public opinion, the National Congress in 1924 passed a resolution recording its view that poppy cultivation should be restricted to supplying 'medical and scientific requirements only'.[72] This laid the foundation for the protests made by the dominant political party against the manufacture of opium for addiction.

Alongside the public agitation, the non-official members of the legislative assemblies argued strongly in favour of prohibition of intoxicating drugs. In August 1921 a motion had been moved by Professor S.C. Mukherji in the Bengal legislature requiring the government to take immediate measures for a total prohibition within three years. He argued that 'the enormous increase in revenue means a very appreciable increase in consumption'. Demanding total restriction, he further argued:

> The excise policy of the government is not the policy of the people of the country. We want restricted consumption and we do not mind if it means shrinkage in revenue. Our ultimate goal is total prohibition and we are praying for the day when the whole of the excise revenue will be blotted out of our provincial budget.[73]

The motion was supported by others members, who referred to the texts of the great religions of India – Islam, Hinduism and Buddhism.

After a two-day debate and exhaustive discussion, the motion was lost, 48 to 41. Similar motions were subsequently tabled in Bombay, the UP and other legislative assemblies, but were faced with the parliamentary defeats.

Nevertheless, launching their persistent attacks and a political battle both outside and inside the government, Gandhi and other nationalist leaders created an unpleasant situation for the colonial government. To bring an end to the colonial rule in India, the Indian National Congress politicized public opinion to help reduce the revenue of the alien rulers by boycotting the drug shops. Before the movement was totally suppressed, the Assam Provincial Congress Committee in June 1924 appointed a non-government Opium Commission in Assam to investigate the impact of opium addiction in the province.

The 'hush-hush' Assam Enquiry

In line with international preparations for the Geneva Convention of 1924, the Congress leaders set up the Assam Opium Enquiry Committee to void medical evidence that had been maintained by the colonial authorities on opium addiction. Headed by the President and the Secretary of the Assam Provincial Congress Committee, the Committee of Enquiry was composed of lawyers, journalists, medical practitioners and political leaders from a variety of party backgrounds. While all the previous commissions – the British Royal Commission, the Philippines Opium Commission and Ceylon Opium Commission – had been state sponsored, the Assam Opium Enquiry Committee was set up by the Indian National Congress, the leading political party opposed to a continuation of colonial rule.

To make the investigation people-oriented the Committee conducted its interviews mostly in the Assamese language, and travelled to remote areas to interview 345 witnesses. Within three months, the Committee had completed its 'non-party lines' report, and this report was published in daily newspapers, including the *Indian Annual Register*, in 1925. The report provided an abundance of information about opium sales, consumption and addiction in Assam. It regarded opium as an evil and 'a national disaster'.[74] The report's findings provided an insight into the level of opium abuse in Assam in particular and India in general. However, the colonial authorities maintained silence about the findings of the Report.

The Assam Enquiry Committee Report provided detailed historical evidence of opium abuse and trade in Assam. Unlike the Royal Commission, which emphasized the Burmese connection in the introduction of the opium habit in the region,[75] the Assam Report provided a different interpretation. Referring to Captain Butler's *Travels and Adventures in Assam*, published in 1853, the Report stated that the poppy culture was virtually unknown in Assam before 'it was introduced by the Rajput troops, who were brought into Assam either by the Koch Chiefs or by the British'. The report further held that:

> When finally the British came ... from 1826 to 1860, they practically followed a policy of drift on the opium question. Their one care was to introduce their own opium for revenue purposes in order to undersell the indigenous product. ... It [the government] allowed the terrible evil to spread among the people.[76]

In 1860, opium was made a government monopoly in Assam, and the government between 1884 and 1921 sold licences at public auction to the highest bidder, and thus received in each year more and more revenue. The consumption of opium in Assam ranged between 70 metric tons in 1875–6 and 65 metric tons in 1919–20, while opium revenue rose from Rs1.2 million to Rs4.4 million during the same period.[77] This rise in opium revenue took place mainly due to the increase in the opium price from Rs5 per *seer* (0.9331 kilo) in 1835 to Rs65 per *seer* in 1924. Thus the investigating body observed that while the maximization of opium revenue had been a policy of the government, the policy of minimum consumption had been dealt with 'only half-heartedly'.

The observations of the Assam Opium Enquiry Committee were, courageous and radical for the time, as they completely abandoned the conclusions of the Royal Commission, and branded the government's opium policy tardy and superficial. It disagreed with the assertion of the British delegates at the Hague Conference that if the reduction were carried beyond a certain limit, then opium consumers would take 'more deleterious drugs'.[78] The Assam Report claimed that as a result of the Non-Cooperation Movement opium taking in Assam had dropped from 65 metric tons to 33 metric tons between 1919 and 1924, while during the same period cannabis had declined from 25 metric tons to 13 metric tons.[79] It also provided evidence opposing the government's defence that a reduction in the number of licensed shops would increase the smuggling of opium. The report thus concluded that due to anti-drug agitation, there had been a remarkable decrease in illicit trafficking as well as in consumption. The report noted that 'when public opinion is awake and active', then the solution to drug problems becomes easier.

The Assam Committee's findings also differed with the Royal Commission about the medicinal use of opium in Assam, and the diplomatic position maintained by the government of India in international forums. The *Final Report of the Royal Commission* observed that 58 per cent of the Assamese population in 1892–3 were habitual opium-eaters and that they required opium in order to protect themselves from disease in the very damp and malarial climate.[80] Replying to this, a medical expert in Assam held that it was 'a preposterous suggestion' that opium had any preventive action against kala-azar or malaria.[81] Compiling similar evidence, the Assam Report noted:

> In the whole of the medical evidence given by our witnesses, among whom were many doctors with a life-long experience of Assam conditions, ... pointed out to us that opium addiction among the Assamese villagers reduced the power of resistance and rendered severe attacks of infectious diseases, such as kala-azar and cholera, more liable to end fatally.[82]

The Committee also asserted that before the Assamese became subject to the opium habit, they were healthy and vigorous, but afterwards they became 'debilitated and outworn owing chiefly to opium addiction'. This finding directly rejected the government's classical argument in defence of its opium policy and supported international moves against South Asian drugs. Rejecting the contention of the Royal Commission that the banning of opium was 'impracticable', the Assam Report claimed that the sale of opium and its derivatives should be limited to the 'medical and scientific needs' of the province. The Assam recommendations contradicted the British government's assertions in international forums, and were identical to the US demand in the Opium Advisory Committee of the League of Nations in 1923. Going beyond the recommendations of the Philippines Opium Commission and the Ceylon Opium Commission, which suggested a rationed supply for adult opium addicts of 21 years of age or more, the Assam Committee suggested 40 years as the minimum age limit to qualify for the registration. They recommended that the rest of the opium addicts in Assam should be dealt with as 'medical patients'.

As an independent investigating body, the Assam Opium Enquiry Committee echoed international demands to limit the use of drugs for medicinal and scientific purposes in South Asia and elsewhere. Its findings helped in the eventual change in the traditional defence of the colonial opium policy, both in the region and internationally. To expedite the observations of the Assam Committee, the All India Congress Committee in 1924 passed a resolution declaring that the opium policy of the government of India was 'contrary to the moral welfare' of the indigenous people.[83] The Assam Committee provided a judgement in favour of the Non-Cooperation Movement of Gandhi, and of the US-led international struggle against South Asian narcotic drugs.

Although the government was silent on the findings of the report, it announced in 1924 its readiness to appoint a Committee to examine the judgements of the 1893 Commission. There is no known record available on the government's proposed committee. The findings of the Assam Opium Enquiry Committee significantly undermined the British position on the opium issue. As it provided fresh evidence in support of international pressure to control the South Asian opium trade, the Assam Report contributed significantly to a modification of British political mind about opium during the Second Geneva Summit in February 1925.

The Geneva Opium Summit

Under political pressure in India and diplomatic pressure from the US and China, the British government ratified the Geneva Convention, of 1925, but refrained from the total execution of its principles. After its boycotting of the Hague Opium Summits of 1912–14, the government of British India during 1924–5 participated at the First and Second Opium Summits in Geneva that were convened to resolve outstanding issues. However, the delegates from British India persistently tried to defend the findings of the British Royal Commission on Opium of 1895. After a two-year-long diplomatic battle, the government of British India accepted the Geneva Convention, but pursued half-hearted policies in controlling the opium habit in South Asia.

At the first summit, India's delegate John Campbell opposed the US resolution to control the manufacture of opium for medical and scientific requirements. In accordance with the findings of the British Royal Commission on Opium, Campbell argued that in India the abuse of opium was so much overlapping with medical uses that it was almost impossible 'to draw a distinction between them'.[84] However, the US representatives continued to press for acceptance of a proposal relating to the immediate control of the production and distribution of South Asian opium.[85] Opposed to the US proposal, India's delegate Campbell urged for the amendment of some technical points of the Hague Convention.[86] The US delegates expressed their inability to sign any agreement 'which does not fulfil the conditions necessary for the narcotic drug traffic as set forth in the preamble'. Disgruntled, the US delegation resigned from the summits on 6 February 1925. They were followed by the resignation of the Chinese delegates on the following day. The Sino-US withdrawal was an indication of the diplomatic protest against the arbitrary of British drug policies in South Asia.

Until the findings of the Assam Opium Enquiry Committee were available in late 1924, the impact of the withdrawal of the US and China from the Geneva summits had been minimal on the British diplomatic stand. In an attempt to prolong the constitutional stalemate, the British delegates to the Second Geneva Summit echoed the drug principles pursued by the government of India. In defence of the government's opium policy the delegates from India argued that it was lawful. Defending the position of the government of India, Clayton insisted that:

> It holds that the present system of opium control in India is legitimate, in the fullest sense of the word, under the Hague Convention of 1912. It also holds that this system is the best and

most effective method of putting into force under the conditions that prevail in India, the principles, which underlie the government of India. [87]

Their assertion was based on an estimate that the annual per-head opium consumption in India, which was 26 grains, did not exceed the cultural and quasi-medicinal requirements of the country. The judgement provided by the colonial authorities in India was about four times higher than the optimum standard assessed by the Health Committee of the League of Nations in February 1924. On publication of the Assam Report in October 1924, both Gandhi and Tagore sent a cable to the League of Nations conveying their anxiety about 'the growing addiction to narcotic drugs' in India. They further requested that the League adopt adequate measures 'for the total extirpation of the plants, from which these drugs originate, except as found necessary for medicine and science in the judgement of the best medical opinion of the world'.[88] Nobel Prize recipient Kabiguru Rabindranath Tagore joined the public statements condemning the harm that Indians were suffering as a result of the abuse of opium. Given political demands in India as well as diplomatic pressure from the US and China, the British government during the Second Geneva Summit on 19 February accepted the Geneva Protocol and the Final Act of 1925.

The end of colonial opium trade

The ratification of the Geneva Convention by the government of British India marked the cessation of colonial opium trade in South Asia by 1935, but increased opium trafficking from central India. Alexander notes that facing immense pressure created by the political leaders in India and international opinion led by the US, the colonial authorities suffered a 'conversion of hearts.'[89] With the increase of international demand, both the production and export of opium in India fell gradually. *India in 1932–33,* indicates that the area under poppy cultivation in the UP in 1931–2 was decreased to 20.8 per cent of the area cultivated in 1913–14, and about 52.1 per cent of the area sown in 1925–6. The first remarkable drop took place as a consequence of the decimation of Imperial opium trade in China, and the second major reduction occurred as a result of India's ratification of the Geneva Convention of 1925.

Under the principles of the Geneva Convention, the government of British India was constrained to take steps to prevent illicit opium traffic completely within five years. In September 1925 the government declared that the process would be accomplished by 31 December 1935, in ten years instead of five years as required by the Protocol. Referring to the ratification of the Geneva Protocol, Governor General Lord Reading, in the following year, said:

> It is desirable that we should declare publicly our intention to reduce progressively the exports of opium from India so as to extinguish them altogether within a definite period, except as regards exports of opium for strictly medical purposes.[90]

Reading's statement indicated a phenomenal shift in the government's opium export policy. In March 1926 the Legislative Assembly adopted an official resolution for the gradual reduction of opium exports, except for medicinal and scientific purposes. Justifying the motion, the Finance Minister, Sir Basil Blackett, argued that revenue from opium export had been declining: whereas the revenue in 1911–12 from this source was Rs10 *crores*, it was now Rs2 *crores*.[91] The circulars of the Opium Advisory Committee of June 1926 expedited the colonial action at this stage. It urged the government of India not to delay in taking effective steps to stop the contraband traffic in opium. Consequently, the Indian government announced an annual 10 per cent reduction of opium exports, taking the rate to 90 per cent in 1927, then 80 per cent in 1928, until it ceased in 1935. The 10 per cent policy, a process applied to the withdrawal of colonial opium trade to China in 1907, was restated in 1926 in violation of the Geneva Protocol.

Nevertheless, through its policy of progressive reduction in supply, the government of India finally came into line with other countries on opium export. Following the adaptation of the Import Certificate system in 1923 and then the Geneva Convention of 1925, the government of India regulated its opium exports for medicinal purposes. Figure 3.3 shows that as a result of this change in policy, the net revenue receipts from opium fell to Rs22.6 million for 1926–7, Rs5.9 million below the previous year.[92] Figure 3.3 also indicates that following the ratification of the Geneva Convention, the government of India's opium exports decreased from 512 metric

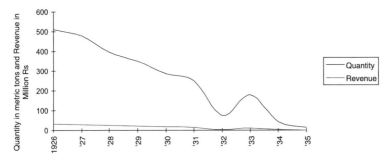

Figure 3.3 Cessation of India's opium exports, 1926–36
Source: *Asian Review Series*, vol. 34, no. 4, 1938, p. 355

tons in 1926–7 to 481 metric tons in 1927–8 and 427 metric tons in
1928–9.[93] This declining trend is evident during the post-Shanghai
era, when the total export of non-medicinal opium to China
and the Asia-Pacific region fell from 1,004 metric tons in 1913 to
544 metric tons in 1923.[94] By withdrawing gradually from this
traffic, the government was finally putting a stop to its export of
opium for non-medicinal purposes. As a result of this decision, the
discredit attached to India as the principal exporter of opium
declined. In accordance with the Geneva Convention, the government further restricted opium shipments at any port in India unless
covered by an authorization by the importing country. Thus the
government policy in the post-Geneva years was confined to its
international obligations to control opium exports in accordance
with the medicinal needs of the importing countries, while the
smuggling of contraband opium from India increased.

The cessation of colonial opium trade in South Asia witnessed the
proliferation of contraband drug trade in the region during the early
twentieth century. There were seizures of contraband Indian opium in
Chinese ports, after supplies of Indian opium had officially ceased
in 1917. Also, illicit Indian opium was detected in Australia, South
Africa, Chile, Peru, Mexico and the United States.[95] As a result of this,
the legality of India's official opium export programme came under
attack by US delegates during the fifth session of the Advisory
Committee in May–June 1923. They argued that while about
100 metric tons of raw opium were required to satisfy the medicinal

and scientific needs of the world, the annual production of the drug
was about 1,500 metric tons, with the surplus being smuggled to the
West.[96] After lengthy discussion, all the opium producing countries
agreed to the US proposals, while the government of British India, the
biggest exporter of opium, disagreed on the need to control opium
production for the medical and scientific needs of world. This disagreement had significant influence on post-Geneva opium smuggling in
the region.

As I mentioned before, the ratification of the Geneva Convention
by India imposed delicate obligations on the colonial authorities by
formally acceding to its principles on opium export. In accordance
with international pressure, India gradually decreased its purchasing
of Malwa opium from 425 metric tons in 1924–5 to 243 metric
tones in 1925–6.[97] This change in government policy created an
enormous opium stockpiles in about 30 central Indian states.[98] A
similar situation also occurred in the government-run opium industry in UP. As a result of this, opium smuggling both from central
Indian states and Benares increased during and after the Geneva
Convention. During 1928–9, customs authorities in China seized
Benares opium, despite the end of official supply in 1917.
Illegitimate Indian opium had also been seized in South Africa and
Australia. Explaining the post-Geneva reality, H.G. Alexander, in
1930, wrote:

> The smuggling trade is a source of embarrassment to the
> government of India; for, although the Malwa States are not
> under its control, the government of India is alone responsible to
> the League of Nations for drug control in the whole of India. ...
> In Bombay, for instance, I was assured that every mail-boat
> leaving for South Africa probably had smuggled opium on
> board.[99]

As a matter of fact, to meet post-First World War international
demands, the British government introduced its own poppy cultivation in the Malwa territories, and thereby became responsible for
controlling the illicit smuggling. Nevertheless, it is evident from the
above information that central Indian opium was continuing to be
smuggled through Indian territories, causing disgrace and embarrassment for the government of India. In an attempt to alleviate the

situation in May 1927 the Viceroy, Lord Irwin, called a summit between the officials of the government of India and the princes of various Indian states. Emphasizing the delicacy of the situation with regard to the enormous opium production and stocks in the central Indian states, Irwin argued:

> So long as there is this immense stock and this considerable area under poppy in their midst, the government of India will be severely handicapped in effectively discharging their international obligations in regard to the smuggling of opium.[100]

The Viceroy urged substitution of wheat and other economic crops for the poppy to compensate for the states' loss of opium revenue. To end poppy cultivation in the central Indian states, Lord Irwin suggested that those states supply opium in accordance with the requirements of the government of India. The Viceroy's proposal was a new approach in the history of opium trade, but could not resolve the problems of opium stockpiles and trafficking. To investigate the opium in central India, the Viceroy appointed a three-member Enquiry Committee, which was presided over by Sir Basil Blackett, a British officer with special knowledge on opium. In 1928, the Committee in its report observed:

> That the main smuggling problem can be solved if the government of India is prepared to spend about £800,000 on buying up the old stocks which could be gradually used for the manufacture of medicinal opium at Ghazipur. The substitution of other crops was likely to prove more difficult than had been originally hoped.[101]

The Report concluded that the substitution of other crops and achieving the conformity of Rajputana with the opium policy of British India were likely to be slow processes. However, this Report was not published until 1930, nor was any action taken on its recommendations. Given this tardy process, opium smuggling from both British India and central India to foreign countries continued. As the region was heading towards independence, cross-border and interprovincial smuggling continued during the 1940s, and the principal sources of supply of contraband opium were the states of

Rajputana, central India and the Punjab hills. The League of Nations, Advisory Committee on Traffic in Opium and Other Dangerous Drugs in 1945 indicated that the Punjab hill opium was smuggled into the Patiala and other neighbouring areas for local consumption as well for transit traffic to Burma and Ceylon. To control this widespread trafficking and local abuse of drugs, the adoption of anti-drug, legislation became imperative.

Anti-drug legislation

During the early 1930s the government of India introduced assorted legislation that failed to stamp out the abuse of drugs in South Asia. The international summits helped influence the government of India in framing drug laws to limit the manufacture, sale and use of narcotic drugs to medicinal and scientific needs. Legal controls were thus introduced in India on the production and distribution of raw opium, including opium smoking. Nevertheless, the government's new drug laws were only half-hearted and allowed the non-medicinal use of opium and other intoxicants. During the post-Geneva era the government introduced some strong provisions against the production and trafficking of harmful drugs, while the distribution of 'dangerous drugs' by the provincial authorities continued .

In an attempt to satisfy international demands, the government of India adopted the Dangerous Drugs Act of 1930, and treated it as a landmark in the history of anti-drug legislation in India. Under the Geneva Dangerous Drugs Convention of 1925,[102] the government of India felt diplomatic pressure to adopt competent laws to limit the manufacture, trade and consumption of opium and other injurious drugs in the region. A similar proposal, for 'a Dangerous Drugs Act', was raised by the Assam Opium Enquiry Committee in 1924. In response to the above demands, the British government in February 1930 passed the Dangerous Drugs Act that partly altered the long-standing official notion about the legality of opium trade and consumption of narcotic drugs.

In line with the international regulations, the Dangerous Drugs Act incorporated all kinds of intoxicants, especially opium and its derivatives (morphine, diacetylmorphine (heroin)), as dangerous drugs. As indicated before, opiates had been identified as poisonous drugs in the Pharmacy Act of 1868 in Great Britain, and their importation into that country was 'restricted' under the Dangerous Drugs

Act of 1930.[103] There had been demand in Sri Lanka and India over four decades for the adoption of similar legislation. Under the Dangerous Drugs Act, the Central government retained total authority over the production and supply of opium, and of other dangerous drugs, and sanctioned provincial governments with controls over traffic in same. The Act prohibited import into and export from British India, and transhipment or selling of prepared opium without licence from the local government.[104] Under this provision, the century-long involvement of the British government with intra-regional opium trafficking was officially denounced. A major drawback of this legislation, however, was its failure to subscribe to a policy of total prohibition.

The Dangerous Drugs Act amended many important provisions of existing drug laws that were framed for revenue purposes. Redefining the 'raw opium' of the Opium Act of 1878, the Dangerous Drugs Act listed every form of poppy capsule as poisonous. In a revision of the Opium Act of 1878, the Dangerous Drugs Act increased the penalty for serious drug offences: the maximum punishment for unlawful manufacture or possession, transhipment or selling of illicit opium became three years' imprisonment and an unlimited fine.[105] The Dangerous Drugs Act increased the punishment for an abettor who violated any of the narcotics laws through cooperation with drug traffickers. It also suggested enhanced punishments for offenders who had previously been convicted on similar charges. Overall the Act was an improvement of the Opium Act of 1878, as it regulated the export and import of narcotic drugs for the colonial authorities.

The Dangerous Drugs Act also provided an option to the provincial governments to introduce legislation on opium smoking in accordance with the international regulations. A provision had been adopted in the First Geneva Opium Summit for legislation on opium smoking.[106] Table 3.1 shows that to meet the international obligations of the government of India, some of the provincial governments adopted legislation on opium smoking, while other provinces refrained. The government of Bihar and Orissa, under the Opium Smoking Act of 1928, allowed licensed smokers to indulge in the vice either individually or jointly, but prosecuted unlicensed smokers under the penal code.[107] After Orissa province's separation from Bihar, the Orissa government duplicated a similar legislation

Table 3.1 *Provincial opium smoking laws in India*

Province	Legislation enacted	Punishment for smoking	Punishment for sale
Bengal	Sept. 1932	6 months jail/ fine Rs 500	2 yrs jail/fine Rs 2000
UP	April 1934	3 months jail/fine Rs 500	1 year jail/fine Rs 1000
Bihar & Orissa	Feb. 1928	1 year jail/fine or both	1 year jail/fine Rs 1000
Bombay	July 1936	3 months jail/fine Rs 500	1 year jail/fine Rs 2000
Assam	March 1933	6 months jail and Rs 500 fine	1 year jail/fine Rs 2000

Sources: The Bengal Opium Smoking Act, 1932 (Act 10 of 1932), pp. 1–6; J.P. Bhatnagar, *Commentary on the Law of Excise in Bihar and Orissa* (Allahabad: Ashoka Law House, 1969), pp. 125–8; V.K.S. Chaudhury, *The Uttar Pradesh Legal Acts: 1825–1967* (Allahabad: Central Law Agency, 1967), pp. 84–91; and Ram Lal Gupta, *Law of Opium and Opium Smuggling* (Allahabad: Law Book Co. 1971), pp. 156–7.

in 1939. The Indian critics, who were mostly nationalists, opposed the measures taken by the provincial governments as inadequate to combat the opium habit in 'black spots'.[108] However, aiming at discouraging opium smoking, the Central Provinces (CP) government adopted an Act in 1929 and prohibited use of *chandu* and *madak*. In July 1933, the CP government imposed a ban on possession of a 'pipe or an apparatus for the purpose of smoking or of preparing opium for smoking purposes'. Under the Bombay Opium Control Act of 1936 (Act 20 of 1936), penalties were imposed for smoking opium and for possessing instruments used in opium smoking. As a result of the reluctance in the central legislation, provincial laws on opium smoking were merely symbolic, as they were not enforced universally.

Under the Geneva Protocol of 1925 the government failed to adopt any central legislation on opium smoking. Instead, the government entitled the provincial authorities to introduce legislation on opium smoking if they chose. By means of opium smoking laws between 1932 and 1935, only about one-third of provincial governments suppressed the habit, while two-thirds remained reluctant to implement the international control. The legislation passed by certain provincial governments and the measures taken under them to control opium smoking and eating were generally defective and ineffectual. Such measures were motivated more by the desire to alleviate international criticism than to resolve the opium problem once and for all.

Nevertheless, in line with some other provinces, the Bengal government adopted the Bengal Opium Smoking Act of 1932 (Bengal Act 10 of 1932). This Act altered the Bengal Excise Act of 1909 and made opium smoking without registration a penal offence. The Act also prohibited unregistered persons from possessing prepared opium or any instrument used 'for the smoking of, or in the manufacture of, prepared opium', while registered smokers were allowed to possess a maximum of one *tola* (0.011 gram) of prepared opium.[109] Compared to Bihar and Orissa, MP and Bombay, the opium smoking legislation in Bengal was stricter and more closely resembled the Burmese experience in the late 1890s. To implement India's undertaking given at the Geneva Opium Summit, the UP government also passed the Opium Smoking Act of 1934. In line with Bengal, this legislation provided a registration system for opium smokers above 25 years, fixed a limit for the possession of prepared opium, and increased punishment for opium smoking in groups. Punishments were imposed on unregistered smokers or members of groups smoking *chandu*, *madak* and other forms of prepared opium.[110] In 1933, the Assam government imposed a total prohibition on opium smoking in all the plain districts of Assam and in some parts of the Khasia and Jaintia hills.

As a result of the new laws on opium smoking, the consumption of opium dropped significantly. The League of Nations document indicated that the Bengal government in 1940 distributed 25 metric tons of excise opium amongst consumers, the Bombay government sold 10 metric tons, the Assam government two metric tons, the MP government 6 metric tons, the Orissa government 15 metric tons, and the UP government 9 metric tons.[111] Compared to the level of opium distribution in 1892–3, these amounts were nominal. The variations in the opium smoking legislation, as well as the denial of similar laws by other provinces, caused major hindrances to the implementation of these laws. Although the legislation enacted by some provinces attempted to bring India closer to the end of opium smoking, these steps could not stop drug addiction altogether.

Due to pressure both at home and abroad, the colonial government in 1935 withdrew in principle from the South Asian opium trade; however, it continued to rely heavily on various excise revenues drawn from domestic consumption of intoxicating drugs. In violation of the international regulations a contrast policy was pursued, especially in Burma and the Punjab, for revenue purposes. Ignoring its gradual extinction policy of the 1890s, the government of Burma continued the excise policies of the 1920s. *India in 1932–33*, indicates that instead of permanently closing down licensed opium dens, the Burmese authorities reopened the dens from April 1932 to provide facilities for opium smoking.[112] With a view to generating excise revenue, the government of Burma passed a series of excise (amendment) laws during the 1930s and 1940s.[113] In harmony with Burma, the Punjab government also pursued a pro-revenue drugs policy and avoided opium smoking legislation. By the late 1930s, there was 'a great increase in the number of excise licenses in the Punjab' and some other provinces, thereby increasing excise revenue. The Punjab authorities distributed about 30 metric tons of opium in 1940. This amount was much higher than the opium distributed for other provinces during the period.

The adoption of total prohibition received political support from the provincial governments after elections were held in 1937. After assuming power, Congress ministers in different provincial legislatures accepted prohibition as a state policy. The Madras government adopted the Madras Prohibition Act (No. 10) of 1937. A similar debate took place in the Bombay Legislative Assembly to consider a 'real prohibition' on intoxicants. In 1938, the Bihar government adopted the Bihar Prohibition Act and banned the consumption and sale of intoxicating drugs in the province.[114] Under the CP and Berar Act (No. 7) of 1938, Ahmedabad city, Surat district and a number of rural areas were declared dry. As a result of the banning policy, the government of India lost a substantial amount of revenue from the distribution of liquor, which was outside the international regulations. The critics of the prohibition policy argued that it was 'unnecessary and impractical'[115] from a financial point of view. They considered the policy as depriving the government of badly needed revenue and that would require costly administrative machinery to enact. In 1939, in protest at the outbreak of the Second World War, the Congress ministry resigned from power and left the prohibition policy unfinished.

During the war period, the government of India received an increased amount of revenue from drugs. Following the outbreak of the Second World War and the resignation of the Congress ministry, the proportion of excise revenue rose to 20 per cent of the total provincial revenue.[116] In 1946–7, the Madras government received about Rs130 million from provincial excise, which was 'the largest head under the Revenue',[117] contributing about 25 per cent of Madras's total revenue.[118] Receipts from intoxicants were Rs50 million in UP in 1944–5, about 20 per cent of the province's total revenue. The *Report of the Indian Statutory Commission* indicated that in 1929–30, the excise revenue in Madras had been Rs52.4 million, and in the UP Rs13.7 million.[119] Thus, the consumption of intoxicating drugs continued in South Asia, largely as a result of the colonial excise policy. In 1946, the return of the Congress Ministry to power led to the introduction of a gradual reduction programme on drugs in Bombay from April 1947. Towards the end of colonial rule in South Asia average revenue from intoxicating drugs remained in second place after land revenue.

Nevertheless, the Sino-US diplomatic union finally succeeded in the mid-1920s when the British accepted international regulations about the universality of drug addiction in India, China and elsewhere as a matter of international concern. The Sino-US compatibility on a universal opium charter replaced the bilateral treaty approach of the government of India. As an outcome of narco-diplomacy, China was released from the British opium trade by 1917, but remained entangled in poppy cultivation. Following the adoption of international control, the contraband opium trades in India and China eventually went under the influence of the traffickers. As the prepared opium used by addicts was also coming from government sources, the abuse of drugs continued when the region achieved its independence in 1947.

4
Indian Resurgence, 1947–97

Narratives about the resurgence of India as a major consumer and supplier of contraband drugs in the world during the early 1980s are complex and numerous. India's re-entry in international drug trafficking came about as a result of a number of factors associated with domestic, cross-border and cross-regional issues. The Indian authorities claim that as it is geographically located at the heart of three opium regions, it is used by traffickers from Pakistan in the west, Burma (Myanmar) in the northeast and Nepal in the north. I argue that, in regard to its drug policies, India is in the grip of a colonial mode of thought that goes back to the British opium trade in South Asia during the nineteenth century.

The post-independence government in India continued for a prolonged period with the colonial drug laws and a partial prohibition programme, instead of attempting to stamp out the drug menace permanently. Until the 1980s, the government of India adopted about 30 different central and provincial legislative Acts to deal with dangerous drugs. Every piece of legislation was strongly influenced by colonial practice and experience. To maintain its source of revenue from intoxicating drugs, the government pursued a weak banning schedule. These outdated and confused laws were unable to combat cross-border drug traffickers, who have allegedly helped separatist guerrillas in the northwest and the northeast India to draw money from drug trafficking.

Furthermore, India's setback in the world pharmaceutical market, largely as an outcome of the Indo-Australia trade war in medicinal opium, has contributed substantially to the diversion of licit opium into illicit channels and also encouraged the illegal production of heroin chemical and psychotropic substances within India in recent years. India's own yield of illicit drugs and the diversion of acetic anhydride now exceed supplies from neighbouring countries. As a result of the above factors the effects of the strict legislation recently introduced under international obligations, have largely failed to curb the domestic consumption and illicit supply of drugs from India.

Multiple drug policies

In fulfilment of its obligations towards the UN and guided by revenue concerns, the Indian government pursued manifold policies on intoxicating drugs during the post-independence period. As part of India's pre-independence commitment to the Geneva Conventions, and the ratification of the Paris Protocol of 1948, the Indian government was under international obligation to follow suit. At the same time, India relied heavily on excise revenue to help build its post-colonial economy. In view of the above objectives the government pursued policies on drugs, which were often contradictory and overlapped with each other. These policies came about as a result of: (1) rejection of a complete prohibition that had been patronized by Mahatma Gandhi; (2) rejection of the findings of the Prohibition Enquiry Committee; and (3) adherence to colonial drug laws to earn revenue from opium. The present section focuses on the above points and examines their influence in the spread of drug addiction and drug trafficking in India in the 1980s.

The denial of Mahatma Gandhi

The multiplicity of Indian drug policies begins with the dismissal of Gandhi's prohibition programme during the aftermath of independence, when the Constitution Drafting Committee made no reference to this issue. In November 1948, a Muslim League Member from Madhya Pradesh, Kazi Syed Karimuddin, urged the Constituent Assembly to adopt the Gandhian prohibition approach to control the production, sale and use of liquors. Referring to Gandhi, who had launched a sweeping prohibition programme as part of his anti-colonial strategies, Karimuddin stressed that denial of this amendment would amount to rejection of the Mahatma's desires. Other Muslim

League members, who from a religious point of view opted for the inclusion of this provision in the Indian Constitution, supported Karimuddin's motion. However, Gandhi argued that his prohibition was part of a programme of moral and socio-economic uplift and emancipation from the 'satanic influence' of drugs.[1] The Muslim League member's submission was confined to liquor and did not include other intoxicating drugs, as originally proposed by Gandhi during the Non-Cooperation Movement.

Some leading Congress members, including the Chairman of the Constitution Drafting Committee, Dr B.R. Ambedkar, opposed Karimuddin's proposal on financial grounds and attempted to put to rest the anti-drug crusade of Gandhi after his assassination. In opposition to the motion, Biswanath Das warned the Constituent Assembly that 'nothing can be gained by appealing to sentiments in the name of Mahatma Gandhi'. Referring to the financial loss which would result from prohibition, Professor Shibban Lal Saksena informed the Constituent Assembly that 'we shall be voluntarily forgoing' about Rs250 million in excise revenue.[2] The Congress members further reiterated that enforcement of prohibition would involve a much bigger financial loss. They argued that drug revenue was needed for the support of government action in politically volatile Kashmir and troubled Hyderabad, and justified the sector as an important source of capital.

As in the principal legislation on narcotics introduced by the colonial government during the previous century, the founding fathers of the Indian Constitution strove to protect excise revenue, even though this was derived chiefly at the ruination of the indigenous population. After a marathon discussion, the Drafting Committee of the Indian Constitution incorporated as Article 47 the following:

> The State shall endeavour to bring about prohibition of the consumption except for medicinal purposes of intoxicating drinks and of drugs, which are injurious to health.[3]

By the use of the word 'endeavour' in this Article, the nation's commitment to prohibition was somewhat down-played. As a result of this, India's policy of prohibition became discretionary for the states. Moreover, H.N. Giri, in his book *Consumers, Crimes and the Law* maintains that the word 'drugs' in the Constitution, in relation to the subject matter, did not specify narcotics.[4] This technical form of prohibition was something new to India and was designed to defeat the very purpose of Gandhi's all-out anti-drug efforts. By contrast, the directive principle Article 47 shrewdly allowed for an optional policy on drugs, without any link to the ideas of Gandhi. The central government invited the state governments to apply this principle on intoxicants depending on the state of their finances. Instead of imposing a complete ban on intoxicating drugs, the Congress government pursued an arbitrary prohibition policy under the Constitution.

Tripartite prohibition policies

To elude any financial engagement, the Indian State governments pursued a chaotic prohibition programme that helped promote excise revenue and the persistence of colonial drug culture in liquor, opium and cannabis. Under a tripartite prohibition programme, some states introduced total banning, some other states partial prohibition; and the rest went without any restrains.

The states that officially declared complete prohibition were Bombay, Madras and Saurashtra, which covered about 28 per cent of the total population and 36 per cent of the total area of India. In pursuance of the banning programme, the Bombay government adopted the Bombay Prohibition Act (No. 25) of 1949 and forbade the abuse of intoxicants in the state. This Act outlawed the possession, consumption and sale of all intoxicants and provided six months to one year imprisonment with a penalty from Rs500 to Rs1,000 for violation of the provisions.[5] Following the adoption of this Act, the licit consumption of country spirit was almost eradicated, with a sharp decrease in opium, *toddy*, hemp, *charas* and foreign liquors.[6] The prohibition programme in Bombay was hailed as a masterstroke during a Lok Sabha debate in March 1955. However, a 1950 study conducted by the Bombay University School of Economics and Sociology in three districts observed that large-scale liquor smuggling from the non-prohibition areas was prevalent, while widespread distillation of liquor from *mahua* flowers and illicit distillation of *toddy* were occurring in the province. To counteract illicit supply, the government in 1954 gradually lifted its prohibition programme and allowed distilleries and licensed shops to sell intoxicating drugs to habitual users. While under total prohibition the Bombay government was making gradual progress, the smuggling of illicit liquor from non-prohibition areas negated the benefits of the programme.

In Saurashtra, from April 1950, while prohibition was introduced to wipe out the liquor problem, a soft attitude was maintained towards other intoxicating drugs. In 1951–2, the Saurashtra government maintained three liquor shops against 193 shops for opium, hemp and *bhang*.[7] Within four years of the new regulation, excise revenue from liquor dropped about 50 per cent, while receipts from opium and other drugs remained intact. Under its prohibition manifesto, the Saurashtra government attempted essentially to combat the evil of liquor, and madea lesser priority of the elimination of narcotic drugs. In Madras, the government had already introduced the Madras Prohibition Act (No. 10) of 1947, and restricted alcohol and diverse harmful drugs in three phases. The use of opium came under a 20 per cent annual reduction from October 1949, and registered addicts were allowed to receive a small amount on medical grounds. By 1951–2, the per capita taxation on intoxicants in Madras fell by 50 per cent, making it the lowest excise revenue earner in India. The government of Madras, which derived its highest amount of revenue from drugs and alcohol in 1946–7, suffered heavy financial losses in subsequent years due to implementation of the prohibition policy.

Alongside the above measures, partial control on intoxicants was implemented in varying degrees in Assam, Madhya Pradesh, Orissa, UP, Mysore, the Punjab, Travancore-Cochin and Himachal Pradesh. In Assam, a prohibition programme was adopted under three separate pieces of legislation: (1) the Assam Opium Prohibition Act of 1947, (2) the Assam Liquor Prohibition Act of 1953 and (3) the Prohibition of *Ganja* and *Bhang* of 1959. Under the UP Opium Prohibition Rules, 1947, the UP government restricted opium to addicts with valid permits.[8] As a result of this, excise revenue fell from Rs60.4 million in 1950–1 to Rs50.4 million in 1954–5.[9] In Madhya Pradesh, complete banning was in force in 6 districts with partial regulation in another 5 districts. Until 1951–2, the Orissa government, with its doubtful prohibition policies, received about 17 per cent of its total revenue from drugs. Under the Mysore Prohibition Act (No. 37) of 1948, the prohibition law was in force in 6 districts of Mysore state, while excise revenue dropped from Rs20 million in 1950–1 to Rs10.5 million in 1954–5.[10] Under the Travancore-Cochin Prohibition Act of 1950, some parts in Travancore-Cochin State were declared dry by 1955, but still contributed about 12 per cent in its total revenue. Due to the revenue motive, the prohibition programmes in the Punjab, Himachal Pradesh and Madhya Pradesh were trifling. Until 1956, no restrictions were imposed on opium abuse in the Punjab.[11] The consumption of non-medicinal opium was prohibited in Madhya Pradesh and Punjab from 1 April 1959. From the same date the using of cannabis was restricted in Tripura, Kerala and Delhi.[12] As a result of the implementation of partial prohibition measures, a declining trend in the excise revenue was evident in most of these states and areas.

For income reasons, there was no prohibition, either total or partial, in Bihar, West Bengal, Hyderabad, PEPSU, Rajasthan, Vindhya Pradesh, Bhopal, Kutch and Manipur. In PEPSU, excise revenue during 1950–5 fluctuated between 25 and 33 per cent of the total revenue: the highest rate for any state in India. Until 1955, Hyderabad had no prohibition measures, allowing the state to receive 28 per cent of its total revenue from intoxicating drugs. In 1951–2, the government of Hyderabad received nearly Rs91 million from intoxicants, which was the highest total amount of any states throughout India. The government of West Bengal was hesitant about a prohibition policy because intoxicants contributed about 12 per cent of its total revenue in 1951–2, the amount being nearly Rs61 million, the second highest figure for India in that year. In Bihar in the same year government receipts were over Rs50 million from 16,135 intoxicant shops. In 1951–2, the Rajasthan government earned about Rs30 million from 3,037 shops selling liquor and 2,080 selling other intoxicating drugs. The *Statistical Abstract, India 1952–3* indicates that as a result of prohibition, the excise revenue of the Indian states fell from Rs430 million in 1947–8 to Rs290 million in 1951–2.[13] The heavy proportion of state revenue coming from drugs made the situation delicate for the government of India when it set out to stamp out dependence on excise revenue and establish an uniform prohibition policy throughout the country.

The enquiry committee is overturned

In order to avoid the financial risks of the prohibition programme, the government of India turned down the anti-drug recommendations of the Prohibition Enquiry Committee in 1956. In December 1954, the Planning Commission appointed an eight-member Prohibition Enquiry Committee to examine the difficulties faced by the tripartite prohibition policy. The Committee submitted its Report in less than ten months and recommended a nation-wide prohibition programme from April 1958.

The Prohibition Committee's Report contradicted the recommendations of the Expert Committee of 1952, which had criticized the prohibition policy for creating confusion in the sphere of excise duties. However, influenced by the recommendations of the Expert Committee, the central government increased excise revenue from Rs830 million in 1952–3 to Rs2 billion in 1956–7.[14] This income was largely consolidated through the adoption of the Medicinal and Toilet Preparations (Excise Duties) Act 1955, whereby the production or manufacture of any goods containing opium, hemp, liquor etc. in the pharmaceutical industry became excisable under the terms and conditions prescribed in the license.[15] Nevertheless, the Prohibition Enquiry Committee provided an administrative formula for a phased banning programme throughout India.

After a review of the banning scheme, the Prohibition Committee pointed out that illicit trafficking and administrative corruption occurred because of the fragmented nature of the policy. Recognizing the heavy financial dependence of certain states on excise revenue, the Committee stressed the importance of central assistance to help free these states from the situation. The report was approved by the National Development Council, and was debated in the Indian Parliament in March 1956. During the debate, Feroze Gandhi, the husband of later Prime Minister Indira Gandhi, quoted a verse from classical Hindi literature:

> *Taruvar phal nahin khat hain,*
> *saravar piyat na pani*[16]

[The tree does not eat its own fruit,
the river does not drink its own water.]

Citing this, Feroze Gandhi urged: 'let not the state tempt its own people to ruin from intoxicants'. This comment was made at a time when the Congress government technically had renounced the anti-drug struggles of Mahatma Gandhi and the sacrifices made by his disciples since the 1920s. In defiance of the deadline set by the Prohibition Committee, the Lok Sabha passed a resolution recommending that the Planning Commission should formulate the necessary programme 'to bring about nation-wide prohibition speedily and effectively'.[17] To avoid any specific decision about the target date for a total banning, the Lok Sabha linked the prohibition policy with the Second Five-year Plan. The Planning Commission in its Second Five-year Plan suggested imposing licensing hours on liquor distribution.[18] The Commission also recommended setting up a technical committee to draw up a phased programme to reduce the number of liquor shops, liquor days, but did not suggest any concrete policy on licensed narcotics shops.

Given the half-hearted government policies on drugs, progress towards complete prohibition was slow and uncertain. From April 1956, a gradual prohibition programme was introduced in Rajasthan. The Madras government introduced complete prohibition from October 1958, but excluded the Hill districts of that state from its scheme. In Maharashtra, total prohibition was introduced from April 1959, excepting some remote areas. In July 1959, a ten-mile long 'dry belt zone' was created in the Gulbarga district of the Maharashtra-Mysore border to facilitate the implementation of the prohibition policy of the government of Maharashtra. In most states prohibition was limited to certain districts or to a few days of the week, while allowing individuals to take liquor on medical grounds. Many states, which had begun to implement total prohibition subsequently, relaxed their control for revenue purposes. In the absence of any national target date for prohibition and of any assurance of central government financial assistance for those states dependent on excise revenue, the results of these prohibition schemes were far from satisfactory.

Towards the end of 1960, the Ministry of Home Affairs set up a Central Committee to review the recommendations of the Prohibition Enquiry Committee. In view of the same objectives, the Third Five-year Plan revealed that in any attempt to enforce prohibition the question of loss of revenue would be 'considered first'.[19]

Referring to prohibition as 'essentially a social welfare movement', the Third Five-year Plan put responsibility upon the voluntary organizations to carry out the gigantic tasks of prohibition. The government tried to shift administrative responsibility for intoxicating drugs onto the social workers. The Third Five-year Plan also left it to social organizations to find 'practical solutions to problems' that occurred as a result of the government's pro-revenue drug policies.[20] This Plan further reiterated that state governments should not fix any target dates for implementing complete prohibition, because such timetables in practice would be difficult to comply with. Ignoring the recommendations made by the Prohibition Enquiry Committee about financial assistance to the disadvantaged states, the central government avoided a target date for complete prohibition.

Nevertheless, the Planning Commission on 29 April 1963 set up a Study Team on Prohibition to assess the magnitude of illicit distillation and the financial aspects of implementation of a dry policy. The report also stressed the need for stern action against corrupt officials and politicians who protected illicit traffickers.[21] It urged the implementation of an integrated programme, and reaffirmed the need to work towards the goal of prohibition. In line with the Prohibition Enquiry Report of 1958 the Study Team endorsed an approach which went against government policy. Because of its radical nature, the recommendations of the Study Team were not put into action in the subsequent years. The dilemma, for and against the prohibition policy, created great confusion in the implementation process. This general setback to prohibition continued in subsequent years without any meaningful attempt to implement the programme on a national basis. Along with its jumbled prohibition programme at the state level, the Indian government pursued further complicated policies in regard to the promotion of export trade in medicinal opium.

The promotion of opium exports

Encouraged by the previous policies of the colonial authorities, the Indian government attempted to derive substantial revenue from licit opium trade. In a bid to promote opium export for the world pharmaceutical market, the Indian government pursued colonial legislation on opium, with some modification to accommodate UN regulations. In line with the interim arrangement of the UN Protocol of 1948, the Indian parliament instantaneously reiterated its commitment to continue poppy cultivation for medicinal purposes. In April 1949, the Indian government convened the first Opium Conference and declared that it would ban opium abuse within a span of one decade.[22] With this pronouncement, post-independence India reaffirmed its plan to produce opium for 'medical and scientific needs' of the world and to prevent illicit trafficking in opium.

In order to step-up its adherence to colonial drug laws, the Indian parliament adopted a number legislative measure in the 1950s and 1960s. Through the adoption of the Opium and Revenue Act of 1950, the government legalized official poppy cultivation in the UP, Madhya Pradesh, and Rajasthan.[23] This Act renewed the Opium Act of 1857, the Opium Act of 1878 and the Dangerous Drugs Act of 1930, to promote income from opium exports. To establish unified control of both manufacture and distribution of opium, the Indian government in the same year set up a Narcotics Department.

The Opium and Revenue Laws Extension Act of 1950 provided authority to the state governments to introduce their own legislation in pursuance of licit poppy cultivation. To protect official cultivation from the illicit traffickers, the Madhya Pradesh government in June 1955 introduced the Madhya Bharat Act of 1955, and imposed a penalty of two years' imprisonment, or alternatively a fine of Rs1,000–2,000, or both, for illegal possession of opium.[24] The penalty had originally been imprisonment for one year under the Opium Act of 1878. In Rajasthan, the state government adopted the Rajasthan Opium Rules of 1958, to exercise the powers conferred by the Opium Act of 1878 in regard to the confiscation of goods and articles used in the preparation of illegal opium. These Rules provided authority to the Rajasthan government to confiscate non-governmental opium and to auction it for revenue purposes. In an attempt to establish control over interstate import into and export from its territories, the Rajasthan government adopted the Rajasthan Opium Rules, 1959.[25] Through these rules the government basically revived the Dangerous Drugs Act of 1930 and established its administrative control over the manufacture of medicinal opium.

In order to implement its control over poppy cultivation, the UP government revived the UP Opium Rules of 1931 and the UP Opium Prohibition Rules of 1947. Through legislation, the government renewed the Opium Act of 1878 and established regulations on the sale of opium. To exercise its power over opium consumption, the government also introduced the UP Opium Rules, 1955, and provided authority to the Collector or the District Excise Officer to give permission to the adult opium users to take or possess opium on medical grounds.[26] With a view to appropriating revenue from the medicinal opium, the state government also introduced the UP Opium Rules 1961 and declared that medicinal opium would be imported and exported only on government account. The Orissa, Madhya Pradesh and other state governments in regard to the interstate import and export of medicinal opium or poppy-heads simultaneously adopted similar Opium Rules, with minor variations.

With the consolidation of opium administration at the state level, the Indian government revived the government opium monopoly and established control over poppy cultivation and production of crude opium under licences that were issued by the Narcotics Commissioner. The total area under licit cultivation, which at independence had been between 236,445 and 304,000 hectares, was reduced in 1957 to 33,777 hectares under international regulations.[27] To reshuffle the colonial production system, the central government reduced poppy cultivation in Benaras and Himachal Pradesh, and gradually spread cultivation in certain authorized districts of UP, Rajasthan and Madhya Pradesh. This system was continued to meet the international demands and domestic need for the supply of licit alkaloids for manufacturing morphine, codeine and so on for medicinal purposes. As a result of government controls, the export of raw opium rose from 66 metric tons in 1947–8, to 130 metric tons in 1949–50, to 302 metric tons in 1950–1, while the supply of excise opium declined from 224 metric tons in 1947–8, to 154 metric tons in 1948–9, to 126 metric tons in 1949–50.[28] The adoption of the Opium and Revenue Act of 1950 and the subsequent state legislation helped the central government to sell about 750 metric tons of excise opium and its alkaloids in the 1960s.[29] The volume of production and trade was less than 10 per cent of what it had been in 1909 at the time of the Shanghai

International Opium Commission. The reduction occurred due to an international control over South Asian contraband opium trade.

Nevertheless, under UN protection the Indian government eventually established a monopoly in the international market for medicinal opium. The *Indian Journal of Agronomy* maintained that the Indian government in 1963 exported about 455 metric tons of medicinal opium, highlighting poppy cultivation as 'vital' for its national economy.[30] As a foreign exchange earner, poppy cultivation continued to play a very crucial role in the country's rural economy, especially in the poppy growing areas. However, to combat the domestic and cross-border smugglers who wanted to undermine the government policy, a follow-up by the state governments was required to make the control a success. In order to consolidate its authority over illicit trafficking, the Indian government adopted the Dangerous Drugs Rules of 1957, and renewed the prohibition powers that were conferred by the Dangerous Drugs Act of 1930 and the Drugs Act of 1940.[31] These rules were largely adopted to satisfy international demands made by the UN Protocol of 1953,[32] and the regulation imposed by the twelfth session of the Commission on Narcotic Drugs in April–May 1957.[33] The 1957 Rules forbade the import and export of any dangerous drugs without valid authorization. In the case of exports of dangerous drugs, rules were framed that required that the drugs should be exported only to countries which had ratified the rules of the Geneva Convention regarding the production, distribution and export of dangerous drugs.

The 1957 Rules also adopted some provisions to satisfy international requirements for the promotion of exports in licit cannabis. The Report of the Export Promotion Committee in 1949 stated that 'every encouragement' would be given to producers to raise the production of cannabis to the 1939–40 level and to 'increase exports by at least 25 per cent'.[34] In accordance with UN regulations engineered by the US delegate, Anslinger, the 1957 Dangerous Drugs Rules adopted restrictions on cannabis and *bhang* to help promote the export trade in licit cannabis. This rule also echoed the resolutions of the 1956 Simla Conference that urged for the banning of cannabis and *bhang* abuse by 1959. The inclusion of cannabis on the 'black list' was a significant breakthrough in the Indian government's traditional narcotics policy. Aimed at maintaining excise revenue, the government had a policy to encourage cannabis production in India. In line with the UN Protocol, the Indian government adopted rules that risked the displeasure of *Sadhus* and other traditional users.

To increase its further control on opium derivatives, the Indian government also adopted the Opium Laws (Amendment) Act of 1957. This Act amended some of the technical problems confronted by state governments with regard to the Opium Act of 1878 and the Dangerous Drug Act of 1930. Due to obscurity in the definition of opium, the Nagpur High Court and the Punjab High Court in December 1955 released some poppy capsules (*Bhuki*) traffickers.[35] The central government was approached by the Punjab government to redefine opium in order to establish control over the import and sale of poppy skin in the state. Renowned persons and leaders in the Punjab, who wanted to remove the drug from the streets, also expressed similar concern about *Bhuki*. The opium laws thus included opium husk, poppy capsules and crushed or powdered poppy-heads in the definition of opium, enabling the state governments to exercise control over the trafficking and consumption of these items.

In an attempt to control smuggling from both domestic and external sources, the opium laws of 1957 increased punishments for such offences, from one year to three years, with or without a fine, for opium related offences.[36] This Act also amended some of the important provisions of the Dangerous Drugs Act of 1930 and imposed three years' imprisonment with or without fine for drug related offences. The laws enhanced the punishment for criminal offences that tried to foil official cultivation. To control the diversion of licit opium into illicit channels, the Act empowered specific central government officers to maintain a common centralized intelligence authority and to assist the state government officers in their anti-drug drive. Given the above central and state-level legislative arrangements, the Indian government during the 1960s and 1970s recovered tremendous influence in the international market for medicinal opium.

However, the above Acts also left a wide scope for anomalous interpretation, providing for imprisonment for some offenders under the Dangerous Drugs Act of 1930 and for the release of other offenders under the new law. The wording and objectives of the major narcotics Acts of 1857, 1878, and 1930 were largely repeated and reproduced in state and central legislation during the 1950s and 1960s. The admixture of colonial and post-colonial narcotics laws was unable to deter the activities of the organized drug syndicates, which set up their network inside and outside the country during the early 1980s.

'Sandwiched' between opium regions

A policy reluctant to pay attention to drugs after independence has in recent years resulted in an abundance of illicit supplies of intoxicants, both from local and cross-border sources. Geographically located at the heart of three opium producing regions – the Golden Triangle, the Golden Crescent and the Golden Wedge – India emerged as a major centre in the 1980s for the smuggling of opiates to Western countries. The US Committee on Foreign Affairs report in 1986 indicated that seizures of Indian heroin in Europe and North America rose considerably during the early 1980s.[37] The Indian authorities claimed that the country was used as a transshipment point for heroin from southwest and southeast Asia. They further held that international drug cartels allegedly financed insurgency wars in the northeastern states, in Punjab, and in Kashmir, diverting money earned from the heroin trade. The following discussion examines the nature of transit traffic from Pakistan, Burma and Nepal, and examines India's role in combating the supply of drugs from cross-border sources.

Pakistani transit traffic

In 1985, portraying the supply of Pakistani contraband drugs as a serious threat to Indian national security, an MP from Bombay, Anoopchand Shah, argued:

> Pakistan, ... a country which has never been able to defeat nor can it defeat India in any of the wars may, by demoralising the people by making them addicts of these [narcotics] drugs, defeat this country.[38]

An identical accusation about heroin trafficking from Pakistan was made in the Indian *Rajya Sabha* in August 1997.[39] The Indian Finance

Minister, T.T. Krishnamachari, in a statement had made a similar warning about Pakistan to the Lok Sabha in 1957, when transit traffic in drugs was relatively insignificant.[40] Given the Indo-Pak conflicts that resulted from the religious division of the Indian subcontinent in 1947, the Indian authorities blamed Pakistan for using India as a transit route, and diverting drug money to the militants in Kashmir, Punjab and northeastern states. The following discussion examines the complex nature of Indian security perception with regard to the western border along Pakistan, and its connection with India's propaganda on Pakistani transit trafficking.

The Indian authorities demonstrated that as a result of the blocking of the traditional Balkan drug route to the West by the Islamic Revolutionary Guards in Iran in 1979, and by the erstwhile Soviet Red Army in Afghanistan in 1980, the prospect of Pakistani transit traffic through India had increased tremendously. A 1988 publication by the Indian government claimed that as a result of the cross-border supplies, its enforcement agencies in 1979 confiscated 305 kilos of Pakistani opium, but by 1982 confiscation had risen to 1.5 metric tons, in 1983 reaching 3.4 metric tons, and in 1984 decreasing slightly to 3.1 metric tons.[41] The same report also asserted that seizures of heroin had risen from 28 kilos in 1982 to 202 kilos in 1984 and 761 kilos in 1985. A similar trend was also evident in the seizure of cannabis, *charas* and *hashish* smuggled from Pakistan. In July 1985, the US Committee on Foreign Affairs noted that in a single month 329 kolos of Pakistani heroin was seized off camels' backs after they had crossed onto Indian soil.[42] Referring to the Indian official statistics, the report held that a total of 920 kilos of Pakistani heroin were seized in India during the whole year. Thus, the Indian official reports claimed that the obstacles in the Iranian and Central Asian routes in the early 1980s saw Pakistani traffickers increasingly use India as a transit route for overseas destinations.

Indian sources assert that the trafficking of Pakistani heroin via India has continued throughout the 1980s and 1990s. A contemporary Indian report suggests that the smuggling trade in heroin by 'camel-borne smugglers' through the Thar Desert in Rajasthan took place during the early 1980s.[43] In 1987, the *Statesman* of New Delhi maintained that out of a total capture of about 2.7 metric tons of heroin, over 2.2 metric tons of heroin was of Pakistani origin.[44] In 1989, the US Subcommittee on Crime estimated that 30 to

40 metric tons of Pakistani heroin passed through the Thar Desert into India every year.[45] The difference in the wholesale price of heroin between India and Pakistan was the primary reason for the widespread trafficking. In a 1989 study B.V. Kumar, a member of the Central Board of Excise and Customs, indicated that the cost of heroin per kilo was Rs30,000 in Pakistan, Rs100,000 in New Delhi and Rs200,000 in Bombay, and reached $100,000 on the US wholesale market and one million dollars on the streets of New York.[46] Kumar held that the Pakistani traffickers used Indian embarkation points to avoid rigorous checking by Western law enforcement agencies in Pakistan.

In February 1991, the Bombay enforcement agencies asserted that they arrested three transborder traffickers with a total of 43 kilos of heroin in their possession. In August 1991, *The Times of India* reported that the Bombay 'narcotics cell' detained one Pakistani and seized 61 kilos of heroin from his concealed possession. This was the biggest single seizure conducted throughout the country within the first eight months of the year. A separate unofficial report claimed that in a police encounter 'a Pakistani drug smuggler' was killed at J.B. Nagar, Andheri in Bombay.[47] In August 1997, the Revenue Intelligence authorities in Delhi claimed that they seized 43 kilos of 'Pakistani' heroin from local smugglers on the Delhi–UP border.[48] Entertaining similar news items, the Indian authorities demonstrated the presence of strong Pakistani 'mafia' activities in Bombay and other areas.

Indian authorities also claimed that the cross-border drug trade in India has been closely aligned to the insurgent wars in the country. They maintained that Pakistani drug money was funnelled to Sikh militants to create an independent Khalistan, and to Kashmiri freedom fighters in liberating Jammu and Kashmir. The Indian authorities insist that the Pakistani military intelligence agency, ISI, aid the KLF (Khalistan Liberation Force) and Kashmiri *mujahedins* with money earned from heroin trafficking. In support of India's assertion, a 1993 CIA report indicated that the ISI had assisted the Sikh militants and the *mujahedins* in the 'Indian-controlled Kashmir' with drug money to purchase arms.[49] This report was published after India created diplomatic pressure on the US in 1992 to help end the ISI's strategic warfare in Kashmir.

Some Indian sources maintained that the ISI in 1987 had shifted its attention from Sikh militants in the Punjab to a Kashmir liberation movement led by an ultra-Islamic group, the *Hizb-ul-Mujahedin*. In 1994, *The Hindustan Times* claimed that by funnelling drug money, the ISI helped 40 guerrilla groups in their war of independence in Kashmir.[50] Citing *Drug Dispatch*, a Netherlands magazine, the same report asserted that the Pakistani traffickers worked under the 'Operation K-2/TOPAC' network controlled by the country's military secret agency. Denying the allegations, the Pakistani authorities asserted that 'the brutalities of the Indian security forces' compelled the Kashmiri youths, including the injured persons, to take shelter in the Azad Kashmir.[51] To counteract Indian allegations, the Pakistani Interior Minister, Nasirullah Khan Babar, in 1996 reiterated that the leading Indian intelligence agency RAW (Research and Analysis Wing) was involved in 'bomb blasts' in Pakistan.[52] Thus, accusations of funnelling drug money for cross-border insurgency or terrorist activities have become a regular phenomenon in South Asian politics.

In an attempt largely to block Pakistani infiltration in cross-border politics, the Indian government adopted a programme of fencing and thereby physically sealing its 3,040-kilometres-long western border with Pakistan. The Indian government was concerned about the Khalistan movement and the smuggling of arms through its vulnerable border in Punjab. Explaining the fencing rationale, the Union Minister for Home Affairs, Mohammad Maqbool Dar, in July 1997 maintained that 'to ensure [the] integrity and sovereignty' of the country the measure was essential.[53] The Indian government constructed a fence along the western border in the early 1990s. The sealing of the border saw the supply of Pakistani drugs through India decline significantly. In addition, changes in western drug routes also helped in the reduction of Pakistani transit traffic through India. According to an unofficial report, seizures of Pakistani drugs in India dropped dramatically from 2.7 metric tons in the late 1980s to about 1.0 metric ton in the early 1990s.[54] The opening of the drug route through the Central Asian states after the collapse of the erstwhile Soviet Union and the re-opening of the traditional Balkan drug route, which starts from Pakistan and crosses Iran, to pass through Turkey, Bulgaria, Yugoslavia into western Europe, has contributed to a reduction in Pakistani drug supply through India in recent years. Despite these facts, India in recent years has continued its preoccupation with Pakistani transit trafficking.

In perpetuation of anti-Pakistani propaganda, Indian authorities claimed that following the completion of fencing along the Rajasthan–Punjab border, the drug trafficking through the Jammu and Kashmir border increased substantially. Some Indian officials maintained that Delhi-bound drug trafficking through the Punjab in 1991–2 fell to about 30 per cent, while 70 per cent of Pakistani supplies were passing through the unfenced Jammu and Kashmir border.[55] Given increased military pressure and growing tension along the Kashmir border, it is highly unlikely that traffickers would follow this route. Recent reports suggest that despite the fence, illicit trafficking in arms and drugs has still continued through the Punjab border.[56] In May 1997, *The Indian Express* reported that the cross-border traffickers, in collaboration with BSF officials, used a 116-foot-long tunnel in the Amritsar border for the smuggling of heroin, acetic anhydride and gold between the two countries.[57] The police at a border village in Ferozepore unearthed a similar underground cave, where local BSF officials for seven years maintained a connection with traffickers on the Pakistani side. Evidence thus shows that cross-border trafficking has been taking place along secret channels with the cooperation of branches of the Indian military.

As on the western border, the Indian authorities believe that the Pakistani intelligence agency diverted drug money to secessionist movements in the northeastern region of India. Citing BSF information, *Link* in 1983 claimed that insurgency in the northeastern states of Manipur, Meghalaya and Nagaland had been assisted by Pakistani drug money.[58] Quoting the then Chief Minister of Manipur, R.K. Ranbir Singh, *The Times of India* in 1991 asserted that the Pakistan diplomatic mission in Dhaka, Bangladesh had helped tribal militants with arms and money.[59] Similarly, *India Today* in a special report in 1996 accused Pakistan of allegedly using coastal areas in Chittagong, Bangladesh for arms shipment to the militants in the northeastern states.[60] By binding Bangladesh with Pakistan, India was in fact trying to justify its current role in the Chittagong Hill Tract area. However, in an earlier report Manipur Chief Minister Singh claimed that Burma was arming the PLA and other insurgent groups in northeastern India.[61] Political confusion has prevailed in the geographically isolated northeastern region, providing an environment for cross-border traffickers to conduit heroin from Burma through India to overseas destinations.

The Burmese connection

Heroin smuggled from Burma, through its thousand-kilometre-long border with India in the northeast, has become a major concern for the world in recent years. With the bumper production of illicit poppy during the early 1980s, it was estimated that the Burmese traffickers produced about 50 metric tons of illicit heroin.[62] By 1997, the annual production of heroin in Burma had reached around 188 metric tons of which at least 15 per cent were smuggled overseas via India.[63] In January 1989, *The World Press Review* reported that about 17 heroin refineries and 80 mobile heroin laboratories located in Kachin and Shan provinces in Burma were engaged in heroin production.[64] The mammoth manufacture of heroin in clandestine laboratories in Burma pushed the northeastern states of Manipur, Nagaland, Mizoram, Assam and Arunachal Pradesh to develop as important transit points in international drug trafficking.

As a result of the huge profit margins, a large quantity of Burmese heroin was smuggled through the northeastern states for international destinations. The maximum cost for per kilo heroin in Burma's Shan state was about $1,200, while that produced in India ranged between $12,500 and $14,300. This variation in the price is linked to the superior quality of heroin produced in the area. Generally known as heroin-4, which has 95 per cent drug content and is suitable for intravenous injection, Burmese production is one of the finest qualities in the world.[65]

Illicit heroin was smuggled from Burma by tribal couriers through the dense forests, open fields and rivers; and once inside India it was transported either by road or air. In the *Far Eastern Economic Review* in 1994, Hamish McDonald maintains that Burmese heroin was smuggled along National Highway no. 39, that starts from Moreh, the last Indian town in Manipur.[66] The transborder traffickers used important routes from Tahan in Burma to Moreh, then to Aizawl in Mizoram; and also from Tahan to Champai, a small town on the Mizoram border. Moreh, a remote village on the India–Burma border, has turned into a drug crossroads where Indian drug dealers receive heroin from their counterparts from Tamu in Burma. Other routes, which have also expanded over the past few years, as suggested by a 1989 study, are (1) Tamu–Moreh–Imphal; (2) Mandalay–Tiddim–Singhat–Churachandpur–Imphal and (3) Mandalay–Tiddam–Champai–Aizawal. McDonald further claims that the Burmese couriers moved heroin through different jungle paths into Assam. Once heroin reached Assam or any other states in the northeastern region, it was transported to Calcutta and Bombay, then overseas. It is generally carried through the Siliguri Gateway, a narrow passage between Bangladesh and Nepal that connects the geographically isolated northeastern states with India. To avoid the hazards and risks of lengthy land routes, a portion of Burmese heroin is also smuggled by sea in places around India's east coast.

Throughout the 1980s, illicit heroin trafficking from Burma continued unbridled by the Indian authorities. A recent report suggests that heroin was smuggled through the Imphal airport in Manipur, which lacked any modern facilities to detect it.[67] A local drug dealer estimated that, over one metric ton of heroin entered India from Burma through Moreh every year.[68] In a cosmetic bid to control the cross-border drug trade, the Indian government restricted the movement of trucks at night on the Imphal–Moreh road from early February 1991. Despite the measure there were hardly any checkpoints in the Imphal–Moreh route, which is about 125 kilometres long, to help implement the regulations. Tribal settlements exist on both sides of the international border, sometimes as deep as 150–200 kilometres. In recognition of the traditional rights of the local inhabitants, a 'head load' free trade continued within 10 kilometres of Burma and 40 kilometres of Indian soil.[69] The autonomous movement of the Kukis and Nagas on either side of the international border facilitated the trafficking in heroin, illegal arms and other contraband items from Burma.

Compared to the highly sophisticated weapons carried by infantrymen in the Golden Triangle, security measures and seizures in northeastern India were deficient. In June 1997, *The Washington Post* reported that with 'five guns and one jeep' the enforcement authorities were completely unprepared to combat drug trafficking in Manipur. The report further indicated that, being perplexed by the central government's policies, the legal agencies seized only one kilo of heroin throughout the year. This lack of control over the Burmese drug supply was also evident in other northeastern states. In February 1998, *Organiser* maintained that the total seizures of contraband drug along the Burmese border were only a few grams in 1992–3 and over two kilos in 1994–5. These tiny seizures by local commanders, in contrast to the vastness of the illicit trade, are not even a drop in the ocean.

Besides incompetence, serious allegations about the lack of integrity of the official authorities were mounting. In 1994, McDonald claimed that security personnel collaborated with anti-Indian insurgents for heroin trafficking from Burma, to Assam's Brahmaputra Valley.[70] In October 1989, the *Indian Express* reported that vehicles belonging to the armed forces had been used in drug trafficking.[71] Recently it was revealed that some members of the military 'have been regularly escorting trucks transporting high quality cannabis to Bihar for personal gains'.[72] Referring to official authorities, *The Statesman Weekly* in October 1997 reported that drug money has paralysed a section of political leaders, bureaucrats and security forces.[73] Corruption amongst law enforcement authorities and military personnel hindered any prospects for the success of the drug control programme in the northeast.

The involvement of the law enforcement agencies with drug traffickers in politically volatile northeastern region has been significant for various reasons. A separatist movement for the creation of an independent state comprising Manipur, Nagaland and Mizoram, and other similar ethnic areas, has continued for the last couple of decades. To finance their guerrilla war, some of the underground organizations in Manipur and other northeastern states allegedly became involved in drug trafficking. Unlike Khun Sa's Shan Liberation Army, who themselves grow poppy and manufacture heroin in the Kachin and Shan states in northern Burma,[74] India's tribal militants were essentially runners of the drug trade. Referring to intelligence reports, the Manipur Chief Minister Rishang Keishing in 1996 claimed:

> The insurgents are bringing a staggering quantity of heroin and other forms of drugs through Moreh and New Somtal in Chandel district bordering the international border.[75]

During their assignation a large number of tribal people became addicted to heroin and other hallucinogenic substances in the mid-1980s. In a 1985 study of two villages in Churachandpur district of Manipur, Shibani Roy and S.H.M. Rizvi observed that, besides rice beer (*zu*), nicotine water (*tuibuk*) and opium (*kani*), the local youth also indulged in synthetic drugs. The abuse of pure heroin (locally known as Number 4), has reached alarming proportions among the hill tribe youth in Manipur. Statistics indicated that 11.73 per cent (46 individuals) of one village had become addicted to Number 4, while in another village the proportion was 18.64 per cent (77 individuals).[76] Compared to the average national heroin consumption, Manipur alone represented 38 per cent of the total addicts in India, the top position of any state in the country. *The Washington Post* in 1997 reported that out of its two million population, Manipur has 50,000 heroin addicts.[77] To support their drug habit, most of the addicts became couriers in the illicit trade to earn money for the next shot. Heroin addiction is generally viewed as an emerging big-city vice, but the Manipur evidence provided a unique example which demonstrated that people in rural and semi-rural areas have also become addicted to synthetic drugs.

The sharing of needles amongst addicts in the northeastern region has created an epidemic of HIV infection in the area. By a conservative estimate, government statistics maintained that over 50 per cent of the drug addicts in Manipur were HIV virus carriers. In 1994, the Indian Council of Medical Research indicated that Manipur has about 15,000 intravenous drug users. *The Times of India* in September 1997 reported that 'earlier 100 per cent of HIV positive cases were intravenous drug users', and that the figure is now about 75 per cent.[78] The addict population transmitted their disease amongst their wives and children, many of whom did not report to the health authorities. A study conducted by Manipur Voluntary Health Association in 1991 claimed that, including the undetected cases, the actual number of HIV virus carriers in that state stood between 30,000 and 40,000. Based on reports provided by the NGOs, the Union Health Ministry anticipated that by the new millennium a quarter of the Manipur population 'will die of AIDS'.[79] Intravenous drug addiction was also on the rise amongst youth in politically volatile Nagaland. Despite the geographical proximity of this area to the HIV affected areas of Burma and Thailand, the Indian authorities were apparently reluctant to act to control the drug habit among tribal youth.

In an attempt to suppress the tribal insurgents, Indian authorities pursued a reluctant policy to counter the spread of drug addiction and heroin trafficking in the northeastern states. Recall that the *Calcutta Englishman* in the late nineteenth century observed that the policy of the colonial government was to make 'the Naga a peaceable subject through his developing a taste for opium'.[80] The collaboration of some enforcement authorities in cross-border drug trafficking, and a substantial rise in the number of intravenous drug users in Manipur and other areas, is an indication of government counter-insurgency activities in the northeastern region. To combat drug addiction, the tribal guerrillas have introduced severe restrictions on both heroin addicts and traffickers. The separatist militants have allegedly announced a death penalty for drug addicts, and killed some traffickers in Manipur for their anti-social activities. Except for a few reports of the shooting of heroin addicts in the thigh, it is not known how many addicts had been executed by separatist guerrillas. India's dilemma to prevent the cross-border drug syndrome in the northeastern region also coincided with its policies in regard to illicit delivery of drugs from Nepal.

Supplies from Nepal

As in the case of the Indo-Burma boundary, anti-drug measures along the 1,568 kilometre-long Indo-Nepal international border were porous and inadequate. The Kingdom of Nepal, a landlocked country in the Himalayan belt, was a traditional supplier of licit opium to British India. Official papers indicate that to discourage the Nepalese poppy farmers, who often sold opium to smugglers to take it to the port of Calcutta through British territory, the British government in 1891–2 purchased 5.4 metric tons of opium compared with five metric tons in the previous year.[81] This supply was received at Ekdari in Motihari of Bihar and at the Tirhut Sub-Agency. In 1908, the *Imperial Gazetteer of India, Afghanistan and Nepal* reported that the British government imported 'intoxicating drugs' including *charas* and opium from Nepal.[82] This supply continued until the beginning of international controls on South Asian drug trade.

During the post-independence period, the supply of Nepalese drugs continued and the use of intoxicating drugs was legal in that country. In his biography Rabindra Singh, an Indian heroin addict who died at the age of 21, provided a detailed story about the flourishing of Nepalese drug culture in the early 1970s. He explained the role of the so-called 'Freak Street' in Kathmandu for selling low-cost Nepalese drugs to addict tourists from India and overseas.[83] As a result of this, Nepal eventually in the 1980s emerged as one of the important drug traders' havens in the landlocked Golden Wedge region.

The illicit drugs produced in Nepal used India either as a transit point for overseas markets or for local distribution. The supply of Nepalese opium first received parliamentary attention in India in August 1985, when an MP claimed that illicit poppies were grown in the Indo-Nepalese border region near the police and BSF posts in Indian territory. In 1989, a US intelligence report revealed that Nepal was also used as a corridor for heroin-3 smuggled from Bangkok and utilizing trans-shipment facilities in India.[84] The Indo-Nepalese border has traditionally been used for cannabis trafficking via routes through Siktal, Raxaul, Jainagar and Bhimnagar in Bihar. Indian authorities claimed that the country's law enforcement agencies in 1986 seized about 6 metric tons of cannabis that had been smuggled from Nepal.[85] In 1996, the *Indian Express* reported that along with other organized groups, traffickers from the Golden Wedge region were 'conducting brisk business' in Goa on the West Coast.[86] In October 1997, *Deccan Herald* reported that due to transit trafficking through Nepal, Darjeeling has become a market for Ecstasy and amphetamine-type stimulants (ATS) produced in the UK.[87] Despite the abundance of Nepalese smuggling, India has shown little concern about this channel.

Based on geo-strategic deliberation, India maintained its major concerns about cross-border trafficking from Pakistan while it showed reluctance to undertake any defence measures in the north-east and in the Himalayan region. During the same period, Indian drug policies have largely been patterned by the country's concern about a sharp decrease in the international market for medicinal opium in the 1980s.

The Indo-Australia opium trade war

A decrease in the supply of medicinal opium,[88] largely due to Australia's rise in the international market, has significantly contributed to widespread drug trafficking in India in recent years. Under the UN Protocol of 1953, the production of medicinal opium for export was permitted to seven countries including India.[89] Post-independence India from the late 1950s until the late 1970s retained its supremacy as a traditional supplier of opium. Throughout the 1970s, India was the single largest supplier of medicinal opium to the world market, meeting almost 90 per cent of international demand. However, with the increase in world demand for medicinal opium in the early 1970s, some non-traditional opium exporting countries, including Australia, emerged as opium suppliers.[90] The traditional opium trading nations, Turkey, Spain, France, Holland, also showed renewed interest in the trade. The opium poppy, which had been regarded as the 'Black Gold of India', was now being challenged, especially by the flourishing Tasmanian enterprise. The capturing of international opium trade by the Tasmanian opium industry motivated India to create diplomatic pressure opposing Australia's entry into the same competition.

Pursuit of opium diplomacy

In an attempt to protect its traditional supremacy in the international opium market, India in the early 1980s used diplomatic channels. Due to tremendous competition from high-yielding-opium pods, especially from Australia (85 per cent morphine content), exports of Indian opium (10–15 per cent) fell by almost 50 per cent by 1980.[91] India's export earnings from opium fell from Rs450 million in 1978 to Rs250 million within the next two years. Some of the traditional buyers – the UK, France, Belgium and Germany – have significantly curtailed their imports from India, preferring to buy Australian or Turkish concentrate poppy straw (CPS).[92] In less than three decades the Tasmanian opium industry emerged as one of the most professional and profitable enterprises in the world.

The rise of Tasmanian opium industry significantly swayed the international licit market from India. In 1981, *The Times of India* reported that the UK had cut its opium imports from India by 78 per cent, West Germany by 94 per cent, Italy by 94 per cent, Norway by 80 per cent, and that there was no demand from the US.[93] This report contained some exaggerations. For example, the US statistics indicate that its import of medicinal opium from India fell from 50 metric tons (67.1 per cent) in 1980 to 10 metric tons (31.7 per cent) in 1981.[94] Another reliable source suggested that the UK reduced its opium imports from 144 metric tons in 1979, to 76 metric tons in 1980, with a further reduction to 8 metric tons in the following year. A similar declining trend was evident in the European market, from 303 metric tons in 1977, to 169 metric tons in 1979, and to 29 metric tons in 1981.

To elicit sympathy from the UN, India claimed that due to a tremendous drop in external demand, the country was enduring a financial burden. The Indian government also expressed concern about the stockpiles of opium, which had risen from 1,200 to 2,600 metric tons during the same period, and had inflicted tremendous suffering on poppy growers.[95] Criticizing the flourishing opium industry in Tasmania, a technologically more advanced enterprise jointly run by the leading US pharmaceutical company Johnson and Johnson and Glaxo Australia, India demanded international pressure on Australia to force it to come forward with practical solutions to help India to save its declining opium industry. Endorsing India's concern, the UN Economic and Social Council (ECOSOC), in a resolution in May 1981, urged the major opium importing countries to buy Indian opium and requested Australia and other East European countries to limit their opium production for domestic purposes. The resolution was adopted by 45 votes, while five countries interested in the trade abstained from the voting.[96] Perceiving the growth of the Tasmanian opium industry as a potential threat, India was unhappy that Australia, a non-traditional opium producing country, had entered the world pharmaceutical market.

India revived the issue in a Vienna meeting in 1985 when ECOSOC reiterated the need for immediate measures to help free India from the burden of its huge opium stockpiles. The impact of the Vienna meeting on Australian opium exports was immense. The INCB report in 1990 indicated that Australia's opium exports declined from 411 metric tons in 1985 to 38 kilos in the following year. Data provided by the Australian Bureau of Statistics indicated that Tasmania's export earnings in 'restricted items' fell from A$16.5 million in 1986–7 to A$2.7 million in 1987–8, while interstate export grew substantially.[97] Consequently, at the Ninth Special Session of the UN Commission on Narcotic Drugs (CND) in Vienna in 1986 the Australian delegates demanded unconditional 'eradication of illegal crops' within India.[98] To counter India's diplomatic moves, Australia, Turkey and Spain accused India of producing false reports on the abuse of drugs, and on the effectiveness of the government's control system. In response, India blamed Pakistani cross-border supply, while ignoring India's massive production of illicit opium and its role in drug trafficking.

Having a stockpile of 2,000 metric tons of unsold opium, Indian envoys in February 1988 urged the CND to provide 'economic protection', as had been envisaged by ECOSOC in 1985.[99] At the annual CND meeting in Vienna the Indian delegates claimed that the country needed international assistance to modernize its opium industry, and find alternative economic activities for those who had traditionally grown opium poppies.[100] The Indian delegates defended the '80–20' trade rule of the US, the biggest consumer of licit opium in the world. Under this rule, the US government committed to buy 80 per cent of its opium from the traditional poppy growing countries (for example, India and Turkey), and the remaining 20 per cent from the non-traditional poppy growing countries. In May 1988, India pursued ECOSOC to request the non-traditional poppy growing countries to bring about a quick betterment in the situation in India.

In a counter communiqué in 1990, Julian Ormond Green, Chairman of the Poppy Advisory and Control Board in Tasmania, claimed that the US's policy was unable to prevent the illegal production and diversion of licit opium into illicit channels in India.[101] He urged the gradual abolition of US regulations for a refined trade in medicinal opium. Convinced by Green's assertion, the US *International Narcotics Control Strategy Report* in March 1991 observed that the monitoring system in India was insufficient to deter diversion and side-production for the black market, and noted that 'little has been done' to improve the situation.[102] Following US approval, Wayne Smith, Chairman of the Tasmanian

Oil Poppy Growers Association, lobbied the US Congress in August 1991 to break US trade barriers on Australia's entry into the world opiate market.

In order to deflect the accusations of Western countries, opium authorities in India maintained that poppy cultivation was well regulated and controlled. They held that to prevent the diversion of licit opium to the illegal trade, the government had maintained watchful eye. In an official bulletin the Indian government declared that, as there was little opium grown outside authoritative control there was no plan to eliminate poppy cultivation altogether. It further claimed that India, in an attempt to meet the world's demand for medicinal opium, had increased poppy cultivation in the mid-1970s, but was now burdened with an opium reserve. Figure 4.1 shows that the opium stockpile reached its highest level in 1982, and remained high until 1987. A contemporary US report maintained that reserves of opium gum in 1982–3 was 3,200 metric tons, which fell in 1988–9 to 2,000 metric tons. However, there is some variation in the statistics provided by the US and the Report of the INCB. To refute international allegations about its reluctance 'to devote adequate resources', the government claimed that it had allocated Rs1.2 billion to the NCB out of a total law enforcement budget of Rs28 billion in 1987.[103] To satisfy international pressure, India adopted strict narcotics laws in the late 1980s and attempted to release itself from the burden of the opium stockpile. By 1988, the government had recruited about 60,000 anti-drug personnel, and trained an additional 1,200 enforcement officials. In 1989,

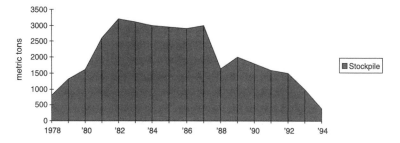

Figure 4.1   Stocks of medicinal opium in India, 1978–94
Sources: Based on data provided by the *Report of the INCB for 1993*, p. 13; *The Licit Importation of Opium*, p. 86

India concluded a bilateral drug control agreement with the US, to demonstrate its full support for the DEA and other intelligence agencies. By 1990, the Indian authorities had convinced the US that 'controls have been bolstered by additional regulatory and enforcement measures'.[104] Through its narco-diplomacy, India in 1991 made a record sale of 370 metric tons to the US, the largest buyer of medicinal opium in the world. In February 1992, India received the Foreign Assistance Certificate from the US for its crusade against drug trafficking. Creating diplomatic pressure on the Tasmanian opium industry, the Indian government by 1995 had successfully disposed of its huge opium stockpile, and prevented Australia from free entrance to the international market.

To clear its opium stockpile, India also maintained the existing price of exportable opium, while Australia, Turkey and France raised their price significantly. In 1990, the Indian rate per kilo of opium gum was US$150, nearly half the price of Australian and Turkish CPS.[105] The government's rebate policy helped relieve the opium stockpile, but only marginally abated the economic hardships of Indian poppy growers. A rise in Indian opium exports since 1990, combined with two subsequent poor harvests in 1993 and 1994, have enabled the country to reduce its opium reserve substantially. Thus, using its price discount policy and diplomatic channels, the Indian government by 1995 had successfully disposed of its huge opium stockpile.

As India wanted to eliminate its reserve, the country's annual opium production was reduced drastically. Figure 4.2 demonstrates that due to immense competition in the international market the production of Indian opium alkaloid between 1980 and 1993 declined from 107 to 37 metric tons (in morphine equivalent). This diminishing return was in fact evident in the late 1970s, when Indian opium exports fell from 1,200 metric tons in 1978, to 750 metric tons in 1979, with a further reduction in the following year.[106] A setback in the international market was coupled with other financial hardships within the opium enterprise. In a 1995 study, Angela S. Burger maintained that at great financial loss the Indian government maintained 1,400 employees in the Ghazipur and Neemuch opium factories.[107] Moreover, the creation of the Central Narcotics Control Bureau, as a result of international pressure, was an additional financial burden for the government.

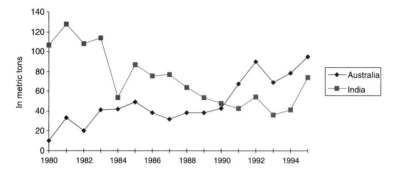

Figure 4.2 Production of medicinal opium in India and Australia in morphine equivalent, 1980–94
Sources: Based on data provided by the *Report of the INCB for 1993*, p. 13; *Report of the INCB for 1995*, p. 15

While the Indian opium industry was a losing concern, Australian production gradually rose from 10 metric tons in 1981 to 95 metric tons in 1995. In 1991, Sheryle Bagwell indicated that the Tasmanian poppy industry during the period supplied 30–40 per cent of licit morphine, codeine and other painkillers in the world pharmaceutical market with an annual return of A$30–40 million.[108] By 1997, according to David Marr and Bernard Lagan, the total annual earnings of the Tasmanian opium industry reached about A$80 million.[109] Another report by Bruce Montgomery in August 1997 maintained that the annual output of this industry amounted to A$100 million.[110] The INCB report for 1990 indicated that extracted mechanically directly from the poppy straw (utilizing stems, leaves and pod), the per hectare yield of Australian opium during 1984–90 had been over 800 kilos, while in India the production of opium latex ranged only between 24 and 30 kilos. The Indian government, during this period, paid little attention to improving the standard of its opium manufacture.

Due to lack of capital and appropriate technology, in India poppy juice is still collected manually. At the Ghazipur factory in UP about 800 workers are involved in processing black opium pastes in the hot sun until it becomes waterless.[111] Many foreign buyers prefer to import the opium alkaloid from India and do their own distilling. Despite the massive cut in poppy cultivation (for example, 200 hectares by 1996) in the UP, the Indian government has continued the century-old opium industry at Ghazipur. Inside the factory, chemists transform the opium alkaloid into morphine, codeine, narcotine and thebaine, which are mostly used in making special painkillers.[112] As a result of an increase in international demand for painkillers and medicines for cancer, AIDS and bronchial ailments, the Indian authorities were optimistic about the acceleration of opium production in the country. In April 1997, *The Indian Express* indicated that licit poppy cultivation took place in eight districts in UP, while illicit poppy cultivation continued in Jaunsar Bhabar of Uttarakhand. During the following month, *The Hindustan Times* reported that the government collected over 1,300 metric tons of opium alkaloid breaking all the previous records.[113] This quantity was 100 metric tons higher than that of the registered production in 1978. Despite the capturing of the international market, India has done little to match the flourishing opium industry in Tasmania.

None the less, India used its diplomatic channels to clear its opium stocks that had been created by its failure in the international licit market. By exerting diplomatic pressure against the Tasmanian opium industry, India achieved three objectives: (1) By 1994, the country was able to clear its huge opium stockpiles; (2) India earned US sympathy in favour of the '80–20 Rule', and through the latter, India was successful in blocking Australia's entry to the international licit market in medicinal opium; and (3) India's narco-diplomacy largely diverted world attention from the proliferation of domestic drugs that allowed traffickers to contribute to the country's black economy. Overall, by 1995, India was successful in influencing the world pharmaceutical market in support of its opium industry, but failed to ensure a tight security system equal to that maintained by the multinational companies in Tasmania.

Licit opium into illicit channels

India's setback in the international opium trade, due to immense competition especially from Australia and Turkey, encouraged many poppy farmers to establish a connection with underworld traffickers. As a result of reversal in the international opium market between 1979 and 1987, many Indian poppy cultivators diverted a substantial amount of domestic licit opium into illicit channels. A nineteenth-century study by C.E. Buckland indicated that mutual 'frauds' and 'paper-cultivation' by the poppy farmers and *gomastas* had existed under the government opium monopoly in India.[114] The post-independence government in India failed either to modify century-old flaws in the drug laws, or to undertake any measures to strengthen the security system in the opium industry. This reluctance in government policy encouraged local traffickers and poppy farmers to engage increasingly in underground trade.

Until 1985, the Indian government was reluctant to enforce a security system in the opium industry required in accordance with the UN Single Nation Convention on Narcotic Drugs, 1961; the UN Convention of Psychotropic Substances, 1971; and the UN Protocol of 1972. In the absence of strong anti-drug laws, the international drug syndicates established their influence in the Indian heroin trade, and helped create a flourishing black economy in India throughout the 1980s and early 1990s. Confronted by the government's reduction in the area under cultivation, poppy farmers of Madhya Pradesh, Rajasthan and the UP suffered severe financial hardship. As I discussed in Chapter 1, once a cultivator broke his connection with the opium management, it was difficult to get him back in poppy cultivation. Unlike their predecessors in the previous century, the poppy cultivators in India were now keen to continue growing the 'money plant' which offered them economic prosperity and social dignity.[115] However, a gradual decline has taken place in recent years, both in terms of the poppy growing areas and the work force involved in the opium industry. Figure 4.3 shows that the area under poppy cultivation was reduced from 62,684 hectares in 1978 to 15,000 hectares in 1989, while the number of poppy farmers declined from 245,161 in 1978 to 129,000 in 1987. As a result of the reduction policy in poppy cultivation, the poppy farmers in UP, Rajasthan and Madhya Pradesh diverted large-scale licit opium into illicit channels. Compared to the loosely administered opium industry in India, about 750 farmers are engaged in about 12,000 hectares of poppy cultivation in Tasmania.[116] The immense rise in poppy cultivation in Australia has occurred in less than two decades. During 1984–94, the total area under poppy cultivation in Tasmania ranged between 3,500 and 8,000 hectares. While the production of opium poppy gradually increased in Australia, poppy cultivation in India

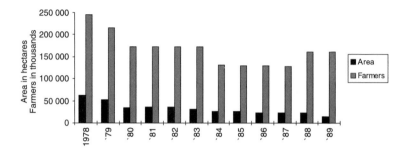

Figure 4.3   Reduction in the area of poppy cultivation and the number of
poppy farmers in India, 1978–89
Source: *The Licit Importation of Opium,* p. 261

between 1978 and 1981 fell about 50 per cent, and the number of
poppy cultivators fell about 35 per cent (see Figure 4.3). During
1988–9, the area under poppy cultivation continuously shrank, but
the number of poppy farmers increased, allowing marginal farmers
to grow poppy on an ad-hoc basis.

As a result of the temporary nature of their engagement, the Indian
poppy farmers started diverting a large quantity of opium from licit to
illicit channels to derive additional profits from the declining industry.
In 1971, the total number of licensed poppy cultivators in India was
approximately half a million, and by the early 1990s this figure had
fallen by 75 per cent. Between 1994 and 1995, about 92 per cent of
poppy licences were cut in Bara Banki district with a corresponding
54 per cent reduction in the total area of poppy cultivation. Given the
uncertainty of the opium industry, a large majority of Indian poppy
farmers were involved in passing opium into traffickers' channels by
numerous methods. In an account of the illegal income accruing to
licensed poppy farmers, a newspaper correspondent from Chittorgarh
(Rajasthan) wrote in 1992:

> The farmer is tempted to make some extra money by not
> declaring the yield produced in excess to the stipulated
> minimum of 34 kg. The lure is all the more when the raw opium
> in the open market fetches 25 times more money. It may not be
> very difficult to hoodwink the officials of the Narcotics
> Department as the fields are in far flung areas.[117]

The report claimed that as a result of regular 'keeping off a substantial quantity' by the poppy growers, over 40 per cent of the opium produced in Chittorgarh district evaded government accounting. Referring to the Superintendent of Police in Chittorgarh in 1994, another report maintained that over 50 metric tons of opium were diverted annually by smugglers to manufacture heroin. There was similar evidence from Bara Banki district of UP, of which D. Gidwani wrote that most farmers' 'siphon off opium to the illegal market' by reporting low-yield harvests or theft.[118] It can be recalled here that frauds and fictitious cultivation by the poppy farmer–gomasta–smuggler nexus also had existed during the previous century.[119] Gidwani also noted that as soon as the time for poppy collection draws near, 'reports of opium theft and looting register an abnormal rise', over 90 per cent of which were false. This situation was largely related to the massive cut in official licences and the reduction in the area of poppy cultivation, which led many poppy farmers to derive a financial benefit from a decaying enterprise by any means.

Nevertheless, the Indian government asserts that 'every inch under [poppy] cultivation was accounted for' by the officials of the Narcotics Department. It also maintains that narcotics personnel monitor the poppy harvest 'round the clock', controlling the diversion within one per cent. Despite these official pronouncements, the existence of a nexus between farmers, smugglers and corrupt officials facilitated huge quantities of opium passing from licit sources to the traffickers. Moreover, due to political corruption some kinsmen manage to get licences issued for the cultivation of opium poppy and earn handsome amounts of blackmarket money by engaging more land than they are allowed.[120] Quoting Indian police authorities, US official reports in 1988 had estimated that 10–20 per cent of India's licit opium crop was diverted into illicit channels.[121] In 1991, the International Narcotics Control Strategy Report (INCSR) stated that in three years the diversion rate had risen by 20–30 per cent. A 1997 report from India indicated that undermining official vigilance, over 50 per cent of opium in UP was 'smuggled to the drug mafia for production of heroin'.[122] Despite these varied rates of diversion, it can be deduced that a significant portion of licit opium was transferred to the traffickers for manufacturing heroin.

A model experiment conducted in 1994 by Karan Sharma, the Mandsaur Deputy Narcotics Commissioner, showed that a substantial amount of official opium went to the underground traffickers. Sharma produced 62 kilos of opium from one hectare, while the minimum qualifying yield (MQY) was 40 kilos. However, Sharma claimed that careful farmers produce on average between 60 and 100 kilos per hectare. Indian licensed farmers cultivated opium poppy on just over 11,000 hectares in 1993. Given the conservative MQY standard of Sharma (for example, the difference between 40 and 60 kilos), poppy farmers in 1993 diverted about 220 metric tons of official opium to the black market.[123] This experiment was identical to the US State Department report of 1985, which estimated that annual diversion could have been approximately 200 metric tons.[124] The INCB statistics in 1990 indicated that per hectare MQY in India ranged between 24 and 31 kilos during 1984–90. Due to the influence of the pro-opium lobby, the Madhya Pradesh legislature in 1991–2 turned down a tabled resolution for the increase of MQY. The Chief Minister, Sunderlal Patwa, opposed a similar attempt in 1994 aimed at increasing the MQY from 40 kilos to 60 kilos in Madhya Pradesh. A senior Congress leader from Madhya Pradesh stated:

> The truth is that the opium lobby is very strong and a number of leaders from both the Congress and the BJP are involved in the business.[125]

Under international pressure, the central government raised the MQY from 46 kilos in 1995–6 to 48 kilos in 1996–7 in Madhya Pradesh and Rajasthan, but for 'low productivity' it was fixed at 40 kilos in UP.[126] Former finance minister R. Prabhu attacked this slow increase of MQY at a press conference in Delhi as 'drug mafia-friendly'.[127] As a result of this 'unholy nexus' amongst poppy cultivators, politicians and drug traffickers, it has been estimated that about 270 metric tons of opium was diverted to the black market in 1996.[128] This assessment was provided by the then collector of Mandsaur district of Madhya Pradesh in an official note to the higher authorities in May 1996. Under the revised poppy cultivation policy, the Indian authorities in October 1996 increased the MQY from 48 kilos per hectare to 54 kilos per hectare. However, only a few poppy farmers reached this target in the following year.[129] Getting political protection, a large quantity of the official opium in India ends up with black marketers who offer a higher price to the poppy farmers to sell their unaccounted daily reserve of opium.

In an unrealistic attempt to encourage farmers to use the licit market, the government in the early 1980s introduced a ceiling system with the principle of greater production and a higher official rate. A study in 1982 indicated that compared to the official rate of Rs220 per kilo of opium smugglers were paying Rs500 to Rs700 in the poppy growing areas. The same amount was sold in northern India from Rs800 to Rs1,000, along the coast from Rs1,500 to Rs1,800, and across the border for between Rs5,000 and Rs8,000.[130] In 1995 the President of the All India Opium Producers Federation, Kanheyalal Dungarwal, claimed that the government paid about Rs250 (US$8) per kilo of opium, while smugglers offered cultivators more than 30 times the official rate.[131] Compared to the government rates, a great disparity also existed in Bara Banki, where farmers received between Rs30,000 and Rs40,000 per kilo on the open market. To protest the government's 'rock-bottom prices', poppy farmers of Madhya Pradesh organized a 15-day strike in the middle of April 1995 and refused to take advance money from the government. Supporting their demand, Digvijay Singh, the Chief Minister of Madhya Pradesh, asked the Central Finance Ministry to pay farmers more. This situation encouraged most licensed poppy farmers to develop an alternative economy by transferring a portion of licit opium into illicit channels. Given the unfavourable world market, the central government was unable to raise the official rate, and alleviate discontent at the grassroots.

Besides the above malpractice, there has been drainage of opium by corrupt officials from the government storehouse to smugglers. Referring to an Indian official report, the US State Department in 1991 indicated that 'storage losses' from the licit stockpile of 1,450 metric tons amounted to about 250 metric tons. However, it is not clear from the above reports whether this loss occurred in a year or in a span of a decade. Whatever may be the case, using this diversion strategy the Indian poppy cultivators and some corrupt officials in the opium department have helped in the growth of clandestine heroin laboratories and widespread drug trafficking with origins in India.

Heroin traffic

As a result of the diversion of official opium to smugglers' channels, and the production of illicit opium within the country, India emerged as a major exporter of heroin in the international market. The US Committee on Foreign Affairs in 1988 observed that the diversion of licit stocks in India was creating 'a billion dollars worth of street heroin'.[132] The Narcotics Control authorities in India in 1996 agreed that a substantial number of heroin factories have flourished in Bombay and other parts of the country during the last few years.[133] Some of the production in these clandestine factories was export oriented, while most of it were consumed locally.

With the easy access to illegal opium and precursor chemicals, heroin production in the poppy growing areas spread very rapidly. In early 1985, a group of research students at Lucknow University used their research laboratory for producing illicit heroin and hashish. Two other heroin-processing laboratories were detected in UP in the following year. In 1988, three clandestine refineries were unearthed by the enforcement agencies, and two makeshift laboratories were seized in 1991.[134] In 1992, a newspaper report from Chittorgarh in Rajasthan showed that there were many home based 'brown sugar' factories.[135] The same source also noted that manufacturing of heroin had become a 'cottage industry' in Pratapgarh and Badi Sadri of Chittorgarh district, and in Ramganjmandi and Jhalrapatan of Kota district. A report in 1994 from Achari, a village of Mandsaur district in Madhya Pradesh, indicated that hidden heroin laboratories had 'mushroomed everywhere' along the MP–Rajasthan border.[136] Another report in 1994 noted that 'large scale clandestine manufacture of heroin and smack' was taking place in Mandsaur district, and Chittorgarh. Thus, with the gradual decline of its licit market, the Indian smugglers were becoming increasingly involved with heroin trafficking.

Given the coolness in the foreign market for Indian medicinal opium, some ex-officials of the Narcotics Department and government factories began processing heroin in clandestine laboratories. For example, Ashwini Bhardwaj, a former Inspector of the Department of Narcotics, ran such a factory in Mandsaur for a decade. This report was first discussed in parliament in 1985, and it again came to public attention nine years later, because Bhardwaj has still not been arrested. In UP, some of the former employees of government-run alkaloid units at Ghazipur were reported to have turned to heroin manufacturing.[137] The simplicity of the extraction process from opium latex to heroin, the easy availability of chemical substances, and the potentially huge profits involved, attracted many exofficials to the 'mafia' underworld. An unofficial report stated that one kilo of pure heroin in Mandsaur or Neemuch in 1994 sold for around Rs100,000. When it reached Bombay, it was mixed with other chemical agents to make it at least four kilos, which was then sold for at least Rs150,000 per kilo. On reaching the retail market, the price shot up to Rs250,000 per kilo.[138] Thus, the availability of underground markets in the big cities in India and overseas animated some narcotics officials to become manufacturers of illegal heroin.

Illicit heroin from UP, Madhya Pradesh, Gujarat and Rajasthan was increasingly passing to international destinations via the West Coast. Evidence from the time from the government of British India, indicates that in the early nineteenth century there had been a traditional route for opium exports from Baroda and Cambay to China, via the Gujarat sea coast and Sind. In order to avoid paying Malwa transit duty to the colonial authorities, the Central Indian rulers until 1843 used Daman and Karachi ports for exit traffic.[139] This route again began to be used by Indian drug traffickers in the mid-1980s, and three exit points were used for trans-shipment: Kutch, Porbandar and Daman (see Map 2). Referring to government officials, Bhim Sain wrote in 1991, 'a large number of cases' of heroin trafficking were detected in the area in recent years.[140] In support, Joginder Singh, the Director General of the NCB, in an official statement observed:

> Smugglers have made inroads into the vast desert of southern Rajasthan and the marshlands of the Rann of Kutch in Gujarat. They use the porous western coastline, particularly Cori Creek and Siv Creek in Gujarat.[141]

A new international narcotics trunk route from Gujarat–Maharashtra to Europe and North America has emerged. In 1996, it was estimated that the total drug trade in this area had reached between Rs50 billion and Rs200 billion.[142] In November 1996, *Frontline* maintained that to avoid all the checkposts along the west coast, heroin and hashish

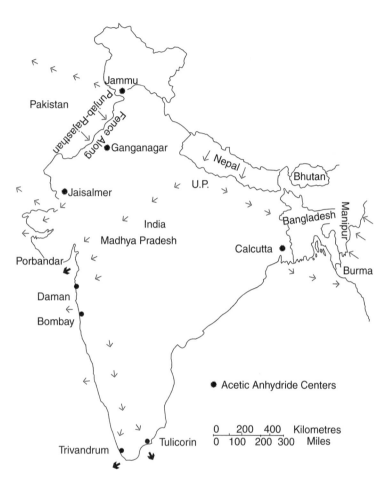

Map 2   India: direction of illicit trafficking

consignments were sent via Chennai in Madras and an inland city of Bangalore, further south.[143] From there, illicit drugs were disbursed to Mangalore, Thiruvananthapuram, Tuticorin and other ports along the coast. Small fishing boats then carried the contraband drugs to larger vessels offshore, for overseas destinations. Heroin, hashish and other psychotropic substances produced in India contributed significantly to the international drug trafficking in the 1980s and 1990s.

With the resurgence of India as a major drug exporting country, drug money has captured an important place in the mainstream Indian economy. In the past, hashish and *charas* were generally smuggled from Pakistan, Nepal and Afghanistan. In recent years, with the increase of illicit drug trade, some Indian farmers began producing hashish and *charas* as cottage industries. A report in 1993 indicated that about 2,000 rural people of Ghazipur district in UP were engaged in the illegal manufacture of hashish, and opium derivatives.[144] An unofficial report indicated that the poppy farmers in Bankura, Burdwan, Purulia, Birbhum, Nadia and the North 24-Pargana were involved in manufacturing hashish and *charas*,[145] and hashish oil was being manufactured in the northern states. Indian hashish, like many other drugs, was then smuggled to Western countries. In June 1985, US officials at Port Elizabeth in New Jersey seized 3 metric tons of hashish, which was labelled as Indian foodstuffs.[146] Israeli customs in July 1994 seized three tons of hashish (worth Rs500 million) from a UK-bound consignment at the port of Ashdod, uncovering a drug cartel led by a top Madras entrepreneur, C. Nagraj, who had masterminded smuggling of over 1,250 metric tons of hasish from India since 1992.[147] The detection of this cartel indicated that hashish trafficking was becoming another important element in the black economy of India.

Encouraged by the illegal export of drugs, Indian pharmaceutical manufacturers produced large quantities of illicit mandrax (methaqualone) to meet the demand of a booming international market. As a sedative-hypnotic, mandrax had been outlawed in the US and also in China. In January 1984, the Indian government officially banned the production of this chemical compound. Nevertheless, a large number of pharmaceutical laboratories in India had established connections with illicit traffickers in Third World countries. This connection was evident in 1987 when four mandrax factories with a stock of over one metric ton of methaqualone powder were discovered by the enforcement agencies. In 1988, an official publication indicated that the enforcement authorities seized 745 kilos of mandrax in 1985 and 1,684 kilos in the following year.[148] Most of the seizures of mandrax were made in Gujarat and Maharastra, where clandestine laboratories were engaged in its illicit production. To meet the growing international demands, illicit production of mandrax in India subsequently increased further, reaching about 24 metric tons in 1994. In early 1997, the Bangalore (Karnataka) customs seized about three metric tons of mandrax tablets worth Rs30 million in the Indian market and Rs1.5 billion in the international market.[149] The sporadic seizures of mandrax reveal that an increasing amount of Indian psychotropic substances was smuggled to markets, especially in the countries in Asia and Africa.

In line with the colonial opium trade, India's drug empire has flourished chiefly in Third World countries, ranging from the Asia-Pacific to South Africa. Indian 'brown sugar', mandrax, hashish and phensedyl are now widespread in Bangladesh, Nepal, Pakistan and other countries in South Asia. In recent years, Indian traffickers have expanded their supply of psychotropic substances mostly in Third World countries, while heroin from local and cross-border sources are destined for Europe and other Western countries. Diversion of licit opium and narcotics chemicals into illicit channels has largely contributed to this disastrous development.

Heroin chemicals

A gap in the chemicals policy between India and neighbouring poppy growing countries helped India to rise as the single largest supplier of acetic anhydride (AA), a key precursor to the refinement of opium into heroin. Indian AA is in great demand in the illicit poppy growing areas of southwest and southeast Asia. India produces this chemical licitly for its textile, pharmaceutical and leather industries. However, due to leakage in production management, a substantial amount of heroin chemical is diverted from licit to unlawful channels for clandestine use in Pakistan, Afghanistan and Burma.

Besides India, China is another country that produces AA in the region. Compared to Chinese AA, the Indian product is more attractive to the traffickers. In 1989, the US Judiciary Subcommittee on Crime observed that laboratory operators in Pakistan and Burma prefer to buy Indian reagent because of its high quality and cheap price, rather than the Chinese article.[150] The chemical, which is just Rs50 a litre in retail markets in India, sold at a 100 times profit margin in the heroin processing areas of Pakistan.[151] Another Indian report suggests that on the local black market this chemical is sold for between Rs2,000 and Rs3,000 per litre, while in Europe and other

Western countries it cost between Rs30,000 and Rs40,000 per liter.[152] As a result of this price difference, Indian AA is continually diverted from licit sources to smugglers' channels in the NWFP and Baluchistan in Pakistan and Afghanistan.

Ignoring the hostilities between the two countries, Indian traffickers continually pass a substantial amount of licit AA to traffickers' channels in Pakistan. In 1997 a mimeograph distributed by the Pakistan High Commission in Canberra claimed that India was 'involved deeply' in the smuggling of heroin chemical to the Pakistani traffickers.[153] Law enforcement agencies in Karachi in April 1990 had confiscated about 20 metric tons of AA, plenty to refine all of Pakistan's annual opium production.[154] This reagent was smuggled from Jaisalmer in southern Rajasthan and destined for clandestine heroin laboratories in Baluchistan. Again in July 1991, legal authorities in NWFP seized about five metric tons of acetic anhydride smuggled from Jammu in India. Similar seizures happened seldom during subsequent years. As a result of the growing demands for AA in Pakistan and Afghanistan, and continued supplies of the product from India, the Pakistani authorities admit that they have failed to halt the cross-border trafficking in AA.

A lucrative trade in the narcotics chemical drew India's attention as early as the 1960s, when Indian delegate Banerji raised the issue at the Third Plenary meeting of the UN Conference of 1961.[155] Paradoxically, at the Vienna meeting in 1985 India was accused of abusing heroin raw materials and of routing AA to the poppy growing regions in southwest and southeast Asia. The Australian delegates in February 1986 at the Ninth Special Session of the Commission on Narcotic Drugs (CND) urged the inclusion of precursor chemicals in the UN Convention.[156] In line with Australia's proposal, the International Narcotics Control Board (INCB) subsequently invited India and other industrialized countries to control the 'availability' of this chemical reagent.[157] Under the UN Convention on Illicit Narcotic Drugs and Psychotropic Substances of 1988, provisions were adopted to formalize the above actions.[158] The Convention, which came into force in November 1990, urged the industrialized countries engaged in the preparation and export of precursor chemicals to present legislation controlling the movement of AA and other narcotics raw materials.[159] The US and some other industrialized countries instantly ratified this Convention, but India hesitated to follow suit.

Due to the lack of administrative control, Indian smugglers became increasingly involved in illicit trafficking of AA by the mid-1980s. In late 1985, India adopted tougher legislation on drugs, while refraining from imposing any restrictions on the diversion of AA from licit sources. As a result, the US Committee on Foreign Affairs in 1986 indicated that India alone furnished almost all the AA to the Golden Crescent, and was one of the major suppliers to the Golden Triangle for the production of heroin. None the less, under the new regulation in 1988 India prohibited the movement of dangerous drugs within 100 kilometres of its international border. This legislation failed to identify AA as such a drug, or to arrest the supply of heroin chemical to the neighbouring poppy growing countries. The Indian government also failed to address the issue under the toughest laws introduced in 1989. In 1993, the Indian government amended the Essential Commodities Act of 1985, which restricted the production of AA to licence holders, and only on government account. Under the Essential Commodities Act, the movement of AA was officially prohibited within 100 kilometres of the Burma border and 50 kilometres of the Pakistan border.[160] In November 1996, AA was finally declared a 'notified drug' in India. However, these legal sanctions have failed to prevent the supply of the chemical to neighbouring poppy growing areas.

In contrast to India, there are no facilities to produce AA either in Pakistan or Afghanistan. The Pakistan government as early as 1991 banned the manufacture of AA, imposed punishment on its smuggling, and tightened controls over its importation by industrial buyers.[161] In May 1993, the Pakistani law enforcement agencies captured four traffickers with one metric ton of heroin chemical in a truck in Hyderabad, and in the following September, 200 litres of AA were seized from camel's back in Lahore.[162] In 1995, the Pakistani law enforcement agencies, in a record-breaking drive, seized about 30 metric tons of Indian heroin chemical from cross-border traffickers. With the frequent seizures of Indian heroin raw material, the Pakistani enforcement agencies attempted to prove the underhand association of India in the clandestine production of heroin in the region.

Under international pressure, sporadic seizures of AA by the Indian enforcement agencies along the western border began in the

1990s. In 1992, Indian authorities first detected the smuggling of AA into Pakistan through the Barmer border in Rajasthan. They seized about 2,730 litres of AA during the operation.[163] A recent report by the Indian authorities admitted that about 8,600 litres of illicit acetic anhydride were confiscated in Barmer district in 1994, and in the following year over 2,000 litres, with a market value of Rs43 million and Rs10 million respectively. Despite sporadic seizures, the INCB report of 1995 suggested that a substantial amount of AA was exported illegally to Pakistan, Afghanistan and diverted within India for the illicit manufacture of heroin. In 1995–6, the Indian Narcotics Control Bureau indicated that seizures of AA on the western border rose from 20,000 litres in 1993 to 48,000 litres in the following year.[164] Another Indian report in 1995 had maintained that smugglers from Jaisalmer in southern Rajasthan and Jammu in the northwest continued to serve as major suppliers of illegal AA to heroin laboratories located in Pakistan and Afghanistan.[165] A 1997 Indian report indicated that heroin chemicals worth 20 to 25 metric tons a month were transported on the flights from Delhi to Jalalabad, the capital of Kandahar, in Afghanistan.[166]

Being involved in a strategic war against Pakistan, the Indian authorities claimed that the sealing of the Punjab–Rajasthan border along Pakistan restricted cross-border trafficking in AA. By January 1997 India had completed the 1,171-kilometre sealing and installed 1,204 kilometres of floodlighting along its 'vulnerable stretches' from Srinagar to Rajasthan. Besides blocking cross-border penetration, the fencing has reduced the prospect of direct supply of AA from Ganganagar, a centre located between Rajasthan and the Punjab in India. However, the Indo-Pakistan border along Jammu and southern Rajasthan has been left open and allows traffickers to continue their contraband trade. The Indian authorities maintain that due to intense tension and 'regular firing' the sealing of the Jammu border was obstructed, while due to lack of funds 400 kilometres remained unfenced in southern Rajasthan. In May 1997, *Frontline* from Delhi indicated that work further south along Jaisalmer and northwards in Jammu will be completed by the year 2000. However, without strict controls in the production management of AA, fencing the entire border might not help reduce the diversion of heroin chemical from industries in Gujarat, Jaisalmer and Jammu.

In contrast to the measures against Pakistan, there has been a lack of control in the northeastern border that allows the open supply of heroin chemical to Burma. As a result, chemical enterprises in Calcutta continually deflect licit AA to hidden laboratories in Burma for manufacturing heroin. The legal measures adopted in the late 1980s and early 1990s had little impact on this cross-border smuggling trade.

The smuggling of AA to poppy growing areas in India and adjoining poppy growing countries of Burma, Pakistan and Nepal helped accelerate the production of heroin in the region. A concerted international effort is essential to control the detour of licit heroin chemical into illicit channels that help the production of clandestine heroin both in the Golden Triangle and the Golden Crescent regions. Besides the effective sealing of the Indian border, the proper implementation of anti-drug laws in the country is essential to combat the cross-border traffickers. After the recovery of its position in the world pharmaceutical market, India now faces a trial of its political will and must implement the international anti-drug conventions and agreements to which it is a signatory.

Anti-drug legislation

In an attempt to satisfy international demand for a reduction of drug trafficking, India has adopted strong anti-narcotics legislation in recent years. The International Narcotics Control Board (INCB) in its report in 1984 blamed India for allowing trans-shipment facilities in Bombay, New Delhi, Calcutta and Madras that concealed heroin in legitimate air or sea freight cargo and permitted couriers to exit for Europe or North America. In belated recognition of the need to combat illicit production and trafficking, the Indian government adopted legislation only in the late 1980s. The present discussion presents the strengths and weaknesses of the strict legislation and assesses the overall impact of these laws on domestic consumption and in reducing the role of India in global drug trafficking. It argues that lack of proper implementation, and the contradictory nature in some provisions made the results of these laws unpromising.

The NDPS Act of 1985

To meet the demand of world bodies in favour of strong anti-drug legislation, the Indian government adopted the Narcotic Drugs and Psychotropic Substances Act of 1985 (NDPSA). This amended Act consolidated the existing drug laws. In the early 1980s India became the subject of international criticism for routing heroin to overseas destinations. In January 1984, drugs worth $103 million were seized by US authorities off the coast of New Jersey from a freighter that was allegedly sent from Cochin in Kerala by an Australian, who planned 'operations from his yacht'.[167] As a party to the UN Single Convention on Narcotic Drugs, 1961, the UN Convention on Psychotropic Substances, February 1971, and the Protocol of the UN Conference at Geneva in March 1972, India was under pressure to translate its previous commitments into action. Given these accusations and obligations, India was compelled to redesign its national legislation in accordance with international conventions.

To strengthen controls over addictive drugs and illicit trafficking, the Indian government, through the NDPSA, repealed the Opium Act of 1857, the Opium Act of 1878 and the Dangerous Drugs Act of 1930. Under the above laws maximum punishment ranged from six months to three years, and offenders were bailable even if they were caught with illegal drugs. The NDPSA provided severe punishment for the violation of this provision, with a minimum imprisonment of ten years, including a Rs100,000 fine, extendable up to 20 years and Rs200,000.[168] Compared to the anti-drug provisions of the UK, France, Germany, Italy and the Netherlands, the Indian legislation was much stronger and quite similar to Greece and Indonesia. The punishment provided by the NDPSA was almost double that of the Assam Opium Prohibition Act of 1947. In order to exercise effective control over narcotics and psychotropic substances, the new Act placed primary emphasis on trafficking and provided sufficient legal strength for the law enforcement agencies. The critics of the legal approach argued that the law helped legal authorities to earn 'bread and butter'.[169] However, the Act also banned activities connected with narcotics or psychotropic substances, except for medicinal or scientific purposes.[170] The penalties imposed under the Indian Act were too general, and made no classification of sentence according to the nature of offence. The Act substantially authorized the Court to grant bail to offenders on the basis of their mental state of affairs.

Due to lack of correct application, the new laws failed to prevent illicit poppy cultivation and heroin manufacturing in the poppy growing areas. In defiance of the existing laws, illicit poppy cultivation continued in UP, Madhya Pradesh and Rajasthan, where opium has been officially cultivated. The US Foreign Affairs Committee report in 1988 indicated that cultivation was detected in Gujarat and on the Kerala–Tamil Nadu border.[171] In 1987, the Indian authorities officially admitted that 21 hectares of illicit poppy, with potential yield of about one metric ton of opium, had been eradicated.[172] In 1988, the enforcement authorities destroyed 20 hectares of illicit poppy in the Chakrata hills of Dehradun district.[173] In 1990, Indian legal agencies destroyed 24 hectares of unlicensed poppy, compared to 99 hectares in the previous year. Despite the sporadic operations, illegal cultivation of opium poppy flourished in Bankura Burdwan, Purulia, Birbhum, Nadia and the North-24 Pargana of West Bengal. A recent article showed that in 1993–4 unauthorized cultivation was detected covering about 115 hectares in Bankura, and 8 hectares in the Kaksa *thana* of Burdwan district.[174] With the spread of forbidden cultivation in neighbouring areas, Calcutta in the recent years has been revived as a centre for drug racketeering. In recent years, poppy farmers have justified the illicit production of opium poppy, and demonstrated 'tough resistance' and confrontational approach with the law enforcing agencies if their actions were challenged. The cheap investment and high cash rewards were making ousted poppy farmers aggressive in defense of what they see as their traditional rights. A number of reports suggested that, in violation of the tougher laws, illegal cultivation has been lasting in Gujarat, on the Kerala–Tamil Nadu border, in the Chin Hills and in the Naga Hills. In 1996, *Frontline* reported that illicit poppy cultivation continued in Kashmir and Himachal Pradesh,[175] where poppy had been licitly grown under the British rule. In the UP, illicit poppy cultivation was protracted in some of the hill districts. The traditional involvement of the poppy cultivators with this rewarding cash crop has encouraged them to aggressively undermine the new legislation.

Cannabis Sativa, or the hemp plant, which is officially cultivated for industrial use, received contradictory treatment under the NDPSA. In India, hemp is commercially utilized in certain industrial products and also consumed in the form of cannabis, *bhang* and *charas*. Cannabis, which grows in abundance and has been used for religious ceremonies in many parts of India, was not viewed as a significant problem by the NDPSA. Article 8 excluded cannabis from the other two varieties, giving the drug 'an inexplicable relaxation'.[176] The Act provided noticeably liberal punishments for cannabis-related offences. Compared to other drugs, punishment in connection with more commonly used cannabis is only half as severe. Contradicting Article 8, which forbade the non-medicinal use of hemp, Article 10 allowed addicts to take *charas* without any control by state governments.

As a result of the 'soft' attitude of the NDPSA, illegal production of cannabis is on the rise in India. A study in 1989 found that large-scale illicit cultivation of cannabis was taking place in the Idukki, Thrissur and Ernakulam districts of Kerala. It was reported in 1996 that the cultivation of cannabis has persisted along the Kodagu–Wyanad border in Kerala. In Andhra Pradesh, cannabis production in recent years has witnessed 'an unprecedented boom', with an estimated return of Rs10 billion.[177] A report in 1993 noted that cannabis was cultivated in 4,050 hectares in Warangal district, and that about 50,000 small farmers were involved. Most of the production was destined for Madras, Bombay, Bangalore, Delhi, Nagpur and Hyderabad for smuggling purposes. Referring to official sources, the *Statesman Weekly*, in 1992, indicated that large-scale illicit cultivation of cannabis was detected in the districts of Nadia and North-24 Pargana of West Bengal.[178] In March 1994, Excise Department officials detected about 7 hectares under cannabis cultivation in Nadia, with an estimated yield of about 4.9 metric tons.[179] *Charas* and cannabis are now also cultivated in Kashmir in fields that previously cultivated vegetables or cereals. A report in 1996 observed:

> It is an open secret that a section of the [narcotics] officials extend tacit support to the ganja lobby. ... The lack of determination on the part of the authorities in the anti-ganja fight is evident from the facilities extended to those involved in it.[180]

In 1996, *The Hindu* indicated that farmers in Imphal, Ukhrul and Senapati districts of Manipur were producing the 'best quality' cannabis in the country.[181] Ignoring the destruction of cannabis by enforcement authorities in 1994 and 1995, the cultivation of this drug remained widespread in the deep forests of the southwestern *ghats* in Tamil Nadu.[182] Sporadic eradication touched 'the tip of the iceberg' and could not prevent the assignation of the cannabis farmers, who were hardly tried by the existing laws. Moreover, the margin on cannabis smuggling has been more lucrative for traffickers: what is worth Rs3,600 per kilo in India reaches $4,300 (about Rs140,000) at the first transit point on the international market, and fetches up to Rs400,000 as it moves to retail points. Evidence shows that an easy attitude towards cannabis, with a ten-fold increase in price from the grower to consumer, encouraged farmers to undermine the NDPSA.

A similar contradiction also exists in provisions regarding the quantity of drugs. While Articles 15 to 18 impose heavy punishment on consumers, Article 27 prescribes a light punishment for addicts for possessing a 'small quantity' of narcotics or other psychotropic substances. In 1985, the *Gazette of India* exempted 500 grams of cannabis, 125 milligrams of cocaine, 250 milligrams of heroin, and 5 grams of hashish and opium from legal punishment.[183] In the absence of any explanation for the variation in the minimum quantity of drugs, it is difficult to find a rationale for the basis of this standard. Moreover, the Act under Article 8 considers addicts as criminals while Article 27 regards them as patients. The contradictory nature of the legislation increases the possibility of malpractice and defeats the very purpose of the Act.

Under the Act, Gazetted Officers of the concerned departments and law enforcement agencies were granted authority to enforce the drug laws. These officers were authorized to search public places at any time and arrest drug offenders with or without warrant.[184] To coordinate their activities the Central government in March 1986 created the Narcotics Control Bureau (NCB), a division of the Department of Revenue under the Ministry Finance. The NCB acts as a coordinating authority for anti-narcotics activities amongst the Directorate of Revenue Intelligence (DRI), the Central Bureau of Investigation (CBI), the Border Security Force (BSF), the Indian Customs Service (ICS) and the Police Department. Despite their managerial authority, the NCB's role in the anti-drug war is far from satisfactory.

Corrupt officials within the enforcement agencies obstructed the proper implementation of anti-drug laws. There are reports that smugglers bribe higher authorities to withdraw honest officers from strategically important border districts. An unofficial report indicated that police and civil officials bribed corrupt bosses for postings to Moreh in Manipur and other transit points in the northeast to make money from the contraband trafficking.[185] Once posted, they abuse the anti-drug laws by grabbing black money from traffickers. In 1993, *Down to Earth* maintained that the mammoth amount of cash involved in the drug trade was 'controlling and regulating [administrative] machinery at every stage'.[186] A study by Bhim Sain indicated that on charge of peddling illicit drugs two police constables had been arrested from Greater Kailash in Delhi in July 1986.[187] In January 1988, two police constables were again arrested in Delhi on a charge of drug trafficking. During the same month, an ex-Superintendent of Customs was arrested in Bombay while trying to smuggle Mandrax tablets worth Rs3 million to Zambia. Another report in 1996 indicated that, defying the NDPSA, some employees in the foreign mail service of the postal department were part of a 'new conduit' for trafficking heroin and hashish overseas.[188] Widespread corruption amongst government officials and misuse of NDPSA by members of enforcement agencies has largely boosted the spread of drug addiction within the country.

Due to weaknesses in enforcing compliance, the rate of drug addiction in India was on the rise. Surveying the situation in Bombay, the Indian drug specialist Dr Yusouf Merchant indicated that an alarming proportion of young people were drug addicts, of whom 80 per cent were slum-dwellers. A report in 1991 estimated that there were 10,000 youth addicts in Mandsaur district, because 'smack' or 'brown sugar' was readily available to them.[189] In January 1997, *India Today* reported that the number of 'junkies' in Mandsaur had reached 40,000. In Neemuch in Madhya Pradesh there are about 2,500 heroin addicts. Another report from Indore claimed that 25 per cent of the population of Madhya Pradesh were drug addicts[190] – this figure presumably included liquor addicts. Drug addiction has also become alarming in Ghazipur district in UP during recent years. Referring to local *Lok Vikas Kendra* (Community Development Centres), an unofficial survey estimated that addiction amongst youth in Ghazipur surpassed 50 per cent; it is very likely that the majority of these addicts were cannabis and *bhang* users. A 1994 study conducted in the four northern states indicated that opium addicts were greatest in number in Rajasthan, in Orissa *bhang* users, in Madhya Pradesh *mahua*, *handia* or alcohol users, and in eastern UP predominantly cannabis and *bhang* users. The INCSR in 1991 estimated that the number of hardcore heroin addicts in India had reached four million. The above reports and studies clearly indicate that drug addiction was flourishing in India at an alarming rate, and the obligations of drug law towards international agreements and conventions remained largely unfulfilled.

The NDPSA, which has been a commendable achievement in the process of anti-drug legislation in India, was undermined by the recommendations of the working group appointed by the Union Welfare Ministry in 1986. Instead of suggesting ways and means for the successful implementation of the recently instituted legislation, the Group demanded reformative measures for traffickers, distributors and pushers of illicit drugs. As a result of the lenient view taken by the Welfare Ministry, the Courts released many of the arrested persons on bail. Statistics show that after the adoption of new laws, the total number of arrests on drug offences throughout India rose during 1985–6, but declined in 1987.[191] A survey of court cases for 1988 noted that 'roughly two-thirds of arrested traffickers were released on bail despite a history of skipping bail', and that judges were also 'allegedly bribed to classify traffickers as addicts'.[192] As a result of this confusion in the NDPSA, the enforcement authorities failed to apprehend inter-state traffickers. So far, drug offenders have been freed on bail, and only a few were handed over by the legal agencies to the Court for further investigation and trial.

The Preventive Detention Act of 1988

With the aim of impressing the CND and other UN anti-narcotics bodies, stringent provisions for dealing with drug traffickers were incorporated in the Preventive Detention Act of 1988. Under the perseverance of the International Conference on Drug Abuse and Illicit Trafficking held in Vienna in June 1987, the Indian Government came under pressure to further modify its laws on drug traffickers. There was also a growing concern amongst social workers in India due to a rise in drug trafficking. In April 1988, the Indian *Lok Sabha* debated the nexus between powerful leaders and the drug traffickers in Rajasthan and Madhya Pradesh.[193] In an attempt to alleviate the domestic pressure and international demand, the President of India in July 1988 proclaimed a Detention Ordinance combating the ruling drug traffickers. Following the adoption of the Ordinance, the law enforcement agencies immediately detained 134 traffickers, of whom 15 were ringleaders of the drug trade and 19 foreign agents.[194] After this initial test, the Detention Ordinance was enacted as the Prevention of Illicit Traffic in Narcotic Drugs and Psychotropic Substances (PITNDPS) Act, in September 1988.

In order to halt drug traffickers, the PITNDPS Act provides for the detention of persons involved in drug trafficking. Under the Act, officers of the central government with the rank of Joint Secretary or above and the Secretary of the state government are authorized to issue detention orders to persons engaged in organized drug trafficking for a maximum of one year.[195] Despite the legal attempts, the patronization of drug trafficking by some political leaders hindered the implementation of PITNDPS in the subsequent years. The connection between some political leaders and drug traffickers was evident in Gujarat. In 1991, Bhim Sain maintained that because of their personal involvement some MLAs and MPs opposed the application of anti-drug laws in the area.[196] Allegations were brought against the then Chief Minister of Madhya Pradesh, Sunderlal Patwa, for his shady links with drug traffickers, and for providing them with political shelter and protection. A Bangladeshi columnist also made allegations against Sharad Pawar, the then Chief Minister of Maharahstra, for his involvement with prominent drug cartel leaders in Bombay.[197] The writer did not provide any evidence in support of his assertion. However, following the adoption of the PITNDPS Act, the traffickers–politician nexus has continued to undermine the toughness of anti-drug legislation.

The PITNDPS Act also gives elite officials the authority to arrest suspected offenders engaged in drug trafficking in 'highly vulnerable' areas (for example, international airports, sea ports, international borders with other countries) and to hold them for up to two years under detention. A general lack of coordination amongst the law enforcement agencies regarding the provision for 'search and seizure' and 'arrest', as incorporated in Article 42 of the NDPSA, complicated the process. Laxity of important formalities, and inefficiency amongst officials, allowed many genuine offenders to be released by the courts. A north Indian newspaper in 1996 claimed that an 'inefficient police department' in almost 90 per cent of cases was applying short-term punishments only to addicts and petty peddlers.[198] In many cases arrests were made without any evidence, while the law requires at least two witnesses. There was also evidence that in Bombay police used false witnesses in many cases. Due to lack of witnesses, many accused persons managed to get bail because of legal loopholes in the NDPSA.

Given the above complications, the NCB failed in 1995 to establish any legal case against Memon, an alleged drug criminal otherwise known as 'Tiger' Memon, whose so-called 'mandrax empire' reached from South Asia to West Asia and South Africa. Memon was arrested by Interpol in London in 1995, but was subsequently freed due to lack of evidence. Referring to the limited application of the Act, a former director general of the NCB admitted that the conviction rate in NDPSA cases was only 33 per cent. Due to problems with collection of evidence and the persistence of looseness in the judicial process, most suspected offenders were freed during the first half of the 1990s. In an attempt to accelerate the effectiveness of the PITNDPS, the Indian Government in 1996 amended Article 10 of the Act and increased the detention period to a maximum three-year period.[199] Similar to other recent anti-drug legislation, the amendment was conducted as a sign of India's willingness to cooperate with international bodies.

The NDPS (Amendment) Act of 1989

In an immediate response to the UN Convention against Illicit Traffic in Narcotic Drugs and Psychotropic Substances in 1988, the Indian Government passed The Narcotic Drugs and Psychotropic Substances (Amendment) Act of 1989. These new laws provided for tougher bail provisions, the death penalty for a second offence and forfeiture of property derived from or used in illicit traffic. Under the amendments to the NDPSA, bail was made an exception replacing the existing general rule. It allows no bail to an accused that has received a 5-year or more mandatory sentence for possession of illicit narcotic drugs and psychotropic substances.[200] The law now restricts the granting of bail to the Sessions Court and above, which hears the prosecution's arguments and justifies all bail orders before releasing the accused.

Despite the adoption of tougher bail provisions under the NDPS (Amendment) Act, the Indian Courts have not demonstrated an ability to apply the law effectively. Referring to a survey of Court cases for 1988, the US Subcommittee on Crime noted that 'roughly two-thirds of arrested traffickers were released on bail despite a history of skipping bail', and that 'judges were also bribed to classify traffickers as addicts'.[201] Producing a 'one-line bail order' to a reporter, a senior Indian Narcotics Control Bureau (NCB) official claimed that the judgment did not explain the reasons for granting bail. The enforcement of anti-drug laws has remained minimal due to the arbitrary decisions of judges. Reports from various sources indicate that the Session Court judges often adopt a generous attitude in granting bail because of the serious human consequences of a narcotics case. In a judgment in 1991, S.M. Daud of Bombay High Court noted:

> Once bail is denied he [the accused] has to languish in jail for several years as experience shows that trials do not take place for at least a couple of years. The consequences are indeed serious.[202]

Taking advantage of the bail provisions incorporated in Article 37 of the NDPSA, most of the lower court judges consistently follow the traditional maxim of 'bail, not jail'. When a case comes up for hearing, the courts take a lenient view and in many cases lets accused persons go free on 'minor technical grounds', instead of sentencing them to 10 years – the minimum punishment under the NDPSA. In a contrasting report, the United Nations Drug Control Programme (UNDCP) in May 1994 maintained that due to 'intensive competition between enforcement agencies,' the NCB had lost its credibility as a managing authority. Incomplete paperwork by law enforcement agencies in a complicated investigation process also adds to the malfunctioning of the stringent anti-drug laws in India.

In order to combat leading drug dealers, the NDPS (Amendment) Act approved the death sentence for a second large-scale offence involving specified quantities of certain drugs. Aimed at controlling bigger drug crimes, the law exempts the death penalty from presidential pardon except where the sentence is given for small quantities possessed by addicts.[203] In an attempt to control money laundering, which is often conducted by the drug syndicates, the NDPS (Amendment) Act expands asset forfeiture legislation in India. The adoption of this law was greatly influenced by the regulations of the 1961 Convention and the provisions of the 1971 Convention. In order to enable the enforcement agencies to cooperate with Interpol and the Customs Cooperation Council, the Indian Government in 1989 extended the existing anti-smuggling laws.[204] The new law provides authority to the Court to freeze the assets of an offender who has been convicted of a drug offence either in India or abroad. The legislation applies to criminals who had been charged with a drug offence and detained for a five-year period or more under the PITNDPS Act, 1988.[205] Thus, property acquired through drug trafficking up to six years prior to the date of apprehension or held in the name of relatives or associates now comes under confiscation. A conviction for money laundering abroad also counts as a first major offence in India. In accordance with this legislation, deposits or property of convicted offenders held in Swiss Banks or outside India also became liable to seizure.

Compared to the stern US forfeiture laws, Indian legislation is more open and obscure. Under the US laws, if there are genuine doubts about an individual's involvement in drug trafficking, criminal agencies take information from the Internal Revenue Service (IRS). If there are any irregularities in the known income and expenditure levels, most of the assets are immediately frozen, requiring the person to justify any claim that the income is not connected with the narcotics trade. This legislation is aimed at controlling the gravity of crime. By contrast, the Indian legislation is unable to control drug cartels and trafficking groups that are organized and structured to function efficiently both within the national economy, and at the international level. Before freezing someone's assets, the government has to wait for the conviction of the offender either under the law of the land or by a foreign government, which is not very easy in the Indian context. These laws are inadequate to deal with the 'sophisticated *havala* system and electronic transactions' that resulted from the economic liberalization in 1993–4.[206] Defective banking regulations and liberal policies governing corporations and the stock market are contrary to the NDPS Amendment Act, and help promote such transactions.

The NDPS (Amendment) Act exempts an addict who voluntarily agrees to undergo medical treatment at a place recognized by the government provided it is a first offence. As a result of this rehabilitation policy the budget allocation of the central Welfare Ministry shot up from Rs3.4 million in 1985–6 to Rs54.5 million in 1989–90. To avoid direct involvement, the Ministry of Welfare in 1990 delegated the responsibility to 86 counselling centres, 24 de-addiction centres and 5 after-care service centres. In 1996, *The Nation* claimed that despite the enormous funds provided by the WHO, the Indian Government has failed to set up specialized detoxification centres in Madhya Pradesh. The report further indicated that, except for some counselling and treatment centres run by the Red Cross, initiatives from central government were rare. To create adequate medical facilities and to develop specialized services, Indian health authorities were urging more financial help for drug addicts, and requesting supplies of Neltrexone, the only effective medicine used in de-addiction, which is hard to obtain in the Indian market. Another recent report from the Punjab shows that a claim by the state government for Rs57.5 million for the construction of de-addiction hospitals and community health centres was not met by the central government.[207] The above reports indicate that the Indian Government was either reluctant or unable to meet the growing demands for adequate rehabilitation facilities needed by the drug addicts in India. Although the Act allows addict offenders the chance of rehabilitation, it provides an opportunity for offenders to exploit mercy on technical grounds.

Despite the enactment of the PITNDPS Act and NDPS (Amendment) Act, the operators, organizers and financiers of the drug trade remained hidden and were rarely caught under legal provisions. In most cases, the law enforcement agencies arrested only carriers and peddlers, and presented them either as the members of the Pakistani drug cartel or Bombay 'Muslim drug mafias'. This factional treatment of drug laws largely ignored the domestic production of illicit drugs and psychotropic substances, and illegal supplies from Burma and Nepal. Consequently, over 200 metric tons of heroin and hashish of local and cross-border origin leave India annually. Of this total amount, India's domestic production could be at least 25 per cent. Through the impersonal use of drug laws, the application of recently introduced property seizure laws, and a sharpening of the investigative machinery, India could maximize its control over trans border drug traffickers. To make the existing legislation a success, enforcement agencies should be given special orientation and training on the formalities of the legal system.

The foregoing discussion also reveals that recent anti-drug laws have failed to prevent Indian poppy growers from dealing with traffickers. Under international pressure, the Indian Government in the late 1980s adopted strict legislation on drugs. In early 1997, at an international conference on global drug laws in New Delhi, Prime Minister H.D. Deve Gowda unveiled another amendment of the NDPS Act providing 'graded punishment for graded quantities of drugs', and laws permitting the tracing of properties acquired by traffickers.[208] However, due to lack of political will on the part of the governing elite, as well as the existence of an attachment between smugglers and some politicians, the implementation of these laws has been minimal. Corruption amongst the enforcement authorities has been another major impediment in the implementation of anti-drug laws in India. Sometimes seizures of outlawed drugs are made purely for purposes of official publicity, but these symbolic seizures are only a fraction of the total contraband trade. In most of the seizure cases, drug couriers are arrested to demonstrate the Pakistani connection, while the leaders of the Indian drug trade remain safe and untouched.

As a result of the prevalence of underhand connections and duplicity, the government's deterrent policies on harmful drugs are losing credibility amongst criminals and in international forums. To combat the resurgence in the contraband drug trade in India, international pressure is essential, as happened in the early twentieth century in opposition to the British opium trade. Immense international pressure could encourage India and other drug producing countries in the region who presently vacillate in their implementation of strict drug laws.

5
Pakistani Dilemmas, 1947–97

The fruitless attempts of the Pakistani leaders to revive the licit opium industry, coupled with the geo-strategic changes in southwest Asia at the beginning of the 1980s, eventually helped the rise of illicit production and transit trafficking of heroin in Pakistan. For revenue purposes, Pakistan retained the century-old drug laws that facilitated the illicit production of opium poppy by *Pathan* cultivators. In 1975, the adoption of Islamic prohibitions by Prime Minister Zulfikar Ali Bhutto produced a form of political mockery. The continuance of a similar policy by General Zia at the beginning of political instability in southwest Asia, failed to control the domestic abuse of drugs.

As a result of the so-called *Saur* (April) Revolution in Afghanistan and the Islamic Revolution in Iran, Pakistan became connected more than ever with the underworld drug trade. The artificial division of the subcontinent in 1947 extended Pakistan territorial disputes with Afghanistan and India. Pakistan's security became vulnerable as a result of the Soviet presence in Afghanistan in December 1979. In an attempt to promote its security interests in southwest Asia, the US government turned a blind eye to strategic use of drug money by some army personnel in Pakistan and by bosses of the Afghan *mujahedin*. I argue that the US government's Cold War strategies in Afghanistan completely ignored the threat posed by a flourishing illicit drug trade in the region. During the post-Cold War era political compromise and coalition with known traffickers, by both Prime Minister Benazir Bhutto and Prime Minister Nawaz Sharif, has further polluted Pakistan's democratic institutions.

Colonial legacies

In 1995, LaMond Tullis wrote

> In 1947 Pakistan became independent and began to license opium production just as had the British. Revenue was a motivator; the British had taught their subjects well. Production and consumption expanded.[1]

Tullis did not provide any explanation for his remark. The following discussion attempts to explain the influence of colonial drug policies in Pakistan during the post-independence era. With independence, Pakistan inherited an official excise system for the distribution of opium and cannabis amongst customers and addicts. Largely to earn revenue by supplying drugs to the population, the government attempted to establish its own opium industry, using a model originally developed by the colonial authorities in Bengal in 1773. Alongside the limited quantity of licit production, illegal cultivation of opium poppies continued in the politically unbridled tribal areas of NWFP and Baluchistan. The Pakistan government also lacked the political will to implement international conventions and agreements on the abuse of drugs. This obstinacy gave rise to an increase in illegal production, smuggling and consumption of drugs in Pakistan by the early 1980s.

Colonial excise policy

Instead of stamping out the use of drugs in accordance with the international regulations, Pakistani leaders during the late 1940s embraced the 'gradual reduction' policy of the colonial authorities for appropriating revenue from intoxicants. An official pronounce-ment was made at a joint conference in Lahore in April 1948, when the central and provincial/state governments expressed their determination to maintain the policies of the foregoing government for at least 15 years.

Given its financial stagnancy, the Pakistan government did not alter the major colonial narcotics laws, including the Punjab Excise Act of 1914, and its subsequent amendments in the 1920s and 1930s. Under these Acts,[2] the post-independence government issued some 330 licences for opium and *chandu* shops throughout the country.

Compared to the dispersal of 1,000 licences in the Northwest Provinces in 1892–3, the figure was progressively reduced. Under the Opium Act of 1878, the Pakistan government allowed vendors to receive supplies from government treasury for legal distribution to habitual users, as well as to *Hakims* and *Kabiraj* for *Tibbi* (medicine introduced by Arab physicians) or *Unani* treatment.[3] Following the regulations of the Dangerous Drugs Act of 1930, vendors were authorized to sell a maximum one kilo of licit opium to *Hakims* and registered addicts at a time.

Until the late 1950s, the Pakistani leaders had failed to replace colonial drug laws in line with international conventions. In 1948, Pakistan ratified the UN Protocol of 1946 and promised the eradication of drugs of addiction under international conventions and agreements of 1912, 1925 and 1931.[4] Due to political instability and a lack of consensus on fundamental issues, the Pakistani authorities failed to devise effective measures to meet these international demands. Instead, the Sind government in April 1949 abandoned the prohibition policy,[5] while the Punjab government in September introduced the Punjab Prohibition and Restriction of Liquor Rules, 1949.[6] As in post-independence India, contradiction and confusion prevailed in the implementation of a prohibition policy in Pakistan. In 1953 Pakistan became a party to the UN Protocol of 1953, and the central government suggested that the provincial authorities in Sind, Baluchistan and NWFP, including the princely states and tribal areas, introduce provisions restricting opium smoking and eating.[7] However, the dissolution of the Constituent Assembly by Governor General Ghulam Mohammad in October 1954 facilitated a reversal of this policy. Applying the Opium Act of 1878, the Pakistan government adopted the West Pakistan Opium Rules of 1956, and authorized the licensed vendors to distribute a limited amount of excise opium or poppy capsules to any individual. Having been involved in a long battle over constitutional arrangements, the civilian governments failed to frame drug laws in line with the international conventions and agreements on narcotics.

Nevertheless, to accord with the international regulations of the 1920s and 1930s, the Martial Law authorities in Pakistan adopted the West Pakistan Dangerous Drugs Rules of 1958. The Ayub regime restricted the sale of opium and hemp on condition that the consumer had a medical prescription from an approved medical practitioner.[8]

In 1959, the government established the first Narcotics Board, which had been initially suggested by the League of Nations in 1931. Under the influence of the Geneva Protocol of 1925, the government also adopted the West Pakistan Prohibition of Opium Smoking Ordinance of 1960. The penalty under the current laws was stricter than the Bengal Opium Smoking Act of 1932, as two years' 'rigorous imprisonment' or a Rs2,000 fine, or both, was imposed for opium smoking. While the earlier laws generally restricted opium smoking to groups or in assemblies, the new law prohibited opium smoking in all situations. The Ayub regime, as part of the 1962 Constitution, adopted policies to halt the consumption of dangerous drugs for non-medicinal purposes.[9] In an attempt to further regulate the external trade in drugs, the Ayub regime adopted the Dangerous Drugs (Import, Export and Transshipment) Rules of 1967.[10] Following the dismemberment of East Pakistan in 1971, Prime Minister Zulfikar Ali Bhutto reversed the anti-drug policies pursued by the Ayub regime during the early 1970s.

To help reconstruct the war-torn economy and the shattered defence system, the Bhutto regime renovated the excise policies of the colonial authorities. For revenue purposes, it loosened control on the consumption of intoxicating drugs. However, considering the alarming proportions of *charas* addiction, which was already posing a substantial threat to society, the regime pursued a hard-line policy on its consumption. The government disdained the recommendations of the newly organized Narcotics Control Board (PNCB) for the abolition of licensed opium shops, which under-cover were distributing unauthorized drugs to the consumers.[11] In violation of the Articles of the 1973 Constitution related to drugs,[12] the government pursued a pro-revenue policy and granted authority to the provincial legislatures to levy on alcohol, opium or other intoxicants. Through this measure, the Bhutto regime revived the excise Acts of the early 1900s, which had allowed Bengal, Punjab and other provinces to contribute substantial earnings to the British Finance Department.

Taking a lead from this pro-revenue action, the government of Sind under the Sind *Abkari* Act of 1973 increased the punishment for unlawful trade and possession of intoxicants from 2 to 7 years, and increased the fines from Rs2,000 to Rs100,000. The Sind government, at the same time, distributed nearly 200 licences for liquor shops in Karachi, Hyderabad and Khairpur divisions by the end of the year.[13] The legislation in Sind was subsequently duplicated in Punjab, Baluchistan and NWFP. Distribution of excise opium, cannabis, *bhang* and other derivatives to addicts became permissible by either licensed vendors or government officials. As a result of the new excise policy, the use of excise opium in 1975 jumped to more than twice what it had been a decade earlier. In the absence of strict regulations, the administration relied on the general provisions of the colonial laws to derive revenue. Given the weaknesses of government policies, the courts were lenient in their action on narcotics cases. A study by Ch. Abdul Wahid maintained that out of a total number of 2,060 cases detected in 1975 in Punjab Province, about 23 per cent were ordered to pay small fines, and 20 per cent were sentenced to short-term imprisonment.[14] In most cases, the courts blamed the enforcement agencies for loopholes in their investigative and prosecution procedures.

This bewilderment in the implementation of drug laws contributed to the rise in the consumption level of intoxicants. A survey in 1976, jointly conducted by the PNCB and WHO, indicated that as a result of the government's policy the annual demand for excise opium in Pakistan rose to about 150 metric tons and another 70 metric tons for *Tibbi* or *Unani* medicine.[15] In addition to that the Sind government alone received almost Rs100 million per year as excise revenue from bars and nightclubs in Karachi immediately before the fall of the Bhutto regime.[16] In the big cities, licensed shops that were auctioned annually by the provincial governments were also earning handsome money distributing intoxicants. As a result of the government's pro-earnings excise policy, the abuse of intoxicating drugs grew gradually during the Bhutto period. Under the perception that drug addiction was an 'American disease', the Bhutto regime was supposedly unwilling to address the problem potently.[17] Like the colonial authorities in the previous century, the government regarded drug addiction as a lesser threat to the indigenous population.

The unrestrained selling of drugs by licensed vendors, and psychotropic substances by pharmacists, both contributed to the upsurge of drug addiction in the country. A 1975 Pakistani study by Ijaz Haider indicated that there was a gradual increase in the hospital admission rate of drug addicts from 2.6 per cent in 1968 to

18.9 per cent in July 1975 in a Mental Hospital in Lahore.[18] In another study guided by the WHO in 1975 it was observed that amongst 71 drug addicts 76 per cent were *charas* users, while 24 per cent used *bhang*.[19] In 1977, a 'Sample Survey' conducted in Sukkar district of Sind indicated that 73 per cent of drug users were dependent on *charas* and the rest were taking opium and *bhang*.[20] Thus, reports and studies conducted by both local and foreign analysts indicated that the problem of drug addiction was on the rise, while the use of *charas* was widespread throughout the country. The increase of drug addiction in the 1970s was closely linked to the bungled attempts of the Pakistani authorities to promote the licit opium industry.

The licit opium industry

As in India, the post-independence government in Pakistan was striving to set up its own licit opium industry to energize a model established by the colonial authorities in Bengal in the 1770s. Under the partition plan, India inherited all the principal poppy growing areas while Pakistan emerged without any opium industry of its own. Due to the establishment of a hemp monopoly, poppy cultivation had been withdrawn in Bengal proper in 1839, and the major licit source in these areas was official opium supplied from Patna and Ghazipur factories in India. The licensed vendors also distributed Kashmiri opium in the Punjab, Baluchistan and in NWFP to discourage the unauthorized supply from Afghanistan.[21] Following independence, the Pakistan government reached a temporary deal with India to buy licit opium for medicinal and recreational use. However, due to conflict and tension over Kashmir, the prospect of regular shipments of opium from India became uncertain.

In order to meet the *Hakimi* and non-medicinal opium needs in the country, the Pakistan government initiated a system of poppy cultivation in the Punjab where a limited quantity of poppy had traditionally been grown. Under the Opium Act of 1857, the Pakistan government attempted official poppy cultivation in an organizational set-up similar to the Indian model. In line with the licensed poppy cultivation system in the pre-partition Punjab, the government in 1948 made an initial experiment in Montgomery District. Nineteenth-century evidence suggests that the average annual production of opium in the united Punjab during the late 1880s had been about 65 metric tons.[22]

However, as a result of administrative mismanagement, poor quality of seed, and lack of interest amongst the cooperative farmers, the Pakistani test crop failed.[23] In 1949, the Pakistan government doubled the area under poppy cultivation to about 333 hectares and the total opium production reached 237 kilos, compared to only 30 kilos in the previous year. In 1950, the production increased to 732 kilos from 397 hectares of crop. Although poppy cultivation in the Punjab was partly under colonial administration, the Pakistan government failed repeatedly to achieve its goal of opium production.

After inaugural experiments, the Pakistan government in 1951 shifted cultivation areas from Punjab to the Mardan district of NWFP, and Rahimyarkhan in the State of Bahawalpur. Cultivation in Rahimyarkhan failed totally, while the per hectare yield in Mardan district ranged between 17 and 60 kilos.[24] Heartened by the production rate in the NWFP, the government in 1952 brought 306 hectares under poppy cultivation that produced 4.6 metric tons of opium. This quantity met only a quarter of Pakistan's total lawful demand for excise and quasi-medicinal opium. In October 1953, official cultivation increased to 810 hectares and the government was able to procure only 7 metric tons of opium from the licit industry. To meet an expanding demand in local consumption, the Pakistani authorities purchased opium from Afghanistan and illegal sources from the NWFP (see Map 3).

Given the arrangements, the Pakistan government pursued a hesitant policy in implementing the major conventions and thereby limiting areas of poppy cultivation. To achieve a 'phenomenal [increase in] foreign exchange' from the opium trade, just as the British had done, the Bhutto regime in 1973 rejected the proposal of the Narcotics Control Board (PNCB) to quit poppy cultivation.[25] In a study in 1977, Sahibzada Rauf Ali, Chairman of the Pakistan Narcotics Control Board, maintained the Pakistani official position. To dissuade the Pakistani leaders from opium production, the US government during the early 1970s offered financial aid to Pakistan to introduce alternative cash crops instead of opium poppies. Under US pressure, Turkey in December 1972 banned poppy cultivation, but Pakistan failed to follow suit until the late 1970s. By 1975, the total area under official poppy cultivation had reached 1,000 hectares, and cultivation was restricted to Swat, Hazara and Parachinar districts in NWFP.[26] The Pakistani authorities

Map 3   Pakistan: drug culture and trafficking channels

maintained that in order to deter illegal supply from the tribal areas of NWFP and Afghanistan, official poppy cultivation was a necessity.

In their efforts to revive the opium industry, the Pakistani authorities utilized the colonial practice. Under the Opium Act of 1857, cultivators were bound to surrender all their raw opium and poppy capsules to the government at a fixed rate. To process the official opium, the Pakistan government in 1950 set up a factory in Lahore that was administered by the Excise and Taxation

Department of the Punjab government. The expertise of Muslim officers and employees, who had experience in the Opium Department in India, and had opted for Pakistani citizenship, was applied in running the industry. The opium factory was the single government agency which received, stored and processed raw opium from licit sources, and issued excise opium to the government treasuries from where the licensed vendors obtained their requisite amounts. The Pakistani authorities asserted that the security system in the opium industry was operated under the Single Convention on Narcotic Drugs of 1961. No matter how efficiently the Opium Industry was run, illegal supplies of drugs continued from the tribal *Pathan* areas and cross-border sources, undermining the official policy of deterrence adopted by the central authorities in the early 1960s.

Pathan poppy culture

The origins of present-day poppy farming in southwest Asia, as I discussed in Chapter 1, go back to the millennium before last. The truth of this was demonstrated in May 1993 when a group of 'fully armed' *Pathan* poppy growers, in Nehag Valley of Sultankhel district, declared to a visiting press delegation from Islamabad that:

> We are growing this [poppy] crop for ages. … We will fight till the last, if government forces try to destroy our standing crops, without giving us an alternative means of livelihood.[27]

Similar tribal avowals, from time to time, challenged the territorial integrity of the country and prevented the Pakistani authorities from ratifying the Convention on Psychotropic Substances of 1971 and the Protocol of 1972. Thus, the origin of the Pakistani poppy dilemma goes back to the partition plan in 1947, when poppy enriched tribal areas of the NWFP, as a legacy of the colonial rule, were merged with Pakistan.

British strategic interests in the northwest frontier had initially developed during the early nineteenth century to control the overland drug route used by the tribal *Pathans* from southwest Asia to China. *Narcotics Control Digest* claims that opium trafficking in NWFP was 'first encouraged by British merchants who bought the sticky black opium gum for sale to China'.[28] Unaware of this assertion, some scholars and historians in their work traditionally maintain that in order to block Russian expansion towards the southeast, the British government created a buffer zone along the tribal areas between Pakistan and Afghanistan. These sources generally ignore the strategic importance of the mountainous areas, which have excellent climatic conditions for poppy cultivation.

As a result of its fitness for poppy growing and the strategic importance of the site as part of the traditional Silk Road, the NWFP became flash point between the Amir of Afghanistan and the government of British India. Nineteenth-century evidence from Hurst indicates that 'a small trade in the drug' existed between the northwestern areas of India and China, 'through the passes of the Himalayan Mountains'.[29] In his book, *The Frontier 1839–1947: The Story of the North-West Frontier of India,* Major-General J.G. Elliot, who took part in the Afghan campaign during the early twentieth century, maintains that as part of a strategy to eventually obtain control over the traditional Silk Road linking China, the British government seized areas from Afghanistan.[30] In 1954, another study by A.E. Wright, a former British Civil Servant who later became a senior bureaucrat in the Pakistan Finance Ministry, asserted that an 'opium road' existed in the previous century from India through the Sinkiang region in China.[31] It is plausible that the tribal *Pathans* passed a portion of their medicinal opium through Sinkiang region into China.

Aiming at establishing control over the mountain paths into southwest China, the British government launched its first military offensive against Afghanistan during the late 1830s. In 1856, Major-General R. Alexander held that the Indo-China opium trade rose sharply from 127 metric tons (2,000 chests) in 1800 to 446 metric tons (7,000 chests) in 1821, and 2,485 metric tons (39,000 chests) in 1837.[32] Given this dramatic rise in the contraband trade, the Chinese government in 1837 exerted vigorous pressure and issued orders and proclamations that the offenders be punished with the utmost harshness. An 1857 study by Matheson indicates that, against strong resistance, some British merchants between 1837 and 1838 smuggled opium into seaports in Canton, Whampoa, Macao and Hong Kong.[33] This led to serious collisions and convulsions for opium traders from India. The physical barrier in the Chinese Sea ports in the late 1930s, conspired with the First Anglo-Afghan War of 1838–42 to force the opening of an alternative overland road through the Sinkiang region into China. After suffering a rout at the hands of the Afghan *Pathans*, the British government dropped the Kabul campaign in 1842.

In an attempt to sustain the China trade in 1840–2, the British government simultaneously fought the First Opium War against China. To this arrogant act we may apply the analogy of the famous historian-diplomat Mountstuart Elphinstone: that it was the act of a 'bully' who is 'kicked in the streets' and goes home to beat his wife in retaliation. In order for Britian to maintain its military morale and to keep control over the sea route to China, the Opium War became a strategic necessity.

Alongside its military manoeuvring, the British government attempted to gradually extend the Bengal opium monopoly in the Hill States of Punjab, Kashmir and UP and procure finest quality opium. In 1849, the British government seized the Lahore Kingdom, an area that had been engaged in poppy cultivation under the Sikh ruler, Ranjit Singh. Contemporary evidence provided by a British employee indicated that before the annexation of the area opium was 'untaxed' in Punjab.[34] Following the invasion of Punjab a tax was imposed on opium imports from non-British territories. Elphinstone, a British emissary to Kabul in 1808, confirmed that opium poppy and *Pustu* (poppy seeds) was grown in abundance in the hilly areas of western Afghanistan. Due to demands for it as a spice amongst both the Hindus and Muslims, poppy seeds were exported to India in 'vast quantities'.[35] In 1908, the *Imperial Gazetteer of India: Afghanistan and Nepal* further indicated that some poppy cultivation had been taking place in the Herat Valley, Kabul, Kandahar and Jalalabad in Afghanistan over the previous century to produce exportable opium.[36] Largely attracted by the region's poppy culture,[37] the British government had fought a series of wars in and around Afghanistan in 1879–80. Despite the long-term campaign, Britian failed to dominate the mountain' *Pathans* or to capture their poppy growing areas. The failure of the military offensives obliged the British in November 1893 to negotiate with Amir Abdur Rahman, at Kabul, to accept the Durand Line as a peaceful demarcation line between the two territories. This peace agreement, which included the payment of an amount of money to the Afghan Amir (King) for the occupied territories of NWFP, divided the *Pathan* people into two parts: one portion fell to British India and the rest to Afghanistan.

As the unruly *Pathan* drug trade was counter-productive, the British government by the late nineteenth century pursued a policy of controlling poppy cultivation in the region. The colonial administration then imported opium by licensed vendors from Amritsar, Shikarpur and Rajanpur of the Punjab and distributed it in Dera Gazi Khan district and other surrounding areas in Baluchistan. *The Imperial Gazetteer of India, 1909* maintains that after paying a requisite fee to the government, licensed dealers were allowed to collect excise opium from Jammu and also from Jalalabad Valley for distribution in the Frontier Province.[38] Despite the official measures, illicit supply of drugs continued from the tribal areas in NWFP and Afghanistan to India and elsewhere. Evidence provided by Finlay notes that 'small quantities of illegal opium' were seized at Quetta-Peshin from tourists coming from Kandahar in Afghanistan.[39]

This cross-border trafficking continued during the early twentieth century. A League of Nations report in 1940 also indicated that *charas* was being smuggled into India from across the border 'by trans-border Pathans'.[40] Law enforcement agencies detected some cases of smuggling of *gardah charas*, inferior quality hashish, from the tribal areas in NWFP. Opium smuggling also continued from the poppy growing areas of Kaya Khabal, Amb, Sher Garh, Phulra and Gandaf situated on the border of Hazara and Mardan Districts of NWFP and the mountainous areas in Afghanistan. With independence, Pakistan inherited some of these politically unrestrained areas where unauthorized poppy cultivation and opium manufacture had been taking place from the pre-independence era.

As under the colonial rulers, the implementation of the Pakistan government's central laws on narcotics remained largely inoperative in the merged areas in NWFP and Baluchistan. At independence, Pakistani leaders inherited complex tripartite administrative arrangements: (1) the semi-autonomous princely states; (2) the centrally administered territories (the Tribal Agencies of the Northwest Frontier, and the chief commissioner's province of Baluchistan); and (3) the locally administered settled districts (the governor's province of the Northwest Frontier).[41] Despite the opposition of the *Pakhtun* leader Khan Abdul Ghaffar Khan, popularly known as the Frontier Gandhi or Bacha Khan, the NWFP was incorporated into the complex Pakistani federal structure. Due to political pressure, the Pakistan government in October 1955 endorsed autonomy for all the tribal areas including the NWFP, a special status which they had held under the British rule. Explaining the situation, Wright observes:

> In the tribal areas adjoining the North West Frontier Province of Pakistan, the ordinary law of the country did not apply, and there was no restriction on the cultivation of the poppy, for consumption or for export.[42]

The illicit opium collected from the tribal areas and across the border from Afghanistan was largely sold undercover by licensed vendors for domestic consumption. The vendors, who purchased their licences for fees ranging from Rs100,000, sold illicit opium to maximize their financial benefit after recovering their initial investment. To bring the illicit poppy cultivation in the NWFP under international regulations, the British government convinced Pakistan to sign the Single Convention on Narcotic Drugs of 1961, and to become the Vice-President of an 18-member narcotics control body.[43] However, due to its inability to enforce federal laws in the politically unbridled poppy growing areas in the NWFP, the country remained reluctant to ratify the international conventions and regulations adopted during 1971–2.[44] With the availability of raw opium and *charas* from illegal channels, the distribution by licensed vendors continued without much official interruption.

The political sensitivity of the tribal areas during the post-independence era created favourable conditions for illegal trade in narcotics. Under the Constitution of 1962, the tribal chiefs of NWFP were approved substantial power to act independently without being interfered with by the central government.[45] Recognizing the prerogatives of the tribal authorities, con-stitutional arrangements in 1973 granted 5 extra seats in the 63 member Pakistani Senate to *Maliks*. Given the political sensitivity in the region, they were provided another 3 seats in the 87-member Upper House in 1985.[46] The *Pathan Maliks*, who have close links with the poppy growers, have played a crucial role in the formation and political stability of Pakistan's coalition governments. They often refuse to accept any legal control over poppy cultivation in their territory. As a result of the weak central policy, the tribal people in 1977 grew about 200 metric tons of opium, of which one-third came from the Bunar subdivision of Swat district.[47] After the banning in 1979, about 90 per cent of illicit poppy cultivation was concentrated into Dir district and the Gadoon-Amazai sub division of Mardan district in NWFP, while 10 per cent was confined in the Khyber Agency controlled by the tribal leaders.[48] The Pakistani leaders maintain that the remote poppy growing mountainous valleys were inaccessible, and therefore out of their jurisdiction. As a result of this loose administrative arrangement, illegal cultivation of poppy and trafficking in drugs were prevalent in the strategically uncontrolled areas.

Nevertheless, the central authorities have involved the Frontier Constabulary, a loyal paramilitia force created by the colonial authorities in the early twentieth century. In the absence of federal forces, the local militias in NWFP were virtually incapable of controlling the seven million *Pathans*, of whom about 80 per cent supposedly 'survive on smuggling'.[49] In 1991, drug traffickers killed five militiamen and kidnapped seven others when they were on duty. Armed with Second World War rifles the militias were unable to compete with the modern kalashnikov rifles, submachine guns, mortars and missiles used by the traffickers. A Pakistani study in 1987 indicated that the Dir people alone owned over 70,000 Russian kalashnikov rifles, that they used to defend their poppy fields in defiance of the central government.[50] In the absence of central control, *Afridi* and *Shinwari Pathans* run heroin conversion facilities at Landi Kotal and other surrounding areas, linking NWFP with the global drug trade.[51] Thus, due to a combination of the drug and gun cultures, central control was largely inoperative in these areas during the 1980s.

The tribal areas in NWFP, which had been largely outside the jurisdiction of the central authorities during the colonial era and its aftermath, now emerged as an important centre for poppy cultivation and the manufacture of heroin. The jumble of administrative districts dating from the colonial era have provided an agreeable environment for an increase in the illicit trade in drugs. In a report from NWFP, Terence White maintains that as 'a legacy of British colonial rule', Pakistani law enforcement is inoperative in Barra, a small town about 15 kilometres south of Peshawar. The area, which enjoyed substantial liberty under British rule, remained outside the control of the central authorities during renewed power games between Pakistan and Afghanistan. As an influence of its pre-independence status, the area has become a traffickers' haven, where hashish, opium, morphine, heroin and every contraband item are available.

In recent years, the Pakistan government has been pressed by Western countries to alter the status of 'administrative autonomy' granted by the colonial authorities through special treaties with each individual ethnic group over the previous century.[52] In order to avoid any adverse political consequences, such as intentionally pushing the tribal people to ally themselves with ethnic groups on the Afghan side, the Pakistan government was reluctant to break the status quo. Besides the legacy of the colonial past, Pakistani drug policy was further complicated by the political implications of *Shariah* (Islamic law) prohibition by Prime Minister Bhutto and his successor General Zia-ul Haq during the late 1970s.

Islamic prohibition, 1977–85

The adoption of *Shariah* laws against intoxicating drugs in the late 1970s and early 1980s was largely determined by the desire of the Pakistani power elite to survive in mainstream national politics. To alleviate the mounting pressure from the *ulema* for an immediate resignation in early 1977, Prime Minister Zulfikar Ali Bhutto hastily announced laws on prohibition. He introduced the complete ban on liquor that had been demanded by the religious groups for three decades. In a military coup, General Mohammad Zia-ul Haq removed Bhutto from power and then eventually adopted the *Hadd* (Qur'anic) Ordinance to supersede the fallen Prime Minister's hurriedly adopted policy on prohibition. The *Shariah* regulations failed to control the spread of drug culture in the country. To gratify the anti-drug campaigners, General Zia in late 1983 amended the *Hadd* order and declared life imprisonment for drug traffickers. However, a lack of clarity and determination by the ruling elite facilitated the strategic use of drug money to support the war in Afghanistan and made the religious approach a political mockery. We shall examine these incidents in greater detail below.

Bhutto's political expediency

Aimed at satisfying the rival *ulema*, Prime Minister Zulfikar Ali Bhutto in March 1977 pronounced laws on prohibition in Islamic line. A struggle for the adoption of *Shariah* prohibition by the religious groups had persisted in Pakistan since independence. Between 1948 and 1954, religious forces had been striving to incorporate Islamic prohibition into the Constitution. To satisfy them, the Basic Principles Committee (BPC) Report of 1951 recommended the banning of intoxicants.[53] The First Constituent Assembly in 1954 also gave close consideration to the *ulema*, which urged that intoxicants be constitutionally prohibited within a three-year time.[54] Instead of relying on the Constituent Assembly, the government in March 1956 adopted provisions created by bureaucrats, who lacked political will to stamp out the abuse of intoxicating drugs. The Westernized forces that dominated the state machinery overran the influence of the religious leaders and stymied the adoption of strict Islamic laws on intoxicants.

In 1972, the NWFP's Chief Minister, Maulana Mufti Mahmud, for the first time introduced an unsuccessful provincial prohibition policy. As in India, an isolated prohibition program in NWFP failed to deter the illegal supply of drugs from those provinces without general prohibition. The prohibition agenda was defeated both by the pro-revenue policy of the central government, and by smugglers who made a ten-fold profit in the black market. Prime Minister Bhutto, who often expressed his liking for whisky, declared in a public meeting in Lahore that he 'drank wine – not people's blood', and thus he came under attack by the Pakistani *ulema*.[55] In expressing his fondness Bhutto ameliorated Emperor Akber, who in his modish faith found no wrong in liquor-taking and 'forced' many religious dignitaries to drink wine at the New Year's festival.[56] None the less, under the guidance of Maulana Mufti Mahmud Bhutto's un-Islamic life-style, his amorality in politics and ultra-secularism came under attack from the *ulema*. Under the banner of Pakistan National Alliance (PNA), a combination of religious political parties launched vigorous anti-Bhutto demonstrations during the mid-1970s. They created civil unrest by boycotting the provincial and Senate elections, and agitated to unseat the Prime Minister, accusing him of rigging the National Assembly elections in March 1977.

In a deceitful attempt to stay in power, Bhutto at a press conference in Lahore in April 1977 declared an immediate closure of 'bars and night clubs'. His proposal was welcomed by the loyal Chief Minister of Sind, Ghulam Mustafa Jatoi, but rejected as 'dishonest' by the PNA leaders who urged Bhutto 'to quit' his office without any delay.[57] In early May, a Prohibition Bill was passed by the parliament, which urged the rival *ulema* to help implement the policy. It forbade liquor for every Muslim citizen in Pakistan, but endorsed the provincial authorities to issue licences for foreigners and other religious minorities.[58] Maximum six months' imprisonment or a maximum penalty of Rs5,000, or both, was imposed for violations. Following this, Bhutto invited PNA leaders to join in the Islamic Ideology Council and introduce the political system of the Prophet Mohammad (*PBUH*) in the country.[59] Terming these 'dishonest proposals', the PNA leaders accused the Prime Minister of trying to divert people's observance from his electoral rigging. As a result of the massive unrest created by the PNA, General Zia captured political power on 5 July 1977, and executed Bhutto on 18 March 1978, after a judicial verdict of the Lahore High Court.

General Zia's *Shariah* approach

Identifying himself as the benevolent soldier of Islam, General Zia pursued an Islamic line on intoxicants in the late 1970s. Unlike the hypocritical attempts of the former Prime Minister, General Zia enthusiastically adopted Islamic prohibition, an approach which had never been pursued by any central government in Pakistan. Zia, who invariably avoided wine, also banned intoxicating drugs to ally himself with the powerful *ulema*. In accordance with Qur'anic laws[60] which forbade intoxicants as *haram* (unlawful, forbidden and a punishable crime), and regarded use or traffic in them as the 'act of Satan', General Zia adopted Islamic prohibition as a political stance. His prohibition laws were an elaborate version of the Punjab Prohibition Act of 1949, which was relaxed by Bhutto during the early 1970s.

The adoption of the *Hadd* Ordinance by General Zia on 10 February 1979 had a number of implications. Firstly, recommendations in favour of an Islamic approach had been made by the drug control authorities during the mid-1970s. At the 1975 National Workshop on the Prevention of Drug Abuse, a resolution was adopted condemning the 'foreign influences and pseudo-cults' that were leading Pakistani youth to drug addiction.[61] A similar observation had also been made by the Pakistan Narcotics Board in 1973 about the entry of 'human rats' (hippies from the West) who were spreading the disease of drug addiction amongst the country's younger generation.[62] Suggestions in favour of Islamic prohibition were again made at the Pakistan–Colombo Plan Workshop on Drug Abuse Prevention Education in 1977. This workshop, which was convened immediately after the assumption of political power by General Zia, urged the implementation of *Shariah* laws and the need for a greater role for religious preachers – *Khatibs*, *Mobaligians* and *Pirs* – to arouse the anti-drug conscience of the people. In his paper Mohammad Aslam Azam, Deputy Drugs Controller of the Health Division in Islamabad, emphasized that this method would be useful to handle rural addicts, who had great respect for religious leaders.[63] Influenced by the above recommendations, General Zia attempted to employ the service of the religious leaders to help free the country from intoxicating drugs.

On the birthday eve of the Holy Prophet (*Eid-e-Milad-un-Nabi*) in 1979, General Zia promulgated the Prohibition (*Hadd*) Order to mark the religious importance of the legislation. Zia argued in the National Assembly that prohibition was necessary 'to wipe out' the vice of intoxicants.[64] Zia's move was largely motivated by the need to deal with the rising drug addiction problem in Pakistan during the late 1970s.

Secondly, following the assumption of political power, the Martial Law authorities announced punishments against the manufacture and sale of intoxicants, and they opened 'round-the-clock' reporting centres in the big cities.[65] The government restricted the use of morphine and pethidine to hospitals and maternity clinics, and imposed a ban on their sale by pharmacists.[66] As a result of the banning programme, 'panic gripped the addict population', and sensational stories of death and anguish began to appear in the press, while some addicts appealed to hospitals and medical practitioners for withdrawal help.[67] Zia's initial hard-line policies were further consolidated by the *Hadd* Ordinance, and were key to establishing the legitimacy of the military regime.

Compared to Bhutto's approach, Zia's policy was modified in accordance with the injunctions of Islam as set out in the Holy Qur'an and *Sunnah*.[68] While under the abortive Prohibition Bill of 1977 the consumption of opium and hemp had been tolerated by the Bhutto regime, the *Hadd* Ordinance banned activities connected with intoxicants. Under this law, the manufacture and sale of intoxicants became punishable with a maximum of five years' imprisonment with thirty lashes, including a fine. Pakistan's ordinance on physical punishment for drug related offences was an exception amongst the South Asian countries. In Islam, the objective of this punishment is to deter, reform and prevent a person from indulging in a similar crime, rather than just inflicting physical injury or humiliation. Nevertheless, Zia revived the public floggings which had last been imposed by the Martial Law authorities in the late 1960s to suppress political opposition in former East Pakistan.

To avoid any counter-productive results, the Zia regime distributed opium tablets through the hospitals to addicts. The WHO report in 1980 observed that following the adoption the Prohibition Order, over 7,000 addicts received opium tablets from the hospitals in Punjab in one month. For better treatment, some addicts went to the Mayo Hospital in Lahore, and the Treatment, Rehabilitation and Research Centter at Lyari, in Karachi. An article published in *Dawn* in 1983 indicated that some drug peddlers prevented addicts from going to hospital because they feared disclosure of the source of illicit drugs to the enforcement agencies.[69] Organized traffickers were undermining official attempts to curb the spread of drug addiction in Pakistan. As a deterrent, the *Hadd* Order was found to be deficient to deal with the complex situation existing during the early 1980s. It also failed to adopt extensive policies in accordance with religious principles, which were only idealistically covered by the regulations.

Thirdly, Pakistan in 1947 emerged as a Muslim country and supposedly adhered to many cultural and religious institutions introduced by the Mughal rulers. Through his prohibition policy, General Zia hoped to revive the Islamic prohibition instituted by the Mughal Emperor Aurangzeb, in medieval India. Impressed by the prohibition policies of General Zia, eminent Pakistani anthropologist Akbar S. Ahmed once compared him to Aurangzeb.[70] Indulgence in liquor by the Mughal nobility as well as by commoners was widespread when Aurangzeb, the son of Emperor Shahjahan, ascended the throne during the mid-seventeenth century. In order to control this,

Emperor Aurangzeb directed Police personnel (*Kotwal*) to punish anyone who sold spirits.[71] Describing the regulations on intoxicating drugs, the European tourist Bernier wrote:

> Wine, that essential part of every entertainment, can be obtained in none of the shops at *Delhi*, although it might be made from the native grape, were not the use of that liquor prohibited equally by the *Gentile* and *Mahometan* [Mohammedan] Law. I drank some at *Ahmed-abad* and *Golkonda* in Dutch and English houses.[72]

Jadunath Sarkar argued that the Emperor ordered the administrators (*Mufitasib*) to implement the Prophet's commands 'by putting down the drinking of distilled spirits, *bhang* and other liquid intoxicants'.[73] In a similar attempt, General Zia prohibited the illegal manufacture, sale and use of intoxicating drugs. A report published in *The New York Times* in 1988 admitted that as a result of the tougher penalties in Pakistan, the consumption of 'alcohol was virtually banished'.[74] During the earlier attempt, Aurangzeb had permitted Europeans to prepare and drink liquor on condition that 'they did not sell them'.[75] In line with Aurangzeb, Zia authorized the provincial governments to issue liquor permits to foreigners and non-Muslims, but they were prohibited from consuming liquor in public places. In 1991, a current-affairs book by Christina Lamb notes that as part of its anti-drug campaign, the Zia regime expelled some diplomats for drinking liquor in public places in Islamabad.[76] Another journalistic work by Emma Duncan in 1989 suggests that during the days of strict control, some diplomatic missions in Islamabad supplied liquor at midnight using signals from car headlights.[77] Both Lamb and Duncan describe the offering of liquor in teapots in Chinese restaurants, and it being served by high officials and the business elite at home. Most of the liquor supply continued to come through tribal channels or illegal imports that were organized by corrupt officials.

To help implement the punishments for drug related offences; Zia attempted to revive the judicial institutions of the medieval *Qazis*, because analogical deduction (*Ijma*) and consensus amongst the Islamic jurists (*Qias*) has a definite role in the Islamic judicial system. While in Iran, 'Revolutionary Courts' run by the Islamic judges handled drug related cases, the institution of Islamic courts in Pakistan was delayed. A National Assembly report in 1985 indicated that due to 'certain administrative difficulties' the government was unable to set up *Qazi* courts.[78] In June 1985, *Dawn* commented that the whipping punishment of the medieval *Qazis* 'has no place in modern penal science'.[79] Secular intellectuals, who tried to undermine the *Shariah* prohibition, explored this critique. The military regime was unable either to induce the active support of religious political forces, like the *Jamiatul Ulema-i-Islami* or the ruling Muslim League, or to help motivate people in accordance with Qur'anic injunctions and laws made from the prescriptions of the sayings and practices of Prophet Mohammad (*PBUH*). For the implementation of the *Hadd* Ordinance, General Zia relied on secular-minded bureaucrats, who had blocked the introduction of Islamic prohibition in the 1950s and in many cases themselves indulged in the drinking habit.[80] Thus the Islamic prohibition declared by General Zia was confined to political rhetoric rather than the institutionalization of the *Qazis* in the enforcement of Islamic drug laws.

As a result of the above difficulties, combined with the increase of illicit poppy cultivation in the region, the consumption of drugs, especially heroin, rose during the early 1980s. Use of heroin was almost unknown in Pakistan until 1980, but its availability and abuse became widespread in subsequent years. (The trends of heroin addiction in Pakistan are discussed later in this chapter.) In 1991, a Peshawar-based physician argued that prior to official banning, addiction had been confined to alcohol or *charas*, but after the banning the abuse of heroin and psychotropic substances became widespread.[81] *Dawn* in 1983 claimed that flaws in the country's anti-drug laws had helped corrupt enforcement agencies to make extra money by conspiring with traffickers.[82] The *Hadd* ordinance failed to specify heroin and other psychotropic substances in the prohibition list, and refrained from defining the role of the narcotics laws introduced by the previous regimes. Besides this lack of clarity and absence of political determination, General Zia also failed to apply *Shariah* laws in the tribal areas.

As there was an overlap between current criminal laws and Islamic provisions, the *Shariah* prohibition failed to deter illicit supplies and abuse of intoxicants. In an attempt to arrest this, General Zia in December 1983 adopted the Prohibition (Enforcement of *Hadd*) (Amendment) Ordinance that refined the Dangerous Drugs Act of

1930, and the *Hadd* Ordinance of 1979. This amendment came about due to pressure from anti-drug campaigners, and to recommendations of the Islah-i-Muashera Committee, headed by the Federal Information Minister. In order to remove the obstruction of the existing laws, the government banned the manufacture of 'raw opium' and heroin in the country and imposed a maximum life imprisonment for the possession of 10 grams of heroin or one kilo of raw opium or its derivatives.[83] The 1983 Ordinance was extended to the tribal areas, banning the establishment of heroin laboratories in NWFP and Baluchistan.[84] It was the first central action to bring tribal offenders under the drug laws of the land.

The extension of drug laws to source areas theoretically empowered the enforcement agencies, but the application of these laws in the tribal areas was inconsistent. Due to lack of control over the merged areas, the enforcement authorities relied on the goodwill of the tribal leaders for the implementation of central laws. Following the adoption of the latest amendment order, several dozen heroin laboratories were seized in the Khyber Agency of the NWFP by the arbitrary power of the tribal authorities. The tribal chiefs helped sporadically in the seizure of heroin laboratories, but were reluctant to eradicate poppy cultivation altogether. In most cases the tribal *Maliks* favoured the poppy growers, who argued that 'to avoid death by starvation', drug money was theologically permissible (*halal*) for them.[85] In 1983, an Indian estimate indicated that the *Pathan* cultivators in the NWFP produced about 105 to 126 metric tons of opium between 1980 and 1982.[86] The 1983 Ordinance made little sense to the tribal *Pathans* who relied on poppy cultivation as a traditional livelihood. From the beginning of the Afghan crisis, drug trade in the Golden Crescent region had gone practically out of control.

Geo-strategic changes in southwest Asia

The emergence of Pakistan in underworld drug trafficking occurred largely as a result of geo strategic changes in southwest Asia at the turn of the 1970s. Pakistan involved its principal military intelligence unit, ISI, to help CIA 'covert' operations against the expansion of Soviet influence in southwest Asia. Political instability in Afghanistan in connection with the assassination of the US Ambassador Adolph Dubs in February 1979 and President Taraki in September, expedited direct

Soviet military intervention in Afghanistan in December of that year. As a result, millions of Afghan migrants took shelter in the NWFP, and the possibility of disintegration along ethnic lines increased in Pakistan. The presence of the Soviet Red Army in Afghanistan, and the Iranian Revolution in 1979, had created great concerns for US security interests in the Persian Gulf. The following discussion analyses the shady links between the geo-political changes occurring in southwest Asia during the Cold War era and the promotion of drug trade in the region.

The Afghan crisis

The moves towards the Sovietization of Afghanistan and the challenge made to the territorial integrity of Pakistan by President Nur Mohammad Taraki in 1978 caused common concerns for both Pakistan and the US. In 1947, Afghanistan had voted against the entry of Pakistan to the UN and questioned the legality of the Durand Line. In 1973, the Daoud regime extended its moral support on the *Pakhtunistan* issue with the purpose of eventually reuniting Baluchistan and the NWFP with Afghanistan. To nullify the latest threat from a pro-Soviet government in Afghanistan, Pakistan invited the US to come forward and defend non-Communist interests in Afghanistan. The political instability and the socialist reforms programme in Afghanistan were, further, in many ways conducive to the promotion of drug trade in Pakistan.

With the advent of the Soviet-backed Taraki regime in Afghanistan, Pakistani leaders at the turn of the 1970s adopted as a means to safeguard national sovereignty a defence strategy needing drug money. In an interview with Christina Lamb in Rawalpindi on 15 February 1989, General Fazle Haq, the former Governor and the Zonal Marshal Law Administrator in NWFP, maintained that he pursued Brezinski, the US National Security Adviser of the Carter Administration, to win its ideological battle in Afghanistan after its earlier messy results in Korea and Vietnam.[87] Hamidullah Amin and Gordon B. Schiltz argue that in mid-1978, the Pakistani secret agency, ISI, coordinated and organized the three Afghan *mujahedin* (Islamic militant) groups – (1) *Milli Islami Mahaz* (Pir Ahmed Gilani); (2) *Jabha Nijat-il Milli* (Sibghat Ullah Mujaddidi); (3) *Harakat-i-Islami* (Nabi Mahammadi) – to jointly oust Taraki from power.[88] This came about due to Taraki's recognition of the Baluchistan People's

Liberation Front (BPLF), and the declaration of the Pakistani *Baluch* ethnic community that they constituted a separate nation.[89] Aimed at protecting the Durand Line legality, the Afghan guerrilla war facilitated opium production and heroin processing along the international border between Pakistan and Afghanistan.

The assassination of Taraki in a military coup in mid-1979 hastened the Soviet military offensive in Afghanistan in late December. Taraki's socialist reforms programme and Afghanistan's alignment with a hostile superpower, the Soviet Union, became an essential part of US strategic considerations. A Moscow publication by Y. Volkov and his colleagues in 1980 claimed that to help oust the pro-US government of Hafizullah Amin who removed Taraki, the intrusion was vital.[90] In February 1980, speaking at a New Delhi banquet, the Soviet Foreign Minister Andrei Gromyko warned Pakistan that it would jeopardize its sovereignty if it continued acting as a 'springboard' for the US interests.[91] The appearance of an unfriendly superpower at its doorstep created grave security questions for the sovereignty and geographical integrity of Pakistan.

The political instability in Afghanistan drove three million *Pathan* refugees into Pakistan. Local *Pathans*, who had been separated politically from their Afghan counterparts by the colonial authorities during the late nineteenth century, welcomed them. This ethnic relationship was a security concern to the Pakistan government, which feared the prospect of greater cross-border solidarity amongst the *Pathans*. After the dismemberment of East Pakistan (now Bangladesh) in 1971, the Pakistani leaders perceived further threats to Pakistan's territorial integrity would come from the *Baluchis* and *Pathans*. Being hypersensitive over this issue, the Pakistani army in 1973 brutally killed thousands of *Baluch* militants and arrested Sher Mohammad Marri, a tribal leader known as 'General Sher'.[92] Selig S. Harrison maintains that Marri commanded about 20,000 guerillas, supposedly with the help of Kabul and the USSR.[93] Alfred W. McCoy argues that in an attempt to alleviate the centrifugal tendency of the minority ethnic groups, the Zia regime built the ISI into a 'powerful covert operations unit', and engaged the agency in providing total support for the Afghan resistance war.[94] Unlike Iran, which extended only humanitarian support to the one million Afghan refugees in its territory, Pakistan provided both military and humanitarian assistance, and allowed *mujahedins* to operate about 300 camps in NWFP, as their base for insurgency across the border. Remember that in addition to its military involvement on the western front, Pakistan was also confronting a threat in the east from its traditional enemy, India.

Given the fragility of its national security, the Pakistan government was desperately looking for viable sources to help finance its defence strategies. In early 1980 Pakistan was offered by the Carter administration $400 million in military assistance, which was rejected by General Zia as 'peanuts'. Before a $3 billion military aid package was made available by the Reagan administration, some of the rich Afghan migrants invested money in poppy cultivation for 'hard currency' to be used in an effort to eventually expel the Soviet Army from Afghanistan.[95] Many of the Afghan refugees were traditional poppy farmers in the country's eastern poppy-enriched areas. Encouraged by the absence of central laws the immigrant *Pathans*, in collaboration with locals, started poppy cultivation in NWFP and along the 1,400-kilometre border between Afghanistan and Pakistan. In response to this, the Pakistan government in February 1979 abandoned its long-cherished opium industry and banned poppy cultivation.

But, the banning of poppy cultivation aside, there is hardly any evidence available that the Pakistan government tried to impede the new development in the Afghan drug trade. Referring to a Pakistani news report, *The Hindustan Times* claimed that with the rise of the Afghan crisis 'a foreign trained adviser' had suggested to General Zia that he use drug money for meeting the military challenge.[96] This unnamed counselor was presumably General Fazle Haq, whose role in the Pakistani drug trade I shall discuss later. The *Review of United States Narcotics Control Efforts in the Middle East and South Asia* indicates that *Pathan* cultivators in 1979 engaged about 32,600 hectares in poppy cultivation and produced about 800 metric tons of illicit opium.[97] This rise in opium production helped facilitate *de facto* status for the drug trade in the region and in the strategic use of drug money during the Afghan battle.

Nevertheless, the promotion of poppy cultivation in NWFP coincided with a sharp rise in international demand for both medicinal and non-medicinal opium. A demand was created in the international black market for opium as a result of a drought in the Golden Triangle region in 1977–9.[98] On 1 April 1979, Iran banned poppy cultivation in an attempt to control the illicit trade and abuse of opium in the country. The prohibition of poppy cultivation by Iran, a traditional poppy growing country in southwest Asia, had a profound impact on the illicit market. The legal sanction in Iran and the crop failure in Burma provided an impetus to the international drug syndicates to become involved in illicit production in Pakistan and Afghanistan. The absence of legal controls, coinciding with the political instability in the region, attracted Western drug cartels and 'scientists' to establish heroin processing facilities in the tribal belt, without any fear of being locked up by Islamabad.[99] The Soviet army's blocking of the traditional Silk Route that passed through Afghanistan, the Central Asian republics and Yugoslavia, also influenced international drug syndicates to use conversion facilities in NWFP and Pakistani exit points to overseas destinations. Given these preconditions, some 'fortune-seekers' from Europe and the US paid visits to the tribal areas in the late 1970s and helped the locals to set up clandestine laboratories. The tribal *Pathans*, who had no idea about opium conversion processes and facilities, now became familiar with heroin processing technologies.

During this transition, the Pakistani military intelligence agency tacitly ignored the involvement of the *mujahedin* leaders, especially Gulbuddin Hekmatyar, who drew money from the drug trade to support insurgency war in Afghanistan. A contemporary study from Kabul indicates that Hekmatyar and his *Hesb-i-Islami* group were almost non-existent during the formation of an organized Afghan resistance in Pakistan in mid-1978.[100] Championing his support for tying Afghanistan to Pakistan 'ideologically and strategically', Hekmatyar very soon earned the whole-hearted support of General Zia.[101] During mid-1980, Hekmatyar was the lone representative, out of 170 splinter groups and 7 dominant leaders, who signed a paper confirming that if he gained power in Afghanistan, he would respect the Durand Line (see Map 3, above). Lamb argued that to secure a maximum allocation in military hardware for Hekmatyar, the ISI convinced the US to use him as 'a worm to catch a fish' in the Afghan turmoil.[102] In a report in 1988, Lawrence Lifschultz maintained that the ISI funnelled secret US arms deliveries to the Afghan *mujahedin*, thereby safeguarding Pakistan's own defence strategies in the war.[103] In pursuance of Pakistani strategic interests, the ISI funnelled most US arms shipments to Hekmatyar, who had taken shelter in Pakistan long before the Afghan war broke out.[104] *The Washington Post* in May 1990 reported that the ISI delivered to Hekmatyar and his *Hesb-i-Islami* group a large share of the $3 billion channelled by the CIA to Pakistan.[105]

Besides the backing of the CIA through the ISI, Hekmatyar attached himself to the illicit opium trade, to consolidate his power base in Afghanistan. In 1986, Kabul Radio accused Hekmatyar and other anti-Communist Afghan leaders of procuring money from the drug trade.[106] Although the journalistic integrity of Kabul Radio was questionable, it provided a sense of the pro-Soviet regime's view of Hekmatyar. To win the support of the *Pathan* tribes for the promotion of his future political plans, he identified himself as the protector of poppy fields in NWFP and northeastern Afghanistan. Under his command Dera Adam Khel, a small town between Peshawar and Kohat, eventually emerged as a centre for heroin processing as well as gun manufacturing.[107] The Hekmatyar lieutenants operated some of the heroin laboratories at Rabat, a small town at the meeting point of Pakistan, Iran and Afghanistan. A large number of *mujahedin* camps and heroin laboratories were located in the Koh-i-Sultan region, where the ISI was in total control. After the Soviet pull-out from Afghanistan in 1990, the Pakistani troops helped Hekmatyar to control Kabul's 'multi-billion dollar opium trade', which had emerged as 'a key factor' in the Afghan power struggle.[108] With Pakistani backing Hekmatyar eventually emerged as Prime Minister in Burhanuddin's government in late 1993. Nevertheless, Hekmatyar's new political role in Kabul during 1994–5 failed to accomplish the strategic objectives of Pakistani leaders.

Following the collapse of the USSR, Pakistan was eager to promote its trade relations with the Central Asian states of Kazakstan, Kyrgyzstan, Tajikstan, Turkmenistan and Uzbekistan. Pakistan failed to convince the Afghan leaders, including the newly installed Prime Minister Hekmatyar, to carry out its Central Asian trade plans. On the contrary, Afghanistan closed down the Pakistan embassy in Kabul in March 1994 and captured a Pakistani convoy with 40 army personnel and senior ISI officers at Kandahar in late 1995. These measures by the Afghan bosses obstructed the expansion of Pakistan's overland trade link with Central Asian states through the 1,284 kilometres along the Karakorum Highway.

To help free hostages the ISI used the *Taleban*, 2,500 armed *Pathan* students influenced by the radical philosophy of the *Jamiatul Ulema-i-Islami*. Commanded by Maulana Fazlur Rehman, they launched a series of successful military offensives in Afghanistan.[109] To secure US support, the *Taleban* in late 1994 initiated some symbolic operations by burning poppy fields and executing some drug traffickers.[110] In September 1997, *The Middle East* maintained that to finance their war in Afghanistan, the *Taleban* collected 10 per cent opium tax (*usher*) from poppy growers in the eight provinces where poppies were chiefly grown.[111] As a result of this unspoken approval, the UNDCP estimated that opium production in Afghanistan had risen from 2,066 metric tons in 1995 to 2,248 metric tons in 1996.[112] The long-term political instability in Afghanistan pushed Pakistan to emerge as the biggest supplier and transit country for illicit heroin in southwest Asia. Civil war in Afghanistan, which originated from the Pakistan's need to defend its territorial integrity, and the Cold War strategies of the US, now extended close to the border of Tajikstan in an ambitious *Taleban* plan to take over Afghanistan.

The US Cold War strategy

During its Cold War engagement in southwest Asia, the US government winked at the strategic use of drug money by some leaders of the Pakistan army and the Afghan militants. For strategic purposes, the US maintained a hotline with Pakistan, a 'front-line' country facing the Soviet Red Army in Afghanistan. To combat Soviet hegemony in southwest Asia, the US overlooked its century-long crusade against the drug trade. In a statement N. Dorn and N. Smith revealed the US's Cold War drug policy as follows:

> There is evidence that whilst one arm of US foreign policy was working to eradicate opium and heroin production, the other arm was forming political and economic alliances with local anti-Communist groups heavily involved in the opium trade.[113]

This contradictory line had been initiated during the early 1950s when the CIA allegedly diverted drug money in the formation of Kuomintang Nationalist Chinese guerrilla army to destabilize the Communist government in China.[114] A number of experts have examined the involvement of the CIA in diverting drug money made in the 'Golden Triangle' region to combat Communism in Laos, Vietnam, Burma and Cambodia in the 1970s.[115] Larry Collins, in his book *Black Eagles*, maintains that the CIA depended on drug money to fight the expansion of world Communism in Central America in the 1980s. The following discussion demonstrates that the equivocation of the US's Cold War strategy in Afghanistan substantially helped increase illicit production and transit trafficking of heroin in Pakistan.

Prompted by its security interests in the Persian Gulf and the Indian Ocean, the US government in 1980 ignored its crusade against the drug trade and extended unconditional support to the military rulers in Pakistan. Until 1979, Iran, under the reign of Shah Mohammed Reza Pahlavi, had been a faithful ally of the US in an ideological battle against the expansion of Soviet omni-potence in the Persian Gulf. With the fall of the Shah in Iran and the Soviet intrusion in Afghanistan, US policy planners perceived a great threat to their security interests in southwest Asia. Anticipating a Soviet thrust towards the Persian Gulf, the US special emissary Clark Clifford, in New Delhi in January 1980, warned that it would inevitably lead to a 'war'.[116] In May 1984, similar concerns about the Soviets using Afghanistan as 'a stepping stone' were expressed by the then Vice-President George Bush, during his visit to Pakistan. In December 1985, President Gorbachev ruled out the apprehensions of the US at the Geneva summit, where he asserted that the Soviet Union had no blueprints for an expansion towards Iran or the Indian Ocean.[117] Gorbachev's declaration was a turning point that permitted US diplomats to resolve the Afghan crisis amicably.

The US concern over the Pakistani drug trade moved up the agenda after Gorbachev's affirmation. Revealing the current 'mistake', President Reagan, at the Tokyo economic summit in October 1986, declared that international drug control would in future be the number one priority of US foreign policy objectives.[118] Nevertheless, until the Soviet regime agreed in 1988 to withdraw its military pres-ence from Afghanistan, the US government pursued its strategic support to the *mujahedin* leaders supposedly involved in the drug trade. A State Department report in 1987 indicates that the Soviet occupation of Afghanistan was the 'core of the Administration's agenda' and surpassed all other foreign policy considerations.[119] The 'superpower posturing' facilitated the illegal production of opium poppy in NWFP and beyond its border in Afghanistan.[120] With the running of heroin laboratories along its western borders, the status of Pakistan changed dramatically from a limited supplier of raw opium to a major manufacturer of Number 4 heroin for the underworld market.

The US policy in Afghanistan backfired when a substantial amount of Pakistani heroin started to arrive in the US and other Western countries. A report by the US Committee on Foreign Affairs in 1986 indicated that the smuggling of southwest Asian heroin into the country accounted for only 3 per cent in 1978 while this figure rose to 51 per cent by 1980.[121] Referring to British enforcement agencies, *The Times* of London in 1983 maintained that 80 per cent of heroin sold on the streets of England came from Pakistan.[122] By 1985–6, Pakistan had emerged as a major refiner of southwest Asian opium into heroin, and a principal channel for heroin destined for US markets.[123] *The International Narcotics Control Strategy Report 1985* asserted that over 50 per cent of heroin smuggled into the US in the previous year had originated in southwest Asia, and Pakistan was 'the key to that trade'.[124] Despite an increase in the drug trade from Pakistan, official US reports were cautious in regard to the strategic relationship with Pakistan. A work by Jonathan Kwitny, an investigative journalist, claims that in pursuit of its anti-Communist foreign policy, the CIA committed a 'civil crime' against its own people in the US.[125] Kwitny's general observation, however, does not specify the impact of US Cold War policies on the Afghan resistance war.

Nevertheless, to appease their Cold War partners, US officials publicly hailed Pakistan's drug policy, although it contradicted US drug war strategies in southwest Asia. In December 1983, at a meeting with Pakistani leaders in Karachi, Dr Carlton Turner, Adviser to the US President, praised the 'coordinated efforts' made by the enforcement agencies to overthrow drugs.[126] During his visit to Pakistan in 1984, the then US Vice-President George Bush, who was also the Chairman of the National Narcotics Border Interdiction System, commended the efforts made by Pakistan 'to curb narcotics menace'.[127] In an expression of political solidarity with General Zia, he ignored a sharp rise in the Pakistani supply of heroin to the US black market. His statement also contradicted the DEA's (Drug Enforcement Agency) Congressional report in 1983, which claimed that about 52 per cent of the heroin smuggled into the US in the previous year had come through Pakistani channels.[128] Interpol suggested that Pakistan alone supplied about 70 per cent of heroin in the world market in 1984, when George Bush paid a visit to this country. Thus, there were great social costs to the US and other Western countries from the ideological battle that evicted the Soviets from Afghanistan.

The controversial policy pursued by the US government also created anxiety amongst some of its high officials. In September 1984, *The New York Times* reported that US Under-Secretary Lawrence S. Eagleburger regarded US drug policy in regard to the supply-side countries as flimsy.[129] Despite his contention, as a confidence building measure to a leading ally the Reagan Administration in March 1986 extended $4.02 billion in military assistance to Pakistan.[130] In 1986, the DEA postulated that 'there exists a serious cooperative relationship' on drugs with leaders in Pakistan.[131] Despite the claim about the diversion of *mujahedin* arms 'for the protection of illicit drug trade', the US government was reluctant to review its strategic relationship with Pakistan.[132] In 1990, *The Washington Post* blamed the US government for its refusal to inquire into the alleged involvement of some Pakistani leaders and their Afghan co-partners in illicit drug production and trafficking.[133] Without being affected by the criticisms, the State Department in 1992 expressed satisfaction with the steps of the Pakistan government against drug trafficking. This official approval by the US, a century-long crusader against the drug trade, animated the Pakistani traffickers to proceed with their business enthusiastically.

Ignoring the alleged involvement of some Pakistani Generals and Afghan *mujahedin* leaders with drug trade, US State Department officials maintained a 'blind eye' policy. In the late 1980s, the US defence strategist Selig S. Harrison verified that the US secret agencies maintained political connections with 'a bunch of Noriegas' in the Pakistani military.[134] During the US presidential elections in 1988, Michael Dukakis criticized the 'hypocrisy' of the Reagan administration for its failure to deal with the branded Pakistani Generals, while it had intercepted Panama's General Manuel Antonio Noriega on charges of drug trafficking.[135] Referring to the DEA officials, *The Washington Post* in 1983 reported that Afghan militants were 'financing their battle' to some extent through the sale of drugs to the West.[136] Some reports hinted that the DEA officials wanted to ensure that the Afghans forced the Soviets out of Afghanistan at any cost.

Despite the numerous allegations, the US government showed little enthusiasm to investigate the CIA's role in the insurgencies in Afghanistan. In 1981, a left-wing Indian magazine, *Link*, claimed that some DEA representatives stationed in Pakistan were privately involved in the drug trade to secure Cold War objectives.[137] Another Pakistani report in 1994 observed that, in protest at the CIA's 'refusal to pinpoint' its official representatives and known *mujahedin* leaders involved in the drug trade, one of the DEA members posted in Islamabad had quit his job in the early 1980s.[138] William O. Walker III, in a North American study, asserts that the CIA over-looked Afghan militants who helped receive weapons in exchange for drug money.[139] In January 1993, the *Knight-Ridder* news service criticized outgoing President George Bush, a former chief of the CIA, after he pardoned a Pakistani drug trafficker who had been sen-tenced to 50 years' imprisonment in the US.[140] Until recently, the US State Department or the INCSR refrained from releasing any reports on this crucial point. The silence of the US officials, if taken as a sign, suggests that there were secret links between the CIA and the ISI, and that they implicitly overlooked the use of drug money in their campaign for Cold War victory in Afghanistan.

US anti-drug measures in Pakistan have largely been subservient to its superpower security postures in southwest Asia. Driven by its strategic objectives, a US State Department report in 1985 main-tained that Pakistan's annual opium production during 1983 to 1985 ranged between 40 and 60 metric tons[141] (see Figure 5.1). These figures were contradicted by Edith T. Mirante, an inquisitive journalist who estimates that the Pakistani production in 1985 was 200 metric tons.[142] The State Department report on Afghanistan was also contradicted by a US Congressional report in 1986, which suggested that opium production in Afghanistan in 1985 was as high as 750 to 880 metric tons.[143]

Overall, State Department statistics claimed that due to climatic conditions opium production in Pakistan and Afghanistan dropped in the 1980s. Nevertheless, the *Department of State Bulletin* in

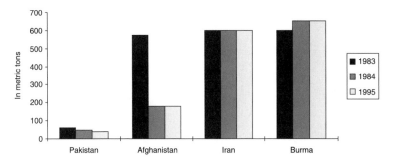

Figure 5.1 Opium production estimated by the US State Department, 1983–5
Source: Based on data provided by the *International Narcotics Control Strategy Report 1985*, p. 4

October 1989 admitted that due to 'limited or no access' in Iran, Afghanistan and Burma, it was difficult for the government to have accurate information on production.[144] The Iranian statistics shown in Figure 5.1 were politically motivated and intended to undermine the anti-drug crusade of Imam Ayatullah Khomeini. (Iranian drug policy is discussed in the following section). As a matter of fact, with the outbreak of the Gulf War in 1980, cross-border drug traffickers from Pakistan and Afghanistan used Iranian territory. In 1994, the Pakistani freelance journalist Ahmed Rashid argued that US statistics differed greatly from all the contemporary reports maintained by the UNDCP.[145] The UNDCP report in 1994 claimed that illegal production in Afghanistan reached 2,000 tons, but the US estimate was less than half that. This contortion of official figures in regard to poppy cultivation in Pakistan and Afghanistan largely helped encourage illicit drug trade in the region.

So it was that Pakistan by the mid-1980s emerged as major refiner of southwest Asian opium into heroin intended for the international black markets. Pakistani drug syndicates controlled most of the opium produced in Afghanistan and Iran. A report by Edward Girardet in 1989 indicated that about 50 per cent of Pakistan's heroin processing was taking place within 10 miles of the Afghan border.[146] Despite this fact, the US authorities were not equipped to stop the flow. During their anti-Soviet campaign, US State Department officials assumed that after 'stability' returned in

Afghanistan, they would be able to address Pakistani poppy politics effectively.[147] As a result, the massive supply of cross-border opium, combined with the domestic illicit production in NWFP, helped Pakistan become the world's largest supplier of heroin by the time a peace accord had been reached between the superpowers in April 1988. Through the Afghan crisis, the US won its ultimate victory against the former Soviet Union, but lost ground in the battle against drugs in southwest Asia.

The promotion of drug trade in southwest Asia during the Cold War era helped expand addiction to drugs, especially heroin, in Pakistan. Figure 5.2 shows that drug addiction in Pakistan increased from 1.2 million in 1980 to 1.6 million in 1985.[148] These drugs included opium, heroin, *charas*, *bhang*, mandrax and alcohol. Of all these drugs, the increase in heroin addiction was conspicuous. Figure 5.2 indicates that between 1980 and 1985 the number of heroin addicts rose from a few thousands to over 365,000. Statistics provided by contemporary Pakistani sources asserted that heroin addiction rose steadily from 0.4 per cent in 1980, to 1.5 per cent in 1981, 3.8 per cent in 1982, 7.4 per cent in 1983, 15 per cent in 1984, and 22.8 per cent in 1985 of the total drug addicts.[149] The PNCB authorities claimed that during the 1980s the number of heroin addicts increased from a few thousand to one million; and 1.7 million in 1993.[150] In September 1996, the Interior Minister, Naseerullah Khan Babar, told the National Assembly that the country's total addict population was 3.5 million, while the number

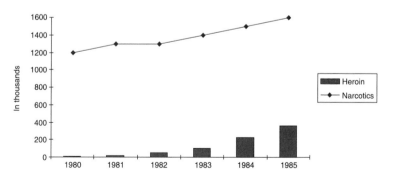

Figure 5.2   Growth of heroin addiction in Pakistan, 1980–5
Source: *National Survey on Drug Abuse in Pakistan 1986*, p. 314

of heroin addicts reached 2 million in 1996. These official assertions were echoed by contemporary studies conducted on drug addiction in diverse areas of Pakistan. A study of 1,020 drug addicts admitted to Lyari Hospital in Karachi between 1985 and 1988 revealed that out of these patients about 99 per cent were heroin addicts. Because of the deadly nature of heroin abuse, the admission of heroin addicts was dominant compared to other drugs. A 1987 survey conducted on drug addicts at the Services Hospital in Lahore indicated that amongst the total number of patients, 98 per cent were heroin addicts.[151] The availability of high-grade heroin at cheap rates contributed substantially to the increase of heroin addiction in Pakistan during the Cold War era. With the arrival of heroin in the illicit market, opium, *charas* and *bhang* were replaced as outdated drugs. Figure 5.3 shows that within four years, heroin addiction rose by 33 per cent, while the consumption of *charas*, opium and *bhang* had declined significantly. The growth of this calamity in Pakistan was noted with keen interest in some quarters in the US, where heroin addiction was already immense. Quoting Clyde D. Taylor, the Acting Assistant Secretary of State for International Narcotics Matters, *The New York Times* in 1984 acknowledged that as Cold War syndrome 'we have developed an attitude [heroin abuse] in Pakistan that wasn't there before'.[152] Thus, being involved in the Cold War strategies, Pakistan assisted in bringing about the withdrawal of Soviets from Afghanistan, but it now confronted a massive problem of heroin addiction.

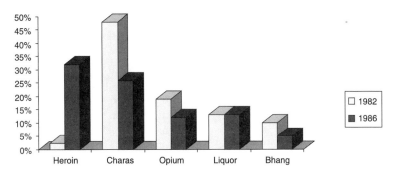

Figure 5.3   Changing patterns of drug abuse in Pakistan, 1982–6
Source: Data based on the *National Survey on Drug Abuse in Pakistan 1986*

Under its amended strategies during the post-Cold War era, the US government has drastically cut its funding for anti-drug programmes abroad. In the two years between 1992 and 1994, this budget has been reduced 50 per cent. As a result of this revised policy, a gap was created between the US and Pakistan in the early 1990s, which significantly affected the drug control programmes in Pakistan. Besides the Cold War disease that resulted from contra-dictory US policies and the Pakistani strategic dilemmas to which followed suit, heroin addiction also had escalated as an outcome of the radical anti-drug laws adopted in Iran in 1979.

The Iranian revolution

The harsh treatment of the drug offenders by the radical govern-ment in Iran in many ways contributed to the spread of drug addic-tion in, and trafficking from, Pakistan. Under Reja Shah Pahlavi, Iran had been a producer of licit opium both for the international medicinal market and for local consumption. Following the assump-tion of political power in February 1979 Imam Ayatollah Khomeini adopted stern measures against drug traffickers and declared them a memorial of colonialism. The anti-drug laws introduced by the Khomeini regime sent many cross-border criminals to take shelter in the remote tribal areas in NWFP and Baluchistan. The death penalty was imposed on traffickers possessing more than 30 grams of heroin and 5 kilos of opium. In July 1980, a report published in *The Washington Post* indicated that during a 7-week period 170 drug offenders were executed in Iran.[153] Another 1981 study by Arnold S. Trebach observes that under the directives of Ayatullah Sadegh Khalkhali, drug dealers and sometimes addicts were tried by the Islamic Courts, and were shot publicly if found guilty.[154] Compared to the Iranian laws, the maximum punishment for drug-related offences in Pakistan were two years' imprisonment.

The lenient central laws, which were largely inoperative in the tribal areas of Pakistan, attracted international drug syndicates to set up heroin laboratories in NWFP. A Pakistani administrator claimed that a heroin laboratory was first detected in Quetta in 1980, a city close to the tribal areas of NWFP. The US State Department Report of 1985 maintained that soon after the Iranian revolution, 'several active heroin labs' started operating at Rabat, the meeting point of the Iran, Pakistan and Afghanistan borders.[155] As a result of the suppression of heroin conversion facilities by the Iranian revolutionary guards, the tribal areas in NWFP and Baluchistan became the 'world's largest haven for heroin processors'.[156] The abundance of opium supplies from local and cross-border sources facilitated the running of clandestine heroin laboratories, a technology which was almost unknown in the country before.[157] With the availability of heroin transformation expertise, tribal areas along the Pakistan and Afghanistan border turned into important centres in the global drug trade in the early 1980s.

Iranian drug addicts, who arrived in Karachi and Quetta, contributed to the spreading of heroin addiction in Pakistan. Reports published in *The Herald* indicated that the Iranian insurrection was responsible for the decision of Shah supporters, including members of several left- and right-wing groups, to take shelter in Pakistan.[158] Besides political migrants, the country also absorbed a huge number of drug addicts who helped spread the habit amongst the locals. A 1992 Pakistani study maintained that before the fall of the Shah, Iran, with 11 per cent opium smokers, was the largest opium consuming country in the world.[159] Under the Shah, opium was served to registered addicts and methadone to heroin addicts in public hospitals, resulting in an increase in the drug addiction problem in the country. The declaration that drug addiction is a crime by Imam Khomeini created grave concerns amongst addicts and forced many of them to seek political refuge in the tribal areas of NWFP or Baluchistan. Moreover, the high price of drugs in the illegal market, in consequence of official banning of poppy cultivation, also encouraged many addicts to cross the border into the Pakistani tribal areas, where high-grade heroin was cheap. The arrival of Iranian addicts in Pakistan helped to introduce heroin addiction to the local population, who was virtually unaware of the vice before.

The blocking of the traditional Balkan drug route by the Khomeini government in 1979–80 contributed to the promotion of the drug menace in Pakistan. Prior to the Islamic Revolution, the vast area of trackless desert in central Iran was used as corridor by drug traffickers from Afghanistan and Pakistan who rendered an brisk trade in opium and hashish. These traffickers supplied illicit opium for conversion into heroin in clandestine laboratories in Iran and Turkey, from which it eventually passed to Italy and North America.[160] Following the fall of the Shah, drug running through the Iranian territories declined substantially. The blocking of the Balkan route, coinciding with bumper production in the Pakistani tribal areas, created a huge stockpile of illicit opium and an abundance of pure heroin, causing a massive increase in heroin consumption within Pakistan. Moreover, in connection with the elimination of heroin processing facilities in Turkey during the early 1970s, many Kurdish traffickers moved their heroin refineries into Baluchistan–Sistan to take advantage of the political instability in Iran.[161] The Revolution then forced cross-border traffickers to shift their heroin laboratories from Iran into Pakistan. The entrance of migrant traffickers coincided with the patronage of the drug trade by some bosses in the Armed forces, and both helped contribute to the rise in drug addiction in Pakistan.

Militarization of the drug trade

The growth of the drug trade under the Zia regime witnessed a nexus between drug dealers and some army personnel who became beneficiaries of the underground heroin trade. A Pakistani Human Rights Lawyer, Ikramul Haq, made this claim in his work entitled *Pakistan: From Hash to Heroin*.[162] During the military dictatorship of General Zia between 1979 and 1988 there was strong international criticism of a chain of command that involved some top bosses in the military with Pakistani heroin trade. Explaining the nature and influence of the drug dealers under General Zia, Hussain wrote:

> They [drug dealers] are the new billionaires. Rising from different social and class backgrounds, they now form part of a brotherhood. Each runs his own empire, its network reaching to almost every institution of the state. They finance political parties and a change of face at the top does not affect their position. They run a parallel economy and are capable of destabilising any government if their business is threatened. Many of them are socially respectable people, public figures such as politicians, industrialists, sportsmen, businessmen, military men, publishing magnates and even philanthropists. They are the barons who control the most lucrative trade in Pakistan today: narcotics.[163]

The following discussion demonstrates an alliance amongst certain members of the Pakistani armed forces who exploited their official immunity for the promotion drug trade in Pakistan.

One of General Zia's closest associates and trusted confidants, General Fazle Haq, fostered the increase of the military role in the Pakistani drug trade in the early 1980s. During his 8-year rule, first as a Governor and then Chief Minister in NWFP, Lieutenant General Fazle Haq, sometimes known as the Pakistani 'Noriega', protected poppy cultivation and the operations of heroin factories in the tribal areas. For his likely links in underground drug trade, General Fazle Haq was described as the 'notorious Pakistani' by *International Intelligence* during his official visit to Washington in April 1982.[164] His drug connections became an open secret in 1985, when at a tribal caucus at Wana in South Waziristan, Governor Fazle Haq declared heroin a Pakistani 'mineral'.[165] Despite his open advocacy of the drug trade, and reputation as the 'poppy General', General Haq remained in the good books of General Zia. A Pakistani newspaper in 1993 reported that his son had been convicted of charges of drug trafficking in New York, and this compelled General Haq to resign after 'the story became a public property' in Pakistan.[166] General Haq was re-appointed by his companion General Zia as the Chief Minister of NWFP in late May 1988.

Besides Fazle Haq, some other close associates of General Zia were also entangled with the Pakistani drug trade. In an article in *The Nation* the South Asia specialist Lawrence Lifschultz maintained that the Pakistani Federal Investigation Agency (FIA) in October 1985 arrested Hamid Hasnain, the chief executive of Habib Bank in Islamabad, on charges of drug trafficking.[167] The case was linked to the arrest of a Pakistani smuggler at Fornebu airport in Oslo, Norway in December 1983. Lifschultz points out that during the arrest the FIA retrieved from Hasnain's possession personal banking documents and cheque-books of President Zia and his family members. President Zia and his wife, Shafiqa Zia, attempted to personally intervene in the case. However, due to Norwegian pressure, the Pakistani court was compelled to put Hasnain in jail. Munir Bhatti, the lawyer for the accused, indicated to Lifschultz that his client had been made a 'scapegoat' to rescue the biggest smugglers in the case. To suppress the indistinct links of the

Pakistani higher authorities in the drug trade, the copies of *The Nation* (14 November 1988) that outlined Zia's drug links were confiscated and destroyed publicly.

A trafficking chain existed right up to the President's innermost circles, and it involved some of the most influential Generals in the Pakistan army. Selig S. Harrison, a senior US strategic analyst, maintained that drug corruption flourished in the 1980s 'throughout the military structure', involving about '10 Noriegas' in key positions whose names were risky to disclose.[168] Referring to Interlop, a Bangladeshi columnist in 1993 named the members of the military high command that ran a secret network for Pakistani heroin trafficking.[169] *The Hindustan Times* in 1994 indicated that former Air Vice-Marshall Anwar Shamim, a close associate of General Zia, had a reputation for his alleged involvement in drug trafficking.[170] Shamim was designated as Pakistan's Ambassador to Canada and to Saudi Arabia, but was rejected by both countries because of these drug-running allegations. The connection of Islamabad's high-ranking officials to the promotion of drug trafficking was damaging the international reputation of the country.

Drug syndicates also flourished among some members of the armed forces, which General Zia had termed '*momin*' (honest) in his first address to the nation. The *Narcotics Review in Southeast/Southwest Asia and Middle East, and Africa* in 1988 maintained that within a two-month period in 1986, Pakistani police had arrested two army officers with 900 kilos of heroin in their possession. The street value of these drugs was estimated at $4 billion, almost double the US budget for the 8-year-long Afghan resistance war. These were two separate cases in Karachi with identical results. In one case an Airport intelligence officer, Major Zahooruddin, was detected with a large quantity of heroin. To keep him under surveillance, Zahooruddin was transferred from police custody to a military base. From here he escaped, miraculously![171] It was reported that Lal Mohammad Matti, an alleged Pakistani drug trafficker, first hired Zahooruddin as a courier.[172] Matti also involved a number of Airforce and customs officials in his drug syndicate. Flight Lieutenant Kharur Rehman, another recruit of Matti, was arrested with a large quantity of heroin while approaching Karachi. Feigning illness, Rehman was admitted to hospital from where he escaped.[173] In addition, 14 other army officers were arrested by 1989, on charges of drug trafficking both inside and outside the country. In April 1997, the DEA officials arrested Squadron Leader Farooq Ahmed with two kilograms of heroin in New York, while his alleged pathfinder Squadron Leader Qasim was apprehended in Karachi by the Pakistani authorities within a week.[174] These incidents reveal that some members of the Pakistani armed forces have aided traffickers at the important exit points in passing heroin to the international black market.

Drug-running activities were also conducted through specific channels under the protective umbrella of the Pakistan military intelligence agency. The links between the CIA and the Pakistani ISI are evident in Alfred W. McCoy's book on *The Politics of Heroin: CIA Complicity in the Global Drug Trade*. McCoy demonstrates that in the wake of Afghan crisis the Pakistani secret agency had become involved in drug trafficking. Trafficking was conducted via channels which normally carried arms and goods to Afghan refugee camps. Under the CIA's auspices, arms were collected from Romania, Czechoslovakia, Egypt, China, Israel and East Germany.[175] These were mainly carried from Karachi to Peshawar by the National Logistic Cell (NLC), the largest army transport organization in the country. The NLC armoured vehicles were beyond the inspection of the police or customs authorities. With this extra advantage, the NLC trucks carried heroin from Peshawar to Karachi. In corroboration of this, *The Herald* in September 1985 observed:

> The drug is carried in NLC trucks, which come sealed from NWFP and are never checked by the police. They come down from Peshawar to Pirpri, Jungshahi, Jhimpir, where they deliver their cargo, sacks of grain, to government godowns. Some of these sacks contain packets of heroin ... This has been going on now for about three and a half years.[176]

Support for this allegation against the NLC's protective covering vehicles was to be found in a road accident at Bula Khan *Thana* in mid-1985. An eyewitness of the incident, Dr Manzoor, a physician at Lyari clinic, maintained that 'a white powder' was spilled all over the road from upside-down carrier. This heroin was being smuggled from Peshawar to overseas destinations allegedly by Pakistan's National Shipping Company in Karachi.[177] In January 1993, Turkish monitoring agencies stationed in Karachi seized a US-bound heroin consignment weighing about 10 metric tons that was being transported by NLC trucks.[178] It is highly unlikely that these were isolated incidents. Citing numerous reports, a CIA intelligence document in late 1992 asserted that a group of ISI officials used heroin profits 'to fund separatist movements in India and the civil war in Afghanistan'.[179] Under international pressure, the Pakistan government in October 1997 arrested some servants of the NLC who intrigued with corrupt officials of the secret agency to pass heroin while in transit between Lahore and Karachi.[180] The connection between some members of the ISI and the organized drug mafia was evident in the above reports.

The promotion of drug trade in specific army channels coincided with the liberal banking policy in Pakistan during the early 1980s. Due to inflation and debt repayment, the Pakistan economy at the turn of the 1970s had gone into immense crisis. The Pakistan State Bank was in bankruptcy and the IMF or US economic assistance was unavailable due to country's nuclear proliferation policy. To overcome this financial shortfall, General Zia in 1983 allowed Pakistani traffickers to deposit their black money in the scandal-ridden Bank of Credit and Commerce International (BCCI). For its alleged involvement in money laundering, fraud and irregularities the Bank was closed in 1991. The BCCI Bank, which was 77 per cent owned by Abu Dhabi, had helped facilitate an annual turnover of Pakistani drug money that rose to $4 billion, an amount exceeding the country's total legal exports, by 1989. In December 1989, an article by Zahid Hussain indicated that the drug trade was 'fetching for its dealers a revenue of over $8 billion'. This growth in the drug trade continued under civilian rule during the subsequent years. An unclassified CIA report in 1992 claimed that the Pakistani drug trade was 'virtually the same size as the legitimate economy'. In 1993, a Pakistani report estimated that the country's annual share of the world drug trade was about $120 billion.[181] As a result of the promotion of drug trade, a big change has occurred in the Pakistani underground economy within a span of one decade.

The proliferation of the drug trade has resulted in youths becoming both addicts and drug peddlers in some areas. This development was allegedly assisted by the important parts of the state machinery. In 1985, *The Herald* indicated that enforcement agencies were 'forcing' drug peddlers to distribute drug amongst the youths in Karachi to destroy the strong support base of the slain Prime Minister Zulfikar Ali Bhutto.[182] As indicated in the previous chapter, some members of the Indian armed forces were involved in the promotion of drug culture amongst the tribal youths in northeast India. Being involved in a similar conspiratorial crime some members of the enforcement agencies, allegedly under an orderly plan, propitiated the spread of the drug habit in Sind and Baluchistan.

In December 1983, at a seminar sponsored by the Pakistan National Centre, social workers and representatives from a dozen youth organizations accused Police and Excise authorities of involvement in advancing the narcotics trade in different parts of Karachi. Yusuf Qureshi, a representative of the *Pakistan Himayet Tehrik*, maintained that drug addiction was spreading like a bush fire, and social workers who tried to prevent it were 'harassed, maltreated and implicated in false cases' by corrupt police officials.[183] President of the *Majlis Samaji Karkunan*, Syeed Warsi, warned that an anti-drug 'long march' from Karachi to Islamabad would be organized if the authorities failed to adopt measures controlling drug pushers. Unfortunately, the march never occurred. Thus, the militarization of the drug trade during the geo-political changes in southwest Asia helped increase the participation of corrupt officials and traffickers in the cross-border drug trade. This put at risk the survival of democracy in the country.

The growth of narco-democracy, 1985–97

The combination of state power and drug money under Zia helped spread the pollution of democratic institutions in Pakistan. As a legacy of the colonial past, the country had not had an Industrial Revolution or a the bourgeois revolution as had taken place in Britain itself. At independence, Pakistan inherited an over-developed bureaucracy that led to the dominance of civil-military bureaucracy in the state machinery. After a brief trial of parliamentary democracy under Prime Minister Zulfikar Ali Bhutto during the early 1970s, General Zia announced Martial Law in mid-1977. In an attempt to legitimize military supremacy in politics, General Zia in 1985 created a putative non-partisan Islamic parliament (*Majlis-e-Shura*) where, nevertheless, loyal friends of the government were elected who had no grassroots support. He used the civilian parliament as a 'sandbag'[184] in the wake of Western criticism about Pakistan not having a representative government. The absence of a responsible government, coupled with the covert operations of the military regime, made drug money cardinal in the national polity. This trend continued over successive regimes and resulted in the blighting of the country's growing democratic institutions.

Gadoon poppy politics

During the so-called Gadoon Poppy War in early 1986, a discord emerged between General Zia and his humble Prime Minister Mohammed Khan Junejo over the eradication of poppy cultivation in the Pakistani tribal areas. This event had links with General (President) Zia's dual policies of handling international expectations for anti-drug programmes, as well as protecting the interests of poppy cultivators in NWFP. Junejo, whom General Zia recruited as a yesman in 1985, contested his tolerant policies on poppy cultivation. To win the US's post-Geneva (1985) reliance, Junejo contradicted Zia's 'hardline Afghan policy' as well as his policy to allow the farming of opium poppy in NWFP. Zia's policy on poppy cultivation was evident at the third Interpol conference of the heads of the national drug control services in the Gulf areas in January 1986, when he emphasized the need for measures 'firstly on the international front'.[185] Unlike General Zia, Junejo opted for evolving strong anti-drug measures on the internal front. The Pakistan Muslim League led by Junejo adopted a resolution in January 1986 asking for the introduction of a death penalty for the drug traffickers.[186] However, Junejo was confronted by the opium lobby both inside and outside parliament, and was unable to mobilize public opinion in accordance with US pressure.

Nevertheless, to satisfy the US, which was a major strategic ally in the regional power game, the Junejo parliament in June 1985 intro-duced a Bill to confiscate properties derived from the drug trade. The official objective of this legislation was that it was a protective measures against the illicit traffic in drugs. During the legislative session, the pro-opium MNAs, who opposed the introduction of property seizure laws and its extension to the tribal areas, staged a 'walk-out'.[187] To justify their stand, the boycotting MNAs claimed that the cultivation of poppy and production of opium had been lawful both under the colonial and post-colonial administrations. Their political stand was very much in line with Pakistan's international policy on poppy cultivation. Being placed in the 'corridors of power' by General Zia, the pro-opium MNAs were trying to protect the traditional rights of the poppy cultivators, which they had enjoyed during the colonial period and afterwards. The Bill was carried by the *Majlis-e-Shura*, but as a result of the pressure from the opium lobby Zia delayed the enactment of the law for two years. Zia's reluctance to implement the forfeiture laws delayed the anti-drug drive of the civilian authorities. The tactic bought time for poppy growers, who sought alternative employment opportunities from the central government before giving up their traditional rights.

The crop substitution technique had been initiated by Prime Minister Zulfikar Ali Bhutto in July 1976, with a $5 million UN package that provided better irrigation facilities to the poppy growers in Boner Subdivision of Swat district. General Zia continued this policy in the Boner area, once responsible for one-third of Pakistan's illicit opium production.[188] Due to economic reasons the alternative approach, which aimed at substituting other cash crops for poppy cultivation, provided only a temporary remedy. A marginal farmer cultivating wheat in a small piece of land (*kanal*) could earn only a few hundred rupees, but if he engaged the same area in poppy cultivation he made between Rs2,000 and Rs2,400.[189] These incentives from the black market meant that farmers preferred the money on offer from drug dealers.

However, the Pakistan government in 1983 received USAID amounting to $20 million (Rs256 million) for development projects in the poppy growing areas. In June 1985, the NWFP Chief Minister, Arbab Jehangir Khan, told the provincial assembly that a gigantic 'project involving Rs420 million was launched for the socio-economic uplift' in the poppy-growing Gadoon–Amazai area of Mardan District.[190] The programme was announced as part of General Zia's policy of gradually reducing poppy cultivation by alternative means. However, due to official corruption this policy failed to benefit the tribal poppy growers, or to curb opium production. An extensive report published in *The Herald* in 1986 indicated that instead of making a direct investment amongst the poppy growers for employment opportunities, most of the initial allocations in 1984–5 were made on infrastructure build-up.[191] The government supposedly misused huge amounts of the aid that was received to reduce poppy cultivation.

In an attempt to meet the demands of the US, a country with considerable influence in Pakistani politics, Prime Minister Junejo resorted to force to eradicate poppy cultivation. However, for the tribal *Pathans*, who lived in poor, isolated villages with limited or no water supplies, poppy cultivation was the main source of income. In mid-February 1986, they raised a 'human barricade' of women and children, and attempted to stop the enforcement agencies from an operation to eradicate poppy cultivation in the Gadoon-Amazai area near Swabi. After a strategic retreat, the central authorities decided on a forceful solution to this long-standing issue. On 8 March, a 10,000-strong force comprised of police and paramilitaries launched an operation to destroy poppy fields in the Gadoon area. The attempt resulted in a fierce battle between the enforcement agencies and the tribal poppy farmers; 13 people were killed and over 150 injured on both sides. During the campaign, the authorities destroyed only about 20 per cent of the poppy growing areas along the roadside, while between 2,000 and 2,400 acres in the interior areas remained untouched.[192] Due to tough resistance by 20,000 to 30,000 people armed with deadly weapons, a complete eradication was impossible. The attempt was abandoned after the angry tribesmen shot down a helicopter used for aerial spraying of the crop.

None the less, during the campaign the enforcement authorities arrested over 100 people including the local MNA, Yakoob Khan Jadoon, MPA Ghafoor Khan and the chairman of the Gandaf union council Gul Bahadur Khan. A report published in *The Herald* in 1986 indicated that during the previous election Yakoob Khan promised his voters 'to get poppy cultivation legalized'.[193] The report also hinted that some close relatives of Ghafoor Khan were drug dealers. Because it had support from the local political leaders, the results of the Gadoon campaign went exclusively in favour of the poppy growers as well as the dealers of the drug trade. Almost all the major political parties in NWFP, including the Pakistan Peoples' Party (PPP), the National Democratic Party (NDP), the *Jamiatul Ulema-i-Islam* (JUI-Mufti Mahmood Group) and the PNP condemned the operation. They formed an 'action committee' to mobilize public opinion against the destruction of opium crops. Addressing a protest rally, the NDP Chief, Khan Abdul Wali Khan, the son of Khan Abdul Ghaffar Khan, declared:

This is our land and we will grow whatever we like on it. We are not subject to the orders of the Americans nor do we need their arms. They cannot dictate to us, and we are resolved to resist. Our resolution has become stronger after the March 8 incident.[194]

Organized anger against the central government and the US erupted in the midst of the tribal *Pathans* who demanded compensation for their damaged crops. They claimed Rs40,000 in compensation from the government for every acre of opium poppy destroyed.[195] The protesters blamed the central authorities for acting under pressure and burnt a portrait of the US President. They also accused the government of sheltering known leaders of the drug trade and permitting them to use the state apparatus as a stepping-stone for drug trafficking. To suppress the tribal reactions the police authorities, arrested and held the *Pakhtun* leader Wali Khan 'among others' for a short period. However, the Gadoon incident created political 'shock waves' for the civilian authorities, and ethnic tensions among the tribal *Pathans*, who were still engaged in a strategic war which could damage both the US and Pakistan.

The legal justification for the Gadoon operation was obvious, but the confused situation led the Pakistani leaders to elude responsibility for the tribal tension. Facing tremendous criticism created by the pro-opium lobby, both inside and outside the National Assembly, Federal Interior Minister Aslam Khattak, denied charges. In a counter-statement the Chief Minister of NWFP accused the Interior Minister of arbitrarily launching the operation.[196] Almost all the leading political parties including the civilian authorities blamed the enforcement agencies, and refrained from taking any political risk. Through this denial of responsibility, both by the central and provincial governments, the Pakistan government provided legality to poppy cultivation. These actions created a precedent and encouraged drug dealers to block any similar future attempt under foreign influence. Through the Gadoon incident, Prime Minister Junejo lost ground to the pro-opium lobby both inside and outside the parliament, while the pro-opium lobby embraced the policy of General Zia, who sought the gradual withdrawal of poppy cultivation.

To alleviate the international pressure, however, the Zia regime in 1987 approved the property seizure law that had been passed by the Junejo parliament two years before. This Act changed some of the important provisions of the colonial drug laws, but made the implementation of such regulations more problematic. Under the Dangerous Drugs (Forfeiture of Assets) Act of 1985, the Pakistan government declared that the assets of an accused would be liable to forfeiture if he were sentenced to life imprisonment for a narcotics offence. This provision 'complicated' the nature of the property seizure law, which enforcement agencies and most judges have found difficult to interpret.[197] Consequently, the illegal activities of the drug syndicates continued without much control. As a result of the confused anti-drug laws about 30 to 40 business organizations were involved in heroin trafficking from Pakistan.[198] Because of their financial position and influence in national politics, the Forfeiture of Assets Act or international pressure had little impact over the drug running activities of traffickers.

General Zia sacked Junejo in May 1988, and Zia was assassinated in a mysterious plane crash in August 1988. Following his death, a new set of political leaders emerged in Pakistani politics that maintained the pact with known drug dealers, and thereby further polluted the political institutions of the country.

Benazir's anti-drug fanfare

Benazir Bhutto pursued contradictory drug policies to survive in the Pakistani power politics. Upon taking office in December 1988, Benazir, the daughter of executed Prime Minister Zulfikar Ali Bhutto, declared that illicit drugs were the country's number one problem. In her campaign against the drug offenders, she emphasized that no one would be spared from the laws of the land.[199] In line with her election promise on drugs, she took a number of measures which the previous regimes had either ignored or viewed as too difficult. Benazir followed up her anti-drug propaganda for two reasons: (1) to express her solidarity with the US war on drugs after a peace settlement was reached on Afghanistan, and (2) to address the alarming heroin addiction problem that had risen to one million by 1988. But, although these objectives helped her to come to power, they were unfavourable to keep her there in a country where many organized groups were known beneficiaries of the drug trade. Benazir negotiated with some of the known drug dealers, both at the provincial and central levels, for the very survival of her PPP regime.

To win US support, the pursuance of an anti-drug agenda was vital for Benazir's regime. It is widely known that her father was engaged in an anti-American battle, and he was deposed from power in 1977. Avoiding unpleasantness with the US, Benazir adopted a number of measures and patched up the post-Cold War anti-drug drive. In early 1989, the Benazir regime created the Narcotics Control Division (NCD) within the Ministry of Interior and strengthened the antinarcotics bureaucracy. The NCD was a parallel institution of the PNCB, which had proven ineffective at the implementation of narcotics laws under Zia. The government also established a new cabinet-level drug control authority, directly accountable to the Prime Minister. This elite Anti-Narcotics Enforcement Unit comprised 'the best personnel available', and replaced the ineffective Joint Narcotic Task Force Units. The impact of these administrative measures was apparently minimal. Corruption amongst members of the law enforcement agencies continued to cause major hindrance to the successful implementation of the anti-narcotics drive of the Benazir regime. As head of this drive, Benazir in April 1989 attempted to remove enforcement authorities that had previously helped in the promotion of the drug trade. The Benazir regime arrested some top-ranking drug smugglers. Despite her gesture, many of the corrupt officials were freed on political grounds, while several absconded and took refuge in trafficker's camps in NWFP and Baluchistan.

As part of a reworking of its power relationship with the US, the PPP regime in January 1989 began an official programme to eradicate poppy fields in NWFP. To satisfy US Congressional Drug Certification requirements, the Benazir regime allowed several US Thrush aircraft to undertake aerial spraying in the poppy growing areas. As had happened in the Gadoon operation in 1986, aerial spraying evoked an aggressive response from the poppy growers. The attempt was abandoned after poppy farmers fired 'mounted anti-aircraft guns' at the aircraft and their escorting helicopters.[200] As a result of this assistance, there were domestic repercussions, as poppy cultivators maintained that besides opium poppy, the 2.4-D herbicide used in the spray also destroyed other standing crops – mustard and wheat – in the same area. The use of this chemical is banned in the US, as it causes cancer.[201] Under US laws, similar aerial spraying requires a public announcement and 'strong environmental guarantees'. However, by permitting the spraying the Benazir regime managed to receive the US Presidential Certification from George Bush in March 1989. During her visit to the US in June, Benazir also received $1.5 million assistance to modernize the drug enforcement agencies.[202] This amount doubled previous anti-drug aid to Pakistan, but was far less than the previous allocation for the poppy substitution programmes in NWFP.

To appease the poppy farmers, Benazir encouraged the entrepreneurs to set up industries in NWFP and provide employment opportunities to the *Pathan* cultivators under the low interest-rate policy. This low-cost strategy evolved in the US in the mid-1980s in an attempt to accommodate poppy farmers with alternative employment opportunities. The *Department of State Bulletin* in October 1989 indicated that, as part of the Tribal Areas Development Agreement with the US in late 1988, Benazir undertook a new industrial scheme in the Bajaur and Mohmand Tribal areas.[203] The industrial policy provided financial benefits for investors and political benefits for the Benazir regime, but failed to diminish poppy cultivation in the tribal areas. The recruitment of skilled labourers from neighbouring cities negated possible job chances for the unskilled poppy farmers. Thus, the new investment policy failed to prove an alternative to poppy cultivation.

Alongside its poppy eradication programmes, the Benazir regime also cooperated in arresting and extraditing known traffickers. To please the US, the Prime Minister asked the Anti-Narcotics Enforcement Unit to target, arrest and prosecute known traffickers. Warrants were issued for the arrest of Ayub Khan Afridi, otherwise known as Ayub Zakha Khel, on charges of drug trafficking. The US government had wanted him for allegedly smuggling over a hundred tons of hashish and heroin from the mid-1980s. Under the existing Extradition Treaty, the PPP regime was obliged to arrest and hand over Afridi to the US. However, Afridi remained a fugitive for two years and avoided arrest. Another ringleader in the Pakistani heroin trade, Mirza Iqbal Baig, had been a principal target of US drug enforcement agencies, and was arrested in 1989. In a 1988 study, Lawrence Lifschultz indicated that Baig's leadership in the Pakistani drug trade had been exposed in May 1983, when a Japanese courier named Hisayoshi Maruyama was arrested in Amsterdam with 17.5 kilos of high-quality heroin.[204] The owner of a Lahore cinema and Baig introduced this bogus Japanese doctor to

General Zia. This story appeared on Pakistan Television (PTV) after Baig was arrested by the Benazir regime.

Benazir's part in the anti-drug battle was peripheral for two reasons: Firstly, due to personal connections of the dominant drugs dealers with the ruling elites; and secondly, because traffickers made threats to the legal authorities. The nexus between political leaders and drug dealers was evident in numerous cases. For example, Baig surrendered to the enforcement agencies in July 1989, and was freed by the Lahore High Court for lack of evidence. In December, Zahid Hussain in an article in *Newsline* commented that Baig's release was 'a deep mystery', and it occurred as a result of his close links with some of the influential figures in Benazir's government.[205] In 1993, Khan maintained that Baig financed Mirja Khalid, Speaker in the National Assembly, during the 1988 elections.[206] Besides his political connections, Baig's colleagues allegedly prevented the enforcement agencies from giving any official evidence and offered a $250,000 reward for the head of anyone willing to give such evidence.[207] In October 1989, Pakistani drug criminals assassinated Altaf Ali Khan, the regional director of the PNCB in Karachi, and this provided a warning to other enforcement authorities to maintain a low profile. To foil the anti-drug drive of the Benazir regime, they killed several officials in the narcotics department. These mafia-type activities marked a watershed in the political crusade of the Benazir regime and made clear the helpless situation of those attempting to move against suspects in the drug trade.

In spite of her political commitment, Benazir also failed to break the powerful drug lobby within the army. In May 1989, she fired the chief of ISI, Lt. General Hamid Gul, who was controversial for his alleged involvement in the drug trade under the Zia regime.[208] In July, the government arrested General Fazle Haq, the former Governor and Chief Minister of NWFP, who allegedly promoted the Pakistani drug trade. The government later charged him with the murder of a *Shia* leader, Arif Al-Hussaini, who was waging a war against the flourishing heroin trade in the Punjab.[209] Benazir also sacked the ISI Bureau Chief, Brigadier Imtiaz (retired), who allegedly involved himself in running a 'smuggling racket' under cover of Afghan arms transportation.[210] Benazir's actions against leading Army personnel greatly dissatisfied the top military leadership. In late 1989, Pakistani senior Army officers expressed their resentment of the Benazir regime for its interference in the activities of the defence forces. Benazir invited political instability for her government with these actions against the highest-level army officers. *The Christian Science Monitor* reported that 'the drug mafia' in the dominant opposition political party was 'urging the Army to declare martial law'.[211] As in many other leading drug producing and transit trafficking countries, black money and corruption were threatening the political stability of the Benazir regime.

Benazir's anti-drug crusade was weakened by the dominance of the drug lobby in Pakistani polity. Pakistani drug traffickers and their powerful mentors within the leading political parties undermined the deterrent measures of the country's first female Prime Minister. They allegedly consulted religious experts on a ruling that a woman cannot lead an Islamic state. In early March 1989, at a convention in Rawalpindi, over 2,000 *ulema* claimed that a government led by a woman was un-Islamic, and urged the people to overthrow it.[212] In early June, eight opposition parties formed the Islamic Democratic Alliance (IDA), a new parliamentary coalition under the leadership of Ghulam Jatoi. The IDA, which accommodated the pro-opium MNAs under its political umbrella, placed a motion of no confidence on 1 November 1989 to topple the Benazir regime. After narrowly surviving the motion of no confidence, Benazir accused the IDA leaders of spending about Rs195 million of drug money for bribing MNAs to vote against her.

In an attempt to balance the influence of drug money in politics, Benazir compromised with some of the leading figures of the Pakistani drug trade. A *Newsline* report asserted that the Minister for Parliamentary Affairs, Tariq Rahim, allegedly negotiated with a convicted drug baron and the tribal MNAs to support the falling PPP regime.[213] Thus, legislators linked with the tribal poppy growers were playing a decisive role in the political survival of Benazir's coalition government. In the Pakistani National Assembly, the powerful drug lobby had the capacity to either stabilize or destabilize the Benazir regime.

To survive in this power struggle, Benazir provided political status to many known traffickers in violation of her election promise. Benazir offered a PPP ticket to an infamous trafficker, Malik Waris Khan Afridi, who was elected from the Khyber Agency and became a state minister for tribal affairs in her cabinet. Contemporary reports indicated that Malik Afridi allegedly helped Benazir in the 1988 elections and in her political battle against Nawaz Sharif during the early 1990s.[214] Benazir also accommodated Amanullah Gihki, a major drug trafficker in Baluchistan, as the president of the PPP provincial committee. To secure her position in Baluchistan, Benazir welcomed Mohammad Ali Rind, a drug baron who had collaborated previously with General Zia, and made him the provincial revenue minister. The Benazir regime also recruited another dominant trafficker, Malik Moin Khan Afridi, who was elected in the 1988 National Assembly elections on the PPP label. While Benazir was striving to consolidate her position in the parliament by power-sharing with the traffickers, the US government under the Pressler Amendment in 1990 stopped all direct economic and military aid, including anti-drug development assistance to Pakistan. Benazir was accused of corruption and mismanagement, and sacked by President Ghulam Ishak Khan in August 1990. The sacking of a 20-month-old elected government allowed the counter-drug lobby to power share with the Sharif regime in the general elections in November 1990 (which I am going to discuss later).

Nevertheless, reiterating her promise to help free the national economy and democratic institutions from the influence of drug dealers, Benazir returned to political power for second term in October 1993. During her election campaign, she had accused Prime Minister Nawaz Sharif's party of allegedly using 'drug money to dislodge the PPP government', and she declared that once back in power she would destroy the 'activities of drug mafia'.[215] Upon her re-election as Prime Minister, Benazir reaffirmed her election word on the anti-drug crusade. To get US sympathy, Benazir extended her support to the anti-drug measures taken by the caretaker government of Moeen Qureshi. Under the Dangerous Drugs (Amendment) Act 1993, the Qureshi regime had imposed a death penalty or life imprisonment for trafficking and financing in the narcotics trade, and revised almost all the major provisions of the Dangerous Drugs Act of 1930.[216] In an effort to deter drug trafficking from Pakistan and to help control local consumption of drugs, the PPP regime invited international agencies and non-governmental organizations. The Benazir regime also passed the Anti-Narcotics Task Force (ANTF) Ordinance of 1994 and arrested a recognized trafficker, Mirza Iqbal Baig, who had been freed earlier due to lack of evidence.

To gain credibility in the eyes of the US, the Benazir regime expressed its readiness to cooperate with the former to help control drug trafficking from Pakistan. Prior to her visit to the US, the Benazir regime in January 1995 made a huge seizure of narcotics at Illamgudor in the Khyber Agency.[217] In the presence of US officials, the ANTF seized and burnt about 125 metric tons of *charas* and 480 kilos of heroin, and arrested 33 workers from the drug processing factories. In December 1993, the operation was conducted with approval from Senators of the Federally Administered Tribal Areas (FATA).[218] However, the seizure was termed unfair by local *ulema*, who demonstrated at Bara and demanded the return of the hashish and the release of the detainees. The elders and Maliks of the *zirga*, which included the MNA of the Khyber Agency, Mohammed Shah, also supported tribal resentment. During a meeting with administration they condemned the ANTF action as interference in the 'internal affairs' of the tribal areas and demanded 'immediate release' of the arrested people.[219] The *zirga* also conveyed the message to the government that the manufacturing of *charas* would continue in tribal areas because it was 'a traditional and lawful means of earning' for the tribal people. Despite the risk of tribal resentment, the operation was launched largely to revive US assistance, which had been suspended due to the Pressler Amendment in 1990.

As part of its pro-US policy, the Benazir regime in January 1995 restructured the narcotics control administration and merged the PNCB and ANTF into one organization. In 1995, the Federal government froze properties worth Rs2.16 billion of seven dominant drug dealers.[220] The authorities arrested Ayub Afridi, one of the ringleaders of the Pakistani drug trade and a former National Assembly member who had fled the country in late 1994, and extradited him to the US for trial.[221] The Benazir regime was trying to remove the tensions in the country's post-Cold War relations with the US. However, due to the Pressler Amendment the Prime Minister returned empty handed from the US in April 1995, and this lack of US support seriously hindered the war on drugs in Pakistan. As a result of US policy, the amount of property seizures from the traffickers dropped sharply during early 1996. The adoption of the Narcotics Control Ordinance 1995, that had been drawn up by the Minister for Interior Major General (retired) Nasirullah Khan Babar in January 1995, also became uncertain.

The lack of financial support as the well as the limited political will of the national leaders to fight back against traffickers also hindered the successful implementation of the existing drug laws. In the absence of moral and material commitment, the results of the stringent laws were confined to routine work in response to international pressure. Consequently, the framing comprehensive drug laws or the removal of existing flaws, and the introduction of the death penalty for traffickers, remained unaccomplished. As a result of the confused nature of narcotics laws, the drug and gun culture prevailed in Karachi and other big cities under the Benazir regime.[222] The gangster activities of the Pakistani drug mafias posed a tremendous threat to public life, especially in Sind, Baluchistan and Punjab.

Benazir's anti-drug campaign was eventually messed-up by the alleged involvement of her husband and the water and power minister in her cabinet, Assef Ali Zardari. Quoting John Banks, a former British trafficker who later became a secret DEA informer, the *Sunday Times* in January 1997 reported that Zardari 'financed' large heroin shipments to Britain and the US in the late 1980s and early 1990s.[223] Benazir usually denied the charge as a political conspiracy. On 5 November 1996, President Farooq Ahmed Leghari dismissed the Bhutto regime on charges of corruption and mismanagement. The newspaper story damaged the political reputation of the Bhutto family and the credibility of 'democratic institutions' in the country.

Drug dealers in the Sharif parliament

The post-Pressler Amendment years in Pakistan between 1990 and 1993 witnessed power sharing with known drug traffickers in the democratically elected Prime Minister Mian Mohammad Nawaz Sharif's parliament. As a device to neutralize Western opinion about the Pakistani democracy the Sharif regime created a separate ministry for narcotics in 1991, and burnt about 3.5 metric tons of heroin and 39 metric tons of hashish near Karachi in early 1992.[224] In 1992 the government also became a party to the 1988 Convention and accepted extradition laws for drug traffickers. Sharif's anti-drug actions were aimed at deflecting the growing criticism about Pakistani drug trade both at home and abroad.

While confronting international denunciation, the government was equally faced with a number of local animosities. The government introduced the Special Courts for Speedy Trial Act of 1992, but failed to extend the jurisdiction of special courts to the tribal areas for the trial of drug smugglers. Mere legislation could not control the illegal production of opium or eradicate small laboratories involved in heroin manufacturing in NWFP. *The Washington Post* in early 1993 reported that the PNCB with its 'meager resources' was unable to combat the powerful drug traffickers in the country.[225] A study published by the DEA in early 1993 indicated that over 1,000 tons of opium was smuggled annually from Afghanistan and processed in heroin refineries between the Khyber Pass and Peshawar.[226] To block this channel, the government at the beginning of 1993 undertook a big road construction project linking the 'rugged valley' in NWFP where most of the heroin refineries were located. The road-building programme was abandoned after the drug dealers killed two bulldozer drivers and resisted the enforcement agencies in the Tihar Valley.[227] It was the third time since 1986 that central government failed to implement a programme in accordance with the US demands.

Compared to the US pressure on poppy cultivation, the anti-drug measures taken by the Sharif regime were only window dressing. Given this reluctance, the tribal *Maliks* at a press Conference in Nehag Pass in early May 1993 argued that by demanding an end to poppy cultivation Western countries were maintaining a double standard. In the presence of a group of journalists from Islamabad they claimed that it was unjust for the US government 'to ask poor *Pathans* to give up their traditional livelihood' while the country itself was exporting 'liquor, bombs, missiles and other deadly products'.[228] The declaration of the tribal elders helped consolidate the political base of the leading traffickers, who used heroin money and were elected as legislators both in the national and provincial assemblies. As a result of this, the heroin trade was penetrating the ruling elites in Pakistan and becoming the 'lifeblood' of the economy. In 1992, a US State Department report maintained that Pakistan had turned into the world's largest heroin producing country, with 70 metric tons annual production.[229] In 1993, a UNDCP report observed that by using drug money leading drug traffickers had reached a stage where they were operating 'a parallel government' protecting the interests of the illicit trade.[230] The Pakistani leaders, who have never admitted the influence of drug money in politics, 'denied' the accuracy of the above report.

Nevertheless, the power of drug money helped some of the branded traffickers, especially Ayub Afridi, to receive parliamentary nominations and to become a part of the political system. In an attempt to block the return of Benazir Bhutto, who tried to arrest Afridi previously, Ayub Afridi allegedly helped finance Sharif's *Islamic Jamhuri Ittehad* party. After winning the IDA nominations, the so-called 'Khyber King' paid approximately $2,000 (Rs50,000) for every single vote to become a member of the National Assembly.[231] The power of drug money assisted Afridi to defeat another tribal leader Nadir Khan by winning 70 per cent of the total votes. As a result of this large investment, Afridi received political shelter and evaded US diplomatic pressure for his extradition. Under the UN Convention of 1988, the US urged Pakistan to hand over its leading drug dealers, including Ayub Khan Afridi. A CIA document in 1992 indicated that, in gratitude, the Sharif regime 'promptly quashed' Afridi's warrants issued by the Benazir regime. His ostensible connections with Prime Minister Nawaz Sharif and President Ghulam Ishak Khan and the leading military intelligence agency, ISI, allowed Afridi to enjoy a freedom in the 'Fortress' in the Khyber Valley. In a diplomatic mission in 1992, Afridi led a 60-member parliamentary delegation to Kabul to organize a peace settlement between the battling *mujahedin* factions. Avoiding international criticism, the Sharif regime endorsed Afridi to participate in parliamentary politics.

While the US applied pressure for the incorporation of drug issues as an important item on the agenda of its bilateral relations, the Sharif regime was reluctant to adopt the same. Pakistan ignored US pressure to arrest Seth Saifullah, a dominant drug dealer, or to extradite him to the US. Saifullah had contested the Provincial Assembly elections from Kohat in Peshawar, as a nominee of Sharif's *Islamic Jamhuri Ittehad* party.[232] US pressure on the Sharif regime largely failed because the former had cut off its logistic support to Pakistan during the post-Cold War era. In February 1993, Zahoor Malik, press attaché of the Pakistan embassy in Washington, argued:

America [the US] used us like a condom [*sic*] ... and turned its back on Pakistan by cutting off military aid and sharply reducing economic assistance when the Soviet troops left Afghanistan.[233]

In response to US post-Cold War strategies in Pakistan, the Sharif regime in 1993 allegedly freed a leading drug trafficker from a public hospital in Dera Ismail Khan in Peshawar in April 1993.[234] He was undergoing life imprisonment for his involvement in international drug smuggling, but was permitted to visit his house regularly after sunset. To achieve a parliamentary majority in Baluchistan, Sharif also accommodated about six MNAs, one Senator and three provincial ministers who had connections in the drug trade.[235] One of these MNAs engaged in a gun battle with the enforcement agencies as they tried to seize 500 kilos of heroin from his possession. These are only a few examples of the power of the drug money that eventually perverted democratic institutions in Pakistan.

Allegations were made about political corruption and a lack of integrity within the administration that affected the working of parliamentary democracy in Pakistan. During the early 1990s, Prime Minister Nawaz Sharif reinstated the ISI Bureau Chief Brigadier Imtiaz, who had been sacked by the Benazir administration on charges of drug trafficking.[236] However, to punish some of the drug dealers who had belonged to the opposition camp, the Sharif regime arrested Malik Waris Khan, a political colleague of the former Prime Minister. In line with the political vicious cycle of arrests and counter arrests, some of the police personnel in Islamabad and elsewhere became involved in the promotion of the drug trade.[237] Given the susceptibility of the enforcement agencies to manipulation and corruption, the implementation of anti-drug laws was uncertain. As a result of this, an 'organized gang' within the postal department in Karachi was collaborating with traffickers in smuggling heroin through registered parcels.[238]

The smuggling of Pakistani drugs also continued through the participation of some members of Pakistan Airlines during the early 1990s. Alfred W. McCoy and Larry Collins maintain that drug-running operations had been conducted by US Airlines in Korea, Vietnam and in South America. As a legacy of the Cold War in Afghanistan, some crews of the Pakistan Air services were involved in drug-running operations. These activities grew during the first term of the Sharif regime.[239] Due to its inability to control the air traffickers, international pressure was intensifying against the Sharif administration during the early 1990s. *The Washington Post* in 1993 maintained that US enforcement agencies between 1987 and 1992 seized about 775 kilos of illegal heroin from PIA flights in which a group of employees were involved in drug trafficking from Pakistan.[240] The same report also asserted that replacing cocaine, heroin emerged as the number one drug in the US black market, Pakistan alone being the supplier of 20 per cent of this drug. Consequently, US aviation authorities in 1992 threatened 'to cancel landing rights' of PIA, and imposed a penalty of $5 million on the airline after its crews were found involved in drug trafficking. *Dawn* in early 1993 indicated that two PIA security staff were arrested at Manchester airport while they were carrying 3 kilos of heroin (estimated market value £25,000).[241] During the same week, another seizure from a PIA flight took place at London's Heathrow airport, when two Pakistanis were trying to release 10 kilos of heroin worth £1.2 million onto the wholesale market. Following repeated seizures and US threats, the Pakistani law enforcement agencies arrested a former PIA employee for his alleged involvement with the Pakistani drug 'mafia', after smuggling illicit drugs into Europe and Middle East.[242] In April 1997, a Pakistan Airforce officer, Farook Ahmed Khan, was arrested in the US while he was trying to sell two kilos of heroin to a secret DEA agent from Pakistan.[243] Compared to the involvement of the PIA officials in drug trafficking, official attempts to stop smuggling were inadequate.

The Pakistan government also came under pressure from the Saudi authorities to stop the illicit supply of heroin. In Saudi Arabia, Pakistan has about 2 million workers and employees, who bring the biggest amount of foreign exchange to the country. As a result of the spread of drug trafficking, every Pakistani was regarded as 'a prime suspect' by the Saudi authorities, and in February 1993 Saudi Arabia threatened closure of labour imports from Pakistan. This threat came at a time when the number of seizures of Pakistani drugs in that country had reached alarming proportions. A Pakistani report in February 1993 maintained that over a period of six months 260 Pakistanis were arrested by the custom authorities on charges of drug trafficking into Saudi Arabia.[244] A report published in *The Washington Post* indicated that King Fahd in March 1993 warned the Sharif government that the country's weak efforts to stop drug trafficking could cause 'irreparable damage to relations'.[245] As a result of the misuse of licit labour channels by Pakistani air traffickers, the conventional bilateral relationship between these two countries was threatened during the first term of the Sharif regime.

Besides the diplomatic pressure, the Saudi government continued with the death penalty for Pakistani drug offenders in the early 1990s. Between 1987 and 1992, over 50 Pakistani drug traffickers were beheaded under the Saudi *Shariah* laws.[246] In 1993, *Dawn* reported that Pakistani traffickers represented over 50 per cent of the total executed in Saudi Arabia.[247] During the same year, *The Washington Post* reported that, breaking all other previous records, 38 Pakistani traffickers were beheaded by the Saudi authorities in 1992 alone.[248] In July 1993, executions of one Pakistani and one Afghan smuggler were carried out in Jeddah. After witnessing the incident, a Bangladeshi onlooker wrote in the weekly *Bichitra* that whoever witnesses a beheading would never commit such crimes. A large number of Pakistani traffickers were also sentenced to death in the Sultanate of Oman, in Egypt, in the United Arab Emirates (UAE), and the Kingdom of Kuwait, and imprisoned by the Turkish authorities. Nevertheless, Pakistani drug traffickers remained largely undaunted and managed to find new recruits who were willing to risk their lives smuggling heroin. On charges of drug trafficking into its territory, the Saudi government beheaded 48 Pakistanis in 1995 and another 46 in the following year.[249] The increase occurred while Benazir Bhutto was in power. While the couriers were arrested or executed in foreign countries, their bosses in Pakistan, being well placed in the legislative assemblies, practised democracy as political mockery.

During the early 1990s, as a result of the cross-border drug trafficking, the bilateral relationship between Pakistan and Iran also deteriorated. In January 1993, two Iranian border security guards were killed and several others injured in a gun-battle with cross-border traffickers in Jali Rabat, where the Iranian border meets Pakistan and Afghanistan. In a campaign to stop a big heroin convoy, 20 Iranian soldiers were killed and traffickers at the same spot took 80 others hostage on the following day.[250] Recall that opium vessels armed with canon and guns had sailed from India, violating the resistance of the Chinese navy in the previous century.[251] Following a similar modus operandi, the Pak-Afghan traffickers used rocket launchers, missiles and other heavy weapons to break the Iranian blockade. In 1993, the Iranian authorities claimed that in one year they seized about 65 metric tons of contraband drugs smuggled from Pakistan, more than 40 per cent higher than the previous year.[252] They accused the Pakistan government of reluctance in the control of illegal poppy cultivation and heroin processing in the tribal areas.

In May 1993, the Iranian border forces, in an operation in the southeastern part of Sistan-Baluchistan province, seized 11 metric tons of illicit drugs and killed 20 cross-border traffickers.[253] To control northeastern caravans and trucks loaded with illicit heroin or morphine base, the Iranian government constructed a 450-kilometres road and built a strong wall across their eastern frontier, with the aspirations of the Chinese Great Wall. The government also set up over 100 observation towers and built about 1,000 kilometres of connecting roads along the Pakistan and Afghanistan border to monitor the movements of overland traffickers carrying heroin and hashish through Iranian territories.[254] In the wake of international criticism and isolation, the cleansing of the Pakistan's governmental machinery was becoming imperative. President Ghulam Ishak Khan sacked Nawaz Sharif on charges of corruption in April 1993.

Following the stampede of traffickers into Sharif parliament, Western countries attempted to prevent traffickers from becoming lawmakers. The US government in late July 1993 pursued the caretaker Prime Minister Moeen Quereshi to help free the country's fragile democracy from drug dealers. This realization struck home in the US, the leader of world democracy, after a warning made by Khan Abdul Wali Khan that by dint of drug money any leading trafficker could become the prime minister of Pakistan.[255] Besides US, a number of Western countries that cared for democracy also urged the Pakistan government and its leading political parties to avoid giving tickets to smugglers in the October 1993 polls.[256] In accordance with their approach, Qureshi took some positive steps to conduct fair elections in October 1993. The regime disqualified the 12 branded traffickers who had been elected to the national and provincial assemblies during the elections. Although the caretaker government was successful in preventing drug traffickers from taking part in the elections, it failed to control the use of drug money in influencing voting behaviour.

Defying the electioneering rules, influential traffickers spent money in favour of major political parties in the parliamentary polls. During her election campaign at Sargodha, Benazir accused Sharif of allegedly grabbing Rs200 *crore* from the drug dealers and the industrialists to purchase votes.[257] A similar complaint had been raised previously against Benazir by Sharif: that she made one trafficker a Senator in exchange for drug money. In an article in *Dawn*, Akhtar Payami wrote:

> Nobody will ever know how much drug money has been injected into the campaigns for the 4 October elections. Neither will it be easy for the elected government to take appropriate steps against a well-entrenched mafia having vital links with the political elite walking in the corridors of power.[258]

To protect their black money, the leading drug traffickers allegedly funded the dominant political parties. Due to lack of absolute majority in the election results, the major political parties also welcomed black money to buy support from the elected members of the splinter groups and political parties.[259] Despite the good intentions, the interim government failed to help free democratic institutions from the influence of drug money. The old links between the leaders of the narcotics trade and some leading political figures undermined the regulations of the short-lived government. Nevertheless, the strict measures adopted by the caretaker government in a way helped Benazir to return to power for a second term in October 1993. However, she was sacked on corruption charges by President Farook Ahmed Leghari in November 1996.

In an attempt to proclaim his innocence and to divert international attention, Nawaz Sharif in 1994 blamed some of the top figures in the Pakistan military for their underworld connections. In an interview given to *The Washington Post*, Sharif claimed that General Aslam Beg, then chief of the Pakistani army, and General Asad Durrani, then head of the ISI, had proposed a 'blueprint' to the then Prime Minister for organizing 'covert military operations' in early 1991.[260] Sharif maintained that he 'categorically' rejected the proposal, but he had 'no sources' to prove that the ISI had carried out his suggestion. Brigadier General S.M.A. Iqbal, a spokesman for the Pakistan armed forces, rejected Sharif's claim. To appease the top brass, Sharif later argued that he would take this matter to the Court for $100 million compensation for the annoyance.[261] *The Washington Post* accepted the challenge, but Sharif stepped aside. Through this tripartite debate, Nawaz Sharif gained politically by indicating that the smuggling network existed outside the sphere of his political authority. Nevertheless, the massive influence of drug money in electoral politics now created political apathy amongst the voters, and this was evident in February 1997 elections.

The perversion of democratic institutions during the 1980s and early 1990s allowed many branded drug dealers to acquire a share of power in the central and provincial legislatures. It involved many recognized figures in the illicit business and reaped fabulous profits. The alleged involvement of the family members of both Benazir and Nawaz Sharif,[262] and many other political leaders, has substantially undermined the supremacy of laws on drugs. In some cases drug partisans have blocked the passing and implementation of strong anti-drug laws in the national and provincial assemblies. The dominance of the drug traffickers in national politics has hindered the growth of democratic institutions in the country. The anti-drug drive of Prime Minister Benazir Bhutto was largely limited to political propaganda rather than making any serious political commitment. Prime Minister Nawaz Sharif was accused both at home and abroad for allegedly allowing known traffickers to share power. Because of political expediency, the governments of General Zia, Benazir Bhutto and Nawaz Sharif did not attempt to help free democratic institutions from the influence of drug money.

6
The Bangladeshi Panorama, 1972–97

The rise of Bangladesh as a major consumer of and geographical crossroad for contraband drugs, occurred as a result of colonial drug laws at the beginning of twentieth century, coupled with the spread of the illicit drug trade in South Asia during the 1980s. The implications of colonial drug laws in the then East Bengal[1] and their ramifications on the ensuing drug policies in former East Pakistan and then in post-independence Bangladesh were profound. Besides some technical changes to suit the needs of the time, no basic change had taken place in the government's drug policies during the Pakistani days or in the aftermath of independence in 1971.

As a result of the half-hearted legistative procedure and the abundance of illicit supplies from neighbouring countries (Burma, India and Pakistan), Bangladesh gradually has become a corridor for South Asian drug trafficking in recent years. With the influx of 'brown sugar' (low-grade heroin), phensedyl, and other contraband drugs from India, Bangladesh has emerged as an external market for the Indian drug trade. To combat the cross-border challenge, the Ershad regime adopted strict anti-drug laws during the late 1980s. In line with international and regional agreements, the Khaleda regime also pursued an anti-narcotics drive. However, due to political unrest, lack of logistical support, and an increase in administrative corruption, the country was unable to deter the emergence of Mafia culture and suppress the evils of drug addiction. These trends remained unabated under the regime of Sheikh Hasina.

Colonial excise policy

The origins of drug policies in Bangladesh and the drawing of revenue from intoxicating drugs go back to British colonial era during the 1790s. Contraband trade and the *Swadeshi* Movement undermined colonial excise policies in the early twentieth century. In an attempt to consolidate its control over the local drug market, the colonial government adopted the Bengal Excise Act of 1909 that helped promote excise revenue in subsequent years. Until the early 1930s, the government encouraged the consumption of intoxicants under the principle of the maximization of revenue. The unwillingness of the political authorities to bring about any effective change in colonial drug policies during the Pakistani period and the post-independence era has spurred the cross-border drug trade in Bangladesh in recent years.

The results of the pro-revenue excise policies pursued by the colonial government in East Bengal were minimal for about a hundred years. In 1895, the *Final Report of the Royal Commission Report on Opium* noted that the average per head consumption of excise opium in Orissa Division was 47 grains,[2] in the City of Calcutta it was 276 grains, but the consumption in the Dhaka Division was nominal (only five grains).[3] In 1896, *Chamber's Journal* indicated that in East Bengal opium was mostly taken as 'household remedy' to fight malarial fever.[4] As in the case of opium, the low consumption of cannabis by the local population was evident in the contemporary official reports. In his administrative report in 1908, L.S.S. O'Malley indicated that the total income from excise duty and licence fees from the cannabias in the province was only Rs40,000 in 1905–6.[5] The lower rate of consumption of drugs in the Muslim majority East Bengal was probably influenced by the religious principles of Islam that forbade intoxicants.

Nevertheless, claiming a better administration of the liquor industry, the colonial authorities set up distillers in 1890, and distributed liquor amongst vendors at a fixed rate. As a result of the official policies, excise revenue in Dhaka district increased from Rs121,000 in 1865–6 to Rs272,000 in 1892–3, and reached Rs413,000 in 1906–7.[6] The liquor revenue in Bogra district also steadily rose from Rs51,000 in 1886–7 to Rs123,000 in 1906–7, but declined afterwards.[7] The main buyers of liquor in these districts were from minority groups, while the local Muslims generally avoided drinks. Despite the flourishing of the liquor trade, the receipts of excise revenue in most districts in East Bengal were unstable for two reasons: (1) the spread of the smuggling trade in opium and (2) the diffusion of political unrest in the area.

The supply of contraband opium from unofficial sources threatened the overall receipts in excise revenue at the beginning of the twentieth century. O'Malley held that due to widespread smuggling of opium, excise revenue in Chittagong declined during 1900–8. The report also asserted that the excise revenue declined from Rs228,000 in 1895–6 to Rs173,000 in 1900–1, and further fell in 1906–7 to Rs147,000.[8] Over 50 per cent of the excise revenues in Chittagong district were drawn from the sale of opium. To meet this greater demand, opium was smuggled from the UP and Patna via Calcutta into Chittagong. A substantial amount of this smuggled opium transited Chittagong for Akyab in Burma, where almost 40 per cent of the population were heavy opium eaters.[9] The *District Gazetteer of Eastern Bengal and Assam* in 1910 claimed that a considerable amount of excise opium was also smuggled from Bogra to other districts where the rate of consumption and price were higher.[10] The supply of opium from private traders was weakening government revenue policy both in East Bengal and Burma.

Moreover, political violence to nullify the partition of Bengal between 1905 and 1911 manifested instability in the overall excise receipts in East Bengal. In 1908, O'Malley an noted that the revenue income from the sale of intoxicants was becoming trifling in East Bengal during the period.[11] In many districts, the revenue decline was attributable to political unrest led by the secret societies, such as *Swadesh Bandhab*, *Brati Dhaka Anushilan*, *Suhrid*, *Sadhana*. In East Bengal, the *Swadeshi* activities were mostly concentrated in Barisal, Chittagong, Rangpur, Faridpur and Mymensingh, and aimed at bringing an end to the government actions in Bengal.[12] The emergence of numerous ultra-Hindu organizations in the district towns in East Bengal largely affected receipts from the official distribution of drugs. Figure 6.1 shows that the excise revenue in the Dhaka district declined in 1908, in Bakarganj (Barisal) district in 1907, in Chittagong district in 1904 and in Faridpur district in 1907. The above developments in Bengal in the early twentieth century created major uncertainty in the colonial economy.

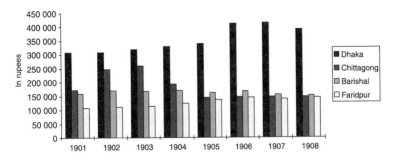

Figure 6.1   Revenue from intoxicating drugs in four districts in East Bengal, 1900–11
Source: Based on the *Bengal District Gazetteer* Statistics, 1900–11

To arrest the declining trend in drug revenue, the Bengal government adopted the Bengal Excise Act of 1909, and prohibited the manufacture and sale of all intoxicants without a licence. This Act provided exclusive authority to the provincial government to issue licences for marketing wholesale and retail country liquor or intoxicants within any specified area.[13] Under the new law, power was vested amongst the officials to impose duty on the sale and manufacture of any excisable intoxicating drugs. The government introduced this legislation, as in other parts of India, in the aftermath of the Shanghai Opium Conference that had questioned the legality of opium trade in China and elsewhere. With the imposition of new excise laws, and peace restored after the annulment of Bengal partition in 1911, the revenue from excisable items – for example, liquors, *tari*, *pachwai*, opium, hemp drugs – rose gradually.

After the adoption of the Bengal Excise Act, there was a take-off in excise revenue from the sale of narcotic drugs. The *Eastern Bengal District Gazetteers: Dacca District* in 1912 maintained that following the implementation of the new regulations, the Dhaka District authorities in 1909–10 earned Rs522,000 from distributing licences to opium vendors.[14] In addition, the sale of opium in Dhaka district rose from Rs33,000 in 1907–8 to Rs144,000 in 1929–30. As in Dhaka, the sale of opium in Barisal increased from Rs52,000 in 1907–08 to Rs72,000 in 1921–2 and Rs170,000 in 1930–1.[15] A similar trend was also evident in Chittagong, Faridpur, Dinajpur

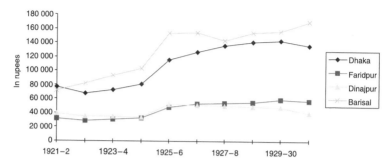

Figure 6.2   Revenue from opium in four districts in East Bengal during the 1920s
Source: Based on the *Bengal District Gazetteer* Statistics, 1921–31

and other districts (see Figure 6.2). *Bengal Legislative Council Proceedings/Debates* in 1921 maintained that, as with opium, the excise revenue in liquor rose from Rs6.2 million in 1916–17, to Rs8 million in 1918–19.[16] The Bengal government encouraged the use of intoxicants and made necessary provision for the advantage of habitual drinkers that facilitated a steady rise in excise revenue during the mid-1920s.[17] In violation of the current international agreements, the government increased its receipts from opium revenue in major districts during 1925–9, after the cessation of the opium supply to China.

To tackle both domestic and international pressure that opposed the distribution of narcotics, the government of Bengal in late 1932 adopted legislation on opium smoking. As I discussed in Chapter 3, Mahatma Gandhi's opposition to the distribution of intoxicating drugs through the licensed vendors in the early 1920s created an immense pressure. The government was also under obligation to control the distribution of narcotics in accordance with the Geneva principles. Under the Bengal Opium Smoking Act, opium smoking became a penal offence, with the penalty being six months in jail or a fine to a maximum of Rs500, or both.[18] Aimed at licensing opium smokers, the Bengal Opium Smoking Act 1932 banned opium smoking without registration. The registration system which had first been recommended by Henry J. Wilson, MP, in his Note of Dissent in the Royal Commission Report of 1895, after about half a century came about through international pressure.[19] The Act prohibited unregistered persons from opium smoking facilities, and allowed registered smokers to possess about 12 grams (one *tola*) of prepared opium. Under this Act, the illicit marketing of opium became a punishable offence with a maximum of two years' imprisonment or fine of Rs2,000, or both, and opium smoking in pair groups became a penal offence.[20] In line with the Burmese experience in the early 1890s,[21] the Bengal Act provided authority to local government to make rules for registration of opium smokers, the minimum age limit being 25 years or more. The adoption of these regulations on opium smoking had some impact in reducing the consumption of excise opium in areas within Bangladesh. With these regulatory measures, opium vendors in 1940 distributed 25 metric tons[22] of excise opium amongst consumers, who used it mostly for smoking, and some for semi-medicinal purposes. This amount was second highest after Punjab, where 29 metric tons of official opium was distributed to addicts and consumers.

As a legacy of the colonial past the Pakistan government, during the post-independence era, continued the distribution of excise opium for revenue purposes. In line with Pakistani policy, the Bangladesh government continued the distribution of excise opium and allowed registered addicts to buy opium from licensed shops. *The Bangladesh Country Report to the Commonwealth Regional Working Group on Illicit Drugs* in 1979 claimed that during the mid-1970s about 1,600 'chronic opium addicts' existed in the country.[23] Compared to the size of the addict population in the early twentieth century, this figure was almost consistent.

To propitiate the pro-revenue drug policy, the Bengal administration at the beginning of the twentieth century attempted to increase the sale of cannabis in different districts. Following the enactment of the Bengal Excise Act, the Dhaka District authorities in 1909–10 earned Rs133,000 from licence fees from cannabis distributors, as compared to Rs40,000 in 1905–6.[24] Through a similar process, official wholesale dealers opened licensed shops in every district and subdivision for the distribution of cannabis. In an attempt to consolidate the revenue from cannabis consumption the government, under the Bengal Excise (Amendment) Act of 1914, levied revenue on the cultivation or collection of the hemp plant. The provincial government

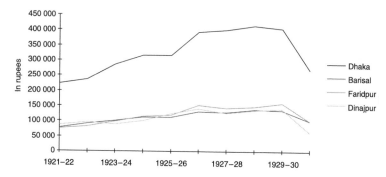

Figure 6.3   Revenue from cannabis in four districts in East Bengal during the 1920s
Source: Based on the *Bengal District Gazetteer* Statistics, 1921–31

continued the licit cultivation[25] of cannabis in Naogaon of Rajshahi, where it had been grown traditionally. The government also 'increased the vigilance' of Excise Department officials to control the smuggling of cannabis, and eventually raised the revenue from official sales (see Figure 6.3). From 1947 to 1971, the then East Pakistan government continued the cultivation of cannabis under a cooperative system. Following independence, the Bangladesh government allowed the cultivation of cannabis in a compact area of about 40 hectares in Rajshahi. The official authorities regulated the production and the sale of cannabis through approved retail vendor shops. Except for two years' imprisonment for the selling of cannabis resin (*charas*), there were no restrictions on the production of cannabis and its use.[26] Through this system, the government partly revived the British and Pakistani arrangements of cannabis cultivation in north Bengal.

As a result of diffident official policy, the abuse and trafficking of cannabis, opium, *bhang* and *charas* has never been completely eradicated from the country. The colonial excise policies introduced during the early twentieth century were hardly changed during the Pakistani period and after the independence of Bangladesh. This reluctance to engage in anti-narcotics drives meant that the country was open to the cross-border supply of contraband drugs during the early 1980s.

A crossroads for drugs

Its multiple communications with the poppy growing countries, made Bangladesh a geographical crossroads for illicit drugs from Burma, India, Nepal and Pakistan. Geographically the country is located at the heart of three drug producing regions: in the east the Golden Triangle, in the north the Golden Wedge and in the west, across India, the Golden Crescent. Bangladesh have direct air, sea and road communications with almost all the heroin producing countries in the region. Most of the supplies, except those from the Golden Crescent, enter the country by road, and depart by air or sea. As a result of this development, the Paris-based Interpol organization in 1996 suggested that roughly 5 per cent of world drug trafficking is 'routed through Bangladesh'.[27] In view of this assertion, the following discussion examines the dimensions and nature of transit trafficking via Bangladesh throughout the 1980s and early 1990s.

The Burmese link

In recent years, as noted above, Bangladesh has emerged as a transit country for illicit drugs produced in the so-called Golden Triangle region. In the northeast, Bangladesh has a 283-kilometre border with Burma, one of the largest heroin producing countries in the world since the 1970s. The 59-kilometre hilly and reverie border along Technaff in Cox's Bazar district has turned into a parade route for international drug traffickers. Besides this, the country has about 2,725 kilometres of coastline in the Bay of Bengal, which from southeast along the Naff River has emerged as an important route for Burmese drug trafficking. The seacoast areas along Technaff, Cox's Bazar and Anwara have assumed greater strategic importance for international drug syndicates.

With the bumper production of illicit heroin in Burma at the beginning of 1980s, Bangladesh gradually assumed a new role in the cross-border drug trafficking. After two years of drought, the Golden Traingle region in 1980 produced about 700 metric tons of opium.[28] Following the enormous production of opium poppies, the smuggling of heroin from Burma progressively increased in Bangladesh in recent years. The first case was detected in 1981, when a considerable amount of illicit drug was seized from the *Banglar Progoti*, at sea after its departure from Chittagong port towards Europe. The Chittagong customs authorities made another seizure from *Banglar Bani* during the same year. In 1982, Interpol claimed that international drug traffickers were increasingly using Bangladesh as a corridor for underworld drug trafficking. Following this assertion, the smuggling of Burmese heroin was first detected at a local Hotel in Chittagong in 1983. The *Review of the 1990 International Narcotics Control Strategy Report* asserted that in two months the enforcement authorities in Chittagong district seized 128 kilos of heroin, which exceeded the total amount seized in the previous 10-year period.[29] The trend of this cross-border trafficking and seizure along the Technaff–Chittagong route continued during subsequent years.

Due to big profit margins in the trade, many local criminals became involved in cross-border drug trafficking from Burma. Different sources indicated that one kilo of heroin in Technaff and its surrounding areas was sold between Tk100,000 and Tk300,000, which rose to Tk1500,000 after reaching Chittagong, and about Tk10 million once it reached the international market. Heroin was smuggled from Maungdaw in Akyab of Burma to Technaff by organized smugglers in powerboats, small boats (*shampans*) or via mountain paths. From Technaff, this drug was carried by local agents of the big drug dealers of Cox's Bazar district and then passed through interior channels to Chittagong.[30] Buses or other vehicles also secretly took the smuggled heroin from Technaff to Chittagong and Dhaka. In early September 1993, the BDR members at Duhazari check-post on the Cox's Bazar–Arakan road seized one kilo of heroin from a Chittagong-bound bus.[31] It was the second seizure by the BDR at the same spot during a week. To pass this smuggled heroin from Burma, a number of criminal groups have evolved along the Mongdu–Technaff–Chittagong route. These criminals, trained in judo, kung fu and firearms use, help in passing heroin from local spots to Dhaka for overseas destinations. With the growth of smuggling, the so-called 'White Sugar' heroin produced in the Golden Triangle was available in Bangladesh under different brand names such as Double Lions, Tiger, OK, Dragon.

Drug trafficking in southeastern Bangladesh has had political links. The suppression of the *Rohinga* Muslims in Arakan by the Burmese army aided in the spread of drug trafficking in Technaff and the Cox's Bazar area. As a result of military oppression, some

140,000 *Rohinga* refugees took shelter in Bangladesh in early March 1992.[32] By the end of the month, this figure had reached 250,000. With the arrival of these migrants, many of whom emerged as carriers of heroin from Burma, the law and order situation deteriorated in the area. As a result of their organized criminal activities, the smuggling of heroin through Technaff–Cox's Bazar and Chittagong increased substantially. Some of the Buddhist *Rakhain* settlers, who migrated from Arakan to Cox's Bazar over the previous centuries, also acted as couriers for Burmese drug trafficking.

Along the eastern border, there has been a large amount of transit trafficking of Burmese heroin via Indian territory. It comes through the northeastern Indian states of Manipur, Mijoram, Nagaland, Tripura, Meghalaya and Assam into Bangladesh for overseas. In February 1991 *The Times of India* reported that in the previous two months 8 kilos of Dhaka-bound Burmese heroin were seized in Manipur compared to 3 kilos seized in 1990.[33]

Following the dramatic surrender of the Drug Lord Khun Sa in 1996, heroin trafficking from the Golden Triangle region suffered a major setback, and now large consignments of 'brown sugar' from UP are finding their way to the northeast. For strategic reasons, the Indian government has sought transit facilities from Bangladesh for the geographically isolated northeastern states with Calcutta. During his visit to Dhaka in November 1996, the former External Affairs Minister, I.K. Gujral, proposed that the Awami League regime provide such communication facilities.[34] The government agreed with the proposal, but the leading opposition party, BNP, vowed to 'resist' any such attempt.[35] Given the present trafficking trend, it is possible that such a system would expedite the transit trafficking of Indian heroin into Bangladesh territory.

Drugs from India

Enveloped by India on three sides, Bangladesh became both an external market and a 'launching-pad' for illicit drugs from the former country. Bangladesh shares a 4,144-kilometre border with India, which is dotted by smuggling routes for illicit drugs. In this contraband trade, many cross-border drug syndicates, including some leading pharmaceutical companies, were involved.

Due to the reluctance of the Indian authorities, the extent of the cross-border illicit trade has become increasingly unmistakable in recent years.

In western Bangladesh, illicit trafficking of Indian drugs has been carried out by drug cartels from Calcutta. The smuggling of Indian heroin has occurred along the borders of Murshidabad, Nadia and Bongaon districts of North 24 (*Chobbish*) Pargana. Referring to intelligence sources, an Indian report suggested that the cross-border criminals have expanded their drug-running activities along the Nadia border.[36] From here, drugs were smuggled through the district's 94-kilometre reverie border and some strategically important islands (*char*) located in the river Padma. Police authorities in West Bengal asserted that 'the kingpins of the criminal gangs' operating along the West Bengal border were based in Calcutta.[37] Trans-border traffickers with consignments from Calcutta were crossing through the Benapole border in Jessore, mostly with false passports. In October 1987, the immigration police caught two Sri Lankan smugglers who entered Bangladesh through the Calcutta channel. They were trying to board a flight at the Zia International Airport with heroin worth Tk20 million. In 1992, the BDR seized over 38 kilos of heroin from the Shatkhira–Jessore border within 24 days and subsequently seized another 25 kilos of heroin in two separate operations from residential hotels in Shatkhira.[38] The volume of the illicit drug trafficking from Calcutta has increased tremendously and created a serious concern for the law enforcement authorities in Bangladesh.

Among the other smuggling routes in the west, the Gudagari border in Rajshahi has emerged as one of the most important corridors for Indian illicit drugs. In April 1991, the Gudagari BDR seized about one kilo of heroin from a labourer who had been engaged by local stockbrokers.[39] Recent reports from India indicate that illicit heroin produced in clandestine laboratories in Barabanki of UP was smuggled by organized traffickers into Bihar, and then passed via Farakka to various smuggling centres along the Gudagari border.[40] Almost every day large quantities of illicit drugs from Lalgola and Bhagwangola were smuggled into Bangladesh in this way. On 20 September 1991, *Dainik Ittefaq* reported that the Bangladesh Narcotics Control authorities in March 1990 arrested an Indian smuggler from a Dhaka hotel with 3 kilos of smuggled heroin. The enforcement authorities in India have showed little or no control over this cross-border trafficking. *The Statesman Weekly* reported that the seizures of illicit drug along the Indo-Bangladesh border in 1994 were about Rs347 *crores* at international prices, and that amounted to 'at best only a fraction of the quantity being smuggled out'.[41]

In the northwest, heroin produced in the so-called Golden Wedge region passed through the Siliguri corridor into Bangladesh, bound for countries far beyond. In 1990, a report published by the French Central Narcotics Office indicated that some heroin was produced in the 'Golden Wedge' region.[42] This report suggested that sporadic poppy cultivation has continued in the mountain valleys in Tibet, Nepal and Bhutan. Like many other southeast and southwest Asian countries Nepal has opium which is converted into heroin. In recent years, some of this heroin began arriving in Bangladesh via India. Compared to other heroin producing areas in Asia, the resurgence of the Himalayan region in global drug trafficking is apparently recent, and quantity of production is minimal.

As a result of the massive trafficking from cross-border sources, especially from India, Bangladesh has emerged as a major consumer of illicit drugs during the 1980s. The *Report of the International Narcotics Control Board for 1989* asserted that 'substantial illicit traffic entering Bangladesh across the Indian border' was destined for local consumption.[43] In June 1991, *Dainik Inqilab* claimed that students, rickshaw pullers and daily labourers in border districts were becoming addicted to Indian heroin. The supply of adulterated heroin from India was causing a big concern for the country. The *Report of the International Narcotics Control Board for 1994* estimated that the number of cannabis smokers in Bangladesh was 300,000.[44] While hemp cultivation was banned in Bangladesh, its production in India was outrageous. With the increase of drug trafficking from India, addiction to heroin, cannabis, pethidine and other psychotropic substances has increased tremendously, while the abuse of Indian phensedyl has reached alarming proportions.

The market for Indian phensedyl

As a result of the gap in government policies between Bangladesh and India, phensedyl, a codeine-based cough linctus, has been causing deleterious effects amongst the Bangladesh youth. In Chapter 2, I demonstrated that during the nineteenth century addiction to blended opium had been widespread in UK and US. In recent years a parallel situation has emerged in Bangladesh with regard to the abuse of illicit phensedyl smuggled from India. During the early eighties, phensedyl had been banned in Bangladesh and in many other countries in the region, yet it is produced licitly by a leading pharmaceutical company in Bombay. The massive smuggling of this contraband drug is now affecting the young population in Bangladesh. The problem has now become acute.

Colonial policy retrieved

In line with the colonial opium trade of the nineteenth century, some Indian pharmaceutical companies have created an external market for deleterious phensedyl in Bangladesh in recent years. Under legal protection, the British colonial authorities in India supplied non-medicinal opium to China and the Asia-Pacific region throughout the nineteenth century. Masters in 1892 maintained that the supply of contraband opium from India made 30 per cent of the Chinese population addicted to the drug, while 10 per cent of them were heavily dependent.[45] During the same period, the abuse of opium chocolates was evident in Turkey and Iran, where pharmaceutical industries marketed them under numerous brands: *Mash-Allah*, and the 'Gift of God'.[46] About a hundred years later, some medical enterprises in India have revived the colonial way by manufacturing phensedyl and other sedative drugs for Bangladesh and some other countries where these drugs are officially banned.

As in China in the previous century, the increased supply of phensedyl from India has continued in violation of Bangladeshi laws. To arrest the opium addiction in China, as early as 1800 the Chinese Emperor issued an edict prohibiting the import of the Indian drug altogether.[47] In 1856, Alexander wrote that the Chinese authorities denounced opium as poison, while it was treated by the Indian customs as a 'medicinal drug'.[48] As a result of gaps in the medical policies, a similar paradoxical situation has emerged between Bangladesh and India in recent years. Under the Drug Ordinance of 1982, the Ershad regime banned the manufacture and marketing of phensedyl cough syrup. In November 1986, the Ordinance was ratified by the Ershad regime after the civilian parliament passed the national medicine amendment bill. By the existing laws, Bangladeshi offenders normally get from two to five years' imprisonment with or without a fine.[49] However, Rhone-Poulenc pharmaceutical company in Bombay licitly produces this drug. As a result, unlawful supplies of phensedyl continue from India, breaking the Bangladeshi proscription.

To capture the underground market in Bangladesh and other Third World countries, some Indian pharmaceutical companies increasingly produced phensedyl, mandrax, buprenorphine and so on. As I demonstrated in Chapter 4, after a major setback in the international market, the Indian opium industry was facing tremendous problems with its huge stockpiles of medicinal opium. In an attempt to alleviate its loss from the international market, the Ghazipur factory in UP expanded the domestic use of medicinal opium.[50] This came about after a diplomatic defeat at the CND in the mid-1980s, to help protect the shrinking opium industry in India.[51] Taking advantage of opium diplomacy, some pharmaceutical companies in India outfitted the production of other drugs, which were regarded as dangerous in other countries. In 1996, in an interview to the *Indian Express*, Dr Harsh Shetty, a psychiatrist attached to the Narcotics Addiction Research Centre in Bombay, called the Indian pharmaceutical companies the 'drug dons' of the country.[52] Despite the criticism both at home and abroad, these pharmaceutical companies continued their controversial production unremittingly. This situation largely worsened when the Indian opium industry, to compensate for its losses in the international market, enthusiastically increased the supply of opium to the local manufacturers.

Under the protection of Indian medical policies, some organized traffickers have launched illicit trade in psychotropic substances in recent years. Contemporary Bangladeshi reports suggest that under cover of the 'licit' trade, classified traffickers along Bangladesh borders were producing contraband phensedyl. In 1992 *Shaptahik Purnima* claimed that impure phensedyl was manufactured across the borders to feed the country's teenagers.[53] Another Bangladeshi study in 1993 asserted that, attracted by the underground market, Indian drug traffickers were sending all their 'date-expired and waste consignments' of phensedyl, which were then expeditiously sold, to Bangladeshi customers.[54] Like the nineteenth-century Chinese addicts who could only afford adulterated opium,[55] the Bangladeshi addicts were mostly grabbing impure phensedyl. The hazard of adulterated phensedyl was twice that of normal cough syrups.

With the sprouting of Indian drug trafficking, supplies of phensedyl continued via various channels that accelerated local demands in Bangladesh. The supply lines were multiplied from the production management to the distribution level. In December 1997 *The Statesman* reported that a pharmaceutical business group of North 24 Parganas was involved in the cross-border drug trade.[56] This report further held that dishonest pharmacies and shopkeepers in the Bongaon and Basirhat areas have cooperated with underground traffickers and supplied phensedyl from licit stocks. Given these secure stock-supply arrangements, the cough suppressant has achieved the top spot amongst the Bangladeshi youth that were abusing the drug recklessly. In 1995, the *Report of the International Narcotics Control Board Report* held that phensedyl has become the main abused drug amongst young people in the city areas, including Dhaka.[57] To meet the swelling demands, the smuggling of phensedyl continued in abundance from India into Bangladesh.

The mounting trend in phensedyl smuggling was undermining the credibility of the country's legal system. As a result of the large profit margins achieved from phensedyl, smuggling has continued through the bordering districts of Jessore, Rajshahi, Kushtia, Khulna, Brahmanbaria and Comilla (see Map 4). In India, the maximum retail price for this medicine is about Rs29 for one bottle, while it sold in the bordering districts between Tk60 and 70 (nearly US$1.5) and in Dhaka for Tk120 or more. Consequently, once available only in 100 ml bottles smuggled into Bangladesh out of India, phensedyl can now also be found in large barrels. In 1992, the Bangladeshi weekly *Bichitra* reported that traffickers smuggled phensedyl in plastic drums and containers, which they then supplied in bottles to the local market to meet the enormous local demand.[58] In an attempt to combat cross-border traffickers, the BDR personnel in August 1994 met in 'Flag' meetings with the Indian Border Security Force (BSF) authorities at Mujib Nagar in Meherpur.[59] Similar 'Flag' meetings continued during the subsequent years, when the Bangladeshi authorities agreed on measures in vain on drug traffickers with their counterparts in India.

Map 4   Bangladesh: cross-border trafficking route

Surpassing all other drugs smuggled from India, the smuggling of phensedyl emerged as the number one contraband drug during the early 1990s. Like many other smuggled drugs – for example, heroin (commonly known as 'brown sugar') and cannabis – phensedyl was generally smuggled at night and stored at centres along the India and Bangladesh border. The Dhaka-bound passenger trains, day and night coaches from North Bengal secretly carried a huge quantity of phensedyl. On 9 June 1991 *Dainik Inquilab* reported that clearing agents in Jessore–Benapol border were involved in passing phensedyl undercover as licitly imported goods from India. The Indian phensedyl was also smuggled by water using fishing trawlers and launches from Pakshi, Nagarbari, Baghabari and Shirajgonj of North Bengal and Khulna, Daulatpur, Mongla and Barisal of Southern Bangladesh. Hidden in trucks which carry vegetables, fruits, or other commodities, bigger consignments are smuggled by road to Dhaka and other cities.

To arrest the massive supply from India, the seizures of contraband phensedyl became an everyday phenomenon in Bangladesh. In 1993, the Dhaka enforcement authorities recovered over 1,400 bottles of phensedyl from the newly constructed Gabtali bus terminal building in Mirpur.[60] The seizures of phensedyl by the Department of Narcotics Control (DNC) increased from 89 in 1989 to 35,000 bottles in 1993, while the cases against the phensedyl offenders rose from 8 to 292 during the period.[61] The *Narcotics Control Bulletin* in 1995 asserted that the DNC, between 1990 and 1995, seized 164,000 bottles and 1,650 litres of phensedyl, while the total number of arrests was 806.[62] Compared to the extent of the underground trade, these seizures were trifling. However, the Bangladesh Narcotics Control authorities emphatically claimed that one out of every twenty cases of smuggling was detected.[63] The UNI Reports on Bangladesh in 1996 suggested that the quantity of phensedyl seized increased by more than 3,000 per cent during the five-year period 1990–5.[64] On 21 August 1999, police recovered 17 thousand bottles of India phensedyl syrup worth about Tk2 million from the TT para slum area in Dhaka. In view of the above reports, it could be assumed that the size of the underground phensedyl trade in Bangladesh is frightening.

As happened with the Indo-China opium trade in the previous century, the economic value of the Indo-Bangladesh drug trade is mounting. Contemporary reports reveal that the annual distribution of phensedyl in the Dhaka City by 1996 had crossed 10 million bottles. Given that the average cost for each bottle of phensedyl in Dhaka is Tk120, Tk3.3 million worth of phensedyl was sold each day and Tk1,200 million every year at the major centres in the capital city. This amount of money is nearly a quarter of the total annual budget of the Dhaka City Corporation. Given the size of the contraband trade in phensedyl, and its sedative impact amongst users, a big threat has been created for the country's economy and the health of its younger generation.

Phensedyl addiction

The abuse of phensedyl in Bangladesh in recent years is comparable to the non-medicinal use of opium alkaloid in England and the US in the nineteenth century. These were available under various brand names: for example, Dover's Powder, Laudanum, Ayer's Cherry Pectoral, Mrs Winslow's Soothing Syrup, McMunn's Elixir, Magendie's Solution, Godfrey's Cordial, and Hamlin's Wizard Oil.[65] Compared to the above patent medicines, phensedyl is causing greater harm to its addicts in Bangladesh. Negligence in disseminating information about the psychophysical and physical reactions of opium alkaloid in India is largely responsible for the outbreak of phensedyl epidemic in Bangladesh today.

As was the case with the cough linctus in the West during the nineteenth century, phensedyl addiction is widespread in almost all the urban and industrial areas in Bangladesh in recent years. In Britian, opium syrups were readily available for customers both in the chemist shops and in the groceries, and were sold in violation of the poison laws of 1818 and 1868.[66] In 1867, Ludlow attacked the wrong prescription of opium tincture by medical practitioners that led to the spread of opium diseases amongst the 'vast majority of Anglo-Saxon opium-eaters'.[67] Similarly, until 1982 phensedyl was legal in Bangladesh, and medical practitioners prescribed it for the remission of cough ailments. As in Britian in the nineteenth century, any Bangladeshi could purchase this drug from the local pharmacists even without a prescription. With the banning of this medicine in the early 1980s, the phensedyl supply from traffickers promoted the addiction problem in the country.

Amongst the phensedyl blackspot areas, Dhaka, Narayanganj and Gazipur have the highest concentration, while almost all the districts and *thanas* (sub-district centres) are generally affected. In a letter to the daily *Shangbad* in 1993, one reader from Jessore reported that everyday after sunset young boys assembled at a sweet shop on the Shatkhira road to drink phensedyl.[68] During the same year the present author was told by reliable sources that phensedyl was sold in teacups in isolated rooms of some restaurants in Brahmanbaria. In August 1992,

Dainik Inquilab had reported that phensedyl syrup was sold in the back rooms of some pharmacies, and in hotels and restaurants in Barisal. Contemporary sources also claim that there were about 150 phensedyl distribution centres in Dhaka City, the principal spots being Sayedabad, Gabtali and Mohakhali bus terminals and their adjacent areas. This endemic trade has employed many street boys aged 10 to 14, commonly known as *Tokais*, as couriers of the drug in different parts of the capital city. As a result of the above operations, the total number of phensedyl addicts in Bangladesh is now approaching one and a half million.

Without realizing the harmful consequences of this codeine-based[69] cough syrup, Bangladeshi youth feel that it is smart and fashionable to use phensedyl. Obvious reasons – for example, good taste, cheaper price, an abundance of supply from cross-border sources, and easy use of it with no external signs – have made the drug popular amongst addicts. Many of them abuse this drug to forget the grim reality of their existence. However, the 'magic' substance in the phensedyl syrup is codeine-phosphate, and this eventually makes users addicted to the drug. Although codeine-phosphate is less strong than morphine or heroin, it creates both mental and physical dependency amongst its users. Recognizing the excessive use of this ingredient in exportable phensedyl syrup, the *Report of the International Narcotics Control Board for 1995* noted:

> Increasing abuse of Phensedyl was reported in Bangladesh. ... The codeine phosphate content of some Phensedyl batches found on the illicit markets in Bangladesh ... is much higher than that of the Phensedyl that is licitly available in India.[70]

A similar concern, about the 'alarming situation' in regard to phensedyl addiction amongst the South Asian population, was expressed by the United Nations International Drug Control Programme (UNDCP) in 1996.[71] During the same year, the Indian press also highlighted the hazards of codeine-based cough syrups: for example, phensedyl, corex or bendryl. Phensedyl addiction has now expanded from Bombay to Bangladesh, Nepal, Burma and the Philippines as a powerful tranquillizer.

Phensedyl euphoria offers a novel form of excitement and provides an illusory sense of adventure. In an interview in the *Indian Express*,

Dr Shetty admitted that addiction to phensedyl or any other cough tincture is 'more dangerous than the episodic use of marijuana or grass'.[72] Compared to marijuana or hashish, which produce hallucinations, phensedyl, as a byproduct of opium, induces deep sleep. Intellectuals in England depicted an identical euphoria after using opiates in the late eighteenth and early nineteenth century. Describing the horror of the opium euphoria, De Quincey in his work *The Confessions of an English Opium Eater* wrote that he 'shed tears' as he looked around on his familiar objects: the chair, the fireplace, writing-table, as if he were looking upon them 'for the last time'.[73] At a later date many other English writers like Dickens and Francis Thompson also became a slave to the opium habit.[74] To get such a romantic experience, Bangladeshi youth are increasingly indulging in phensedyl.

The initial impacts of phensedyl addiction are euphoria, drowsiness, nausea, respiratory depression, allergy and constipation. After the dependency is established addicts become victims of many physical ailments. Describing the danger of the phensedyl habit, Gedu Chacha, a popular Bengali fantasy writer, in a letter to the then Prime Minister Khaleda Zia, in 1992 wrote:

Beloved Mother, sometimes I feel that the whole country is stirring in intoxicating dizziness. [You have] heard about *bidi* (Indian cheroot) and *tamak* (mixture of tobacco). *Gaja* (cannabis) and *afim* (opium) had been the whim of the rich people. These could not cause much evil to the mass of the population. In the old days, the young boys secretly smoked *bidi* and *tamak*. ... However, the boys of the new generation consider tobacco as a trifling thing. Their main meal is heroin and the newly incorporated phensedyl. By taking all these, the glittering kids are marching towards the graveyard.[75]

A number of medical experts in Bangladesh suggest that regular use of phensedyl or codeine-phosphate destroys white blood corpuscles and prevents production of new ones. They further hold that phensedyl causes chronic blood diseases like aplastic anaemia and a total failure of the body's immune system which is very similar to AIDS.[76] It also creates hallucination, pressure on the gall bladder, lung problems, liver pain, intestinal obstruction, jaundice, clammy skin, convulsions and coma, and possible death. As a result of these ailments, a local Awami League leader in Dhaka died in mid-1997. This is a single instance amongst many other phensedyl-related deaths in Bangladesh.

The presence of ephedrine hydrochloride in phensedyl creates high blood pressure and can cause sudden death due to cardio myopathy or heart failure. Administration of phensedyl along with any sedative, hypnotic or tranquillizer drugs multiplies its chemical effects and creates a depression so deep that it may end in death. Regular abuse of phensedyl decreases sexual ability and ultimately makes the user disinterested in women.[77] During withdrawal treatments, runny nose, yawning, loss of appetite, irritability, tremors, panic, cramps, nausea, chills, sweating and so on occur. As phensedyl or codeine has a tolerance-developing capacity, users need to increase their doses with regular use.

Official reports indicate that amongst all the admissions recorded at the Central Drug Addiction Treatment Hospital in Dhaka, phensedyl addicts in 1992 represented 8 per cent,[78] in 1993 16 per cent[79] and by 1995 they rose to 22 per cent, always second to heroin addicts.[80] In an interview to *Bichitra* Dr Qureshi in 1992 claimed that in his drug addiction treatment centre almost 50 per cent of patients were phensedyl addicts. In 1996, the then chief consultant and director of the Central Drug Addiction Control Centre in Dhaka, Syed Kamaluddin Ahmed, asserted that the number of phensedyl addicts had increased 'seven-fold' over the previous five years.[81] Given the above information, it could be concluded that phensedyl is an alarming risk to the public health of the country. Despite the adoption of strong anti-narcotics legal measures in recent years, Bangladeshi authorities have failed to stamp out phensedyl or other drug menaces in the country altogether.

The weak crusade against drugs

Despite its signing of all the major international agreements, the Bangladesh government, due to political instability and administrative difficulties, has failed to launch an all-out effort to deter the cross-border supply of drugs. In early May 1980, President Ziaur Rahman (popularly known as General Zia) ratified the 1961 Single Convention on Narcotic Drugs, and the UN Protocol of 1972. This was done as part of Bangladesh's commitment to UN anti-drug programmes. Following this ratification, the Zia regime attempted to stop the cultivation of cannabis, and to eliminate its non-medicinal use in the country. In late May 1980, General Zia was assassinated in a military coup and the implementation of the UN principles became uncertain for the time being.

To earn US pleasure, the government of Begum Khaleda Zia in 1991 ratified the Convention against Illicit Trafficking in Narcotic Drugs and Psychotropic Substances of 1988. The process had been initiated by the Ershad regime, which provided stringent sanctions for the examination of suspects' bank accounts and tax files and extradition of suspects' drug offenders to the US in certain circumstances. In January 1991, Bangladesh ratified the SAARC Convention on Narcotic Drugs and Psychotropic Substances of 1990 and reached a bilateral agreement with Burma and a Memorandum of Understanding with Iran. Despite the pledging of diplomatic measures, the flow of drugs from India and Burma continued as a result of political instability, administrative mismanagement and the lack of logistical support in the country.

The opium trial

In the mid-1970s, Bangladesh attempted to revive the licit poppy cultivation that had existed in north Bengal during the late eighteenth and early nineteenth centuries. This decision was probably taken in connection with the scarcity of medicinal opium in the international market in the early 1970s. The following discussion demonstrates the sketchy information that is currently available about the momentary opium experiment in Bangladesh.

British official records indicated that the East India Company began poppy cultivation on an experimental basis in north Bengal during the 1780s. In April 1796, a letter by D. Scott and his colleagues to the Governor General at Fort William in Bengal indicated that the demand for Rangpur opium was gradually increasing as it price rose and it made a greater profit for the colonial administration.[82] As the local production of opium was increasing, the government in 1795 brought opium and its derivatives under the taxation system and opium itself was taxed in the following year. Cornwallis in 1797, along with other areas in Bengal proper, incorporated poppy growing areas in north Bengal under the government opium monopoly system in Patna. However, Dane in 1927 maintained that because of inferior production, the East India Company 'abandoned' its attempt to produce opium in the area.[83] This factor, coupled with the previous records of growing superior cannabis in Rajshahi and the surrounding areas, contributed to the banning of poppy cultivation in north Bengal in 1839.

None the less, in an attempt to revive opium production, the Zia regime initiated, on an experimental basis, poppy cultivation in Bogra district, while the possession of illegal opium exceeding one ounce became liable to two years' maximum imprisonment.[84] General Zia was probably attempting to help reconstruct an opium industry similar to those operating in India and Pakistan. Compared to colonial experiments over six decades, the current attempt to produce opium was very short-lived. Due to political instability and the lack of visibility, the successive governments deserted Zia's opium policies.

At the peak of the heroin trade in Pakistan, Burma and India in the early 1980s, the Ershad regime in 1984 banned the production, sale and consumption of opium in Bangladesh. Under the Opium Ordinance of 1984 the punishment for the unauthorized dealing of opium was substantially increased from a maximum of two years' imprisonment to ten years, including a penalty of between Tk20,000 and Tk100,000.[85] The Ershad regime's ban on poppy cultivation was the second such attempt since 1838, and coincided with those of Pakistan and Iran. Although the banning in Iran and Pakistan was either partially or completely unsuccessful, the Bangladeshi restriction remained intact and totally implemented. Nevertheless, the entry of heroin and other psychotropic substances to the local market from cross-border sources, especially from Burma and India, and their abuse by the local people was posing an increasing threat to the country.

To ensure that General Ershad's policies complied with the international conventions, the Bangladesh Jatio Sangsad (National Assembly) in early July 1988 passed the Dangerous Drugs (Amendment) Bill 1988. Under this Act, the Ershad regime stopped the import of opium for official distribution and imposed restrictions on possession of opium exceeding 25 grams.[86] An amendment of the Dangerous Drugs Act of 1930 and the Opium Act of 1878, this Act imposed the death penalty, or life imprisonment, or a maximum rigorous imprisonment of 20 years including a fine, for offenders. However, a London-based features service Panos in mid-1989 claimed that poppy plants were still being cultivated in the northern districts of Bangladesh in violation of the newly instituted laws.[87] The Narcotics Department authorities dismissed this report as completely 'baseless'. The Panos report was probably based on information that existed in the late 1970s, or misreported smuggled 'brown sugar' from India as Bangladeshi heroin. The 1992 *Yearbook of the United Nations* rejected any possibility of illicit opium production in the country.[88] In view of the above reports, it could be assumed that the Panos report was politically motivated to speed up anti-Ershad propaganda.

Nevertheless, recent report suggest that the tribal people of the remote areas of Chittagong Hill Tract have been growing illicit poppy in southeastern Bangladesh. The army patrol teams destroyed such poppy field in about 150 acres of Bandarban district in mid-1999; however, there are some inaccessible areas along the Burmese border where the crop is grown sporadically. I was told by narcotics intelligence sources that the poor tribal people, for their survival, cultivate opium poppies in the 'Kalapahar' (Black Hill) areas of Ragamati district. However, I did not learn from the above source if these people have any access to heroin processing facilities.

The Narcotics Control Act of 1990

In line with the US Drug War strategies and the UN Conventions, the Ershad regime sensibly adopted the Bangladesh Narcotics Control Act of 1990. Through this legislation the Bangladesh Jatio Sangsad (National Assembly) formalized the Narcotics Control Ordinance of 1989 banning the production and trade of intoxicants for non-medicinal purposes. Under this Act, the government repealed the Excise Act of 1909, the Opium Act of 1878, the Dangerous Drugs Act of 1930 and the Opium Smoking Act of 1932.

Under the Narcotics Control Act of 1990, the Ershad regime attempted to stop the production and sale of cannabis, which had traditionally been grown in north Bengal for centuries. This legislation was an extension of the pledge made by the Bangladeshi delegates at the International Conference on Drug Abuse and Illicit Trafficking in 1987, that the country was 'committed' to wiping out the cultivation and use of cannabis 'except for medical and other scientific uses by the end of 1989'.[89] As I discussed in Chapter 1, a cannabis (*ganja*) monopoly run by the colonial authorities had existed in Jessore, Rajshahi, Dinajpur and Pabna during the colonial period. In pursuance of the UN Single Convention of 1961, the Ershad regime banned the licit cultivation of cannabis and closed all shops selling it. With this legislation, the possession of cannabis became a serious punishable offence. Despite the ban, illicit supplies of cannabis continued from both local and cross-border sources, and this supply undermined official regulations.

With an abundance of illicit supplies, the consumption and cross-border trafficking of cannabis continued throughout the 1990s. In an unpublished report on the 'Drug Situation in Bangladesh', the Narcotics Control Department in 1996 indicated that the authorities seized 1,330 kilos of cannabis and 16,000 hemp plants, and made 790 prosecutions during the previous year.[90] In 1994, the enforcement authorities seized a total of 7,000 cannabis cigarettes, while during the following year it seized 6,550.[91] Most of this cannabis was smuggled from India in transit to other countries. In early May 1991, Jessore Narcotics Department officials arrested three brothers on charges of smuggling 6 kilos of cannabis and 300 cannabis plants from India.[92] Sometimes these operations were conducted to prove the effectiveness of the enforcement authorities against the drug traffickers.

To propitiate the execution of international and regional Conventions, the Ershad regime in early 1990 adopted measures modernizing the anti-narcotics bureaucracy. The government separated the Narcotics Control Department from the Ministry of Finance and placed it under the Ministry of Home, and enlarged the total working force to 1,300. In an attempt to abolish the colonial revenue administration arrangements, the government also replaced the Department of Narcotics and Liquor, which had been created for revenue purposes. Compared to the previous system and current bureaucratic arrangements in India, it was a fresh administrative move. To make the Narcotics Control Department a focal-point for anti-drug activities, the new apparatus was established under the President's Secretariat. In an attempt to reshuffle the anti-narcotics bureaucracy, senior officers were drawn from the Civil Service, Police and Customs while medical practitioners were taken from the Health Ministry. In some cases the collection of less efficient officers from other departments has slowed the anti-drug initiatives. As a result of strong political opposition Ershad was ousted from power in late 1990.

With the change of political system in 1991, the Narcotics Control Board was shifted to the control of the Prime Minister to facilitate policy-making and implementation. In early December 1993 the Khaleda regime amended some of the important provisions of the Narcotics Control Act of 1990 and appointed the Home Minister as Chairman of the Narcotics Control Board.[93] Under these alterations, the Khaleda regime adopted provisions regarding forfeiture of assets, controlled delivery, extradition and international cooperation. In its battle against drug traffickers, the Khaleda regime organized an anti-smuggling task force comprising members of the BDR, Police and Magistracy. This task force suffered from coordination problems during anti-drug operations. In spite of its professional training and skill in dealing with the smugglers, the BDR's authority was confined to five kilometres of border area.[94] In any operation against traffickers beyond these areas, the BDR had to contact other sections of the task force. The resulting delay in communication plus the lack of coordination, meant most smuggling consignments remained beyond the reach of the enforcement authorities.

Furthermore, in accordance with UN Conventions, the Act of 1990 classified all kinds of drugs into three categories, and provided specific punishments for sedative, hypnotic and tranquillizer drugs. The law provided different degrees of punishments, including the death penalty, according to the gravity of the drug offence. In September 1991, the death penalty had been given to an Indian smuggler on charges of heroin trafficking by the anti-smuggling Special Court. Until 1994, Bangladesh had executed about 10 cross-border traffickers of Indian, Pakistani and Sri Lankan origin. However, due to some complexities in the application process, the anti-narcotics legislation has lost its bite during the subsequent years. Contemporary reports suggest that under the Act, many couriers were imprisoned on charges of drug trafficking in different parts of the country.[95] Despite the application of strict punishment, cross-border traffickers were increasingly involved in using transit facilities in Bangladesh for underground drug trade.

⟹ (The Narcotics Control Act of 1990 has largely been unable to deter cross-border traffickers, who have great influence. For example, the arrest of a teen-age US girl, Eliadah McCord, on charge of heroin trafficking created a breath-taking story in Bangladesh. In February 1992, McCord was captured at Zia International Airport while she was carrying 3.3 kilos of Thai heroin strapped to her body.) As the largest seizure up until that time, this incident was widely reported in the mass media. Under the Act of 1990, McCord and her Nigerian trafficking aid, Robert Blankson, were given a life sentence in July 1993.[97] McCord's case suggested that Nigerian drug syndicates were using hired people, on payment of huge sums, to carry drugs from South Asia to Europe, Canada or the US. After two years, McCord came into the limelight when local Human Rights leaders challenged the case in the High Court.[98] In August 1995, the High Court overturned the life sentence while the Bangladesh Supreme Court in July 1996 ordered that the case be proved beyond all reasonable doubts.[99] Despite being in possession of the biggest amount of heroin seized until that time, McCord escaped the death penalty due under the existing laws, thanks to the superpower influence pulled off her release from Bangladesh imprisonment in mid-1997.

Under the Act of 1990, stringent regulations were also imposed on the sale and consumption of liquor. This legislation changed liquor policies that had initially been adopted by the colonial authorities and remained in force under subsequent governments. A maximum 15-year imprisonment was imposed for the production or possession of over 10 litres of alcohol and a maximum 3-year imprisonment for unlicensed consumption of liquor.[100] However, these laws did not work well all the time. A Bangladeshi weekly, *Bichitra*, reported that three drunken police constables in August 1993 lost their firearms and official uniforms at the Jamburi Field in Chittagong.[101] Other police recovered the constables in a unconscious state from a nearby drain the following day. In an alarming incident in April 1998 as many as 70 people died by taking illicit spurious liquor in Gaibanda. Adulterated liquor took about 90 lives on another occasion in

Narshingdi in May 1999. Nevertheless, given these pro-revenue arrangements the government from April to December 1992 earned Tk14.8 million, which rose to Tk18 million during the same duration in 1993.[102] Pursuing a pro-revenue liquor policy, the government in 1994–5, earned Tk20 million from this sector. As a result of duplicity in official policy, it has been difficult to enforce the existing liquor laws.

The lack of control of enforcement agencies encouraged smugglers to supply liquor from illicit sources. A report published in the weekly magazine *Shugandha* in 1992 maintained that Indian liquor mixed with 'Koneya Bartige',[103] a strong sedative that quickly creates physical dependency, was smuggled into Bangladesh. This special brand of liquor was smuggled for the tea planters in northeast Bangladesh. In early August 1992, *Dainik Inquilab* reported that some youths in collaboration with Indian smugglers were openly selling 'Three Rum' to local consumers in Shatkhira. The intrusion of Indian liquor has been challenging both for the country's licit liquor industry in Darsana and the government's revenue policy in liquor.

Corruption amongst enforcement authorities has been a major impediment in the war against traffickers under the strict legislation of 1990. A study conducted by the Bangladesh Institute of Development Studies (BIDS) in 1991 observed that traffickers 'maintain constant liaison with officials of the law enforcement agencies' – for example, customs, police, and the BDR who patrol the country's border.[104] The smuggler's representatives, everywhere known as 'linemen', conduct this liaison and pay off officials. The BIDS report further held that:

> The size of the bribes to the law enforcers is fixed well in advance and regular payments are made which are distributed down to the ranks. The system works smoothly though occasional mis-understandings occur, leading to raids by the authorities and confiscation of some consignments. Sometimes such raids are carried out merely to show the public that the authorities are doing their job.[105]

Lucrative postings at the strategically important locations for customs, police and the BDR are distributed at a high price. The smugglers often take advantage of internal conflicts among the enforcement authorities. Also, political instability caused by *hartals* and strikes gives the smugglers honeymoon periods for their drug running activities. The political instability that helped cross-border traffickers to use Bangladesh as an internal market, and its transit facilities for overseas, has weakened the value of the anti-narcotics laws in Bangladesh. The failure of the courts to deal with the traffickers effectively has been another obstacle for the anti-narcotics drive in the country. The BIDS report asserted that out of 1,200 smugglers arrested in 1992, the courts punished only 10 per cent. In most of the cases, the exchange of money or bribes played an important role in the release of traffickers from police custody. The lack of evidence and contradictory witnesses also helped smugglers to secure release from the courts.

A three-tier chain runs drug trafficking in Bangladesh. The big dealers, who generally do not come on the scene, finance the business. In the second level, brokers usually buy and sell illicit drugs at different strategic points within and beyond the borders of the country. At the grassroots, couriers, linemen and spies operate on a commission basis.[106] While carriers pass narcotics from one spot to another, the linemen keep contact with corrupt members of the enforcement agencies and spies give signals to the couriers about the movements of the enforcement authorities. If, in any case, the courier is caught by the enforcement agencies, his associates quickly disappear.

The anti-narcotics drive of the enforcement authorities in Bangladesh also suffers from a shortage of funds and modern facilities. Because of its meagre resources, Bangladesh has been unable to translate into reality the important provisions of the international agreements, and launch an all-out effort against transnational traffickers. The Khaleda regime in late 1993 signed a bilateral agreement with the US. Under this 'Technical Assistance' agreement, the Department of Narcotics Control received only $89,000 dollars from the US to increase its operational capabilities and for the procurement of equipment.[107] This small allocation was made as a result of a change in the US overseas anti-narcotics programme under the Pressler Amendment Act of 1990. In 1995, the Khaleda regime signed another bilateral treaty with the US. With this assistance, the regime established a 'national coastguard' with adequate trained personnel and equipment to control the illicit supply of drug along the Bay of Bengal.[108] Despite inadequate logistical support and continuing financial constraints, this measure has marginally improved the government's anti-smuggling capabilities in the coastal area.

Also, to help expedite the execution of the anti-narcotics laws, Bangladesh undertook a UNDCP assistance programme in 1993, under which the government from April 1994 launched various anti-narcotics activities: for instance, legal assistance and law enforcement, preventive education and information, treatment and rehabilitation.[109] However, complaints about the absence of an independent forensic laboratory were prevalent within the Narcotics Department. Lack of trained and specialized officials also contributed to the ineffectiveness of the Department. Under existing arrangements, narcotics were tested in the single forensic laboratory run by the CID of Police. As a result, narcotics cases were delayed and there were more opportunities for corruption.

Notwithstanding this situation, the Bangladesh authorities under the Act of 1990 imposed government-funded compulsory withdrawal treatment for known drug addicts.[110] To help provide medical facilities for drug addicts, the Khaleda regime under a 5-year masterplan (1994–8) received financial help from the European Commission.[111] This assistance helped run a 40-bed central Treatment Centre for Drug Addicts at Tejgaon in Dhaka and 5-bed Regional Treatment Centres at Divisional Headquarters in Chittagong, Rajshahi and Khulna. In the face of a population of about 1.5 million phensedyl addicts and over 1.5 million-heroin addicts, these treatment facilities were inadequate. The Khaleda regime also involved about 150 non-governmental organizations (NGOs) to help coordinate the UN drug control programme in Bangladesh, and to take part in a mass awareness campaign against drug addiction. In the past, the success of these programmes has been only marginal.

Finally, despite the adoption of stringent legal measures the Bangladesh authorities have failed to control the flow of illicit heroin and other narcotics and psychotropic substances from cross-border sources. With its ineffectual administrative capacities, Bangladesh is now confronted by a tremendous rise in drug addiction and in the anti-social activities of the trans-border drug criminals. Lack of political stability, shortage of logistical support, and the prevalence of administrative corruption have been major impediments to the successful implementation of strict narcotics laws in Bangladesh in recent years. Alone, Bangladesh is incapable of waging the gigantic war against a drug menace that has mostly been created or tolerated during the last two hundred years for the revenue purposes of colonial and post-colonial authorities.

Epilogue

Drug problems in South Asia are the manifestation of complex issues that have a lengthy history. In any attempt to address the current drug issues in South Asia, an understanding of its past is imperative. Present-day drug problems in South Asia came about through a historical process that includes five phases: first, pre-colonial (seventeenth to mid-eighteenth century); secondly, colonial (mid-eighteenth century to 1947); thirdly, post-colonial (1947 to 1978); fourthly, the Cold War decade (1978 to 1988); and fifthly, the post-Cold War era (1988 to the present). Except for during the pre-colonial period, the central motivating force of almost all the South Asian governments' drug policies has been 'money', while human concerns remained peripheral. Money provided the attraction for traffickers and policy planners alike. Due to its economic value, the opium poppy emerged as one of the most sensitive agricultural products, both within the region and beyond.

The pre-colonial drug trade grew out of mercantile trading companies which discovered the commercial merit of opium during the seventeenth century. The sporadic cultivation of opium poppies that had existed in Afghanistan, India and Nepal for centuries for household use and quasi-medicinal purposes, now became a commodity in business competition between Western trading companies. There is no record available to suggest that before the arrival of European merchants an opium monopoly had ever existed in India, nor had there been any central taxation on such a trade during the Mughal period. Under the umbrella of their governments' policies, organized business groups, for example, the Dutch, Portuguese and British, contributed to the spread of the non-medicinal uses of drugs in South Asia, China, the Asia-Pacific region and elsewhere. Ignoring the long-term consequences of the drug habit, many European trading companies, purely for the accumulation of wealth, participated in the South Asian drug trade, which, by the end of eighteenth century, provided the region with its status as the centre of the world's opium trade. The legitimacy of the opium trade was established by the British East India Company, which monopolized the trade in South Asia in 1773 and sent opium to China and the Asia-Pacific to accumulate capital.

The rise of the British East India Company as one of the most powerful business groups in South Asia brought with it the creation of an opium monopoly by the late eighteenth century. During its 190-year rule in the region, British imperial power emerged as an addict of drug revenue. Due to the importance attached to the accumulation of wealth, the government failed to provide any rational legal system to regulate drugs. As a result of international pressure, especially from the US, the British government by 1935 had surrendered its freedom in the opium trade. The opium policies, pursued by colonial authorities were considered in the US, the UK, China, South Asia, and the Asia-Pacific region, as a crime against humanity. During its colonial rule in South Asia, the British government gained over a quarter of its finance through manifold tax systems on drugs. In defence of the colonial revenue policies, the British Royal Commission on Opium highlighted medical evidence that ignored the socio-economic and human aspects of the issue. Nevertheless, a group of Chinese addict migrants who settled in the big cities along the West Coast of the US and the Asia-Pacific region transmitted the habit of opium smoking to the overseas population during the mid-nineteenth century. This dissemination of the drug habit to the US, the Philippines and elsewhere helped China to draw international attention to issues of control of the colonial opium trade in South Asia.

The failure of the post-independence governments in South Asia to make the existing drug laws more stringent helped to escalate drug problems in the 1980s. Due to a lack of political will amongst the governing elites, the introduction of strict anti-drug legislation, or the enforcement of existing drug laws (introduced mostly in the 1930s) were treated as peripheral issues. For revenue purposes, the post-independence leaders in India dropped anti-drug strategies that they had pursued before the fall of colonial power. They ignored the political crusades of anti-opiumists in the UK, the Non-Cooperation workers in India, and temperance workers elsewhere. To protect its earnings from the international market for medicinal opium, India by the 1960s had adjusted its legislation according to international conventions, but had failed to ensure strict controls in the production and management system.

As a result, when the country faced a setback in the world pharmaceutical market in the late 1970s and 1980s, Indian poppy growers started diverting licit opium into illicit channels. Instead of clamping down on illicit diversion and production, India pursued diplomacy to block Australia, a 'newcomer' to opium production, from entering the international licit market for medicinal opium. In line with the colonial mode of thought, India has re-emerged as the major supplier of narcotic drugs and psychotropic substances to Third World countries in recent years. As a result of this, Bangladesh, Pakistan, the Philippines, Nepal, South Africa, the Middle East and some Western countries have become an external market for Indian drugs. Just as it was in colonial India, drug money is important in the mainstream Indian economy. A nexus between traffickers and some political leaders in India has promoted the drug trade, and corruption has become rampant in the government machinery. A major international initiative has become imperative to stop India from illicit diversion of opium, heroin chemicals, and the supply of illicit heroin, mandrax and phensedyl syrup.

To break the smugglers–cultivators connection, a total ban on poppy cultivation could be an appropriate measure. In that case about 150,000 poppy growers might claim compensation from and look to the government for an alternative crop as a result of being deprived of their traditional rights. A related issue is the fate of 350,000 ex-poppy farmers who have already been eliminated from the government opium industry during the last two decades. These farmers, without their occupation, may be involved in the illicit cultivation of opium poppy in different parts of India. The government's eradication efforts should be coordinated with long-term integrated development projects involving the ousted poppy farmers, and accompanied by law enforcement agencies as required. The maintenance of a strict security system in the management of the opium industry would help India free itself from underworld drug trafficking. Without supplies from India the world pharmaceutical market would suffer a shortage of medicinal opium of at least 50 metric tons of morphine equivalent. Moreover, as a traditional poppy growing country India can claim to continue its 'legitimate' status in the global trade in medicinal opium.

As in India, post-independence Pakistan attempted to revive its own opium industry, but relied in reality on illicit production from the tribal areas of NWFP. This policy, without any significant control in the poppy growing areas, eventually attracted international drug syndicates, which sought to establish control over illicit drugs in the region. Pakistan failed to implement the Single Convention on Narcotics of 1961, and refrained from ratifying the Single Convention on Narcotic Drugs and Psychotropic Substances of 1971. The country was reluctant to pursue tough measures in NWFP, largely to avoid political sensitivity over the Durand Line, which was inherited as a legacy of British war strategies in southwest Asia. For the protection of its security along the western border, Pakistan became involved in the superpower rivalry during the early 1980s.

The strategic use of drug money by some elements of the state apparatus during the Afghan War made the religious approach by General Zia a political mockery. In response to international blame, the Pakistani leaders in 1985 adopted some strong anti-drug legislation that marginally filled a gap in the *Shariah* legal system. As a result of weaknesses in the legal approach, some members of the country's leading military intelligence agency, bureaucracy and democratic institutions came to promote the drug trade. Under the new legislation most of the offenders taken to court by the enforcement agencies were generally addicts and couriers of the trade, and were treated leniently. Due to a lack of evidence, or confusion in the legal provisions, many traffickers evaded punishment. Although sporadic seizures were made, action against key offenders in Pakistan has been minimal. The failure of the Pakistani rulers to try indigenous traffickers under Pakistani laws let the US, Saudi Arabia, Turkey, Germany and other countries continually punish Pakistani offenders under their own provisions. This unfortunate development, which transpired largely from the Afghan crisis, raised a question of credibility about the Pakistani legal system.

The long-term attachment of the tribal *Pathans* to poppy cultivation has created a social and economic bond with opium production. On different occasions, Pakistani poppy growers have violently expressed their 'legitimate' claim, as the British did in the previous century, to the continuation of opium production, as it provides a lucrative means of livelihood in hilly areas. The *Pathans* forcefully resisted the poppy eradication programme of the central authorities and regarded poppy cultivation as their birthright. They demonstrated their grievances against the 'interference' of central authorities and the extension of the international regulations in the tribal areas.

Due to political vulnerability, the central authorities avoided any serious confrontation with the tribal poppy growers. In the absence of central control, the tribal areas in NWFP and Baluchistan emerged as the Columbia of the East. It would be a difficult task to stop them from growing opium poppy, without providing some economic assistance or alternative job opportunities. Any attempt to suppress poppy growing will escalate long-term political tensions in Pakistan along ethnic lines, especially in NWFP and Baluchistan. The setting up of intermediate technologies in the tribal areas will offer the tribal people an option to survive without the opium poppy. The promotion of education and creation of employment opportunities would help to improve the situation economically, and create public awareness among tribal poppy growers about the calamity of heroin addiction both within and outside the region.

Nevertheless, the US's Cold War strategies in Afghanistan were conducive to the diffusion of the heroin trade, and were contradictory to its earlier anti-narcotics crusade. As in southeast Asia, US Cold War strategies in southwest Asia encouraged some Pakistani authorities and Afghan militants to use the money derived from heroin trafficking to support the war in Afghanistan. Following the Cold War era the US governmenthas significantly changed its 'drug war' strategies in South Asia. Instead of pursuing socio-economic policies which would disengage growers from poppies, the US government in the 1990s adopted defensive measures using the country's military in the interdiction of US-bound drugs.

This change in the US, the biggest crusader against the international drug trade, has left many issues outstanding in Afghanistan and Pakistan. At the beginning of the post-Cold War era, Pakistan accommodated some known traffickers in the democratic system, and thereby introduced the influence of drug money in politics. This trend created a new phase in democratic institutions in South Asia. In Pakistan, drug money has pushed many leading politicians, army personnel and high officials into the illicit trade. As a result of recent US pressure, domestic production of opium poppies has decreased, but transit trafficking from Afghanistan has increased tremendously. A large amount of cross-border heroin has continued transiting through Pakistan, while the country has an estimated 2 million heroin addicts. Recent evidence suggests that in an attempt to extend their underground activities, the Pakistani drug cartels are using Bangladesh both as an external market and a passage for heroin from southwest Asia. On 20 September 1999 the officials of the Narcotics Control Department, in their biggest ever drug haul in Dhaka, arrested three Pakistani traffickers and recovered over 24 kilos of heroin worth about Tk250 million, equivalent to US$5 million. A major international initiative is required to crack down on this cross-border trade. The confiscation of property from genuine traffickers and the use of this money for further anti-narcotics drives might help the country economically.

The post-Cold War era also witnessed the funnelling of drug money into ethnic conflicts in South Asia. The alleged connections of the Pakistani ISI in Afghanistan and India, *vis-à-vis* India's alleged involvement in the sectarian violence in Pakistan, have become evident. Without political solutions to some of the major regional conflicts, a permanent solution to the drug trafficking in South Asia is infeasible. The Pakistani connection in the *Taleban* campaign in Afghanistan has been apparent in newspaper reports. Under an ambitious plan to conquer Afghanistan, as the British did in the previous century, the Pakistani military intelligence agency became involved in the Afghan campaign during the post-Cold War era. During colonial rule, after massive defeats, the British government left Afghanistan alone. In the current era, the *Taleban* aided by Pakistani secret agencies now control two-thirds of the territory of Afghanistan. Massive poppy cultivation has continued in *Taleban*-controlled Afghanistan, while the drug trade in Pakistan has assumed a new and expanded dimension. The continuance of this situation will allow clandestine laboratory operators on the Pak-Afghan border to lean on heroin chemicals manufactured in some of the Central Asian States. It will also help traffickers in southwest Asia to use the traditional Silk Road route to Europe and elsewhere. Unless an unified international effort is made to control the illicit drug trade in the region, Pakistan will continue to serve as a conduit for trafficking Afghanistan's uncontrolled heroin, as well as its own production in NWFP.

A broad-based understanding between the nations in South Asia with the participation of world's leading countries might help to resolve many of the outstanding regional issues, including the use of drug money in politics. In the past, international Conventions and Agreements played a major role in regulating the colonial drug policies during the early twentieth century. As a result of international regulations, national legislation on narcotics was tightened in the 1980s. However, the results are still unsatisfactory. Further global action is required to stop the resurgence of the drug trade in India and Pakistan, and to halt the strategic links between drug money and politics. Immense international pressure could deter India and other drug producing countries in the region who presently vacillate in their implementation of strict narcotics laws.

The cross-regional and cross-country differences in legal provisions also helped some pharmaceutical companies's efforts to make undue profits. As I have shown in Chapter 2, in nineteenth-century Britian and the USA, some leading medicine companies were involved in the promotion of opiates. Over the last two decades, for incomparable profits, some leading pharmaceutical companies and chemical industries in India became involved in the promotion of regional drug trade. Under cover of the licit trade, pharmaceutical companies in Bombay have been marketing phensedyl cough syrup. This 'medicine' is causing massive addiction problems in Bangladesh and some other neighbouring countries, where it is designated as contraband. For financial gain, Indian clandestine laboratories became involved in manufacturing heroin and mandrax both for local and foreign customers.

As in India, some multinational companies across the world have shown an impetus in the legalization of hard drugs. They often use writers, journalist and medical experts to argue in favour of their trade policies, and invite politicians to frame laws and policies in accordance with their business interests. Under diverse 'harm minimization' programmes, they have presented alternative drugs that have prolonged drug dependence. This chain of experiments began with the opium trial in China, then morphine in the US, heroin in the UK, and now is perpetuated in the methadone programme in Australia. At every stage, modified medicine was introduced to cure dependency on the previous one, but the end result was adverse. To stop such medical catastrophies, uniform international control is required in South Asia and elsewhere.

The adoption of coordinated legislation on drugs across the globe would help reduce the problem of drug trafficking. While the countries in South Asia have adopted tougher drug laws, some Western countries still prefer to undertake alternative 'trials' of particular drugs. With meagre resources, South Asian countries cannot afford such gigantic costs. Moreover, the differences in legal provision, which vary from region to region, have always been favourable for underground traffickers. For example, to control opium traffic the Chinese authorities in the late 1830s implemented the death penalty for local offenders; however, in India at that time the production and supply of opium was legal, and it was sent to China by traffickers in violation of Chinese laws. In the absence of harmonious policies, the prohibition of intoxicating drugs failed in India during the 1940s, and also after independence. Due to a variation in provincial anti-narcotics laws, a similar affliction occurred in post-independence Pakistan.

Despite the differences between countries within the region, and the uniqueness of each country's situation, the pain of drug addiction and illicit trafficking have become common to each, and are intensifying. Without the application of unvarying laws, it will be difficult to handle such a gigantic problem with such complex global connections. An international summit would facilitate the adoption of unvaried laws on narcotics and introduce a strict international monitoring system on cross-border and cross-regional drug trafficking. The summit could also extract reparations from countries for past misdeeds in the drug trade, and present a quota system for medicinal opium, which would help reduce the global drug problem in the new millennium.

Notes

Abbreviations for publications used in the notes

A	*Australian*
AT	*Asia Times*, Bombay
BO	*Bangladesh Observer*, Dhaka
CSM	*Christian Science Monitor*
D	*Dawn*, Karachi
DB	*Dainik Bangla*, Dhaka
DE	*Down to Earth*, New Delhi
DH	*Deccan Herald*
DI	*Dainik Inqilab*, Dhaka
DJ	*Dainik Janokontho*, Dhaka
EBDG	*Eastern Bengal District Gazetteers*
ET	*Economic Times*
FEER	*Far Eastern Economic Review*, Hong Kong
FR	*Financial Review*, Melbourne
FT	*Financial Times*
H	*Hindu*
HS	*Herald Sun*, Melbourne
HT	*Hindustan Times*, New Delhi
I	*Dainik Ittefaq*, Dhaka
IE	*Indian Express*
IEO	*Indian Economy Overview*
INCSR	*International Narcotics Control Strategy Report*
N	*Nation*, Lahore
NCB	*Narcotics Control Bulletin*
NYT	*New York Times*
OHT	*Overseas Hindustan Times*
P	*Pioneer*, New Delhi
S	*Shangbad*, Dhaka
SMH	*Sydney Morning Herald*
ST	*Statesman Weekly*
ST	*Sunday Times*, London
T	*Times*, London
Tel	*Telegraph*, Calcutta
T of I	*Times of India*, New Delhi & Bombay
UNI	*United Nations Investigation*
WA	*Weekend Australian*
WP	*Washington Post*
WT	*Weekend Telegraph*

Prelude

1 In the present study, 'drug' refers to any substance that creates physical dependency, increases tolerance and eventually makes the user slave to its habit. Non-medicinal drugs are generally harmful for the human body, socially disapproved of, and prohibited either by major religions or international regulations or both.

2 Romesh Dutt, *India in the Victorian Age: An Economic History of the People*, Volume 2 (London: Kegan Paul, Trench, Trubner and Co. Ltd., 1906), p. 384.

3 C.R. Haines, *A Vindication of England's Policy with Regard to the Opium Trade* (London: W.H. Allen & Co., 1884), p. 50.

4 *Reports of Commissioners, India (Opium), Royal Commission on Opium, Final Report, Historical Appendices, Index, Glossary*, British Parliamentary Papers, 1895, Volume 42, p. 131. (Hereafter, *Final Report of the Royal Commission on Opium*, Volume 42.)

5 In the east, the Golden Triangle (Burma, Thailand and Laos), in the west, the Golden Crescent (Afghanistan, Pakistan and Iran), and in the north, the Golden Wedge (Nepal, Tibet (China) and Bhutan).

6 Maurice Collis, *Foreign Mud* (London: Faber and Faber Ltd., 1964), p. 17.

1   Colonial drug trade

1 A classical mention of the drug occurs in the ninth century BC in Homer's *Iliad* where he describes the effect of poppy juice in relieving pain and injuries. *The Illiad of Homer*, trans. Richmond Lattimore (Chicago: University of Chicago Press, 1951), p. 152.

2 Cited in *US Narcotics Control Efforts in Southeast Asia*, Hearing Before the Committee on Foreign Affairs, House of Representatives, One Hundredth Congress, First Session, 30 June and 15 July 1987, pp. 12–13.

3 Abu-l-ali-ibn-Sina or Avicenna, *A Treatise on The Canon of Medicine of Avicenna* (London: Luzac and Co., 1930), pp. 374–75.

4 H.B. Dunnicliff, 'The Indian Opium Trade, A Historical Review', *Asian Review Series*, Volume 34, No. 4, 1938, pp. 349–59.

5 E.H. Walsh, 'The Historical Aspects of the Opium Question', *Calcutta Review*, Volume 102, No. 204, April 1896, p. 258.

6 Richard M. Dane, 'Opium in China and India', *Asian Review*, Proceedings of the East India Association (Series 4), No. 23, 1927, p. 57.

7 Haines, *Vindication*, p. 6.

8 Walsh, 'Historical', p. 258.

9 Appendix B, *Final Report of the Royal Commission on Opium*, Volume 42, p. 250.

10 Dane, 'Opium', pp. 57–8.

11 Zahiru'd-din Muhammad Babur Padshah Gazi, *Babur-Nama* (Memoirs of Babur), Volume 1, trans. Annette Susannah Beveridge (New Delhi: Oriental Books Reprint Corporation, 1970), pp. 385–6.

12 Abu'l Fazl Allami, *A'in-I-Akbari*, Volume 1, trans. H. Blochmann (Delhi: Aadiesh Book Depot, 1965), p. 69.

13 Francois Bernier, *Travels in Mughul Empire: AD 1656–1688* (Delhi: S. Chand and Co., 1968), pp. 39–40.

14 Ibid.

15 Walsh, 'Historical', p. 259.

16 Rutherford Alcock, 'The Opium Trade', *Journal of the Society of Arts*, Volume 30, January 1882, p. 205.

17 In 1537 the Portuguese traders established their business settlement at Macao for the promotion of opium trade in the interior of the country.

18 Dane, 'Opium', p. 60.

19 Ibid., p. 61.

20 Quoted in G.H.M. Batten et al., 'The Opium Question', *Journal of the Society of Arts*, Volume 40, 1892, p. 445.

21 Dane, 'Opium', p. 60.

22 Om Prakash, *The Dutch East India Company and the Economy of Bengal, 1630–1720* (Princeton: Princeton University Press, 1985), pp. 24–34.

23 Dane, 'Opium', p. 61.

24 Ibid.

25 *Fort William–India House Correspondence and Other Contemporary Papers Relating Thereto* (Public Series), 1757–9, Volume 2, Delhi, p. 18.

26 In the second decade of the eighteenth century, Bengal achieved its autonomy and emerged as the Kingdom of Bengal that comprised of Bengal, Bihar, Orissa and Assam.

27 *East India (Opium)*, British Parliamentary Papers, 1890–1, Volume 59, p. 460. (Hereafter, *East India (Opium)*, Volume 59.)

28 Appendix 11, *Reports of Commissioners, India (Opium), Royal Commission on Opium, Minutes of Evidences and Appendices*, British Parliamentary Papers, 1894, Volume 61, p. 371. (Hereafter, *British Royal Commission on Opium*, Volume 61.)

29 *Fort William–India House Correspondence and Other Contemporary Papers Relating Thereto* (Public Series), 1757–9, Volume 2, p. 137.

30 Ibid, p. 30.

31 Appendix 11, *British Royal Commission on Opium*, Volume 61, p. 371.

32 The *bigha* in Akbar's time was 3,025 square yards.

33 *East India (Opium)*, Volume 59, p. 456.

34 Dane, 'Opium', p. 61.

35 D.C. Jayasuria, *Narcotics and Drugs in Sri Lanka: Socio-Legal Dimensions* (Nawala: Asian Pathfinders and Booksellers, 1986), pp. 4–5.

36 Quoted by Batten et al., 'Opium', pp. 444–5.

37 *First Report of the Royal Commission on Opium: with Minutes of Evidence and Appendices*, The British Parliamentary Papers, 1894, Volume 60, p. 723. (Hereafter, *British Royal Commission on Opium*, Volume 60.)

38   Robert N. Cust, 'The Indo-Chinese Opium Question as it Stands in 1893', *Calcutta Review*, Volume 97, No. 193, 1893, p. 127.

39   Allami, *A'in-I-Akbari*, p. 410.

40   Niccolao Manucci, *Storia Do Mogor or Mughal India 1653–1708*, trans. William Irvine, Volume 1 (Calcutta: n.p., 1965), p. 393.

41   *Final Report of the Royal Commission on Opium*, Volume 42, p. 3.

42   Nathan Allen, *The Opium Trade Including a Sketch of its History, Extent, Effects, Etc. as Carried on in India and China* (Boston: Longwood Press, 1853), p. 6.

43   G.N. Chandra, 'Some Facts About Opium Monopoly in Bengal Presidency', *Bengal, Past and Present*, Volume 76, 1957, pp. 123–36.

44   Dharma Kumar and Desai (eds), *The Cambridge Economic History of India*, Volume 2 (London: Cambridge University Press, 1983), p. 146.

45   'The East India Company and the Opium Trade', *Meliora*, Volume 1, 1858, p. 29.

46   C.E. Buckland, 'Opium Smuggling in India', *Blackwood's Edinburgh Magazine*, Volume 151, May 1892, p. 670.

47   *East India (Opium)*, Volume 59, p. 460.

48   *Report from the Select Committee on East India Finance: Together with the Proceedings of the Committee, Minutes of Evidence, and Appendix*, The House of Commons, 18 July 1871, p. 340. (Hereafter, *Select Committee on East India Finance*, 1871.)

49   *Report of the Indian Famine Commission*, Part 1, Famine Relief, East India, Accounts and Papers, Volume 52, House of Commons, 1880, p. 405.

50   Jawaharlal Nehru, *The Discovery of India* (Bombay: Asia Publishing House, 1973), p. 275.

51   *Fort William–India House Correspondence and Other Contemporary Papers Relating Thereto* (Public Series), 1773–6, Volume 7, p. 136.

52   Cited in M.E. Monckton Jones, *Oxford Historical and Literary Studies, Warren Hastings in Bengal 1772–74*, Volume 9 (Oxford: Clarendon Press, 1918), p. 253.

53   *Final Report of the Royal Commission on Opium*, Volume 42, p. 122.

54   H.R.C. Wright, 'The Abolition by Cornwallis of the Forced Cultivation of Opium in Bihar', *The Economic History Review*, Volume 12, Numbers 1–3, 1959–60, p. 115.

55   Ibid., p. 114.

56   Ibid., pp. 117–18.

57   Ibid., p. 112.

58   Rajeshwari Prasad, *Some Aspects of British Revenue Policy in India 1773–1833: The Bengal Presidency*, (Delhi: S. Chand and Co., 1970), p. 149.

59   H.R.C. Wright, 'The Emancipation of the Opium Cultivators in Benares', *International Review of Social History*, Volume 4, Number 3, 1959, p. 452.

60   Adam Smith, *An Inquiry into the Nature and Causes of the Wealth of Nations*, Volume 2 (London: Grant Richards, 1904), p. 249.

61 Major-General R. Alexander, *The Rise and Progress of British Opium Smuggling* (London: Judd and Glass, 1856), p. 6.

62 Prasad, *Some*, p. 160.

63 Appendix 9, *British Royal Commission on Opium*, Volume 61, p. 351.

64 E.N. Baker, 'The Opium Industry', *The Economic Journal*, Volume 6, 1896, p. 115.

65 *East India (Opium), Return of Charges to East India government, in Growth and Monopoly of Opium*, The British Parliamentary Papers, 1857, Session 1 (60), Volume 11, p. 124. (Hereafter, *East India (Opium)*, 1857, Volume 11.)

66 *Final Report of the Royal Commission on Opium*, Volume 42, p. 79.

67 'Opium, Cultivation of in India', *Saturday Review* (London), Volume 72, 15 August 1891, p. 191.

68 Cited in Dutt, *India*, pp. 155–6.

69 'Return of Acreage Under Poppy in India', *The British Parliamentary Papers*, Volume 63, 1897, p. 682.

70 *Select Committee on East India Finance*, 1871, Q. 7257, p. 340.

71 William Forbes-Mitchell, *Reminiscences of the Great Mutiny 1857–59* (London: Macmillan and Co., 1893), pp. 293–94.

72 L.S.S. O'Malley (ed.), *Modern India and the West* (London: Oxford University Press, 1941), p. 55.

73 *Colonies East India, British Parliamentary Papers*, Volume 18, Sessions 1859, Q.N. 3934.

74 Cited in Allen, *Opium Trade*, p. 9.

75 Alexander, *Rise*, p. 4.

76 Donald Matheson, *What is the Opium Trade* [?] (Edinburgh: Thomas Constable and Co., 1857), p. 5.

77 Alexander, *Rise*, p. 21.

78 Prasad, *Some*, p. 156.

79 R.Y. Lo, *The Opium Problem in the Far East* (Shanghai: The Commercial Press, 1933), p. 5.

80 *British Royal Commission on Opium*, Volume 60, p. 705.

81 Amongst the British-owned firms, Jardine & Company, Burn, Macivar & Company, Matheson & Company, Dent & Company were prominent, while Russell & Company and Perkins & Company were owned by US merchants. A Parsee firm, Rustomjee & Company, also took part in this state-sponsored trade. Allen, pp. 15–16; Collis, p. 34; Martin Booth, *Opium: A History* (London: Simon and Schuster, 1996), p. 116.

82 Dane, 'Opium', p. 67.

83 Matheson, *What*, p. 38.

84 *East India (Opium)*, 1857, Volume 11, p. 6.

85 Ibid., p. 8.

86 Article 1, *The Law Relating to Opium* (Act No. 13 of 1857), Appendix 48, *British Royal Commission on Opium*, Volume 61, p. 533. (Hereafter, *The Opium Act of 1857*.)

87 Article 11, *The Opium Act of 1857*, p. 533.

88 Appendix 11, *British Royal Commission on Opium*, Volume 61, p. 378.

89   One *seer* is about 0.933 kilos.

90   Buckland, 'Opium', pp. 674–6.

91   Article 11(d), *The Opium Act, 1878* (Act No. 1 of 1878), Appendix 48, *British Royal Commission on Opium*, Volume 61, pp. 539–42. (Hereafter, *The Opium Act of 1878.*)

92   Ibid., p. 540.

93   'Notes on Madras as a Winter Residence', *Medical Times and Gazette*, Volume 3, No. 2, 19 July 1873, p. 73.

94   'Return of Acreage under Poppy in India', *The British Parliamentary Papers*, Volume 66, House of Commons, 1897, p. 684. (Hereafter, *Return of Acreage under Poppy in India*, 1897.)

95   During the mid-nineteenth century, the principal Malwa poppy growing areas were Gwalior, Indore, Bhopal, Jaora, Ratlam, Bhopawar, Narshingarh, Rajghar, Sitamau, Dewas, Sailana, Khilchipur, Piploda in Central India.

96   H.R.C. Wright, 'James Augustus Grant and the Gorkhapur Opium, 1789–1796', *Royal Asiatic Society of Great Britain and Ireland Journal*, April 1960, p. 2.

97   *Fort William–India House Correspondence and Other Contemporary Papers Relating Thereto* (Foreign, Political and Secret), 1796–1800, Volume 18, p. 317.

98   Ibid., pp. 540–4.

99   This rate was initially at Rs175 a *chest* (63.7 kilos) which gradually increased to Rs700 per *chest* by late 1880s.

100 Appendix 11, *British Royal Commission on Opium*, Volume 61, p. 377.

101 Baker, 'Opium Industry', p. 117; Cust, 'Indo-Chinese', p. 132.

102 *British Royal Commission on Opium*, Volume 61, p. 359.

103 D.W.K.B., 'The Indian Opium Revenue', *Calcutta Review*, Volume 63, No. 126, 1876, p. 366.

104 Batten et al., 'Opium', p. 449.

105 G.S. Bajpai, 'India and the Opium Trade', *Atlantic Monthly*, Volume 129, June 1922, p. 742.

106 *Eastern Bengal District Gazetteers: Dacca District* (Allahabad: The Pioneer Press, 1912), p. 140.

107 Ibid., p. 139.

108 Alexander, *Rise*, p. 10.

109 *Report of the Cultivation of, and Trade in, Ganja in Bengal* by Hem Chunder Kerr, *Accounts and Papers, East India 1893–94*, British Parliamentary Papers, Volume 66, p. 107. (Hereafter, *Report of the Cultivation of, and Trade in, Ganja in Bengal, 1893–94*, Volume 66.)

110 *The Saturday Review*, Volume 72, 15 August 1891, p. 192.

111 *Report of the Cultivation of, and Trade in, Ganja in Bengal, 1893–94*, Volume 66, p. 108.

112 Appendix 22, *British Royal Commission on Opium*, Volume 61, pp. 431–32.

113 Under Articles 4 and 5 of the Regulation, excise opium was supplied to the district treasury for distribution at the rate of Rs10 per *seer*. The

unlicensed sale of opium and other intoxicating drugs was restricted under Regulation 10 of 1813.

114 Appendix 22, *British Royal Commission on Opium*, Volume 61, pp. 434–5.

115 *East India Revenue (Opium)*, The British Parliamentary Papers, Volume 58, p. 633.

116 Appendix 30, *British Royal Commission on Opium*, Volume 61, pp. 460–1,

117 Appendix 29, *Reports of Commissioners, India (Opium), Royal Commission on Opium, Minutes of Evidences and Appendices*, British Parliamentary Papers, Volume 62, House of Commons, 1894, pp. 517–19. (Hereafter, *British Royal Commission on Opium*, Volume 62.)

2 Anti-opium pressures

1   Frederich J. Masters, 'The Opium Traffic in California', *Chautauquan*, Volume 24, 1896–7, p. 56.

2   'Treaties and Documents Concerning Opium', *Supplement to the American Journal of International Law*, Volume 3, 1909, p. 253.

3   Mathea Falco, 'US Drug Policy: Addicted to Failure', *Foreign Policy*, Number 102, Spring 1996, p. 120; Paul B. Stares, *Global Habit: The Drug Problem in a Borderless World* (Washington, DC: Bookings Institutions, 1996), p. 16–7.

4   Peter D. Lowes, *The Genesis of International Narcotics Control* (Geneva: Librairie Droz, 1966), p. 91.

5   John Liggins, *Opium: England's Coercive Policy and Its Disastrous Results in China and India, The Spread of Opium Smoking in America* (New York: Funk and Wagnalls, Publishers, 1882), p. 20.

6   C.F. Holder, 'The Opium Industry in America', *Scientific American*, Volume 78, 1898, p. 147.

7   'Opium 'Joints' in the Black Hills', *Chamber's Journal*, 13 October 1888, p. 655.

8   Masters, 'Opium', p. 56.

9   Lowes, *Genesis*, p. 91.

10 Don S. Kirschner, 'The Ambiguous Legacy: Social Justice and Social Control in the Progressive Era', *Historical Reflections*, Volume 2, Summer 1975, pp. 71,73.

11 Liggins, *Opium*, p. 1.

12 Carl D. Chambers, James A. Inciardi and Harvey A. Siegal, *Chemical Coping: A Report on Legal Drug Use in the United States* (New York: Spectrum Publications, Inc., 1975), p. 64.

13 F. Ludlow, 'Opiate Use in Post-Civil War America', *Harper's New Monthly Magazine*, Volume 35, August 1867, p. 377.

14 Henry James Brown, *An Opium Cure: Based upon Science, Skill and Matured Experience* (New York: Fred M. Brown and Co., 1872), pp. 3–13.

15 Hains, *Vindication*, pp. 43–8.

16 H. Wayne Morgan, *Drugs in America: A Social History, 1800–1980* (Syracuse: Syracuse University Press, 1981), p. 12.

17 Brown, *Opium*, p. 20.

18 Cited in Charles E. Terry and Mildred Pellens, *The Opium Problem* (New York: The Bureau of Social Hygiene, Inc., 1928), p. 5.

19. John C. Ball and Carl D. Chambers (eds), *The Epidemiology of Opiate Addiction in the United States* (Chicago: Charles C. Thomas Publishers, 1970), p. 23; David W. Maurer and Victor H. Vogel, *Narcotics and Narcotic Addiction* (Chicago: Charles C. Thomas, 1962), p. 6; William Butler Eldridge, *Narcotics and the Law: A Critique of the American Experiment in Narcotic Drug Control* (Chicago: The University of Chicago Press, 1967), p. 4.

20 Torald Soollman, *A Manual of Pharmacology* (Philadelphia: W.B. Saunders Co., 1932), p. 15.

21 Ludlow, 'Opiate', p. 387.

22 H.J. Anslinger and William F. Tompkins, *The Traffic in Narcotics* (New York: Funk and Wagnalls Company, 1953), p. 263.

23 J.B. Mattison, 'The Prevention of Opium Addiction', *Louisville Medical News*, Volume 17, 23 February 1884, pp. 113–15.

24 Cited in Eva Bertram et al., *Drug War Politics: The Price of Denial* (Berkeley: University of California Press, 1996), p. 61.

25 Jessica de Grazia, *DEA: The War Against Drugs* (London: BBC Books, 1991), p. 3.

26 David F. Musto, *The American Disease: Origins of Narcotic Control* (Oxford: Oxford University Press, 1987), p. 2.

27 Hamilton Wright, 'International Need', *Report of the International Opium Commission*, Shanghai, China, February 1–26, 1909, Volume 2, p. 22. (Hereafter, *Report of the International Opium Commission*, Volume 2, 1909.)

28 *NYT*, 10 June 1900, p. 1.

29 S.D. Stein, *International Diplomacy, State Administrators and Narcotics Control: The Origins of a Social Problem* (Hampshire: Gower Publishing Company Limited, 1985), p. 12.

30 *Report of the Hearings at the American State Department on Petitions to the President to Use his Good Offices for the Release of China from Treaty Compulsion to Tolerate the Opium Traffic, with Additional Papers*. 1905, Senate Document No. 135. 58th Congress, 3rd Session, Washington DC, p. 1. (Hereafter, Senate Document No. 135. 58th Congress, 3rd Session.)

31 Paul Hibbert Clyde, *United States Policy Toward China: Diplomatic and Public Documents 1839–1939* (New York: Russell and Russell Inc. 1964), p. 107.

32 Cited in Arnold H. Taylor, *American Diplomacy and the Narcotics Traffic, 1900–1939: A Study in International Humanitarian Reform* (Durham, N.C.: Duke University Press, 1969), p. 49.

33 A.P. Harper, 'Ravages of the British Opium Trade in Asia', *Our Day: A Record and Review of Current Reform*, Volume 10, 1892, p. 546.

34 Senate Document No. 135. 58th Congress, 3rd Session, p. 5.
35 Ibid., p. 2.
36 Julean Arnold, Department of Commerce, Bureau of Foreign and Domestic Commerce, *Commercial Handbook of China*, Volume 1 (Washington: Government Printing Office, 1919), p. 129.
37 Foster Rhea Dulles, *China and America: The Story of their Relations Since 1784* (Princeton: Princeton University Press, 1967), pp. 100–5.
38 Charles S. Campbell, *Special Business Interests and the Open Door Policy* (New Haven: Yale University Press, 1951), p. 1.
39 M.B. Young, *The Rhetoric of Empire* (Cambridge, Mass: Harvard University Press, 1968), p. 4.
40 Quoted by Dulles, *China*, pp. 104–5.
41 Article 14, 'Commercial Treaty between China and United States', in Julean Arnold, *Commercial Handbook of China*, Volume 2, Department of Commerce, Miscellaneous Series No. 84 (Washington: Government Printing Office, 1920), p. 40.
42 *Return of Acreage Under Poppy in India, 1897*, p. 684.
43 James S. Dennis, *Christian Missions and Social Progress: A Sociological Study of Foreign Missions*, Volume 2 (New York: Fleming H. Revell Company, 1899), p. 130.
44 Jim Zwick (ed.), *Anti-imperialism in the United States, 1898–1935*, http://home.ican.net/~fjzwick/ail98–35.html
45 *Final Report of the Royal Commission on Opium*, Volume 42, p. 131.
46 David E. Owen, *British Opium Policy in China and India* (New Haven: Archon Books, 1968), p. 318.
47 *Hansard*, Volume 158, 1906, p. 508.
48 Arnold Foster, 'The Report of the Opium Commission', *Contemporary Review*, Volume 74, 1898, p. 125.
49 Owen, *British*, pp. 318–19.
50 *Report of the Committee Appointed by the Philippine Commission to Investigate the Use of Opium and the Traffic Therein, and the Rules, Ordinances, and Laws Regarding such Use and Traffic in Japan, Formosa, Shanghai, Hong-Kong, Saigon, Singapore, Burma, Java, and the Philippines Islands*, Senate Document No. 265, 59th Congress, 1st Session, Washington, 1906, p. 53. (Hereafter, *Report of the Philippines Opium Commission*.)
51 Elihu Root, Department of State, Washington, 7 May 1908 to the President, *Correspondence Relative to the International Opium Commission at Shanghai, 1909. China No. 2 (1909)*, Parliamentary Papers, House of Commons, Volume 105, pp. 310–11.
52 *Report of the Philippines Opium Commission*, 1906, p. 55.
53 *Foreign Relations*, the Acting Secretary of State Robert Bacon to Minister Rockhill. Department of State, Washington, 11 July 1906, Volume 1, No. 161, p. 352.
54 Eva Bertram et al., *Drug War Politics: The Price of Denial* (Berkeley: University of California Press, 1996), p. 65.
55 'Bishop Brent to the President', 24 July 1906, 59th Congress, 2nd Session, House of Representatives, Document No. 1 [Inclosure] Great

Britain, *Papers Relating to the Foreign Relations of the United States with the Annual Message of the President Transmitted to Congress*, 3 December 1906, Washington, 1909, p. 362.

56 'The Acting Secretary of State to Ambassador Reid' [No. 297], Ibid., pp. 360–1.

57 'Correspondence Respecting the Opium Question in China', Sir Edward Grey to Sir M. Durand, Foreign Office, 17 October 1906, *The British Parliamentary Papers, China, No. 2, 1908*, Volume 125, p. 83.

58 Hamilton Wright, 'The International Opium Commission', *American Journal of International Law*, Volume 3, July 1909, p. 672.

59 *Hansard*, Fourth Series, Third Session of the Twenty-Eighth Parliament, Volume 188, 1908, p. 366.

60 Cited in Stanley A. Wolpert, *Morley and India: 1906–1910* (Berkeley: University of California Press, 1967), p. 219.

61 *Hansard*, Volume 158, 1906, p. 502.

62 *Hansard*, Volume 188, 1908, p. 367.

63 Cited in James S. Dennis, *Christian Missions and Social Progress: A Sociological Study of Foreign Missions*, Volume 2 (New York: Fleming H. Revell Company), p. 132.

64 *Hansard*, Third Series, Volume 274, 7 November 1882, p. 947.

65 *Hansard*, Third Series, Volume 267, 9 March 1882, pp. 456–7.

66 H.C. Mookerjee, 'Opium at Geneva 1921–1925', *The Calcutta Review*, Volume 102, February/March 1947, p. 107.

67 Ibid., p. 8.

68 Select Committee on East India Finance, pp. 237–51.

69 Ibid., pp. 341–4.

70 *Final Report of the Royal Commission*, Volume 42, p. 113.

71 *Hansard*, Volume 158, 1906, p. 501.

72 Ibid., p. 502.

73 Liggins, *Opium*, p. 14.

74 *British Royal Commission on Opium*, Volume 61, p. 134.

75 Ibid., p. 496.

76 *British Royal Commission on Opium*, Volume 62, p. 91.

77 *Final Report of the Royal Commission on Opium*, Volume 42, p. 23.

78 *Abstract of the Proceedings of The Council of the Governor General of India*, Assembled for the Purpose of Meeting Laws and Regulations, From April 1906 to March 1907, with Index, Volume 45, Calcutta: Office of the Superintendent of Government Printing, India, 1907, p. 1. (Hereafter, *Proceedings of the Council of the Governor General of India*, Volume 45, 1907.)

79 *Final Report of the British Royal Commission on Opium*, Volume 42, p. 130.

80 *Proceedings of the Council of the Governor General of India*, Volume 45, p. 216.

81 Ibid, p. 160.

82 *Hansard*, Volume 188, 1908, p. 370.

83 *Select Committee on East India Finance*, 1871, pp. 168–343.

84 *Report of the Indian Famine Commission*, Part 1, Famine Relief, East India, Accounts and Papers, Volume 52, The House of Commons, 1880, pp. 405–20.

85 John F. Hurst, 'The Story of the Opium Curse in India', *Chautaquaquan*, Volume 12, 1890–1, p. 771.

86 Cyrus Hamim, 'The Anti-opium Resolution in Parliament', *Our Day: A Record and Review of Current Reform*, Volume 8, September 1891, No. 45, p. 154.

87 Dutt, *India*, pp. 155–6.

88 *Hansard*, Volume 188, 1908, p. 368.

89 A.P. Harper, 'Ravages of the British Opium Trade in Asia', *Our Day: A Record and Review of Current Reform*, Volume 10, 1892, p. 554.

90 *Burma, Lower, Papers Relating to Consumption of Opium in British Burma*, Opinions (official and non-official), reports and memoranda submitted in the investigation undertaken by Sir Charles Aitchison, Chief Commissioner, Rangoon, 1881, p. 646.

91 Under Buddhist influence, public opinion in Japan was against the use of opium. Hatred of opium prevailed amongst the Japanese. Having observed the evil effects of the opium addiction amongst the Chinese, the Japanese constitution forbade importation, possession and use of the drug except for medicinal purposes.

92 *T*, 11 April 1891, p. 9.

93 *Burma, Lower, Papers Relating to Consumption of Opium in British Burma*, Opinions (official and non-official), reports and memoranda submitted in the investigation undertaken by Sir Charles Aitchison, Chief Commissioner, Rangoon, 1881, p. 646.

94 Ronald D. Renard, *The Burmese Connection: Illegal Drugs and the Making of the Golden Triangle* (London: Lynne Rienner Publishers, 1996), pp. 15–18.

95 'Copy of Memorandum by C.U. Aitchison, Chief Commissioner of British Burma, Addressed to the government of India 1880, on the Consumption of Opium in British Burma; and other Papers relating thereto', India Office, 25 April 1881. *Opium (British Burma)*, The House of Commons, 2 June 1881, p. 643.

96 Ibid., p. 469.

97 Renard, *Burmese*, p. 22.

98 Appendix 40, *The British Royal Commission on Opium*, Volume 61, 1894, Rule No. 67, p. 496 [502].

99 *Burma (Opium)*, 'Return of the Amount of Indian Opium annually consumed in Burma during the last Thirty Years', India Office, 12 November 1906, Parliamentary Papers, Volume 81, House of Commons, 1906, p. 908.

100 *Report of the Ceylon Committee on Opium*, Ceylon: Correspondence Relating to the Consumption of Opium in Ceylon, Presented to both Houses of Parliament by Command of His Majesty, May 1908, p. 859. (Hereafter, *Report of the Ceylon Commission on Opium*, 1908.)

101 *T*, 15 November 1894, p. 6.

102 *Return of Acreage under Poppy in India*, 1897, p. 684.
103 *Report of the Ceylon Committee on Opium*, 1908, pp. 858–9.
104 Cited in Jayasuriya, *Narcotics*, p. 8.
105 Mary and Marg Leitch, 'Opium and Hemp in Ceylon', *Lend A Hand*, Volume 12, 1893–4, p. 51.
106 *Report of the Ceylon Committee on Opium*, 1908, p. 859.
107 *Royal Commission on Opium, First Report, Minutes of Evidence and Appendices*, Volume 60, 1894, p. 591.
108 Cited in *Report of the Ceylon Committee on Opium*, 1908, p. 855.
109 *British Royal Commission on Opium*, Volume 60, 1894, p. 591.
110 *Report of the Ceylon Committee on Opium*, 1908, p. 859.
111 *Final Report of the Royal Commission on Opium*, Volume 42, p. 131.
112 Virginia Berridge and Griffith Edwards, *Opium and the People: Opiate Use in Nineteenth-Century England* (London: Allen Lane, 1981), p. 186.
113 *Report of the Ceylon Committee on Opium*, 1908, p. 860.
114 Joshua Rowntree, *The Imperial Drug Trade* (London: Methuen and Co., 1905), p. 121.
115 William O. Walker, *Opium and Foreign Policy: The Anglo-American Search for Order in Asia, 1912–1954* (London: The University of North Carolina Press, 1991), p. 14.
116 *Report of the Ceylon Committee on Opium*, 1908, p. 883.
117 'The Birmingham Committee', *The Friend of China*, Volume 6, October 1875, p. 206.
118 F. Stross Turner, 'Opium and England's Duty', *Nineteenth Century*, Volume 11, 1882, p. 249.
119 Hamim, 'Anti-opium', p. 154.
120 Quoted by Liggins, *Opium*, p. 35.
121 Harper, 'Ravages', p. 545.
122 *Hansard*, Fourth Series, Volume 5, 26 June–18 July 1893, p. 603.
123 Gerald N. Grob (ed.), *American Perceptions of Drug Addiction: Five Studies, 1872–1912* (New York: Arno Press, 1981).
124 Wen-Tsao Wu, *The Chinese Opium Question in British Opinion and Action* (New York: The Academy Press, 1928), p. 139.
125 'Appendix to Mr. H.J. Wilson's Dissent', *Final Report of the Royal Commission on Opium*, Volume 42, pp. 197–8.
126 *Letter from the Government of India*, No. 212 (Finance and Commerce), 9 August 1892, with Enclosures, *Papers Relating to the Consumption of Ganja and Other Drugs in India,* The House of Commons, 3 March 1893, p. 82.
127 *Report of the Cultivation of and Trade in Ganja in Bengal*, 1893, p. 231; Oriana Josseau Kalant, 'Report of the Indian Hemp Drugs Commission, 1893–94: A Critical Review', *The International Journal of Addiction*, Volume 7, No. 1, 1972, pp. 90–2.
128 Mary and Margaret Leitch, 'Opium and Hemp in Ceylon', *Lend A Hand*, Volume 12, 1893–4, p. 53.
129 Joseph G. Alexander, 'The Truth About the Opium War', *The North American Review*, Volume 163, 1896, p. 382.

130 Bruce D. Johnson, 'Righteousness Before Revenue: The Forgotten Moral Crusade Against the Indo-China Opium Trade', *Journal of Drug Issues*, Volume 5, No. 4, Fall, 1975, p. 318.
131 *Hansard*, Third Series, Volume 53, 8 April 1840, p. 818.
132 *Hansard*, Third Series, Volume 68, 4 April 1843, p. 362.
133 *Hansard*, Third Series, Volume 144, 9 March 1857, pp. 2027–33.
134 *T*, 11 April 1891, p. 9.
135 Hamim, 'Anti-opium', p. 153.
136 J.F. Stephen, 'The Opium Resolution', *The Nineteenth Century*, Volume 29, No. 172, June 1891, p. 851.
137 For example, in his book Chris Cook neither mentions anti-opium as a prime cause for the Liberal victory nor takes into consideration that there were candidates with anti-opium views. Chris Cook, *A Short History of the Liberal Party 1900–84* (London: Macmillan, 1984), pp. 42–51.
138 J.B. Brown, 'Politics of the Poppy: The Society for the Suppression of the Opium Trade, 1874–1916', *Journal of Contemporary History*, Volume 8, Number 3, July 1973, London, p. 109.
139 *Proceedings of the Council of The Governor General of India*, Assembled for the Purpose of Making Laws and Regulations, From April 1908 to March 1909, with Index, Volume 47, Calcutta, Superintendent Government Printing Press, India, 1909, p. 177.
140 *Hansard*, Volume 158, 1906, p. 494.
141 Ibid., p. 495.
142 Ibid., p. 507.
143 Ibid., pp. 506–11.
144 Stein, *International*, p. 21.
145 Cited in Stanley A. Wolpert, *Morley and India 1906–1910* (Berkeley: University of California Press, 1967), p. 220.
146 *Hansard*, Volume 158, 1906, pp. 505–15.
147 Bruce D. Johnson, 'Righteousness Before Revenue: The Forgotten Moral Crusade Against the Indo-Chinese Opium Trade', *Journal of Drug Issues*, Fall 1975, p. 317.
148 John Viscount Morley, *Recollections*, Volume 2 (London: Macmillan and Co. Ltd., 1917), p. 172.
149 *Hansard*, Volume 188, 1908, pp. 339–40.
150 Wu, *Chinese*, p. 161.
151 *Hansard*, Volume 188, 1908, p. 360.
152 Ibid., p. 376.

3 British narco-diplomacy, 1909–46

1 'Memorandum on Opium in India, Reports from Great Britain and its Possessions, etc.', *Report of the International Opium Commission*, Shanghai, China, Volume 2, 1909, p. 173.
2 H.J. Ansliger and William F. Tompkins, *The Traffic in Narcotics* (New York: Funk and Wagnalls Company, 1953), p. 30.

3 *Correspondence Relative to the International Opium Commission at Shanghai, 1909*, China No. 2, Parliamentary Papers, Volume 105, House of Commons, 1909, pp. 312–13; *Report of the British Delegates to the International Opium Conference Held at The Hague*, December 1911–January 1912, Miscellaneous. No. 11 (1912), Parliamentary Papers, Volume 68, House of Commons, 1912–13, p. 767.

4 Cited in Lowes, *Genesis*, p. 126.

5 Hamilton Wright, 'The International Opium Conference', *The American Journal of International Law*, Volume 6, 1912, p. 872.

6 Vladimir Kusevic, 'Drug Abuse Control and International Treaties', *Journal of Drug Issues*, Volume 7, No. 1, 1977, pp. 35–6.

7 Editorial Comment, 'The International Opium Conference', *The American Journal of International Law*, Volume 5, 1911, p. 467.

8 International Opium Commission, Official Documents, *Supplement to the American Journal of International Law*, Volume 3, 1909, pp. 275–6.

9 'Sir Cecil Clementi Smith to Sir Edward Grey', London, 8 April 1909, *Correspondence Relative to the International Opium Commission at Shanghai, 1909*, China No. 2, Parliamentary Papers, Volume 105, House of Commons, 1909, p. 313.

10 *India Legislative Council Proceedings*, Volume 49, 7 March 1911, p. 290.

11 *India Legislative Council Proceedings*, Volume 50, 22 September 1911, p. 46.

12 *India Legislative Council Proceedings*, Volume 51, 17 March 1913, pp. 453–7.

13 *India Legislative Council Proceedings*, Volume 52, 6 January 1914, p. 98.

14 *East India (Constitutional Reforms), Report on Indian Constitutional Reforms*, Parliamentary Papers, Volume 8, House of Commons, 1918, p. 196.

15 *India, Legislative Council Proceedings*, Volume 48, 4 March 1910, p. 306.

16 For example, the Bengal Excise Act 1909, the Burma Opium Law Amendment Act 1909, the United Provinces Excise Act 1910, the Eastern Bengal and Assam Excise Act 1910, the Punjab Excise Act 1914, the Bihar and Orissa Excise Act 1915, the Central Provinces Excise Act 1915 and the Burma Excise Act 1917.

17 *The Burma Opium Law Amendment Act, 1909* (Act No. 7 of 1909), An Act Further to Amend the Law Relating to Opium in Burma, *Burma Gazette*, 22 January 1910, pp. 1–2.

18 *The Burma Excise Act, 1917* (Burma Act No. 5 of 1917), An Act to Consolidate and Amend the Excise law in Burma, *Burma Gazette*, 19 May 1917, pp. 1–25.

19 Cited in R.L. Gupta, *Law of Opium and Opium Smuggling* (Allahabad: Law Book Co., 1971), p. 151.

20 J. Coatman (ed.), *India 1926–27* (Calcutta: Government of India Central Publication Branch, 1928), p. 157. (Hereafter, *India 1926–27*.)

21 J. Byrne, *Bengal District Gazetteers, Bhagalpur* (Calcutta: Bengal Secretariat Book Depot, 1911), p. 144.

22 H.C. Mookerjee, 'Opium Consumption, 1858–1893', *The Calcutta Review*, December 1946, p. 204.

23 Appendix 1, 'Paper by Sir William Meyer on the Control over the Production, Sale, and Possession of Raw Opium in India, outside Burmah', *Report of the British Delegates to the International Conference Held at The Hague, December 1911–January 1912.* Miscellaneous No. 11 (1912), British Parliamentary Papers, Volume 68, House of Commons, 1912–13, p. 771.

24 *India Legislative Council Proceedings*, Volume 49, 3 January 1911, p. 105.

25 Ibid.

26 *India Legislative Council Proceedings*, Volume 50, 1 March 1912, p. 313.

27 Article 1, *Treaty Series, 1911, No. 13, Agreement Between the United Kingdom and China Relating to Opium.* Signed in English and Chinese Texts at Peking, May 8, 1911, Together with Notes relating thereto exchanged on that day, London, June 1911, pp. 231–36.

28 Alvey A. Adee, Acting Secretary of State, 'Circular Instructions Issued by United States Respecting International Opium Conference', Department of State, Washington, 1 September 1909, as published in *Instructions to the British delegates to the International Opium Conference Held at The Hague*, December 1911–January 1912. Miscellaneous. No. 3 (1913), Parliamentary Papers, Volume 68, House of Commons, 1912–13, p. 738.

29 Appendix 1, 'Paper by Sir William Meyer on the Control over the Production, Sale, and Possession of Raw Opium in India, outside Burmah', *Report of the British Delegates to the International Conference Held at The Hague*, December 1911–January 1912. Miscellaneous No. 11 (1912), Parliamentary Papers, House of Commons, Volume 68, 1912–13, p. 771.

30 Roy K. Anderson, *Drug Smuggling and Taking in India and Burma* (Calcutta: Thacker, Spink and Co., 1922), pp. 57–74.

31 George Barnes, 'Cocaine', *India Legislative Council Proceedings*, Volume 55, 27 September 1916, p. 75.

32 Chapter 1, *International Opium Convention*, Signed at The Hague, 23 January 1912, *League of Nations Document, O.C.I. (1)*, pp. 26–7; *Treaty Series, 1921, No. 17, The International Opium Convention, 1912, and Subsequent Relative Papers*, Presented to Parliament by Command of His Majesty, London, 1921, pp. 236–7.

33 S.K. Chatterjee, *Legal Aspects of International Drug Control* (The Hague: Martinus Nijhoff Publishers, 1981), f.n. 94 (ii), p. 65.

34 Resolution 4, *Correspondence Respecting the Third International Opium Conference Held at The Hague*, June 1914, Miscellaneous No. 4 (1915), Parliamentary Papers, House of Commons, Volume 83, 1914–16, p. 614; International Opium Convention: The Hague, US Treaties, Etc., *Multilateral Agreements, 1776–1917*, Drugs: Opium, Etc. – January 23, 1912, Treaty Series, No. 612, p. 876.

35 G.S. Bajpai, 'India and the Opium trade', *Atlantic Monthly*, Volume 129, June 1922, p. 743.

36 Stanley Reed and S.T. Sheppard (eds), *The Indian Year Book 1930*, A Statistical and Historical Annual of the Indian Empire, with an Explanation of the Principal Topics of the Day (Bombay: Bennet, Coleman & Co., Ltd., 1930), p. 771.

37 *Hansard*, 7 May 1913, Volume 52, Series 5, p. 2181.

38 Ibid., pp. 2150–5.

39 Ibid., p. 2190.

40 Lowes, *Genesis*, p. 168.

41 Ibid., p. 167.

42 Ibid., p. 168.

43 W.W. Willoughby, *Opium as an International Problem: The Geneva Conferences* (Baltimore: The Johns Hopkins Press, 1925), p. 67.

44 L.E.S. Eisenlohr, *International Narcotics Control* (London: George Allen and Unwin Ltd., 1934), p. 223.

45 Dunnicliff, 'Indian', p. 355.

46 Eisenlohr, *International*, p. 229.

47 'Exports of Merchandise', *Review of the Trade of India in 1918–19*, Part 1 – Report, Parliamentary Papers, Volume 35, House of Commons, 1920, pp. 617–18.

48 Enclosure No. 8, *Review of the Trade of India in 1918–19*, Part 2 – Tables, Parliamentary Papers, Volume 35, House of Commons, 1920, p. 643.

49 Enclosure No. 2, *East India (Constitutional Reforms: Provincial Revenues) Recommendations of the Government of India Regarding Demarcation Between Central and Provincial Revenues*, London, 1919, Volume 37, pp. 948–9.

50 *India Legislative Council Proceedings*, Volume 55, 8 February 1917, p. 223.

51 *East India (Constitutional Reforms: Draft Rules Under the government of India Act, 1919), No. 4. Draft Rules Under Sections 1,2,4 (3), 10 (3), 12 and 33 of the Government of India Act, 1919*, Parliamentary Papers, House of Commons, Volume 35, 1920, p. 508–14.

52 *India in 1923–24*, p. 224.

53 *Report of the Indian Statutory Commission*, Volume 1, Survey (London: His Majesty's Stationary Office, 1930), p. 363.

54 *Treaty Series, 1921, No. 17, The International Opium Convention, 1912, and Subsequent Relative Papers*, Presented to Parliament by Command of His Majesty, London, 1921, p. 269.

55 *Bengal District Gazetteer*, B. Volume, Statistics 1921–2 to 1930–1 (Calcutta: Bengal Secretariat Book Depot, 1933), pp. 11–13.

56 Willoughby, *Opium*, p. 66.

57 *India Legislative Council Proceedings*, Volume 49, 7 March 1911, p. 290.

58 'Report of the Assam Opium Enquiry Committee', *The Indian Annual Register*, Volume 2, 1925, p. 110. (Hereafter, *Report of the Assam Opium Enquiry Committee*.)

59 H.G. Alexander, *Narcotics in India and South Asia* (London: Williams and Norgate Ltd, 1930), p. 33.
60 P.C. Bamford, *Histories of the Non-Cooperation and Khilafat Movements* (Delhi: K.K. Book Distributors, 1925), p. 109.
61 L.F. Rushbrook Williams (ed.), *India in 1921–22* (Calcutta: Superintendent Government Printing, 1922), p. 225.
62 David Hardiman, 'From Custom to Crime: The Politics of Drinking in Colonial South Gujarat', in Ranajit Guha (ed.), *Subaltern Studies*, Volume 4 (Delhi: Oxford University Press, 1985), p. 220.
63 Bamford, *Histories*, p. 108.
64 Cited in Eisenlohr, *International*, p. 242.
65 *Report of the Assam Opium Enquiry Committee*, p. 111.
66 Eisenlohr, *International*, p. 235.
67 Hardiman, 'From', p. 216.
68 Eisenlohr, *International*, p. 235.
69 *The Indian Annual Register*, Volume 2, Calcutta, 19 July 1927, pp. 299–300.
70 M.K. Gandhi, *Drink, Drugs and Gambling* (Ahmedabad: Navagivan Publishing House, 1957), p. 109.
71 *Report of the Assam Opium Enquiry Committee*, p. 110.
72 H.C. Mookerjee, 'Opium at Geneva 1921–1925', *The Calcutta Review*, Volume 102, February/March 1947, p. 108.
73 *Bengal Legislative Council Proceedings/Debates*, Volume 4, 31 August–1 September 1921, p. 289.
74 *Report of the Assam Opium Enquiry Committee*, p. 101.
75 *Final Report of the Royal Commission on Opium*, Volume 42, p. 47.
76 *Report of the Assam Opium Enquiry Committee*, pp. 105–6.
77 Ibid., pp. 108–9.
78 Appendix 2, *Report of the British Delegates to the International Conference Held at The Hague*, December 1911–January 1912. Miscellaneous No. 11 (1912), Parliamentary Papers, Volume 68, House of Commons, 1912–13, p. 775.
79 *Report of the Assam Opium Enquiry Committee*, pp. 112(f)–112(g).
80 *Final Report of the Royal Commission on Opium*, Volume 42, p. 47.
81 Gandhi, *Drink*, p. 109.
82 *Report of the Assam Opium Enquiry Committee*, p. 112(j).
83 R.N. Chopra and I.C. Chopra, *Drug Addiction with Special Reference to India* (New Delhi: Council of Scientific and Industrial Research, 1965), p. 221.
84 *The Indian Annual Register*, Calcutta, Volume 2, 1925, p. 210.
85 *Records of the Second Opium Conference*, Volume 2, Plenary Meetings Text of the Debates, Geneva, 17 November 1924–19 February 1925, League of Nations, C. 760. M. 260. 1924. 11, Geneva, August 1925, p. 70. (Hereafter, *Records of the Second Opium Conference*, 1925.)
86 *Index to the Records of the First Opium Conference*, Volume 1, 3 November 1924–11 February 1925, League of Nations, C. 29 M. 15. 11, Geneva, January 1926, p. 53.

87   *Records of the Second Opium Conference*, 1925, p. 70.
88   Cited in Karl Joseph Schmidt, *India's Role in the League of Nations, 1919–1939*, Ph.D. dissertation, Florida State University, UMI Dissertation Services, Printed in 1996, p. 205.
89   Alexander, *Narcotics*, p. 9.
90   Cited in William Paton, 'The Opium Situation in India', *The Contemporary Review*, Volume 132, July 1927, pp. 75–6.
91   *The Indian Annual Register*, Volume 1, 1926, Calcutta, p. 247.
92   Ibid., p. 217.
93   Stanley Reed and S.T. Sheppard (eds), *The Indian Year Book 1930* (Bombay: Bennet, Coleman & Co., Ltd., 1930), pp. 770–1; *Hansard*, Volume 148, Series, 16, December 1921, p. 279.
94   L.F. Rushbrook Williams (ed.), *India in 1924–25* (Calcutta: Government of India Central Publication Branch, 1925), p. 274.
95   H.C. Mookerjee in 'India's International Opium Policy', *The Modern Review*, August 1947, p. 110.
96   *Records of the Second Opium Conference*, 1925, p. 73.
97   *India 1926–7*, p. 156.
98   Paton, 'Opium', p. 82.
99   Alexander, *Narcotics*, p. 48.
100 Ibid., pp. 48–9.
101 Ibid., p. 50.
102 Article 3, *The Dangerous Drugs Act, 1930*, (Act No. 2 of 1930), *Government of India, Legislative Department* (New Delhi: Government of India Press, 1936), p. 5. (Hereafter, *The Dangerous Drugs Act, 1930*.)
103 Frank Logan, 'Drugs of Abuse and the Law', *Law Guardian*, Volume 52, 1969, p. 21.
104 Article 4, *The Dangerous Drugs Act, 1930*, p. 8.
105 Articles 10 and 11, *The Dangerous Drugs Act, 1930*, pp. 11–12.
106 Text of Final Convention, *International Control of Traffic in Opium*, Summary of the Opium Conferences Held at Geneva, November 1924, to February 1925 With Appendices Containing Complete Texts of Final Agreements, and the Hague Convention of 1912, Foreign Policy Association, New York, Pamphlet No. 33, Series of 1924–5, May 1925, pp. 23–4.
107 J.P. Bhatnagar, *Commentary on the Law of Excise in Bihar and Orissa* (Allahabad: Ashoka Law House, 1969), p. 126.
108 H.C. Mookerjee, 'British Reactions to League Attitude', *The Calcutta Review*, Volume 103, March 1947, p. 186.
109 Article 5, *The Bengal Opium Smoking Act, 1932*, p. 2.
110 V.K.S. Chaudhury, *The Uttar Pradesh Legal Acts: 1825–1967* (Allahabad: Central Law Agency, 1967), pp. 84–8.
111 *League of Nations, Advisory Committee on Traffic in Opium and Other Dangerous Drugs, Analytical Study of Annual Reports by Governments on the Traffic in Opium and Other Dangerous Drugs for the Year 1940*, Official No. C. 117 M. 117, 1945, 11, p. 23. (Hereafter, *League of Nations Advisory Committee*, 1940).

112 *India in 1932–33*, p. 173.
113 *The Burma Excise (Amendment) Act, 1925* (Act No. 4 of 1925), *Burma Gazette*, 23 May 1925; *The Burma Excise (Amendment) Act, 1927* (Act No. 1 of 1927), *Burma Gazette*, 30 April 1927; *The Burma Excise (Amendment) Act, 1934* (Act No. 2 of 1934), *Burma Gazette*, 2 June 1934.
114 J.P. Bhatnagar, *Commentary on the Law of Excise in Bihar and Orissa* (Allahabad: Ashoka Law House, 1969), pp. 110–22.
115 P.N. Chopra (ed.), *The Gazetteer of India, Administrative and Public Welfare*, Volume 4 (New Delhi: Ministry of Education and Social Welfare, 1978), p. 680.
116 *Report of the Prohibition Enquiry Committee*, Planning Commission, Government of India, Government of India Press, New Delhi, 1955, p. 28. (Hereafter, *Report of the Prohibition Enquiry Committee*.)
117 'The Government of India, Budget for 1946–47', in *The Indian Annual Register*, Volume 1, 1946, p. 250.
118 *Report of the Prohibition Enquiry Committee*, p. 29.
119 *Report of the Indian Statutory Commission*, Volume 1, Survey (London: His Majesty's Stationary Office, 1930), p. 363.

4 Indian resurgence, 1947–97

1 Gandhi, *Drink*, p. 10.
2 *Constituent Assembly Debates: Official Report*, Constituent Assembly of India, 24 November 1948, Volume 7, p. 556.
3 *The Constitution of India* (As modified up to the 15 August 1983), Government of India, Ministry of Law, Justice and Company Affairs (Legislative Department), New Delhi, 1983, p. 23.
4 H.N. Giri, *Consumers, Crimes and the Law* (New Delhi: Ashish Publishing House, 1987), pp. 56–7.
5 Articles 12 to 17 in Chapter 3, *The Bombay Prohibition Act, 1949*, (Bombay Act No. 25 of 1949): as amended up to 1st January 1963 with Explanatory and Critical Notes, and Exhaustive Commentary (Poona: K.S. Gupte, 1963), pp. 107–18.
6 *Report of the Prohibition Enquiry Committee*, Planning Commission, Government of India, (New Delhi: Government of India Press, 1955), p. 24.
7 *Statistical Abstract, India 1952–53*, New Series, No. 4, Issued by Central Statistical Organization, Cabinet Secretariat, Government of India, Delhi, Manager of Publications, 1955, p. 816. (Hereafter, *Statistical Abstract, India 1952–53*.)
8 *Uttar Pradesh (India) Laws, Statutes, etc.: The Uttar Pradesh Local Acts Containing All the U.P. Acts, Regulations and Other Acts Along with Rules, Orders and Notifications* (Allahabad: Central Law Agency, 1964, 1967), p. 73.
9 *Statistical Abstract, India 1952–53*, p. 816.
10 *Report of the Prohibition Enquiry Committee*, 1955, pp. 28–9.

11 T.S. Doabia (ed.), *The Law of Excise: Being a Commentary on the Punjab Excise Act (1914) As Applicable to the States of Punjab and Haryana* (Chandigarh: Punjab Law Agency, 1976), p. 492.

12 K.C. Markandan, *Directive Principles in the Indian Constitution* (Bombay: Allied Publishers Private Ltd., 1966), p. 293.

13 *Statistical Abstract, India 1952–53*, p. 816.

14 *Statistical Abstract India 1957–58*, New Series No. 8, Issued by Central Statistical Organization Cabinet Secretariat, Government of India (Delhi: Manager of Publications, 1959), p. 211.

15 *The Medicinal and Toilet Preparations (Excise Duties) Act, 1955*, Indian Parliament Act No. 16 of 1955, An Act to provide for the levy and collection of duties of excise on Medicinal and toilet preparations containing alcohol, opium, Indian hemp or other narcotic drug or narcotic, 27 April 1955, p. 123.

16 *Lok Sabha Debates*, Part 2, Volume 3, Twelfth Session, 31 March 1956, New Delhi, p. 3979.

17 Ibid., p. 3971.

18 *Second Five-year Plan: Summary*, Planning Commission, Government of India (New Delhi: The Manage of Publications, 1956), p. 185.

19 *Third Five Year Plan* [1965–70], Government of India, Planning Commission, [1960], p. 723.

20 Ibid., p. 724.

21 Virandra Kumar (ed.), *Committees and Commissions in India 1947–73*, Volume 5, 1962–3 (Delhi: Concept Publishing Company, 1977), p. 200.

22 *T of I*, 26 January 1960, p. 6.

23 *The Opium and Revenue Laws (Extension of Application) Act, 1950*, Indian Parliament Act No. 33 of 1950, (New Delhi: Government of India Press, 1950), p. 154.

24 R.L. Gupta (ed.), *Law of Opium and Opium Smuggling* (Allahabad: Law Book Co., 1971), p. 90.

25 Shivlal Gupta (ed.), *Rajasthan Local Laws 1949–1970 [Civil Criminal Revenue] Containing Acts, Rules, Regulations, Orders, Notifications and Commentaries based on up-to-date Case Law* (Jodhpur: India Publishing House, 1969), p. 300.

26 *Uttar Pradesh (India) Laws, Statutes, etc.: The Uttar Pradesh Local Acts Containing All the U.P. Acts, Regulations and Other Acts Along with Rules, Orders and Notifications* (Allahabad: Central Law Agency, 1964, 1967), p. 73.

27 *Lok Sabha Debates*, Second Series, Volume 9, 25 November–6 December 1957, p. 3002.

28 *Statistical Abstract, India 1953–54*, New Series, No. 5, Issued by Central Statistical Organization, Cabinet Secretariat, Government of India, (Delhi: The Manager of Publications, 1956), p. 900.

29 L.D. Kapoor, 'Poppy Cultivation is Paying', *Indian Farming*, Volume 11, No. 7, October 1961, p. 8.

30 G.S. Shekhawat, 'Cultivation Studies in Poppy', *Indian Journal of Agronomy*, Volume 12, No. 1, 1967, p. 83.

31   Article 3, *The Dangerous Drugs (Import, Export and Transhipment) Rules, 1957*, S.R.O. 3618, dated 5 November 1957, Gazette of India, 1957, Part 2, Section 3, p. 2681.

32   'The United Nations Opium Conference, 1953', *Yearbook of the United Nations, 1953*. Department of Public Information, United Nations, New York, p. 486.

33   'Narcotics Control: A Half Century of Effort', *United Nations Review*, July 1957, Volume 4, No. 1, p. 15.

34   Kumar (ed.), *Committees*, p. 138.

35   Article 2, *The Opium Laws (Amendment) Act, 1957*, Indian Parliament Act No. 52 of 1957, An Act further to amend the Opium Act, 1878 and the Dangerous Drugs Act, 1930, New Delhi, Government of India Press, 1957, p. 112.

36   Article 3, ibid., p. 113.

37   *Review of United States Narcotics Control Efforts in the Middle East and South Asia*, Hearings before the Committee on Foreign Affairs, House of Representatives, Ninety-Ninth Congress, Second Session 13 May and 22 May 1986, p. 19. (Hereafter, *Review of United States Narcotics Control*, 1986.)

38   *Lok Sabha Debates*, 28 August 1985, Volume 9, p. 36.

39   *HT*, 6 August 1997; http://208.219.153.130/ht/060897/seanat02.htm

40   *Lok Sabha Debates*, Second Series, Volume 9, 25 November–6 December 1957, p. 2993.

41   *The Drug Menace*, Lok Sabha Secretariat, New Delhi, 1988, p. 18. (Hereafter, *Drug Menace*.)

42   *Review of United States Narcotics Control*, 1986, p. 27.

43   *OHT*, 31 August 1985, p. 8.

44   Andrew Giarelli, 'India's Drug Byways', *World Press Review*, January 1989, p. 45.

45   *Efforts of the US Government to Reduce the Flow of Illegal Drugs into the United States from Foreign Countries*, Hearing Before the Subcommittee on Crime of the Committee on the Judiciary, House of Representatives, One Hundred First Congress, First Session, 12 April 1989, Serial No. 45, p. 142. (Hereafter, *Efforts of the US government*, 1989.)

46   B.V. Kumar, 'Drug Trafficking – A Historical Perspective', *Indian Journal of Social Work*, January 1989, p. 2.

47   *T of I*, 2 November 1992, p. 5.

48   *H*, 23 August 1997, p. 2, http://www.webpage.com/hindu/daily/970823/04/042318c.htm

49   Knut Royce, 'A Country Run on Drugs: CIA Report Says Heroin is Pakistan's Lifeblood', New York *Newsday*, 23 February 1993, p. 4.

50   *HT*, 24 September 1994, p. 13 (N.C. Menon).

51   *D*, 25 April 1993, p. 4 (A.M. Mir).

52   *D*, 9 September 1996, ftp://usman.imran.com/pub/News/

53   *H*, 21 July 1997, p. 14, http://www.webpage.com/hindu/daily/

54   Shefali Rekhi and Mohammed Hanif, 'Drug Trafficking: The Common Foe', *India Today*, 31 October 1995, p. 58.

55   *T of I*, 2 November 1992, p. 6.

56 Farzand Ahmed, 'Arms Smuggling: A Lethal Invasion', *India Today*, 15 February 1996, pp. 42–55; *T of I*, 15 May 1997, http://www.timesofindia.com

57 *IE*, 23 May 1997, http://www.expressindia.com (Satya Pal Baghi)

58 'Politics of Opium Smuggling', *Link*, 9 January 1983, p. 25.

59 *T of I*, 2 September 1991, p. 1 (Prasun Sonwalkar).

60 Ahmed, 'Arms', p. 53.

61 *T of I*, 28 February 1991, p. 7 (Debashish Munshi).

62 Iboyaima Laithangbam, 'North East: Shared Interests', *Rashtiya Sahara*, March 1996, p. 52.

63 *T of I*, 24 June 1997, http://www.timesofindia.com

64 Andrew Giarelli, 'India's Drug Byways', *World Press Review*, January 1989, p. 45.

65 *SW*, 18 October 1997, p. 7.

66 Hamish McDonald, 'Hooked on Smuggling', *FEER*, 9 June 1994, p. 34.

67 *OHT*, 1 February 1998, p. 4.

68 *T of I*, 25 February 1991, p. 9 (Vijay Jung Thapa).

69 Under the Indo-Burma accords of 31 March 1993, 28 February 1994, and 12 August 1995, the traditional trade rights of the tribal people on both sides of the international border were restored.

70 McDonald, 'Hooked', p. 34.

71 Cited in S.V. Joga Rao, 'Social Legislation, Drug: The Challenge of the Twenty-First Century A Socio-Legal Perspective', *Indian Journal of Social Work*, Volume 51, No. 4, October 1990, p. 716.

72 *H*, 1 March 1997, p. 17, http://www.webpage.com/hindu/daily

73 *SW*, 18 October 1997, p. 7.

74 Bertil Linter, 'Narcotics Pusher With A Cause: Khun Sa Stresses His Role as a Shan Leader', *FEER*, 20 January 1994, pp. 24–6.

75 *H*, 20 August 1997, http://www.webpage.com/hindu/weekly

76 Shibani Roy and S.H.M. Rizvi, 'Report on Tribal Hellucinogenic Tradition: A Case Study of Manipur Village', *Man in India*, Volume 67, 1987, p. 142.

77 *WP*, 16 June 1997, http://search.washingtonpost.com/, (Krishnan Guruswamy).

78 *T of I*, 23 September 1997, http://www.timesofindia.com/today/indi1.htm (Nirmalya Banerjee).

79 *H*, 14 January 1997, p. 15, http://www.webpage.com/hindu/daily

80 *The Friend of China*, March 1882, p. 5.

81 'Copy of Indian Revenue Department's Resolution', No. 2208, 20 April 1894, *East India Revenue (Opium), The British Parliamentary Papers*, Volume 58, p. 633.

82 *Imperial Gazetteer of India*, Afghanistan and Nepal (Calcutta: Superintendent of Government Printing, 1908), p. 120.

83 Rabindra Singh, *I was A Drug Addict* (New Delhi: Orient Paperbacks, 1979), p. 43.

84 *Efforts of the US Government*, 1989, p. 142.

85 *Drug Menace*, p. 18.

86 *IE*, 7 September 1996, http: express.indiaworld.com/ie/daily (J. Dey).

87 *DH*, 19 October 1997, http://www.deccanherald.com/deccanherald/oct19/drugs.htm (Prasanta Paul).

88 Medicinal opium is processed to adapt it solely for pharmaceutical use. It is extracted from opium alkaloid and also from concentrated poppy straw. Including morphine, codeine and thebaine, about 25 elements are manufactured from medicinal opium.

89 *Yearbook of the United Nations*, 1953. Department of Public Information, United Nations, New York, p. 486.

90 Stevedore, 'Record Sales of Opium', *Commerce*, 22 May 1971, p. 952.

91 *FR*, 19 April 1991, p. 29 (Sheryle Bagwell); *Report of the International Narcotics Control Board for 1993*, International Narcotics Control Board, Vienna, (New York: United Nations, 1994), p. 13.

92 From a CPS morphine base thebaine, codeine and noscapine is separated by chemical analysis.

93 *T of I*, 26 June 1981, p. 13 (J.D. Singh).

94 'US Market Share of Narcotic Raw Material', *The Licit Importation of Opium*, Hearing Before the Subcommittee on Crime of the Committee on the Judiciary, House of Representatives, One Hundred First Congress, Second Session, February 27, 1990, Serial No. 89, p. 257. (Hereafter, *The Licit Importation of Opium*, 1990.)

95 *T of I*, 9 November 1981, p. 22 (Shree Sondhi).

96 *Report of the International Narcotics Control Board for 1981*, United Nations, New York, 1981, p. 1060.

97 *Tasmania – A Quarterly Economic Briefing*, Tasmania Development Authority, July 1988 and January 1989, p. 25.

98 'Australia's Attitude', *United Nations Commission on Narcotic Drugs*, Ninth Special Session, Vienna, 10–21 February 1986, Brief for the Australian Delegation, Volume 1, January 1986, Department of Health, Canberra, Australia, p. 92. (Hereafter, *United Nations Commission on Narcotic Drugs*, 1986.)

99 *Report of the International Narcotics Control Board for 1985*, United Nations, New York, 1985, p. 1020.

100 David Guinane, Executive Officer of the Australian Poppy Advisory and Control Board and an Australian delegate to the Vienna meeting, in a personal letter on 15 September 1988 to Professor Robin Jeffrey, Supervisor of the present research, referred to the official position of the Indian Government regarding the Tasmanian project.

101 Appendix 6, *The Licit Importation of Opium*, 1990, p. 263.

102 *Review of the 1991 International Narcotics Control Strategy Report*, p. 276.

103 *Efforts of the US Government*, 1989, p. 144.

104 *The Licit Importation of Opium*, 1990, p. 83.

105 Ibid., p. 93.

106 R.B. Garg, 'Exporting Opium: Need for R & D', *Eastern Economist*, Volume 75, 19 December 1980, p. 1377.

107 Angela S. Burger, 'Narcotic Drugs: Security Threat or Interest to South Asian States?', in Marvin G. Weinbaum and Chetan Kumar (ed.), *South*

Asia Approaches the Millennium (San Francisco: Westview Press, 1995), p. 175.

108 *FR*, 19 April 1991, p. 27 (Sheryle Bagwell).

109 *SMH*, 19 July 1997, p. 6s (David Marr and Bernard Lagan).

110 *WA*, 16–17 August 1997, p. 6 (Bruce Montgomery).

111 *IEO*, 2 May 1997, http://www.m-web.com/opm_proc.html

112 *H*, 12 March 1997, p. 11, http://www.webpage.com/hindu/daily (George Chakko).

113 *HT*, 16 May 1997, http://208.219.153.130/ht/160597/seaeco03.htm

114 Buckland, 'Opium', pp. 669–77.

115 B.L. Mishra and D.K. Marothia, 'Economics of Poppy Cultivation in Mandsaur District of Madhya Pradesh', *Indian Journal of Agricultural Economics*, Volume 29, July–September 1974, No. 3, p. 177.

116 *WA*, 16–17 August 1997, p. 6 (Bruce Montgomery).

117 *H*, International Edition, 14 March 1992, p. 5.

118 D. Gidwani, 'Striking Addiction at the Roots', *India Today*, 30 April 1995, p. 20.

119 Buckland, 'Opium', pp. 669–77.

120 *Lok Sabha Debates*, Sixth Session, Volume 21, No. 40, 7 May 1993, p. 346.

121 *Narcotics Review in Southeast/Southwest Asia and the Middle East, and Africa*, Hearing before the Committee on Foreign Affairs, House of Representatives, One Hundredth Congress, Second Edition, 15 March 1988, p. 87. (Hereafter, *Narcotics Review in Southeast/Southwest Asia*, 1988.)

122 *IE*, 18 April 1997, http://www.expressindia.com/ie/daily/19970418/10851123.html (Sharad Gupta).

123 *H*, 3 January 1997, p. 13, http://www.webpage.com/hindu/daily

124 *International Narcotics Control Strategy Report 1985 to Committee on Foreign Relations, Committee on Foreign Affairs*, United States, Department of State, Bureau of International Narcotics Control Matters, Washington, p. 194.

125 Quoted by Avirook Sen, 'Money Plant: Mandsaur's Heroin Fact-Sheet', *Sunday*, 27 March–2 April 1994, p. 26.

126 *HT*, 10 May 1997, http://38.251/ht

127 *ET*, 27 November 1996, http://www.economictimes.com

128 *SW*, 25 January 1997, p. 7 (Shahid Pervez).

129 *HT*, 16 May 1997, http://208.219.153.130/ht/160597/seaeco03.htm

130 'A Note on Price and Marketing of Opium in Udaipur, Rajasthan', *Indian Journal of Economics*, Volumes 61–2, Number 246, January 1982, pp. 467–8.

131 *Reuter*, 24 April 1995, Bhopal, India.

132 *Narcotics Review in Southeast/Southwest Asia and the Middle East, and Africa*, 1988, pp. 42–3.

133 *Review of the 1992 International Narcotics Control Strategy Report*, Hearings Before the Committee on Foreign Affairs and the Subcommittee on Western Hemisphere Affairs, House of Representatives, One Hundred Second Congress, Second Session, 3, 4, and 12 March 1992, p. 83.

(Hereafter, *Review of the 1992 International Narcotics Control Strategy Report.*)

134 *H*, International Edition, 14 March 1992, p. 5.
135 'Hush Poppy: Opium Cultivators in Mandsaur District of Madhya Pradesh Take to Heroin Production in a Big Way', *Sunday*, 27 March–2 April 1994, p. 22.
136 *T of I*, 26 May 1996, p. 10.
137 *D to E*, 15 May 1993, p. 48 (Parshuram Ray).
138 Sen, 'Money', p. 26.
139 Appendix 11, *The Royal Commission on Opium*, Volume 61, p. 377.
140 Bhim Sain, *Drug Addiction Alcoholism, Smoking Obscenity and Its Impact on Crimes, Terrorism and Social Security* (New Delhi: Millat Publications, 1991), p. 113.
141 William Rhode, 'The Heroin Highway', *Sunday*, 18–24 December 1994, p. 26.
142 *P*, 3 March 1996, p. 9.
143 Satyamurti, 'The Slippery Slope', *Frontline*, 29 November 1996, pp. 77–8,
144 *D to E*, 15 May 1993, p. 48 (Parshuram Ray).
145 *SW*, 21 May 1994, p. 7 (Anindya Sengupta).
146 *Review of United States Narcotics Control*, 1986, p. 28.
147 Rhode, 'Heroin', p. 22.
148 *Drug Menace*, p. 18.
149 *DH*, 28 April 1997, http:/www.deccanherald.com
150 *Efforts of the U.S. Government*, 1989, p. 142.
151 Parveen Swami, 'Revealing Links', *Frontline*, 12 January 1996, p. 46.
152 *HT*, 5 August 1997, http://208.219.153/ht/051097/seacit01.htm
153 A mimeograph titled *Indian Government is Sponsoring Production and Spread of Narco-Chemicals* was distributed by the Pakistan High Commission in Canberra (without a date of publication or the publisher name).
154 *Review of the 1992 International Narcotics Control Strategy Report*, 1992, p. 83.
155 *United Nations Conference for the Adoption of a Single Convention on Narcotic Drugs*, New York: 24 January–25 March 1961, *Official Records*, Volume 1, Summary Records of plenary meetings, United Nations, New York, 1964, p. 8.
156 *United Nations Commission on Narcotic Drugs*, 1986, p. 28.
157 *Yearbook of the United Nations 1986*, Volume 40, Department of Public Information (Boston: Mertinus Nijhoff Publishers, 1990), p. 872.
158 Article 12, *United Nations Convention Against Illicit Traffic in Narcotic Drugs and Psychotropic Substances*, Vienna, Austria, 25 November–30 December 1988, pp. 18–21.
159 *Yearbook of the United Nations 1991*, Volume 45, Department of Public Information (Boston: Nijhoff Publishers, 1992), pp. 732–3.
160 Joginder Singh, 'Fighting Drug Abuse', *Kurukshetra*, Volume 52, No. 11, August 1994, p. 45.

161 Salamat Ali, ' Opiate of the Frontier: Pakistan's Tribes Find it Hard to Give up Poppy Crop', *FEER*, 27 May 1994, p. 18.
162 *D*, 16 May 1993; *D*, 20 September 1993.
163 Swami, 'Revealing', p. 62.
164 Ibid., pp. 46–7.
165 Shefali Rekhi and Mohammed Hanif, 'Drug Trafficking: The Common Foe', *India Today*, 31 October 1995, pp. 58–9.
166 *P*, 29 August 1997, http://www.the-pioneer.com/test/city4.htm (Sidharth Mishra).
167 *Lok Sabha Debates*, 28 August 1985, p. 51.
168 Articles 15 to 18 in A.K. Aggarwal and Tarun Mehta (ed.), *The Narcotic Drugs and Psychotropic Substances Act, 1985, (Act 61 of 1985)* (New Delhi: Metropolitan Book Co., no year), pp. 14–17. (Hereafter, *The Narcotic Drugs and Psychotropic Substances Act, 1985*.)
169 *Lok Sabha Debates*, Sixth Session, Tenth Series, Volume 19, No. 17, 17 March 1993, p. 608.
170 *The Narcotic Drugs and Psychotropic Substances Act, 1985*, pp. 9–10.
171 *Narcotics Review in Southeast/Southwest Asia and the Middle East, and Africa*, 1988, p. 87.
172 Kumar, 'Drug', p. 4.
173 *Efforts of the US Government*, 1989, p. 143.
174 *SW*, 21 May 1994, p. 7 (Anindya Sengupta).
175 Satyamurti, 'Slippery', p. 79.
176 Russell Pinto, 'Narcotic Drugs and Psychotropic Substances Act, 1985', *Indian Journal of Social Work*, January 1989, p. 123.
177 Sarita Rani, 'High on Ganja', *Sunday*, 31 January–6 February 1993, p. 20.
178 *SW*, 14 March 1992, p. 7.
179 *SW*, 21 May 1994, p. 7 (Anindya Sengupta).
180 *H*, 6 March 1996, p. 6, http://www.webpage.com/hindu/daily
181 *H*, 19 August 1996, p. 16, http://www.webpage.com/hindu/weekly
182 *H*, 3 March 1997, http://www.webpage.com/hindu/daily
183 *Notifications Under The Narcotic Drugs and Psychotropic Substances Act, 1985*, Quantity of 'Narcotic Drugs' Specified, Notification No. 12/85 F.N. 664/51/85-Opium, dated 14–11–1985, *Gazette of India*, Ex. Pt. 2, Section 3 (ii), p. 2.
184 Articles 41 and 42, *The Narcotic Drugs and Psychotropic Substances Act, 1985*, pp. 25–6; Appendix 3, *The Drug Menace*, Lok Sabha Secretariat, 1988, p. 153.
185 Iboyaima Laithangbam, 'North East: Shared Interests', *Rashtriya Sahara*, New Delhi, March 1996, p. 52.
186 *DE*, 15 May 1993, p. 48.
187 Bhim Sain, *Drug Addiction Alcoholism, Smoking Obscenity: And Its Impact on Crimes, Terrorism and Social Security*, (New Delhi: Millat Publications, 1991), p. 111–12.
188 *ET*, 25 February 1996, p. 5 (Shailendra).
189 *SW*, 23 March 1991, p. 4.

190 *P*, 17 February 1996, p. 7 (Padma Shastri).
191 S.V. Joga Rao, 'Social Legislation, Drug: The Challenge of the Twenty-First Century A Socio-Legal Perspective', *Indian Journal of Social Work*, Volume 51, No. 4, October 1990, p. 721.
192 *Efforts of the US Government*, 1989, p. 143.
193 *Lok Sabha Debates*, 8th Series, Volume 38, Part 1, 8–19 April 1988, p. 353.
194 *Lok Sabha Debates*, 8 Series, Volume 42, 30 August–5 September 1988, pp. 320–31.
195 Article 3(1), *The Prevention of Illicit Traffic in Narcotic Drugs And Psychotropic Substances Act, 1988 (Act 46 of 1988)* in Pramod Kumar (ed.), *The Narcotic Drugs and Psychotropic Substances Act, 1985 (Act No. 61 of 1985)*, (Allahabad: Ashoka Law House, 1989), p. 110.
196 Sain, *Drug*, p. 114.
197 Shamsur Rahman, 'Bharote Rajnitik-Mafia Shamparka Bitarka', *Shaptahik Bichitra*, Dhaka, 9 September 1994, p. 21.
198 *P*, 20 February 1996, p. 12 (Alam Srinivas).
199 *Prevention of Illicit Traffic in Narcotic Drugs and Psychotropic Substances (Amendment) Bill, 1996*, 26 July 1997, http://alfa.nic.in/BASISCG/nph-b... hri%20Chidambaram%09%26U%3D1
200 Kumar (ed.), *Narcotic*, pp. 26–7.
201 *Efforts of the US Government*, 1989, p. 143.
202 *P*, 20 February 1996, p. 12 (Alam Srinivas).
203 R.N. Kaker, 'Social Legislation: Laws for Controlling Illicit Drug Traffic in Narcotic Drugs and Psychotropic Substances, *Indian Journal of Social Work*, January 1989, p. 116.
204 *Efforts of the US Government*, 1989, p. 143.
205 B.B. Gujral, 'Forfeiture of Illegally Acquired Assets of Drug Traffickers: the Position in India', *Bulletin on Narcotics*, Volume 35, No. 2, April/June 1983, pp. 45–7.
206 Burger, 'Narcotic', in Weinbaum and Kumar, *South Asia*, p. 174.
207 *HT*, 12 February 1996, p. 7.
208 *H*, 4 March 1997, http://www.webpage.com/hindu/today/01/01040005.htm

5 Pakistani dilemmas, 1947–97

1 LaMond Tullis, *Unintended Consequences: Illegal Drugs and Drug Policies in Nine Countries* (London: Lynne Rienner Publishers, 1995), p. 117.
2 *The Punjab Excise Act, 1914* (Act No. 1 of 1914), The Punjab Government Notification No. 112, 23 January 1914. The Act No. 38 of 1920, Act No. 2 of 1925 and the Dangerous Drugs Act of 1930 amended this Act.
3 In the *Tibbi* medical system opium preparations are mostly used in the form of pill or paste against cough, delirium, epilepsy, diarrhoea,

haemorrhage, premature seminal discharge, dysentery, ocular pain, headache and so on.

4 *Yearbook of the United Nations 1947–48*, Department of Public Information, United Nations, New York, 1949, p. 630.

5 *T of I*, Bombay, 4 April 1949, p. 1.

6 M. Anwar Khokhar, *Excise Opium Drugs and Prohibition Laws* (Lahore: Law Publishing Co., 1977), pp. 79–88.

7 A.E. Wright, 'Opium in Pakistan', *Bulletin on Narcotics*, Volume 6, September–December 1954, p. 13.

8 Khokhar, *Excise*, p. 450.

9 Article 20, *The Constitution of the Republic of Pakistan*, 1962, Manager of Publication, Karachi, C.S.-3/19000, p. 15.

10 Khokhar, *Excise*, pp. 462–5.

11 *D*, 28 October 1973, p. 4 (Sagir Ahmed).

12 Article 37(g)(h), Part 2, Chapter 2, *The Constitution of the Islamic Republic of Pakistan*, Amended to 27 May 1981, p. 18.

13 *D*, 15 November 1973, p. 6.

14 Ch. Abdul Wahid, 'Nature and Extent of Control on Supply of Narcotic Drugs in Pakistan', *First National Workshop on Prevention and Control of Drug Abuse in Pakistan,* 25–30 August 1975, Rawalpindi, p. 31.

15 *D*, 8 June 1977, p. 6.

16 *D*, 19 April 1977, p. 4.

17 *Review of United States Narcotics Control*, 1986, p. 49.

18 Ijaz Haider, 'Pattern of Drug Abuse Among Hospitalised Patients in the Province of Punjab-Pakistan', *First National Workshop on Prevention and Control of Drug Abuse Workshop Report*, 25–30 August 1975, Rawalpindi, p. 76.

19 Laeeq Mirza, 'Some Problem Areas of Research on Drug Addiction in Pakistan', *Pakistan-Colombo Plan Workshop on Drug Abuse Prevention Education*, 6–11 August 1977 Nathigali, Workshop Report, June 1978, p. 32.

20 S. Haroon Ahmad, 'Psycho-Social Aspects of Drug Abuse: Results of a Preliminary Survey', ibid., pp. 51–2.

21 *The Imperial Gazetteer of India*, Volume 4, Administrative, new edition, (Oxford: Clarendon Press, 1909), p. 246.

22 *Return of Acreage under Poppy in India*, p. 681.

23 Wright, 'Opium', p. 12.

24 Ibid., p. 13.

25 *D*, 6 August 1977, p. 5.

26 Wahid, 'Nature', p. 36.

27 *D*, 19 May 1993, p. 7.

28 'Pakistani Tribes a Big Hurdle in Drive to Limit Heroin Trade', *Narcotics Control Digest*, Volume 15, No. 14, 10 July 1985, p. 5.

29 Hurst, 'Story', p. 769.

30 Major-General J.G. Elliot, *The Frontier 1839–1947: The Story of the North-West Frontier of India* (London: Cassell, 1968), p. 4.

31 Wright, 'Opium', p. 15.

32 Alexander, *Rise*, p. 2.
33 Matheson, *What*, p. 16.
34 Cust, 'Indo-Chinese', p. 129.
35 Mountstuart Elphinstone, *An Account of the Kingdom of Caubul*, Volume 1 (London: Oxford University Press, First Edition 1815, Reprint 1972), p. 395.
36 *Imperial Gazetteer of India: Afghanistan and Nepal* (Calcutta: Superintendent of Government Printing, 1908), p. 30.
37 Walsh, 'Historical', p. 263.
38 *The Imperial Gazetteer of India*, 1909, p. 246.
39 Appendix 9, *British Royal Commission on Opium, 1894*, Volume 61, p. 354.
40 *Advisory Committee on Traffic in Opium and Other Dangerous Drugs, League of Nations, 1940*, p. 19.
41 Robert G. Wirsing, *The Baluchis and Pathans*, The Minority Rights Group Report No. 48, London, 1987, p. 9.
42 Wright, 'Opium', p. 15.
43 Tullis, *Unintended*, p. 117.
44 *Report of the International Narcotics Control Board for 1995*, United Nations Publications, E/INCB/1995/1, http://undcp.or.at/reports/incb95/incb95en.htm#IB
45 Article 223, *The Constitution of the Republic of Pakistan*, 1962, Manager of Publication, Karachi, C.S.-3/19000, pp. 103–4.
46 Article 59 (b), *The Constitution of the Islamic Republic of Pakistan*, Substituted by P.O. No. 14 of 1985, Federal Judicial Academy, Islamabad, 1990, p. 40.
47 *D*, 27 September 1977, p. 9.
48 Terence White, 'Narcotics: The Drug-abuse Epidemic Coursing through Pakistan', *Far Eastern Economic Review*, 13 June 1985, p. 98.
49 Christina Lamb, *Waiting for Allah: Pakistan's Struggle for Democracy* (New Delhi: Viking, 1991), p. 194.
50 M.H. Askari, 'Pakistan's Security and Drugs/Arms Mafia', *Strategic Digest*, Volume 17, No. 12, December 1987, p. 2306.
51 Kamal Siddiqi, 'Pakistan Smugglers Feel the Pinch', *Asia Times*, http://www.aisatimes.com/ 97/06/12/12069710.html
52 Najma Sadeque, 'God's Medicine Bedevilled' in Michael L. Smith et al., (eds), *Why People Grow Drugs: Narcotics and Development in the Third World* (London: The Panos Institute, 1992), p. 55.
53 Afzal Iqbal, *Islamisation of Pakistan* (Delhi: Idarah-i Adabiyat-i Delli, 1984), p. 137.
54 Cited in G. W. Choudhury, *Documents and Speeches on the Constitution of Pakistan* (Dhaka: Green Book House, 1967), p. 982.
55 Iqbal, *Islamisation*, p. 103.
56 Allami, *A'in-I-Akbari*, p. 207.
57 *D*, 20 April 1977, p. 1.
58 *D*, 13 May 1977, p. 1.
59 *D*, 11 May 1977, p. 1.

60 *Al-Quran, Surah Al-Baqarah, Ayat* (Verse) No. 219; *Al Quran, Sura Al-Ma'idah, Ayat* (Verse) No. 90.
61 *United Nations Information Letter*, Division of Narcotic Drugs, No. 5, May 1976, p. 2.
62 *D*, 28 October 1973, p. 4 (Sagir Ahmed).
63 Mohammad Aslam Azam, *Pakistan-Colombo Plan Workshop on Drug Abuse Prevention Education*, 6–11 August 1977 Nathigali, Workshop Report, June 1978, p. 22.
64 An English translation of President General Mohammad Zia-ul Haq's address on *The Introduction of Islamic System in Pakistan* at the National Assembly Hall, Islamabad, 10 February 1979, pp. 18–19.
65 *D*, 20 July 1977, p. 6.
66 Ibid.
67 G. Edwards and A. Arif (eds), *Drug Problems in the Sociocultural Context: A Basis for Policies and Programme Planning, Public Health Papers 73* (Geneva: World Health Organization, 1980), p. 153.
68 Prohibition (Enforcement of Hadd) Order, 1979, President's Order 4 of 1979, *Gazette of Pakistan, Extraordinary*, Part 1, 9 February 1979, p. 33.
69 *D*, 2 December 1983, p. 6 (Hamdan Amjad Ali).
70 Cited in I.A. Rehman, 'Master of Illusion', *The Herald*, September 1988, p. 56.
71 Manucci, *Storia*, p. 3.
72 Bernier, *Travels*, p. 252.
73 Sir Jadunath Sarkar, *A Short History of Auranzib 1618–1707* (Calcutta: M.C. Sarkar and Sons, 1930), p. 485.
74 *NYT*, 18 August 1988, p. A10 (Henry Kamm).
75 Sarkar, *Short*, p. 485.
76 Lamb, *Waiting*, p. 24.
77 Emma Duncan, *Breaking the Curfew: A Political Journey Through Pakistan* (London: Michael Joseph, 1989), p. 45.
78 *D*, 11 June 1985, p. 2.
79 *D*, 7 June 1985, p. 5.
80 Duncan, *Breaking*, p. 24.
81 Smith et al., (eds), *Why?* p. 55.
82 *D*, 9 December 1983, p. 9.
83 *D*, 5 December 1983, p. 1.
84 *International Narcotics Control Strategy Report 1985: to Committee on Foreign Relations*, Committee on Foreign Affairs, Prepared by the Bureau of International Narcotics Matters, Department of State, Washington, p. 207. (Hereafter: *INCSR 1985*.)
85 Salamat Ali, 'Opiate of the Frontier: Pakistan's Tribes Find it Hard to Give up Poppy Crop', *FEER*, 27 May 1993, p. 18.
86 'Politics of Opium Smuggling', *Link*, 9 January 1983, p. 25.
87 Lamb, *Waiting*, p. 206.
88 Hamidullah Amin and Gordon B. Schiltz, *A Geography of Afghanistan* (Kabul: Centre for Afghanistan Studies, 1984), p. 381.

89 Zalmay Khalilzad, *Security in Southern Asia: The Security of Southwest Asia* (Aldershot: Gower, 1984), p. 154; Tariq Ali, *Can Pakistan Survive? The Death of a State* (London: Penguin Books, 1983), p. 195.
90 Y. Volkov, K. Gevorkyan, M. Mikhailenko, A. M. Polonsky and A. Svetozarov, *The Truth About Afghansitan: Documents, Facts, and Eyewitness Reports* (Moscow: Novosti Press, 1980), p. 85.
91 Selig S. Harrison, 'Dateline Afghanistan: Exit Through Finland?', *Foreign Policy*, Number 45, Winter 1981–2, p. 132.
92 *D*, 5 March 1973, p. 3.
93 Selig S. Harrison, *In Afghanistan's Shadow: Baluch Nationalism and Soviet Temptations* (New York: Carnegie Endowment for International Peace, 1981), 30.
94 Alfred W. McCoy, *The Politics of Heroin: CIA Complicity in Global Drug Trade* (New York: Lawrence Hill Books, 1991), p. 449.
95 *Compilation of Narcotics Laws, Treaties, and Executive Documents*, Report Prepared for the Committee on Foreign Affair, US House of Representatives, 99th Congress, 2nd Session, Congressional Research Service, Washington, 1986, p. 482.
96 *HT*, 1 October 1994, p. 14 (N.C. Menon).
97 *Review of United States Narcotics Control*, 1986, p. 3.
98 *T of I*, 13 September 1980, p. 8 (Henry Kamm).
99 *D*, 8 August 1993, p. 6 (Isac Ali Quazi).
100 Amin & Schiltz, *Geography*, p. 381.
101 Bhabani Sen Gupta, 'CIA-ISI Take Charge of Afghan Issue', *Dhaka Courier*, 13–19 April 1990, p. 30.
102 Lamb, *Waiting*, p. 224.
103 Lawrence Lifschultz, 'Bush, Drugs and Pakistan: Inside the Kingdom of Heroin', *The Nation*, 14 November 1988, Volume 247, p. 492.
104 *NTY*, 18 August 1988, p. A10 (Elaine Sciolino).
105 *WP*, 13 May 1990, p. A1 (James Rupert and Steve Coll).
106 *SWB: Summary of World Broadcasts*, Part 3, Monitoring Service of the British Broadcasting Corporation, 30 January 1986.
107 *D*, 11 July 1996, p. 7 (Melvin A. Goodman).
108 *T*, 27 April 1992, p. 9 (Jawed Naqvi).
109 Ahmed Rashid, 'Enter the Taliban', *The Herald*, February 1995, p. 57.
110 Ahmed Rashid, 'Afghanistan: Sword of Islam', *FEER*, 29 December 1994 and 5 January 1995, p. 22.
111 Peter Willems, 'Current Affairs: Afghanistan's Gold', *The Middle East*, September 1997, pp. 6–7.
112 Cited in 'Enter the Taliban: The Road to Koranistan', *The Economist*, 5 October 1996, p. 21.
113 N. Dorn and N. Smith (eds), *A Land Fit for Heroin?* (London: Macmillan, 1987), p. 167.
114 *WT*, 10 March 1967, p. 23 (Peter Duval Smith and Alexander Low).
115 Edith T. Mirante, 'Indigenous People Mired in "Foreign Mud"', *Cultural Survival Quarterly*, Volume 13, No. 4, 1989, p. 19; 'Solving Burma's Guerrilla War', *CSM*, 30 March 1988, p. 13.

116 Cited in Grant M. Farr and John G. Merriam (eds), *Afghan Resistance: The Politics of Survival* (London: Westview Press, 1987), p. 75.
117 'Behind Closed Doors', *Newsweek*, 2 December 1985, p. 30.
118 John C. Whitehead, 'US International Narcotic Control Programs and Policies', *Department of State Bulletin*, Volume 86, Number 2115, October 1986, p. 37.
119 *Establishment of a South Asia Bureau at the Department of State*, Hearing before the Subcommittee on Asian and Pacific Affairs of the Committee on Foreign Affairs, House of Representatives, One Hundredth Congress, First Session, 10 March 1987, Washington, 1988, p. 16. (Hereafter, *South Asia Bureau at the Department of State*.)
120 David Whynes, 'Illicit Drug Production and Supply-side Drugs Policy in Asia and South America', *Development and Change*, Volume 22, 1991, p. 492.
121 *Review of United States Narcotics Control*, 1986, p. 17.
122 *T*, 6 May 1983, p. 7 (Michael Hamlyn).
123 'Pakistani Tribes A Big Hurdle in Drive to Limit Heroin Trade', *Narcotics Control Digest*, Volume 15, No. 14, 10 July 1985, p. 5.
124 *INCSR 1985*, p. 11.
125 Jonathan Kwitny, *The Crimes of Patriots: A True Tale of Dope, Dirty Money, and the CIA* (New York: A Touchstone Book, 1988), p. 23.
126 *D*, 4 December 1983, p. 12.
127 *D*, 18 May 1984, p. 24.
128 *WP*, 17 December 1983, p. A32 (Mary Thornton).
129 *NYT*, 14 September 1984, p. 1 (Joel Brinkley).
130 *South Asia Bureau at the Department of State*, p. 19.
131 *Review of United States Narcotics Control*, 1986, p. 35.
132 M.H. Askari, 'Pakistan's Security and Drugs/Arms Mafia', *Strategic Digest*, Volume 17, No. 12, December 1987, p. 2304.
133 *WP*, 13 May 1990, p. A29 (James Rupert and Steve Coll).
134 Ibid.
135 *WP*, 23 October 1988, p. C1 (Elaine Shannon).
136 *WP*, 17 December 1983, p. A32 (Mary Thornton).
137 Kalim Bahadur 'Opium Racket in Pakistan', *Link*, 4 January 1981, p. 26.
138 Ahmed Rashid, 'Pakistan: Drug Overdose, Bumper Opium Harvest Threatens Social Order', *FEER*, 15 December 1994, p. 23.
139 William O. Walker III, 'The Foreign Narcotics Policy of the United States Since 1980: An End to the War on Drugs?', *International Journal*, Volume 49, No. 1, Winter 1993, Canadian Institute of International Affairs, pp. 44–5.
140 *D*, 9 April 1993,
141 *INCSR 1985*, p. 4.
142 Mirante, 'Indigenous', p. 19.
143 *Compilation of Narcotics Laws, Treaties, and Executive Documents*, Report Prepared for the Committee on Foreign Affair, U.S. House of Representatives, 99th Congress, 2 Session, Congressional Research Service, Washington, 1986, p. 480.

144 Ann B. Wrobleski, 'Global Narcotics Cooperation and Presidential Certification', *Department of State Bulletin*, Volume 89, Number 2151, October 1989, p. 51.
145 *SMH*, 10 December 1994, p. 23 (Ahmed Rashid).
146 *CSM*, 12 January 1989, p. 6 (Edward Girardet).
147 *NYT*, 13 September 1984, p. A16 (Joel Brikley).
148 *National Survey on Drug Abuse in Pakistan 1986*, Pakistan Narcotics Control Board, Islamabad, p. 314.
149 *D*, 16–22 July 1991, p. 6 (G. Majiz).
150 *WP*, 29 April 1993, p. A32.
151 *D*, 16–22 July 1991, p. 6 (G. Majiz).
152 *NYT*, 13 September 1984, p. A16 (Joel Brinkley).
153 *WP*, 7 July 1980, p. A13.
154 Arnold S. Trebach, 'The Lesson of Ayatullah Khalkhali', *Journal of Drug Issues*, Fall 1981, p. 392.
155 *INCSR 1985*, p. 200.
156 *FT*, 3 March 1989, p. 54.
157 *D*, 18 August 1982, p. 5.
158 Zafar Abbas, 'Karachi's Iranian Connection', *The Herald*, December 1985, pp. 35–6; 'The Revolution Strikes Back: "Teendas" and Pidgin Persian', *The Herald*, August 1987, pp. 31–4.
159 Smith, (eds), *Why?*, p. 55.
160 *D*, 13 May 1973, p. 4.
161 Mark S. Steinitz, 'Insurgents, Terrorists and The Drug Trade', *The Washington Quarterly*, Fall 1985, p. 149.
162 Ikramul Haq, *Pakistan: From Hash to Heroin* (Lahore: Annor Printers and Publishers), p. 17.
163 Cited in Zahid Hussain, 'Narco Power: Pakistan's Parallel Government', *Newsline*, December 1989, p. 14.
164 Ibid., p. 13.
165 A.S. Yusufi, 'National/NWFP: Khyber Crackdown', *The Herald*, January 1986, pp. 59–60.
166 *D*, 27 September 1993, p. 14 (Shabbir H. Kazmi).
167 Lifschultz, 'Bush', pp. 492–4.
168 *WP*, 13 May 1990, p. A29 (James Rupert and Steve Coll).
169 Selim Omrao Khan, 'Pakistan: Heroin Shamrajja', *Shaptahik Bichitra* (Dhaka), 3 December 1993, p. 23.
170 *HT*, 1 October 1994, p. 14 (N.C. Menon).
171 Ravi Shashri, 'Insurgency and Drugs: The Deadly Alliance', *Strategic Analysis*, Volume 12, No. 1, April 1987, p. 43.
172 *D*, 16 September 1993, p. 9 (Faraz Hashmi).
173 Muhammad Sajidin, 'Drugs and Pakistan's Security', *Strategic Digest*, Volume 17, No. 12, December 1987, p. 2302.
174 Ahmed Rashid, 'Marching Orders', *The Herald*, May 1997, p. 38.
175 Pankaj Pachauri, 'International Bazaar: Indian Connection', *India Today*, 15 February 1996, p. 46.
176 Ameneth Azam Ali, 'Crime: The Short Arm of the Law', *The Herald*, September 1985, p. 50.

177 *CSM*, 28 December 1988, p. 1 (Edward Girardet).
178 *ET*, 27 December 1996, (K.N. Daruwala), http://www.economictimes. com/271296/opin7.htm
179 'CIA Report', 1993, p. 6.
180 *D*, http://wnc.fedworld.gov/cgi-bin/r...fy5q&CID= c296264648437500 7765926
181 *D*, 2 October 1993, p. 11 (Akhtar Payami).
182 Ameneh Azam Ali, 'The Short Arm of the Law?', *The Herald*, September 1985, p. 47.
183 *D*, 5 December 1983, p. 1.
184 Ayaz Amir, 'The Rise and Fall of Mohammad Khan Junejo', *The Herald*, June 1988, pp. 60(c)–(d).
185 'Pakistan: Ziaul Haq Addresses Drug Control Conference', British Broadcasting Corporation, *Summary of World Broadcasts*, Part 3, The Far East, 25 January 1986, p. FE/8166/B/1.
186 Husain Haqqani, 'Meagre Compensation', *FEER*, 20 March 1986, p. 51.
187 *Narcotics Review in Southeast/Southwest Asia*, 1988, p. 45.
188 White, ' Narcotics', p. 97
189 Zahid Hussain and A.S. Yusufi, 'The Poppy War', *The Herald*, April 1986, p. 67.
190 *D*, 7 June 1985, p. 2.
191 Zahid Hussain & A.S. Yusufi, 'The Poppy War', *The Herald*, April 1986, p. 68.
192 *Review of United States Narcotics Control*, 1986, p. 9.
193 Hussain & Yusufi, 'Poppy', p. 66.
194 Ibid., p. 73.
195 Husain Haqqani, 'Meagre Compensation', *Far Eastern Economic Review*, 20 March 1986, p. 51.
196 A.S. Yusufi, 'The Interior Minister was in the Picture all the time', *The Herald*, April 1986, pp. 74–5.
197 *Review of the 1990 International Narcotics Control Strategy Report*, Hearings before the Committee on Foreign Affairs, House of Representatives, One Hundred First Congress, Second Session, 1, 6, 8, 13 and 15 March 1990, p. 337.
198 *Review of United States Narcotics Control*, 1986, p. 18.
199 *CSM*, 28 December 1988, p. 1 (Edward Girardet).
200 *FT*, 3 March 1989, p. 54.
201 *CSM*, 30 March 1988, p. 13 (Lucy Komisar); Mary Jo McConabay and Robin Kirk, 'Over There', *Mother Jones*, February/March 1989, p. 41.
202 *CSM*, 28 September 1989, p. 3 (Sheila Tefft).
203 Ann B. Wrobleski, 'Global Narcotics Cooperation and Presidential Certification', *Department of State Bulletin*, Volume 89, Number 2151, October 1989, p. 52.
204 Lifschultz, 'Bush', p. 494.
205 Hussain, 'Narco', p. 14a.
206 Khan, 'Heroin', p. 27.
207 Lamb, *Waiting*, p. 196.

208 *CSM*, 6 November 1989, p. 5 (Sheila Tefft).
209 *IE*, 5 May 1997, http://www.expressindia.com/ie/daily/19970505/12550483.html
210 *D*, 19 May 1993, p. 1.
211 *CSM*, 28 September 1989, p. 3 (Sheila Tefft).
212 Joseph Devimithran, 'Pakistan Chronology 1986–1992', in Albert P. Blaustein and Gisbert H. Flanz (eds), *Constitutions of the Countries of the World* (New York: Oceania Publications, Inc. 1993), p. vi.
213 Hussain, 'Narco', p. 14a.
214 Khan, 'Heroin', p. 26.
215 *D*, 4 October 1993, p. 14.
216 'The Dangerous Drugs (Amendment) Act, 1994', *The Gazette of Pakistan*, Registered No. M-302/L-7646, Extraordinary Published by Authority, Part 1, Acts, Ordinances, President's Orders and Regulations, Senate Secretariat, Islamabad, 7 August 1994, pp. 701–2.
217 *Dawn Wire Service*, Issue 01/04 5 February 1995, ftp://mitrsun.mit.edu/p...hive/1995/dws020595.txt.
218 *D*, 7 December 1993, p. 13.
219 *Dawn Wire Service*, Issue 01/03, 31 January 1995 (Intikhab Amir), ftp://mitrsun.mit.edu/p...hive/1995/dws012995.txt
220 *Dawn Wire Service*, Issue 01/03, 29 January 1995, ftp://mitrsun.mit.edu/p...hive/1995/dws012995.txt
221 Shefali Rekhi and Mohammad Hanif (Karachi), 'Drug Trafficking: The Common Foe', *India Today*, 31 October 1995, p. 59.
222 Robert LaPorte, Jr., 'Pakistan in 1995: The Continuing Crisis', *Asian Survey*, Volume 36, No. 2, February 1996, p. 183.
223 *ST*, 23 February 1997, p. 17 (David Leppard and Jason Burke).
224 *DI*, 5 March 1992, p. 1.
225 *WP*, 29 April 1993, p. A32.
226 *D*, 3 February 1993, p. 13 (M.J. Sayeed).
227 *WP*, 29 April 1993, p. 1 (John Ward Anderson and Molly Moore).
228 *D*, 19 May 1993, p. 7.
229 The 1992 International Narcotics Control Strategy Report cited in 'Pakistan: Drugs and Dividends', *FEER*, 15 April 1993, p. 14.
230 *SMH*, 10 December 1994, p. 23 (Ahmed Rashid).
231 *WP*, 29 April 1993, p. A32 (John Ward Anderson and Molly Moore).
232 *D*, 22 September 1993, p. 9.
233 'CIA Report', 1993, p. 6.
234 *D*, 2 October 1993, p. 11 (Akhtar Payami).
235 Khan, 'Heroin', p. 26.
236 *D*, 8 September 1993, p. 18 (Shaheen Sehbai).
237 *D*, 20 August 1993, p. 7.
238 *D*, 4 April 1993, p. 3.
239 *HT*, 1 October 1994, p. 14 (N.C. Menon).
240 *WP*, 29 April 1993, p. A32.
241 *D*, 21 March 1993, p. 18.
242 *D*, 8 September 1993, p. 3.

243 *N*, 17 April 1997, [International Search], n.p. (Khalid Qayum).
244 *D*, 5 February 1993, p. 13 (Ziaul Islam).
245 *WP*, 29 April 1993, p. A32.
246 *D*, 23 January 1993, p. 1.
247 *D*, 28 May 1993, p. 5 (Mahmudul Aziz).
248 *WP*, 29 April 1993, p. A32 (John Ward Anderson and Molly Moore).
249 *The News*, ftp://usman.imran.com/pub/News/1996/9_September/news 0915
250 *D*, 22 January 1993, p. 1.
251 Alexander, *Rise*, pp. 30–1.
252 *D*, 22 May 1993, p. 9.
253 *D*, 18 May 1993, p. 1.
254 *Report of the International Narcotics Control Board for 1991*, United Nations, Vienna, p. 27.
255 *D*, 5 August 1993, p. 5 (Sultan Ahmed).
256 *D*, 4 August 1993, p. 11 (Haider Rizvi).
257 *D*, 27 September 1993, p. 6.
258 *Dawn*, 2 October 1993, p. 11 (Akhtar Payami).
259 Selim Omrao Khan, 'Pakistane Notun Sarkar: Sangkat Katse Ke', *Bichitra*, (Dhaka), 22 October 1993, p. 22.
260 *WP*, 12 September 1994, p. A13 (John Ward Anderson and Kamran Khan).
261 Ahmed Rashid, 'Pakistan State of Strife: Bhutto's Rivals Call for the Military to Dismiss Her', *FEER*, 6 October 1994, p. 20.
262 'CIA Report', 1993, p. 6.

6 The Bangladeshi panorama, 1972–97

1 Before the annexation by the British East India Company in 1757, present-day Bangladesh was known as the Kingdom of Bengal and included Bengal, Bihar, Orissa and Assam. Between 1905 and 1911, the area was separated from West Bengal and then re-united until 1947. Following partition, Bangladesh became the eastern wing of Pakistan and remained East Bengal until 1956, becoming East Pakistan before the dismemberment. Bangladesh emerged as an independent country in December 1971.
2 7,000 grains = 1 pound.
3 Appendix 22, *British Royal Commission on Opium*, Volume 61, pp. 434–5.
4 'Some Facts About the Opium Habit', *Chamber's Journal*, Volume 73, 9 May 1896, p. 295.
5 *Eastern Bengal District Gazetteer, Chittagong* (Calcutta: The Bengal Secretariat Book Depot, 1908), p. 159. (Hereafter, *EBDG*, 1908.)
6 *Dacca District Gazetteer*, Statistics 1901–2 (Calcutta: The Bengal Secretariat Book Depot, 1905), p. 14; *Eastern Bengal District Gazetteers: Dacca District* (Allahabad: The Pioneer Press, 1912), p. 140. (Hereafter, *EBDG*, 1912.)

7　*District Gazetteer of Eastern Bengal and Assam (Bogra)* (Allahabad: Pioneer Press, 1910), p. 132. (Hereafter, *District Gazetteer of Eastern Bengal and Assam*, 1910.)

8　*EBDG*, 1908, p. 158.

9　*EBDG*, 1908, p. 158.

10　*District Gazetteer of Eastern Bengal and Assam*, 1910, p. 133.

11　*EBDG*, 1908, p. 159.

12　Sumit Sarkar, *The Swadeshi Movement in Bengal 1903–1908* (New Delhi: People's Publishing House, 1973), pp. 376–404.

13　Article 22(e), *The Bengal Excise Act, 1909* (Bengal Act 5 of 1909), Government of East Pakistan, Law (Legislative) Department, Dhaka, 1967, p. 76. (Hereafter, *The Bengal Excise Act, 1909*.)

14　*EBDG*, 1912, p. 141.

15　*Bengal District Gazetteer, B. Volume, Bakarganj District Statistics*, 1921–2 to 1930–31 (Calcutta: Bengal Secretariat Book Depot, 1933), p. 11.

16　*Bengal Legislative Council Proceedings/ Debates*, Volume 4, 31 August, 1921, p. 290.

17　*EBDG*, 1912, p. 140.

18　Article 3, *The Bengal Opium Smoking Act, 1932* (Bengal Act 10 of 1932), Government of British India, Finance Department (Central Revenue), Government of India Press, New Delhi, 1936, p. 2. (Hereafter, *The Bengal Opium Smoking Act, 1932*.)

19　Annexure 4, *Final Report of the Royal Commission on Opium*, Volume 42, p. 184.

20　*The Bengal Opium Smoking Act, 1932*, pp. 2–3.

21　Appendix 37, *British Royal Commission on Opium*, Volume 61, p. 470.

22　*League of Nations, Advisory Committee on Traffic in Opium and Other Dangerous Drugs, Analytical Study of Annual Reports by Governments on the Traffic in Opium and Other Dangerous Drugs for the Year 1940*, p. 23.

23　C.P. Spencer and V. Navaratnam, *Drug Abuse in East Asia* (Kuala Lumpur: Oxford University Press, 1981), p. 63.

24　*EBDG*, 1912, p. 141.

25　*Report of the International Narcotics Control Board for 1992*, International Narcotics Control Board, Vienna, United Nations, p. 26.

26　Spencer and Navaratnam, *Drug*, p. 63.

27　*UNI Reports on Bangladesh*, http://kipcwww.ipc.kanazawa-u.ac (Hereafter, *UNI Reports on Bangladesh*.)

28　*T of I*, 13 September 1980, p. 8 (Henry Kamm).

29　*Review of the 1990 International Narcotics Control Strategy Report*, p. 335.

30　*DI*, 15 August 1993, p. 1 (Mushtaq Ahmed).

31　*Shaptahik Bichitra*, 10 September 1993, p. 17.

32　*BO*, 5 March 1992, p. 1.

33　*T of I*, 25 February 1991, p. 9 (Vijay Jung Thapa).

34　*H*, 14 November 1996, http://webpage.com/hindu/daily/961114/05/05142512.htm

35　*T*, 30 May 1997 (Pranay Sharma), http:/www.telegraphindia.com/national.htm

36　*SW*, 28 January 1995, p. 5.

37 Ibid.
38 *DJ*, 23 June 1993, p. 5.
39 *DI*, 10 May 1991, p. 4.
40 *IE*, 18 April 1997, (Sharad Gupta), http://www.expressindia.com/ie/daily/19970418/10851123. html
41 *SW*, 28 January 1995, p. 5.
42 Cited in *TREVI-Seminar*, Action Against Illegal Drugs Trafficking, Avila, Spain, 7–18 October 1991, p. 9.
43 *Report of the International Narcotics Control Board for 1989*, International Narcotics Control Board, Vienna, United Nations, p. 15.
44 *Report of the International Narcotics Control Board for 1994*, International Narcotics Control Board, Vienna, United Nations, 1995, p. 41.
45 Cited in www.druglibrary.org/schaffer/history/sanfranopium1892.htm
46 Haines, *Vindication*, p. 51.
47 Allen, *Opium*, p. 45.
48 Alexander, *Rise*, p. 21.
49 *NCB*, Volume 8, (January 1994–June 1995), Department of Narcotics Control, Bangladesh, pp. 33–5. (Hereafter, *NCB*, Volume 8.)
50 *IEO*, 2 May 1997, http://www.m-web.com/opm_proc.html
51 *Yearbook of the United Nations 1986*, Volume 40, Department of Public Information, UN, New York (Boston: Martinus Nijhoff Publishers, 1990), p. 864.
52 *IE*, 2 October 1996, (Shalaka Paradkar) http://express.indiaworld.com/ie/daily/1961002/27650132.html
53 Iraj Ahmed, 'Phensedyl: Neshar Notan Painno', *Shaptahik Purnima*, (Dhaka), 29 April 1992: p. 18.
54 Md. Abu Taleb, 'Phensedyl: A Deadly Fashion for the New Generation', *Souvenir*, Department of Narcotics Control, Bangladesh, 26 June1993, p. 67.
55 Cited in www.druglibrary.org/schaffer/history/sanfranopium1892.htm
56 *S*, 6 December 1997, p. 7.
57 *Report of the International Narcotics Control Board for 1995*, p. 45.
58 Ashraf Kaisar, 'Bishakta Nesha Phensedyl' *Shaptahik Bichitra*, Dhaka, 10 July 1992, p. 23.
59 Abdur Rashid Majumder, 'Pashchimanchaley Chorachalan Domon Ovigan' *Shaptahik Bichitra*, 9 September 1994, p. 16.
60 *DI*, 29 June 1993, p. 1.
61 *NCB*, Volume 7, April–December 1993, Department of Narcotics Control, Bangladesh, p. 3. (Hereafter, *NCB*, Volume 7.)
62 *NCB*, Volume 8, p. 61.
63 Taleb, 'Phensedyl', p. 67.
64 *UNI Reports on Bangladesh*, p. 8.
65 Brown, *Opium Cure*, pp. 3–13.
66 'Notes on Madras' as a Winter Residence, *Medical Times and Gazette*, Volume 3, No. 2, 19 July 1873, p. 73.
67 Ludlow, 'Opiate Use', p. 377.
68 *Sangbad*, 10 August 1993, p. 4 (M.F. Haque).

69 Codeine is a Greek word, which means poppy head. In 1932, through the extraction process scientists discovered an impure batch of morphine, which they termed codeine. Crude opium generally contains 0.7 per cent to 2.5 per cent codeine. The scientific name of this reagent is methyl morphine, and it belongs to the phenanthrene group.

70 *Report of the International Narcotics Control Board for 1995*, p. 45.

71 *H*, 21 February 1997, http://www.webpage.com/hindu/daily/ 970221/ 02/02210008.htm

72 Cited in *IE*, 2 October 1996 (Shalaka Paradkar).

73 Thomas de Quincey, *The Confessions of an English Opium-Eater And Other Essays* (London: Macmillan and Co., Limited, 1906), p. 81.

74 Alethea Hayter, *Opium and the Romantic Imagination* (London: Faber and Faber, 1968), p. 273.

75 *Shaptahik Shugandha*, 14 March 1992, p. 6.

76 Kaisar, 'Bishakta', p. 26.

77 Personal interview at Brahmanbaria, Bangladesh in late 1992, with a young phensedyl addict who was undergoing withdrawal treatment.

78 *NCB*, Volume 5, April–June 1992, Department of Narcotics Control, Bangladesh, p. 6.

79 *NCB*, Volume 7, p. 20.

80 *NCB*, Volume 8, p. 22.

81 *UNI Reports on Bangladesh*, p. 8.

82 *Fort William–India House Correspondence and Other Contemporary Papers Relating Thereto* (Pub. Series), Volume 13: 1796–1800 (Delhi: The Manager of Publication, 1959), p. 173.

83 Dane, 'Opium', p. 70.

84 *The Global Legal Framework for Narcotics and Prohibitive Substances*, 29 June 1979, US Department of State, Washington DC, UNI, S1.2: N16/2, p. 1.

85 *BO*, 28 July 1991, p. 10 (A.K.M. Mahbub Ul Haque).

86 Article 10(d), The Dangerous Drugs (Amendment) Act, 1988 (Act No. 36 of 1988), *Bangladesh Gazette*, Volume 5, 10 July 1988, Registered No. V A-1, p. 11304.

87 Mushtaque Ahmed, 'Is Heroin Being Produced in Bangladesh?', *Dhaka Courier*, 10–20 July 1989, p. 18.

88 *Yearbook of the United Nations 1992*, Volume 46, Department of Public Information, United Nations (Boston: Martinus Nijhoff Publishers, 1993), p. 924.

89 *Report of the International Narcotics Control Board for 1989*, p. 11.

90 An unpublished report distributed by the Bangladesh Narcotics Control Department, (n.y., n.p.).

91 *NCB*, Volume 8, pp. 4–5.

92 *DI*, 10 May 1991, 4.

93 *Madokdrobbo Niontron Ayn, Unisha Nobboy Er Shangshudhonkolpey Pronito Ayn* (Act No. 30 of 1993), *Bangladesh Gazette*, Supplementary, 7 December 1993, p. 4259.

94 Shamsur Rahman, 'Chorachalan Kaushal O Protirudh', *Shaptahik Bichitra*, 23 October 1992, p. 25.
95 *DI*, 20 September 1991, p. 4; *Shaptahik Bichitra*, 9 October 1992, p. 18.
96 *BO*, 26 February 1992, p. 1.
97 Article 19 (1), *Madakdrobba Niontron Ayn, Unisha Nobboy*, [translated from Bengali: 'Narcotics Control Act, 1990'], *Bangladesh Gazette*, Additional, Volume 5, Registered No. V A-1, The People's Republic of Bangladesh, 1 February 1990, p. 848.
98 Rafiqul Islam Ratan, 'Heroin Pachare Dondo Prapto Eliadar Boyosh Koto', *Shaptahik Bichitra*, 28 July 1995, p. 19.
99 http://kipcwww.ipc.kanazawa-u.ac...burn Hasina effigy, battle polite, p. 25.
100 Article 19(6), *Narcotics Control Act, 1990*, (Official Text in Bangla), *Gonoprojatontri Bangladesh Sarkar*, Department of Narcotics Control, Dhaka, Bangladesh, p. 10.
101 *Shaptahik Bichitra*, 20 August 1993, p. 17.
102 *NCB*, Volume 7, p. 23.
103 A Jalil khan, 'Cha Sromikder Jonno Varotiyo Mod', *Shugandha*, 31 October 1992, p. 29.
104 Cited in S. Kamaluddin, 'Bangladesh: Trade Without Tariff, the Country has become Smuggler's Paradise', *FEER*, 8 August 1991, p. 17.
105 Ibid.
106 Shamsur Rahman, 'Chorachalan Kaushal O Protirudh', *Shaptahik Bichitra*, 23 October 1992, p. 26.
107 *NCB*, Volume 8, p. 50.
108 *Report of the International Narcotics Control Board for 1995*, p. 44.
109 *NCB*, Volume 8, p. 60.
110 Article 16(8), *Narcotics Control Act, 1990*, p. 7.
111 *UNI Reports on Bangladesh*, p. 8.

Glossary

Abkari: An excise duty drawn from certain domestic commodities. During the British period, this revenue included all forms of intoxicating drugs, as well as liquor.

Acetic Anhydride: A key precursor to refine morphine base into heroin. India is a major producer and exporter of this chemical in South Asia.

Addiction: A state of periodic or chronic intoxication produced by the repeated use of any drug whether it is natural or synthetic. An overpowering desire or need develops to continue abuse of the drug by any means. A psychological tendency and physical dependency grows from frequent use.

Afridi: A dominant poppy growing tribe within the *Pathan* communities in NWFP in Pakistan and in southern Afghanistan.

Anas: 16 *anas* comprise one *rupee*. No longer in modern use.

Ayur-Vedic: The indigenous system of medicine in India, based on the Hindu Scriptures, or Vedas. In Sanskrit, *Ayus-veda* means life knowledge.

Bayparies: A Bengali word used for small businessmen in the countryside.

Bhang: A drink made out of leaves and shoots of hemp is known in Bengali as *bang* and in Sanskrit as *bhanga.* Another name is *siddhi.*

Bidi: In Hindi, a kind of hand-made cigarette normally smoked by ordinary people.

Brown Sugar: Produced in India, this less pure, low-grade heroin is otherwise known as 'no. 3 heroin' and marketed in India, Bangladesh and overseas.

Chandu: It is an extract of opium tar prepared by boiling a strained solution of opium in large copper cauldrons to a thick consistency. The use of *chandu* in India in the nineteenth century was similar to the usual Chinese preparation of opium, and was a new way of opium smoking.

Char: An island in Bangladesh.

Charas: A Hindi word also known as *churrus.* In the West, this resinous exudation of hemp is called *Hashish.* It is brown-black and used without any manipulations other than those necessary for packing and transport. Its influence lasts for an hour or two.

Chest: A unit for weighing export opium in colonial India. Its modern conversion rate is about 63.7 kilos.

Chinatown: Chinese colonies in the western countries are often termed as Chinatown. These areas are not marked upon in any map, but known to the common people under the name.

Diacetylmorphine: The chemical name for heroin. It is also known as *hydrochloride diacetylmorphine* or *diamorphine.*

Diwani: Finance and taxation authority in Mughal India.

Eid-e-Milad-un Nabi: The birthday of the Prophet Mohammad (*PBUH*).

Fium: The local name of opium in NWFP in Pakistan.

Ganja: A Bengali word that denotes the female flowering top of Indian hemp, used for smoking purposes. *Ganja* is also used in Hindi, Sanskrit, and Malayalam. In Greek, the *ganja* plant is known as *kannabis,* while in Latin *cannabis,* in English *hemp* and in Danish *hamp.* Its botanical name *Cannabis L. Sativa.* The female plant bears the seed, while the male plant is the source of pollen. Smoking leaves from the male plant is more potent.

Ganja Mahal: A system of *ganja* monopoly run by licensed traders in north Bengal in the mid-1850s.

Gardah Charas: Inferior-quality hashish in NWFP.

Ghat: A landing-place or a wharf for loading and unloading ships/boats on a riverbank where customs are collected.

Golden Crescent: This region includes poppy growing areas in Pakistan, Afghanistan and Iran.

Golden Triangle: The poppy growing areas of Myanmar (Burma), Thailand and Laos.

Golden Wedge: A new poppy growing region comprising areas from Nepal, Tibet (China), and Bhutan.

Gumashta: Indian agent/controlling officer of the field staff.

Hadd: An Arabic word that denotes Qur'anic laws. To control domestic abuse of narcotics, General Zia in Pakistan introduced the Hadd Ordinance in February 1979.

Hadith: An Arabic word that includes the acts and deed, and sayings of Prophet Mohammad (*PBUH*).

Hakim: An Arabic word that refers to a physician.

Haram: An Arabic word meaning acts that are forbidden or punishable in accordance with Islamic laws and principles.

Hartal: A strike that closes all offices, business activities, and transport from morning to sunset.

Hawala: All implicit authorization that runs through secret financial channels. It is used frequently in India, Pakistan and Bangladesh by drug traffickers to carry forward their illegal transactions.

Heroin no. 4: This high-quality (*diacetylmorphine* content 60 to 95 per cent) heroin is white and designed for injection. For no. 4 heroin, chemist traffickers use a much larger quantity of hydrochloric acid to convert the morphine base into heroin.

Heroin no. 3: This less pure (*diacetylmorphine* content 15 per cent to 45 per cent) heroin is brownish and designed for smoking. In processing this heroin, chemist traffickers use substances like caffeine and minute quantities of strychnine with the morphine base.

Hesb-i-Islami: The political party in Afghanistan led by Gulbuddin Hekmatyer.

Intoxicating Drugs: Includes liquor, cannabis, opium and other narcotics and psychotropic substances that produce drowsiness and create psychological and physical dependency.

Jatio Sangsad: National Parliament in Bangladesh.

Kabiraj: Local physician who prescribes herbal medicine.

Kalashnikov: A Russian-made sophisticated automatic rifle.

Kanal: A small piece of land meant for poppy cultivation.

Khatadar: Middlemen who negotiated between the poppy cultivators and the opium administration.

Kuknar: Mixture of opium and hemp used by some of the Mughal grandies. To some extent Emperor Akbar was dependent on this drug.

Lambardar: Literal meaning is one who gives a serial number. In India, *lambardar* is usually an influential cultivator who assists the government in poppy cultivation.

Majlis-e-Shura: Islamic parliament that exists practically in Iran, and theoretically in Pakistan.

Majum/Majun: It is a favourite form of *ganja* consumption. Boiled with ghee over water, a kind of jelly is prepared from the *ganja* leaves. This jelly is mixed with dried milk and when it hardens it is cut into small tablets for intake.

Madak: A conventional narcotic drug prepared by dissolving crude opium into water and boiling the strained solution until it becomes syrup. A small quantity of sugar was sometimes added. It was then mixed with acacia gum or guava leaves to make it a soft lump. It was divided into small balls for use as *madak*.

Malik: The literal meaning of this term is the sole authority. It refers to the members of the leading *Pathan* families in NWFP, Pakistan.

Malwa: The term was used in British official documents as a non-specific name that refers to the poppy growing areas of the non-British territories in Central India.

Maulana: Islamic religious scholar.

Maund: A traditional unit for weighing in Bangladesh, Pakistan and India. Its conversion rate is 37.34 kilos.

Muashera: Islamic religious consultative body.

Mujahedins: Militants involved in a religious crusade.

Mukhia: A village head. In this context, a general term for a head, who controls poppy cultivation in India.

Narcotics: Substances that induce 'sleep, drowsiness, stupor or insensibility'. In South Asia, this term generally includes opium, *ganja, bhang, tari, charas* and liquor. In recent years, there has been some overlapping of narcotics and psychotropic substances.

Nijam-i-Mustafa: The political system of the Prophet Mohammad (*PBUH*).

NWFP: North West Frontier Province of Pakistan.

Opion: Originally a Greek word (οπιον) which means opium.

Pachwai: Generally known as rice beer. It means fermented rice, millet or other grain, whether mixed with any liquid or not, and any liquid obtained therefrom, whether diluted or undiluted, but does not include beer.

Pathan: Pushtu-speaking population in NWFP of Pakistan and in Afghanistan are otherwise known as *Pakhtun*.

Paua: 235 grams.

PBUH: Peace be upon Him.

Phensedyl: Trade name for a cough syrup containing codeine-phosphate, chlorpheniramine maleate, produced in India by Rhone-Poulenc Co., but banned in Bangladesh, Nepal and other countries for its sedative nature.

Pirs: In Islam, *Pirs* are supposedly persons with spiritual capacities. They guide their followers in accordance with religious principles both in worldly affairs and their life hereafter.

Poppy: The opium poppy – a most politically sensitive agricultural product that grows in Afghanistan, Australia, Burma, India, Iran, Pakistan, Turkey, Lebanon etc. In recent years some South American countries have started poppy growing. Traffickers produce it both licitly under international control and illicitly. In South Asia, the lancing season starts by the end of March.

Provision opium: A technical term used by the government of British India for exportable opium. Following the banning of opium import by the Chinese authorities in 1800, it was introduced as an alternative term for 'medicinal' opium.

Pustu: Poppy seeds are locally known in South Asia by this name. Until the 1990s, these were traditionally used as a popular cooking ingredient to flavour food.

Rupee: An Indian coin. In Urdu it is called *rupiyah.* Abbreviated Rs.

Ryot: Hindi; Indian farmers during the colonial era.

Sabji: Literal meaning vegetable, but traditional street name for *Ganja* leaves in Bengali.

Sardar: Leader of a tribe or group.

Saur: April in the Pushtu language.

Seer: Unit for weighing things equivalent to about 2 1bs.

Shariah: Islamic laws based on *Al-Qur'an* and *Hadith.* It also includes opinion (*Qias*) and analogical explanations (*Ijma*) given by Islamic Jurists.

Shampan: Small boats manually driven along the seaboard areas in Chittagong, Cox's Bazar and Technaff in Bangladesh.

Shinwari: Name of a *Pathan* tribe.

Shia: The second largest sect among the followers of Islam. *Shia* Muslims are mostly concentrated in Iran.

Siddhi: The Sanskrit root *siddha* has the meaning 'accomplished, fulfilled', etc. which derived from the ancient Hindu mythology, the *Vedas,* that postulated the *soma* fluid as the source of courage for warriors. In Bengali, *siddhi* has become a name (in this case meaning 'success giver') for a narcotic.

Sindhi: People of Sind.

Subadarship: Law and order authority in Mughal India

Sunnah: Instruction of Prophet Mohammad (*PBUH*).

Taka: Unit of currency in Bangladesh; abbreviated Tk.

Tanjim Ittehad-i-Ulema: A regional political organization led by the religious activists in NWFP.

Tantras: The art of producing results by attemped control of nature or spirits.

Tari: Fermented and unfermented palm juice. It also includes fermented and unfermented juice drawn from coconut, palmyra, date or other kinds of palm tree.

Tehsil: The lowest unit for the collection of land revenue.
Thana: Local police station and the lowest administrative unit maintained by the colonial authorities in Bangladesh. In 1983, General Ershad renamed it *Upazila* (sub-district), declaring a new programme for rural development.
Toddy: Fermented palm juice or a mixture of spirits, sugar and hot water.
Tola: A traditional unit for weighing; about 14.5 grams.
Ulema: Religious leaders.
Zamindar: Literal meaning is owner of the land. In medieval India they were the landed aristocrats who collected tax for the central authorities.

Index